# ANCIENT INDIAN TRADITION & MYTHOLOGY

*Translated by*
A BOARD OF SCHOLARS

*Edited by*
Dr. G.P. BHATT
Late Prof. J.L. SHASTRI

VOLUME 65

# ANCIENT INDIAN TRADITION AND MYTHOLOGY SERIES

[PURĀṆAS IN TRANSLATION]

*Volumes Released*

ŚIVA 1-4
LIṄGA 5-6
BHĀGAVATA 7-11
GARUḌA 12-14
NĀRADA 15-19
KŪRMA 20-21
BRAHMĀṆḌA 22-26
AGNI 27-30
VARĀHA 31-32
BRAHMA 33-36
VĀYU 37-38
PADMA 39-48
SKANDA 49-71

*Volumes Under Preparation*

VĀMANA 72-73
BHAVIṢYA
BRAHMAVAIVARTA
DEVĪBHĀGAVATA
KĀLIKĀ
MĀRKAṆḌEYA
MATSYA
VIṢṆU
VIṢṆUDHARMOTTARA

# THE SKANDA-PURĀṆA

**PART XVII**

*Translated and Annotated by*

DR. G.V. TAGARE

**Book VI : Nāgara Khaṇḍa**

MOTILAL BANARSIDASS PUBLISHERS
PRIVATE LIMITED • DELHI

*Reprint: Delhi, 2012*
*First Edition: Delhi, 2002*



ISBN: 978-81-208-1872-9

Also available at:

MOTILAL BANARSIDASS

41 U.A. Bungalow Road, Jawahar Nagar, Delhi 110 007
Mahalaxmi Chamber, 22 Bhulabhai Desai Road, Mumbai 400 026
120 Royapettah High Road, Mylapore, Chennai 600 004
236, 9th Main III Block, Jayanagar, Bengaluru 560 011
Sanas Plaza, 1302 Baji Rao Road, Pune 411 002
8 Camac Street, Kolkata 700 017
Ashok Rajpath, Patna 800 004
Chowk, Varanasi 221 001

UNESCO COLLECTION OF REPRESENTATIVE WORKS—*Indian Series*
*This book has been accepted in the Indian Translation Series of the UNESCO Collection of Representative Works, jointly sponsored by the United Nations Educational, Scientific and Cultural Organization (UNESCO) and the Government of India*

*Printed in India*

By RP Jain at NAB Printing Unit,
A-44, Naraina, Phase-I, New Delhi 110 028
and Published by JP Jain for
Motilal Banarsidass Publishers (P) Ltd, 40-41 U.A.
Bungalow Road, Jawahar Nagar, Delhi 110 007

# PUBLISHER'S NOTE

The purest gems lie hidden in the bottom of the ocean or in the depth of rocks. One has to dive into the ocean or delve into the rocks to find them out. Similarly, truth lies concealed in the language which with the passage of time has become obsolete. Man has to learn that language before he discovers that truth.

But he has neither the means nor the leisure to embark on that course. We have, therefore, planned to help him acquire knowledge by an easier course. We have started the series of Ancient Indian Tradition and Mythology in English Translation. Our goal is to universalize knowledge through the most popular international medium of expression. The publication of the Purāṇas in English Translation is a step towards that goal.

**Acknowledgements**

It is our pleasant duty to put on record our sincere thanks to Dr. R.N. Dandekar and the UNESCO authorities for their kind encouragement and valuable help in the publication of the volumes in this series.

# CONTENTS



## SKANDA PURĀṆA
## Book VI: NĀGARA KHAṆḌA

# ABBREVIATIONS

Common and self-evident abbreviations such as Ch (s)—Chapter(s), p—page, pp—pages, v—verse, vv—verses, Ftn—Footnote, Hist. Ind. Philo.—History of Indian Philosophy are not included in this list.

| | |
|---|---|
| AGP | S.M. Ali's *The Geography of Purāṇas,* PPH, New Delhi, 1973 |
| AIHT | *Ancient Indian Historical Tradition,* F.E. Pargiter, Motilal Banarsidass (MLBD), Delhi |
| AITM | *Ancient Indian Tradition and Mythology* Series, MLBD, Delhi |
| AP | *Agni Purāṇa,* Guru Mandal Edition (GM), Calcutta, 1957 |
| AV | *Atharva Veda,* Svādhyāya Maṇḍal, Aundh |
| BdP | *Brahmāṇḍa Purāṇa,* MLBD, Delhi, 1973 |
| BG | *Bhagavadgītā* |
| BhP | *Bhāgavata Purāṇa,* Bhagavat Vidyapeeth, Ahmedabad |
| Br | *Brāhmaṇa* (preceded by name such as Śatapatha) |
| BsP | *Bhaviṣya Purāṇa,* Vishnu Shastri Bapat, Wai |
| BVP | *Brahma Vaivarta Purāṇa,* GM, 1955-57 |
| CC | *Caturvarga Cintāmaṇi* by Hemādri |
| CVS | *Caraṇa Vyūha Sūtra* by Śaunaka, Com. by Mahīdāsa |
| DB | *Devī Bhāgavata,* GM, 1960-61 |
| De or GDAMI | *The Geographical Dictionary of Ancient and Mediaeval India,* N.L. De/Dey, Oriental Reprint, Delhi, 1971 |
| DhS | *Dharma Sūtra* (preceded by the author's name such as Gautama) |
| GP | *Garuḍa Purāṇa,* ed. R.S. Bhattacharya, Chowkhamba, Varanasi, 1964 |
| GS | *Gṛhya Sūtra* (preceded by the name of the author such as Āpastamba) |
| HD | *History of Dharma Śāstra,* P.V. Kane, G.O.S. |
| JP | *Purāṇa* (Journal of the Kashiraj Trust), Varanasi |
| KA | *Kauṭilya Arthaśāstra* |

| | |
|---|---|
| KP | *Kūrma Purāṇa* Veṅkaṭeśvara Press Edn., Bombay; also Kashiraj Trust Edn., Varanasi, 1971 |
| LP | *Liṅga Purāṇa*, GM, 1960; also MLBD, Delhi, 1981 |
| Manu | *Manusmṛti* |
| Mbh | *Mahābhārata*, Gīta Press, Gorakhpur, VS 2014 |
| MkP | *Mārkaṇḍeya Purāṇa* |
| MN | *Mahābhārata Nāmānukramaṇī*, Gītā Press, Gorakhpur, VS 2016 |
| MtP | *Matsya Purāṇa*, GM, 1954 |
| MW | M. Monier-Williams' *Sanskrit-English Dictionary*, MLBD, Delhi, 1976 |
| NP | *Nāradīya* or *Nārada Purāṇa*, Veṅkaṭeśvara Press, Bombay |
| PdP | *Padma Purāṇa*, GM, 1957-59 |
| PE | *Purāṇic Encyclopaedia*, V. Mani, English Version, MLBD, Delhi, 1975 |
| PR or PRHRC | *Puranic Records on Hindu Rites and Customs*, R.C. Hazra, Calcutta, 1948 |
| ṚV | *Ṛg Veda*, Svādhyāya Maṇḍal, Aundh |
| Śat Br | *Śatapatha Brāhmaṇa* |
| SC or SMC | *Smṛti Candrikā* by Devanna Bhaṭṭa |
| SkP | *Skanda Purāṇa* |
| SP | *Śiva Purāṇa* |
| VāP | *Vāyu Purāṇa* |
| VdP | *Viṣṇudharmottara Purāṇa* |
| VmP | *Vāmana Purāṇa* |
| VP | *Viṣṇu Purāṇa* |
| VR | *Vālmīki Rāmāyaṇa* |
| VrP | *Varāha Purāṇa* |

# SKANDA PURĀṆA

## Book VI: NĀGARA KHAṆḌA

### CHAPTER ONE HUNDRED FOUR

### Installation of Kuśeśvara and Laveśvara[1]

*The sages said:*

1. O Sūta, describe the greatness of those Liṅgas which were installed there by Rāksasas endowed with devotion.

*Sūta said:*

2. The terrible Rākṣasas of extraordinary might used to come formerly from the city of Laṅkā in hundreds always for the sake of worshipping them.

3. While coming and going back, they used to devour many people including children and old ones both in the holy spot and on the way.

4. All the human beings in their eagerness to save their lives used to run about here and there.

5. Then many of them went to the great city of Ayodhyā. Exceedingly grief-stricken, they spoke thus to the excellent king Kuśa[2], the son of Rāma:

6-11. "Formerly, the Rākṣasas with Vibhīṣaṇa as their leader had accompanied your father to the holy spot of Hāṭakeśvara. Four-faced Liṅgas were installed by those leading Rākṣasas

---

1. According to Rāmāyaṇa VII. 108.4, Kuśa's capital was Kuśāvatī; no son of Rāma ruled at Ayodhyā.
2. Rāma was succeeded by Kuśa at Ayodhyā but VR notes the desertion (of Ayodhyā after Rāma). Hearing the complaints of people that Rākṣasas who visited their Liṅgas at Hāṭakeśvara devour people, Kuśa sent a messenger to Vibhīṣaṇa to prevent Rākṣasas from coming to Hāṭakeśvara. He got the area of the Rākṣasa Liṅgas buried under dust though that resulted in the burial of other ancient Tīrthas too. VR does not mention this, but our author tells this legend for the glorification of Hāṭakeśvara.

with their own sets of Mantras, in the western zone of that holy spot. In this connection, everyday many of them come to the holy spot and devour people.

If at all any human being were to worship those Liṅgas, he is doomed immediately. This too has become another terrible calamity. Hence, O king, if you do not save us, certainly the entire world will gradually come to ruin. Particularly, that holy spot is going to be doomed, for the Rākṣasas of ruthless activities and covetous of human flesh, frequent it."

12. On hearing it, the king immediately entrusted the ministers with the governance of the kingdom.

Then he went to the holy spot along with his army.

13. On seeing that Kuśa had arrived there, the survivors of the excellent Brāhmaṇas upbraided him with harsh words and said thus:

14-18. "O base Kṣatriya, why do you govern the kingdom in such a manner as to let the people be destroyed by Rākṣasas? You are not born of Rāma; you are born of Rāvaṇa. Hence you are indifferent to us tormented by the Rākṣasas.

Indeed, this fact has already been expressed by the people who are expert in the science of ethics and morality. That caste from which the king hails, enjoys flourishing happiness.

Hence you, begot by a Rākṣasa, neglect all the excellent Brāhmaṇas and others who are being devoured by the Rākṣasas. That king is blameworthy, on account of whose defaults, tears of the distressed people fall on the ground."

*Kuśa said:*

19. O Brāhmaṇas, be consoled. I was not aware of such a thing as this happening, that the Brāhmaṇas have been subjected to harassment by the Rākṣasas.

20. From now onwards, if any Brāhmaṇa or anyone else is destroyed or ruined, it shall be my sin.

21. After saying thus, the irate scion of the family of Raghu despatched a fearless messenger to Vibhīṣaṇa:

22-28. "Do go at once, O messenger, and tell Vibhīṣaṇa: 'The deep affection of Rāma that you have enjoyed, has been very amply requited in my case!

O evil-minded one, with excellent words you made me trust in you, but you are now harassing my realm with your hosts of Rākṣasas.

O base Rākṣasa, it was my father who made you settle down in this prestigious position. Hence, I do not kill you in the way in which your brother was killed by my father.

Even if it be a poisonous tree, how can sensible men cut it off, after once nurturing it with great care!

Hence, after this day, if any demon somehow comes to the northern shore of the ocean, I will immediately invade this city Laṅkā of yours along with my army and destroy it. Further, I will bind you and all the Rākṣasas firmly with fetters. Undoubtedly I will put you in prison."

29-30. On being ordered thus, the messenger went to the Setu quickly. After visiting the deity Rāmeśvara, he was about to proceed further when he was asked by some people: "O dear one, who are you? What is the purpose for which you have come here? Tell us. Usually human beings do not come here'."

*The messenger said:*

31. I have been deputed by King Kuśa to the abode of Vibhīṣaṇa on a certain errand. How shall I go there?

*The people said:*

32. Beyond this no human being can go at all because the Setu was broken in the middle by Rāma of indefatigable actions.

33. Hence, O messenger, all your work with Vibhīṣaṇa can be concluded here by meeting that Rākṣasa.

34. This leading Rākṣasa has adopted this regular practice of worshipping the three deities of Rāmeśvara three times everyday.

35. In the morning Vibhīṣaṇa performs the worship of Maheśvara in the portion of the setu near the gateway of Laṅkā.

36. He worships at noon the deity Rāmeśvara installed in the second portion of the Setu submerged in the water.

37. Always at midnight he comes here with great

devotion and worships this deity. There is no doubt about it. It is the truth that has been uttered (by us).

38. So, wait here unruffled in this very spot with mental concentration, till that noble-souled Rākṣasa comes here.

39. Later you can freely go to his palace in his company or to your own abode if he dismisses you.

40. On hearing their words, the messenger became delighted. "So it shall be", he said and waited there.

41. As midnight approached, Vibhīṣaṇa came to that splendid shrine surrounded by Rākṣasas.

42. He was riding in an excellent aerial chariot. He was eulogized all round by the Rākṣasas in the form of bards. Others sang songs.

43. Coming out of the excellent aerial chariot, he circumambulated the deity Rāmeśvara three times. After bowing down to the deity, he recited the following prayer loudly:

*[Vibhīṣaṇa's prayer]*

44. "Obeisance to you, O Lord of the chiefs of Devas, O bestower of freedom from fear on your devotees. You are endowed with hands and feet all round. You have eyes, heads and faces everywhere.

45. You are Yajña; you are the Vaṣaṭkāra. You are Candra; you are Prabhākara (Sun). You are Viṣṇu; you are the Four-faced One. You are Śakra. You are the great Īśvara.

46. Just as oil is always concealed in gingelly seeds, so also, O Śaṅkara, you stay hidden in all the worlds.

47. Just as fire, latent in wood, is not perceived though it is present in it, similarly you are not perceived by the deluded ones, though you are present everywhere.

48. Just as ghee lies hidden in curd, so also, O Lord, you are stationed (unseen) in all living beings mobile and immobile.

49. Just as a man digging the ground obtains water therefrom, so also one who always worships you attains salvation undoubtedly.

50. As long as you are not pleased with embodied ones, Svarga continues to be difficult of access and the brave are hostile (to them).

51. O Lord of Devas, as long as you are not propitiated and pleased, prosperity remains unsteady and ailments of different kinds begin to assail.

52. O Lord, as long as your are not pleased with embodied beings, so long there is misery arising from one's sons and one's wife."

53. After eulogizing thus he duly bathed the Liṅga and then applied sweet scents and divine unguents.

54-55. With great ardour and faith, he performed an elaborate adoration with the flowers of Pārijāta, Santāna, Mandāra and Kalpa trees. Thereafter, he adorned the Lord with divine ornaments and garments.

56-58. He himself sang, beating time with his hands, where the seven notes of the gamut were remarkable and pleasing with proper intonation and regular fall and rise of the notes. It was characterized by proper *Tānas* (key notes), *Rāgas* and *Grāmas*. Thus, he served the Lord devoutly.

As Vibhīṣaṇa was about to leave for Laṅkā, the messenger came before him and repeated the message of Kuśa.

59. In particular, he repeated the words which Kuśa had uttered in front of him with reddened eyes and great anger.

60. On hearing it, Vibhīṣaṇa stood humbly with palms joined in reverence and spoke to the messenger loudly:

61-62. "O excellent Dūta (Messenger), if the Rākṣasas had behaved thus in the kingdom of Rāma's son, it amounts to this that I too have behaved so (i.e. I accept the responsibility for it). It is indeed a great favour of that noble-souled one, Kuśa, that he sent you to me who have so long been an ignorant fool."

63-64. After saying this, he found out all the Rākṣasas who usually went to the mainland and always caused destruction. He brought them to the presence of the messenger and shedding tears angrily, sternly warned each one of them.

65-67. "Kuśa is my noble-souled overlord. All those Rākṣasas of wicked soul who went to his kingdom and perpetrated the destruction of the people shall become hideous ghosts and spirits in great misery.(Being banished) they will be lurking at the gates of Laṅkā always overwhelmed with hunger and thirst. They will be censured by all the people. They will be deprived of all pleasures and enjoyments. They will have to endure the chill of blizzards and the heat of the scorching sun. Phlegm and urine shall constitute their food intake."

68. After heaping this curse on them, the excellent Rākṣasas said again to the messenger with palms joined in reverence.

69-71. "From now onwards no Rākṣasa will go there. Hence go and tell Kuśa, the excellent one among the descendants of Raghu, in my words: 'May this crime be condoned because this has been perpetrated due to ignorance.'

Rākṣasas as a class are wicked and very greedy for human flesh. They have been punished in your presence, O messenger.

Whatever other duty there may be concerning Devas or human beings can be unhesitatingly communicated to me ever at your service."

*The messenger said:*

72. O Rākṣasa, go there yourself quickly and uproot all those Liṅgas installed by the Rākṣasas.

73-74a. This alone is the greatest task. It will be conducive to the happiness of all people.

These Liṅgas with four faces were installed with the Mantras specially pertaining to the Rākṣasas and worshipped by those Rākṣasas.

74b-75. If a person (being ignorant of the Rākṣasa way of worship) inadvertently worships them, he instantly falls down dead. That is why I request you this, O king of Rākṣasas. The presence of Liṅgas there on the earth (human world) is as good as the continued presence of all the Niśācaras there.

*Vibhīṣaṇa said:*

76. Earlier, in the presence of Rāma it was promised by me that none would go to the mainland beyond Rāmeśvara.

77. There is another reason also for this, O messenger, as stated by learned men. One shall not dislodge a Śivaliṅga installed whether duly or unduly.

78. Being a devotee of Maheśvara myself and having undertaken a solemn pledge, how can I go there and break the Liṅga myself?

79. So, that king should be pacified with these words of mine: "If anything improper or irrelevant has been uttered by me do punish me."

80. After saying so, he adorned the messenger with many jewels taken from the ocean and sent him off to the king.

81. Then the Rākṣasas who had been imprecated by him said to him in great grief, "O Lord of Rākṣasas, grant us all relief from the curse."

*Vibhīṣaṇa said:*

82. O base Rākṣasas, I shall not extend favour to you after you have been cursed, particularly because you are cheats.

83. The most excellent one among the scions of Raghu's family may be favourably disposed towards you undoubtedly by my request. Till then as per my order wait for some time.

84. After saying so, the leading Rākṣasa sent off king Kuśa's messenger, a human being worshipping the deity (with these words):

85. "After going there, tell King Kuśa immediately my message. 'O Lord, bless these Rākṣasas of wicked souls, who have been cursed by me. Let the wretched ones have their food."

86. O excellent Brāhmaṇas, on being told by Vibhīṣaṇa thus, the messenger of Kuśā accompanied by Vibhīṣaṇa's messenger to Kuśa left the place immediately.

87. The messenger went speedily and respectfully reported to Kuśa, after bowing down to him and standing by with humility:

88. "O Lord, Vibhīṣaṇa was seen by me at the shrine of Rāmeśvara where he had come accompanied by many Rākṣasas for the purpose of adoration.

89. O Raghunandana, he was told me all that you wanted me to say. Everything he listened to with great humility.

90. O Lord, the subjects were harrassed by his wicked Rākṣasas greedy of human flesh, without his knowledge.

91. On hearing about it from me, he punished them all. O excellent king, those of them who committed brutality in the mainland were all turned into ghosts and spirits of defiled activities and diet.

92-96. He told them further, 'You will become afflicted with hunger and thirst.'

He was then requested by all of them after bowing down to him repeatedly, 'O Lord, all of us have been cursed. Do this favour to us (by condoning our crime).' On being asked by them thus, he said, 'O base Rākṣasas, I will not condone and bless you. Nor will I give you food. It was at the bidding of Kuśa that ye sinners have been restrained and punished by me. He may be favourably disposed towards you.'

O King, for that purpose a messenger too has been sent to you by that Rākṣasa (i.e. Vibhīṣaṇa). What is proper may be entirely pursued by you. To be sure, there is no need to tell much. There cannot be any other devotee fully endowed with devotion and power like this Vibhīṣaṇa who is your devotee.

97. From now onwards the Rākṣasas will never roam about on the mainland. They will desist from it undoubtedly at the bidding of his. O king, be at ease.

98-99. With regard to the Liṅgas, O king, the Rākṣasa submits: 'O great king, I should not at all come here. At the instance of Lord Rāma, I have no power to step into Jambūdvīpa. Whatever duty I may have to perform, whether divine or human, I shall do it staying here alone even if it be very difficult.'

100. For that purpose, O great king, a human being, a worshipper of the deity Rāmeśvara, has been sent as his messenger. Do meet him."

101. Then at his bidding, the messenger sent by the leader of the Rākṣasas came there along with tributes and presents of various kinds.

102. For the king thirteen *Prastha*-fuls of pearls each of the size of a Dhātrī (Indian gooseberry) fruit were brought by him.

103. O excellent Brāhmaṇas, sixteen *Droṇas* of lapis lazuli, emerald and other jewels of excellent quality and devoid of blemishes were also brought.

104. There were numerous garments of divine quality brought which were pure like fire, and gold of the finest purity without any limit.

105. The messenger displayed all these to the noble-souled Kuśa, O Brāhmaṇas. He circumambulated him and then bowed down to him.

106. "O tiger among kings, Vibhīṣaṇa, the eminent Rākṣasa bows down to you with devotion. He speaks to you through my mouth:

107-109. 'O king, thanks to your father, everything is quite all right in my kingdom. I abide here worshipping every day the deity Hara installed by your father.

O king, whatever has been committed atrociously on the earth (i.e. the mainland) by those wicked-souled ones unknown to me, may be excused.

On account of you, O Lord, these Rākṣasas have been cursed by me. Assign the diet unto them who are in the form ghosts and spirits."

*Kuśa said:*

110. At my bidding let them (ghosts and spirits) come here and fill all the Liṅgas assiduously with dust particles all round.

111. Thereafter, I shall tell you what could be their food on the earth (mainland ). Listen carefully, O worshipper of the deity (priest).

112. Always, when the Sun enters Libra, they must come over to the earth (mainland) and divert themselves earnestly until the Sun is seen to enter Scorpio.

113-114. If during the Pretapakṣa (dark half of Bhādrapada) or during the period of Sun's transit in Virgo as well as Libra, it is my command that those Rākṣasas should assume the form of fever and infest their bodies. Undoubtedly they can feed on them in diverse ways for the period of a month.

115. If people offer anything without resorting to the proper procedure, or if they eat anything in that manner or if Śrāddha is offered and partaken of in this manner, the Rākṣasas should always infest them in the form of *Jvara* (fever).

116. All the ghosts and spirits should be told of my words entirely. Let them come here in the month of Kārttika and do as per my words.

117-119. Further, O messenger, Vibhīṣaṇa should be told by you these words of mine: 'Inadvertently I spoke very harsh words to you. O highly esteemed one, I know (hope) that you are unperturbed thereby. On seeing the people suffer those words were blurted out by me.

Since you, the king of Rākṣasas, continue to stay on the earth I feel that my father Rāma, the foremost among those who wield weapons, also continues to live.'

120. After saying thus the descendant of Raghu honoured the messenger with various kinds of clothes and different kinds of jewels taken from rivers.

121. For Vibhīṣaṇa also, Rāghava sent many things which were ready at hand there as presents.

*Sūta said:*

122. Similarly, the king made all excellent Brāhmaṇas happy and comfortable and gave them all those pearls etc.

123-124. Whatever came as present from Laṅkā was given to them. Documentary charters etc. were presented along with elephants and horses. Towns of wonderful features, villages and cities were gifted away. Whoever asked for anything was given the same immediately.

125-126. The deities of Kuśeśvara and Laveśvara were installed. Those two brothers hailing from the family of Raghu dedicated themselves to the leading Brāhmaṇas and made provision for their proper subsistence. With full satisfaction they (both) returned to the city of Ayodhyā.

CHAPTER ONE HUNDRED FIVE

## Removal of the Rākṣasa Liṅgas

*Sūta said:*

1. Then, O excellent Brāhmaṇas, as the Lord of the day (Sun) entered the zodiac of Libra, the ghosts filled the ground where the Liṅgas had been installed.

2. Whatever was there, namely the original Tīrtha, the shrine etc. was completely filled with dust particles by those ghosts and spirits.

3. As those Liṅgas disappeared, O excellent Brāhmaṇas, there was peace and welfare everywhere in the holy spot and also to other people.

4. Once upon a time, when there was change of the Yuga, King Bṛhadaśva came there from the Śālva land (south of Kurukṣetra).

5. On seeing the extensive ground, O excellent Brāhmaṇas, devoid of palaces, shrines, he became inclined to erect palaces.

6. He summoned many thousands of artisans and craftsmen. He dug up to explore that extensive plot of land from below.

7. As the ground was being dug up, all those numerous four-faced Liṅgas come into view.

8. Thereupon, after seeing the ground fully covered with the Liṅgas, the king as well as the artisans met with their death instantly.

9. Ever since then, out of fear, no man erects palaces or digs lake or well there.

## CHAPTER ONE HUNDRED SIX

# Greatness of the Vanished Tīrthas

*The sages said:*

1-2. Do tell us what those Liṅgas (Tīrthas) were that vanished when the ground was filled with dust-particles by those spirits and ghosts.

*Sūta said:*

Innumerable Tīrthas and Liṅgas got vanished there, O Brāhmaṇas. I shall describe them in the order of their importance. Listen and understand.

3. What is remembered as Cakra Tīrtha vanished. It was there that the discus was placed formerly by Viṣṇu, the all-powerful god.

4. Another Tīrtha that got lost was Mātṛ Tīrtha that bestows all desired things on men. It was there that the Divine Mothers were established by Kārttikeya.

5. There was another excellent Liṅga of the saintly king Mucukunda that got vanished there as well as that of King Sagara.

6-7a. (Liṅgas installed by the following persons were lost:) Liṅgas of (i.e. installed by) Ikṣvāku, Vasuṣeṇa, the noble-souled Kakutstha, Aila (Purūravas), Moon-god (Candradeva), the pious-minded Kāśīrāja, Agniveśa, Raibhya, Cyavana and Bhṛgu.

7b-8. The hermitage of Yājñavalkya got submerged (buried); so also the penance-groves of the great sage Hārīta, the noble-souled Haryaśva, Kutsa, Vasiṣṭha, Nārada and Trita.

9-10a. The Liṅgas installed by many of the wives of these sages got vanished, such as those installed by Kātyāyanī, Śāṇḍilī, and Maitreyī and many other saintly wives whose number cannot be reckoned.

10b-11. When the ground was being filled with dust particles by those Rākṣasas who became ghosts and spirits, a miracle occurred there. O excellent Brāhmaṇas, I shall narrate it to you . You must listen with concentration.

12.[1] On seeing the shower of dust particles let down by the spirits all round, gusts of winds were let loose by the group of Mātṛs (Mother-goddesses).

13. The shower of dust particles was suppressed (blown away) all round externally by the wind and the shower of dust never reached the ground nor was anything buried.

14. The spirits and ghosts became dejected. They lost their hopes for filling up. So they went to King Kuśa and lamented:

15-16. "O king, we created a downpour of dust particles there but it is being blown away in a hundred ways by the gusts of wind let loose by the Mātṛs.

O king, you should consider the means of restraining them, so that we can fill the ground all round with dust particles."

17. On hearing their words, King Kuśa went to that holy spot, O excellent Brāhmanas, and propitiated Rudra.

18. At the end of a year thereafter, Lord Hara became pleased with him and said, "Request for anything that has been desired in your mind."

*Kuśa said:*

19. Kindly see that, with your favour, the plot of land is covered soon by the dust particles poured by these ghosts.

20. O Lord, the group of ghosts was directed by me to fill it up. Since it is being guarded by the Mātṛs it cannot be filled.

21. Further, O Lord, there are Liṅgas there installed with the Mantras of the Rākṣasas. By the contact or sight (i.e. by

---

1. Numeral 10 is assigned to two verses in the printed text. The mistake is corrected in numbering the translated verses.

touching or seeing them) thereof, destruction of the people may take place.

22. There is the just fear as laid down in the scriptures that Liṅgas should not be moved. We do not have recourse to anything else at all such as uprooting them (Liṅgas) etc.

23. Hence, O excellent one among Suras, let a way be adopted to ensure that there is no destruction of the Brāhmaṇas and the sages brought about by the Liṅgas.

24-25. Then Lord Rudra summoned the Mātṛs and said: "Let the spot where you all are stationed be vacated. There, at the bidding of Kuśa and for the benefit of all the worlds, the ghosts and spirits free from worry will shower dust particles day and night."

*The Mātṛs said:*

26. O Bull-emblemed One, at your bidding we shall vacate this spot. But show us some other similar spot (to stay).

27. We would rather stay in this same holy spot created by Skanda by whom we have been installed and directed, "You must all stay here always."

28-30. Then the Lord said: "I shall grant you all severally a spot more auspicious and greater than this spot. O highly esteemed ones, I have already in my possession sixty-eight holy spots where I am always present. All of you, at my bidding, shall divide yourselves into sixty-eight separate groups and stay there. You will all get honoured adoration."

31-32. On hearing the words of that Lord the Mātṛs were delighted. They left the spot established by Skanda. They divided themselves into sixty-eight separate groups and settled in the sixty-eight holy spots forever.

33. The entire terrestrial region abandoned by them was filled with dust-particles by the spirits and ghosts working energetically day and night.

34. After granting him the boon thus, the Bull-vehicled Lord left, O Brāhmaṇas, along with all the Gaṇas.

35. Praised by all the Brāhmaṇas and ascetics Kuśa accepted their benedictions and went from there to the city of Ayodhyā.

# CHAPTER ONE HUNDRED SEVEN

## Installation of Citraśarma Liṅga

*The sages said:*

1-2. O Sūtanandana, it has been mentioned by you that sixty-eight holy spots of the Lord of Devas were established there. How were they installed? Do describe them completely. We are greatly interested therein.

*Sūta said:*

It is a very difficult question that you have put to me. Still I shall describe it after duly bowing down to the Pināka-bearing Lord.

3. Formerly, there was an excellent Brāhmaṇa in the city of Camatkāra here. He hailed from the family (Gotra) of Vatsa. The name of this highly renowned one was Citraśarmā.

4. He thought: 'There is Hāṭakeśvara in Pātāla. I shall bring it here and devoutly worship it day and night.'

5. After resolving thus, he began to perform a penance later. Controlling himself and restricting his diet he reached the highest point of the penance.

6. Only after a long time, O excellent Brāhmaṇas, Lord Śaṁbhu was pleased with him. He spoke to him courteously:

7-8. "O eminent Brāhmaṇa, request for a boon—whatever may be in your mind. Undoubtedly I shall gladly grant you (even) the kingdom of the three worlds. Hence, request for that which has been always lurking in your mind, even if it be very difficult to be obtained by all the human beings and all the Devas in particular."

*Citraśarman said:*

9. O Lord, if you are pleased with me, if you wish to grant me a boon, O Lord of Suras, come here from Pātāla in the form of Liṅga.

10. May that Liṅga named Hāṭakeśvara which was installed by Brahmā and is stationed in Pātāla, come here quickly.

*Śrī Bhagavān said:*

11. O excellent Brāhmaṇa, all the Liṅgas in all the places

are never to be shifted and disturbed. It is all the more so in the case of the primordial one installed by Brahmā himself.

12. Hence, O excellent Brāhmaṇa, install that Liṅga of gold thereof. It will become well-known in the world by the name Hāṭakeśvara.

13-14. A man endowed with devotion who worships it on a Monday or on the fourteenth lunar day in the bright half, O Brāhmaṇa, shall obtain through that adoration the benefit of worshipping the primordial Liṅga as well.

After saying thus, the Lord vanished from there.

15. Citraśarman erected a very charming palace-like shrine and devoutly installed a gold Liṅga there.

16. He performed its worship everyday in the manner enjoined in the scriptures. Thereupon, O Brāhmaṇas, that Liṅga there became well-known in all the three worlds.

17-18a. Thereafter, people from far-off places came there and began to worship it. A great rivalry born of jealousy arose in those Brāhmaṇas of better qualities who were present there. On noticing the activities of Citraśarman, they thought:

18b-24. 'All of us are endowed with good qualities and are born in this same place. But (this Brāhmaṇa) though devoid of good qualities has become famous in all the three worlds by propitiating Hara. Therefore, we shall also propitiate Hara for that purpose so that we may have equality with him.

The holy spots of the Trident-bearing Lord in the world are remembered to be sixty-eight in number and Parameśvara shows his presence there thrice a day.

The number of our Gotras staying here is also sixty-eight having common characteristics with this man of foolish mind.

After propitiating the Three-eyed Lord, the Liṅga stationed in Pātāla has been brought by him.

In the same manner, all of us should propitiate Maheśvara by the power of penance and bring all the Liṅgas of the holy spots.

Śaṅkara will bring them unto the people of all the Gotras and decide which Gotra should be connected with which holy spot. Other things also shall occur as he pleases.'

25. Then all the excellent Brāhmaṇas happily performed penance difficult to be performed by all the creatures.

26. They performed the penance along with Japa, Homa, observance of fast and restraints of different kinds, oblations, adorations, offerings of presents, holy ablution, Dāna, and other things.

27. They installed a Liṅga of the Lord which became well-known by the name Dvijeśvara in a lofty palace comparable to a mountain.

28. They abandoned all their domestic activities and even sacrificial rites as well as everyday duties for the sake of mundane existence and continued to propitiate Maheśvara.

29. Although he was propitiated thus, O Brāhmaṇas, Parameśvara did not become pleased. He never attained the highest satisfaction.

30. When they never got any benefit even at the end of a thousand years of their propitiation of Maheśvara, all of them became angry.

31-33. "O Trident-bearing One, you became very pleased in a very short time with this utter fool Citraśarman. Still, O Parameśvara, we have not been taken into account though we have been worshipping Śaṅkara ever since our childhood and we have grown very old now. Hence all of us should enter fire and immolate ourselves. This is the conclusion we have arrived at. We will do it in front of you."

34. Then all those excellent Brāhmaṇas brought fuel. Meditating upon Īśvara they prepared many funeral pyres.

35-36. They performed all the rites in accordance with the scriptural injunctions such as holy bath, Dāna etc., and kindled the holy fire. Thereafter, all those Brāhmaṇas were about to jump into the fire along with their sons, when the Lord who was pleased, granted them his vision.

37. He laughed boisterously and told all those excellent Brāhmaṇas in a tone as majestic as that of a rumbling cloud. Thereby he seemed to resuscitate them from death:

38-39. "O tigers among Brāhmaṇas, do not commit this rash act. I am particularly pleased. At my instance, you ought not to do so. Tell me what has been cherished within your heart so that I can grant it and go back to my own world."

*The Brāhmaṇas said:*

40. O most excellent one among Suras, the sixty-eight holy spots in this sacred region near this city are glorified by people as the most blessed.

41. O excellent one among Suras, let those primordial Liṅgas be in contact with this holy spot, so that all our indignation may become quelled.

42. Though this fellow is devoid of good qualities he vies with all of us, thanks to the power of your Liṅga. Hence do like this.

*Sūta said:*

43. In the meantime, the Brāhmaṇa Citraśarman came to know that Maheśvara was about to grant the boon. Therefore, he said to Maheśvara out of envious rivalry:

*Citraśarman said:*

44-46. These Brāhmaṇas are arrogant due to their good qualities alone, O Lord of Devas. After performing a great penance they became inclined to abandon their life. Thus, you are propitiated by them. They want only to vie with me. So, O Lord of Suras, nothing should be given to them. If you set me aside and grant them their desire, I will fall into the fire along with these sons and wife, within your sight (presence). So do what is proper.

*Sūta said:*

47-52. On hearing his words the Moon-crested Lord thought thus in his mind: 'What shall be the proper thing to do here? These tigers among Brāhmaṇas will perish on my account. This excellent Brāhmaṇa also who is on a par with the Gaṇas and who has achieved everything (may perish). Hence happiness should be provided to both by me, particularly to these Brāhmaṇas who reside here. I have always been thinking that all my holy spots should be brought by me in one place. The period of Kali age will be very terrible when holy spots and Tīrthas on the earth will perish. All the good Tīrthas have resorted to this holy spot out of the fear thereof. I shall bring all my Kṣetras also here.'

53. Then Maheśvara said to Citraśarman: "Listen to my words and later act accordingly.

54. O excellent Brāhmaṇa, let all my holy spots come here and let the Brāhmaṇas become delighted.

55. If you abide by my advice and abandon your rivalry with the other Brāhmaṇas, O highly intelligent one, I shall make your efficiency too very excellent.

56. Although the order of your Gotra as mentioned in the Vedas is the fourth, yet all those Brāhmaṇas will proclaim it as the first.

57. Further, O Brāhmaṇas, I shall bestow another honour on you. Undoubtedly you shall have sons, grandsons etc. as long as the moon and the sun shine.

58-59. There will be sons and grandsons and others in your family. When the rites of Śrāddha or Tarpaṇa are performed in accordance with the injunctions, the names of the members of the Gotra of the first one named Vatsa and later those of others will he remembered with devotion.

60. Then only they will offer the libations to the Pitṛs and the grandfathers and others, including relatives, friends and allies.

61. In your family, if the members are deluded and offer libations without (uttering) your name, to the Pitṛs, those libations will be fruitless.

62. That will be the case in regard to Śrāddha, Dāna and Tarpaṇa performed by you. So give up your arrogance and simply propitiate me."

63-64. Though, he was already a Siddha, Śiva informed him that he would attain the highest Siddhi of a permanent nature.

After saying thus to the Brāhmaṇas and making him first though he was as yet last, the Lord said to those Brāhmaṇas: "May the palace (shrine of Śiva) be built now. With each of the Gotras kept in view, the excellent Liṅga has to be installed, O Brāhmaṇas, so that my passing into them shall take place."

65. Then those Brāhmaṇas carefully chose the portions of the ground pleasing to the mind and joyously erected the palaces.

66. The palaces numbering sixty-eight were comparable to the peaks of Kailāsa. They installed different kinds of Liṅgas in them. They named them the same as before in the different holy spots.

67. After a lapse of some time, the Three-eyed Lord was

propitiated after the installation of the Liṅgas by means of the power of penance. After some time, the Three-eyed Lord granted them vision and spoke these sweet words:

*Śrī Bhagavān said:*

68. O leading Brāhmaṇas, I am much pleased with you all today. Everything that has to be done in regard to me has been done by you.

69. Our Liṅgas and holy spots (have been changed) due to the fear of Kali age. So you are worthy of my commendation. This would not have been possible through others.

70. Hence, let the excellent Brāhmaṇas request for whatever has been cherished in the mind quickly so that I can immediately grant them even if they happen to be rare.

*The Brāhmaṇas said:*

71-72. O Lord, if you are pleased with us, O Lord of Suras, our names should always be uttered in all the Śrāddha rites in the same way as in the case of Citraśarman who has been made first though he was the last before. This may be done so that we can be on a par with that Citraśarman.

*Śri Bhagavān said:*

73.74. If some young men endowed with the knowledge of scriptures were to come under your control, if they are masters of the Vedic lore, bring them up with the title of "Āmuṣyāyaṇa" (descendant of an illustrious family). They will be the permanent residents of the holy spot and they will perform the Śrāddha perpetually.

75. After saying this, the Lord of Devas vanished. Those Brāhmaṇas were very highly pleased and established themselves in that holy spot.

76. Thus, O leading Brāhmaṇas, all the holy spots and shrines which were afraid of (i.e. in danger of the influence of) Kali age live there permanently.

77. Thus those Brāhmaṇas attained Siddhi by the adoration of Īśvara. They became well-known in all the worlds as the perpetual performers of Śrāddha.

## CHAPTER ONE HUNDRED EIGHT

# The Aṣṭaṣaṣṭi Tīrthas[1]

*The sages said:*

1-2. O Sūtaja, you said that the holy spots numbered sixty-eight. Do narrate and enumerate them mentioning their names. Further, you do describe all the other holy spots and Tīrthas situated on the earth. We are very much eager to listen about them.

*Sūta said:*

3-5. O excellent Brāhmaṇas, the Tīrthas that you asked me about and which number sixty-eight, and other holy spots that are situated on the earth were afraid of Kali age and had entered Rasātala.

O tigers among sages, this Kali yuga is so very sinful. This very same question was put to Parameśvara by Pārvatī formerly. O Brāhmaṇas, for the sake of pilgrimage, you are now asking me about them.

6. Formerly, Lord Maheśvara was seated on the peak of Kailāsa along with all the groups of the Gaṇas. He was occupying an excellent seat.

7. The *Amaras* (Devas) had come for making obeisance to the Lord, O leading Brāhmaṇas, and when all of them had gone back to heaven, the goddess who had occupied half the seat, spoke these words:

*The Devī said:*

8. O Mahādeva, O Lord of Devas whose crest-jewel has been washed by Gaṅgā, do tell me the greatness of the Tīrthas if you consider me your beloved.

9. The number of the Tīrthas on the earth is thirty-five million. Do enumerate them along with their names now:

10. O Lord, O Lord of Devas, do describe the many Tīrthas and holy places to me in a manner easily understood by

1. Chapters 108-110 enumerate the 68 Tīrthas, their locations and names of Śiva associated with them. Hāṭakeśvara is the best Tīrtha.

embodied beings. By glorifying all the Tīrthas great merit is obtained.

*Īśvara said:*

11. O beautiful lady, the word Tīrtha refers to all the righteous rites and all the virtuous holy spots. Do listen with mental concentration.

12. Mother is a Tīrtha; father is a Tīrtha; association with good men is Tīrtha; so is thinking of doing righteous things and also observing restraints and abstentions.

13. So also are the meritorious stories of the celestial sages, the place of resort of excellent sages and Devas too, O My beloved beautiful lady.

14. If parts of lands are holy, they are glorified as Tīrtha. By seeing them, by remembering them and by taking bath in them, all the creatures are liberated from sins arising from hundreds of births.

15. Further, all sinners, all those who commit breach of trust, shall become rid of them by bathing in the Tīrthas.

16. So also, O lady beautiful in every limb, all the sins perish. Even if the embodied beings incur sins by slaying a Brāhmaṇa, those sins undoubtedly get destroyed by the contact of the Tīrthas.

17. Formerly, the skull of Brahmā got stuck up to my hand. By contact with Tīrthas and by taking bath in them it dropped off.

18. In view of this, all should take their holy bath in all the Tīrthas and shrines with the mind fully endowed with devotion, without being diverted to other things.

19. By means of this holy bath, all men attain the benefit thereof. O large-eyed one, my place of resort is destructive of all sins. It bestows all cherished things equally on men and women.

20. O goddess, this has always been maintained as the greatest secret. It has not been mentioned to anyone by me, not even to Devendra who had enquired about it.

21. O fair lady of excellent countenance, it is being mentioned to you because of your being my beloved. The sixty-eight Tīrthas should be frequented by men with adequate devotion.

22. All these are my resorts and they destroy sins. O beautiful lady, by my power they bestow desired things undoubtedly.

23-24. Whatever may be the desire cherished in the heart, a man shall take his holy bath in the Tīrtha and then worship Maheśvara. If Hari is worshipped by men while thinking of one's meritorious deeds, O excellent lady, men are rid of their sins incurred earlier merely by remembering them, let alone their direct sight and touch.

25. O beautiful lady, these Devas beginning with Śakra, and Nārada and others have attained heaven by worshipping me.

26. I shall mention them severally and in detail. With the mind in concentration, O goddess of Devas, listen to them by their names:

*List of Tīrthas:*

27. Vārāṇasī, Prayāga, Naimiṣa the next one, the highly meritorious Gayāśiras, the sacred Kurujāṅgala,

28. Prabhāsa, Puṣkara, Viśveśvara, Aṭṭhāsa[1], Mahendra, Ujjayinī,

29. Marukoṭi, Śaṅkukarṇa[2], Gokarṇa the excellent holy spot, Rudrakoṭi[3], Sthaleśa, Harṣita and Vṛṣabhadhvaja,

30. The holy spot Kedāra, the holy spot Madhyamakeśvara[4], the holy spot Sahasrākṣa and the other one Kārttikeśvara,

31. In the same way, Vastramārga[5], Kanakhala, Bhadrakarṇa, the famous holy spot named Daṇḍaka,

32. The holy spot called Tridaṇḍa and also Kṛmijāṅgala, the holy spot Ekāmra[6], the holy spot Chāgalaka,

33. O goddess of Devas, then the holy spot Kāliñjara[7] and the other one Maṇḍaleśvara, Kāśmīra, Marukeśa, the splendid Hariścandra,

34. Puraścandra, Vāmeśa, Kukkuṭeśvara, Bhasmagātra, Oṁkāra, Trisandhyā and Virajā,

1. Aṭṭhāsa: in Birbhum Dist. of Bengal, a Śakti Pīṭha.
2. Śaṅkukarṇa: the southern portion of Banaras (De 177)
3. Rudrakoṭi : on the Narmadā near its source (De 171)
4. Madhyamakeśvara: A sacred Śaiva place on Mandākinī (De 116)
5. Vastramārga: Region round Girnar.
6. Ekāmra: Śiva Kāñcī, Tamilnadu.
7. Kāliñjara: in Bundelkhand, Madhya Pradesh.

35. Arkeśvara, Nepāla, Duṣkarṇa, Karavīraka[1], Jāgeśvara and then, O goddess, the excellent mountain Śrīśaila,

36. Ayodhyā, Pātāla, the great Kārohaṇa[2], the meritorious river Devikā[3], Bhairava and Pūrvasāgara (eastern ocean in Bay of Bengal),

37. Saptagodāvarī Tīrtha (seven mouths of Godāvarī joining the sea) is also cited, then Nirmaleśa, the splendid Karṇikāra,

38. Kailāsa, Jāhnavītīra, Jalaliṅga, Vāḍava, Badarī, Tīrthavarya and also Kotitīrtha,

39. Vīndhyācala, Hemakūṭa, Gandhamādana, the holy spot Liṅgeśvara, and then Laṅkādvāra,

40. Naleśvara, Madhyeśa, Kedāra, Rudrajālaka, what is named Suvarṇa and the other one, O lady of beautiful thighs, Ṣaṣṭikāpatha.

## CHAPTER ONE HUNDRED NINE

# Greatness of Aṣṭaṣaṣṭi Tīrthas

*Īśvara said:*

1. O lady of excellent countenance, thus everything that I have been asked, has been narrated to you. This group of Tīrthas is the essence of all the Tīrthas.

2. O lady of great beauty, I abide in all these Tīrthas by my name. So also in the other Tīrthas for the benefit of Devas.

3. A man who takes his holy bath in all these Tīrthas, visits me, and glorifies me with eulogies addressed to me by name shall certainly attain salvation.

*Śrī Devī said:*

4. O Lord, what is the name whereby you should be glorified in a specific holy spot? If I am your beloved, O Lord, say this fully.

1. Karavīraka: Kolhapur, Maharashtra.
2. Kārohaṇa: Karwan in Baroda District, Gujarat, It was the native place of Nakulīśa, the founder of Pāśupata Sect.
3. Devikā: southern portion of Sarayū in Oudh, Uttar Pradesh.

*[List of Kṣetras and Names of Śiva associated with each[1]]*

*Īśvara said:*

5. Mahādeva (is the name) in Vārāṇasī; Maheśvara in Prayāga; Devadeva in Naimiṣa; and Prapitāmaha in Gayā.

6. They know that it is Sthāṇu in Kurukṣetra; Śaśiśekhara in Prabhāsa; Ajagandhi in Puṣkara, and Viśva in Viśveśvara.

7-8. Mahānāda in Aṭṭahāsa; Mahāvrata in Mahendra; Mahākāla in Ujjayinī; Mahotkaṭa in Marukoṭa; Mahāteja in Śaṅkukarṇa; Mahābala in Gokarṇa; Mahāyoga in Rudrakoṭi and Mahāliṅga in Sthaleśvara.

9. Harṣa in Harṣita; Vṛṣabha in Vṛṣabhadhvaja; Īśāna in Kedāra; and Śarva in Madhyamakeśvara.

10. Suparṇākṣa in Sahasrākṣa; Susūkṣma in Kārttikeśvara; Bhava in Vastrāpatha, O goddess; and Ugra in Kanakhala.

11. Śiva in Bhadrakarṇa; Daṇḍin in Daṇḍaka; Ūrdhvareta in Tridaṇḍa; Caṇḍīśa in Kṛmijāñgala.

12. Kṛttivāsa in Ekāmra and Kapardin in Chāgaleya. Nīlakaṇṭha in Kāliñjara and Śrīkaṇṭha in Maṇḍaleśvara.

13. Vijaya in Kāśmīra; Jayanta in Marukeśvara; Hara in Hariścandra and Śaṅkara in Puraścandra.

14. It should be known that Jaṭī is the name in Vāmeśvara and Saumya in Kukkuṭeśvara; Bhūteśvara in Bhasmagātra and Amarakaṇṭaka in Oṁkāra.

15. Tryaṁbaka in Trisandhyā; Trilocana in Virajā; Dīpta should be known as the name in Arkeśvara; and Paśupālaka in Nepāla.

16. Yamaliṅga in Duṣkarṇa; Kapālin in Karavīraka; Triśūlin in Jāgeśvara; and Tripurāntaka in Śrīśaila.

17. Rohaṇa in Ayodhyā; and Hāṭakeśvara in Pātāla; Nakulīśa in Kārohaṇa; and Umāpati in Devikā.

18. Bhairavākāra in Bhairava; Amara in Pūrvasāgara; Bhīma in Saptagodāvara and Svayaṁbhū in Nirmaleśvara;

19. Gaṇādhyakṣa in Karṇikāra; Gaṇādhipa in Kailāsa; Himasthāna in Gaṅgādvāra; and Jalapriya in Jalaliṅga.

20. Anala in Vāḍava Agni; and Bhīma in Badarikāśrama; Koṭīśvara in Śreṣtha and Vārāha in Vindhya Parvata.

1. After giving the list of 68 Tīrthas, this chapter gives the different names of Śiva associated with each.

21. Virūpākṣa in Hemakūṭa; Bhūrbhuva in Gandhamādana; Varada in Liṅgeśvara and Narāntaka in Laṅkā.

22. Thus, O goddess, the sixty-eight of them have been specifically enumerated to you. It is destructive of all the sins in the case of those who read or listen to them.

23. Hence, all clever (sensible) persons should assiduously glorify these names three times a day. They should remain pure. Especially those with the initiation in Śaiva doctrines should recite these.

24. O excellent lady, if these names are kept written in the house, no defect arising from spirits and ghosts can happen in that house.

25. O lady of excellent countenance, there shall be no fear of ailments, serpents, thieves or others such as kings at any time or any place.

## CHAPTER ONE HUNDRED TEN

# Greatness of Sixty-eight Tīrthas

*Śrī Devī said:*

1-2. O most excellent one among Suras, men on the earth are not able at all to take their baths in these Tīrthas even if they be long-lived. Hence tell me the most important ones out of these Tīrthas so that a man taking his holy bath in them perfectly can attain the benefit of all of them.

*Īśvara said:*

3. O fair lady, among these, eight Tīrthas are the most excellent ones. If people take their bath in them, they will attain the benefit of all.

4. They are: Naimiṣa, Kedāra, Puṣkara, Kṛmi (Kuru?)-Jāṅgala, Vārāṇasī, Kurukṣetra, Prabhāsa and Hāṭakeśvara.

5. One who takes his holy bath in all these eight perfectly and faithfully gets the benefit of taking the holy bath in all the sixty-eight Tīrthas. The truth has been mentioned by me.

*Śrī Devī said:*

6. O Mahādeva, holy bath in Kali age will take place with very great difficulty. Hence tell me the most important Tīrtha from among these.

7. O Three-eyed Lord of Devas, if I am your favourite, devout beloved behaving in accordance with your mental inclination, mention the most important of all these eight.

*Īśvara said:*

8. O goddess of Devas, that holy spot named Hāṭakeśvara is the most excellent of all these eight Tīrthas.

9. At my bidding, all the holy places are present here. So also the other Tīrthas even when Kali age has arrived.

10. Hence, with all efforts that holy spot should be resorted to by men who wish for salvation. The truth has been said by me.

*Sūta said:*

11. Thus, O excellent Brāhmaṇas, everything connected with the sixty-eight Kṣetras along with the names and the deities has been narrated to you.

12-13. This is the secret narrated to Pārvatī by the Lord. I have joyously detailed them to you entirely. He who reads this and listens to this with devotion regarding the sixty-eight Kṣetras attains the merit of bath therein.

## CHAPTER ONE HUNDRED ELEVEN

# Lamentation of the King of Ānarta

*The sages said:*

1-4. O Sūtaja, mention in detail all the Gotras of those Brāhmaṇas by whom the Śivakṣetras were brought and which holy spot was brought by which Brāhmaṇa of which Gotra, thanks to the favour of Śaṅkara, at the advent of that Kali age.

How many Gotras were established in the excellent city of

Camatkāra by the highly devout (King as) Ānarta? Earlier, you had mentioned that the city was built and bequeathed to Brāhmaṇas; but you had not mentioned their number. So do tell us now.

*Sūta said:*

5. Advice was imparted earlier by seventy-two leading sages. Formerly, the Lord of Ānarta was afflicted by the disease of leprosy. He hurriedly went to the Śaṅkha Tīrtha and had his holy bath.

6. Thereby, the leprosy of the king was instantly cured and disappeared, thanks to the greatness of that Tīrtha, though he had been dejected with the condition of his body at first.

7. When he was rid of the disease, he became extremely delighted. He bowed down to the excellent sages repeatedly and said:

8-9. "O excellent Brāhmaṇas tell me what appeals to you and how much thereof. Is it gold? Or an elephant? Or a horse? Or my entire kingdom? Or any other thing? I shall give them unto you. I am in a wretched plight. I am bowing down to you. May I be favoured."

*The Brāhmaṇas said:*

10. We are Brāhmaṇas of the third stage (Vānaprastha) of life with non-acceptance of gifts as our virtue. We are those who wash off immediately (i.e. who spend money on sacred rites without hoarding it). Of what avail to us are riches and kingdom?

*The king said:*

11. One who does not help others in return after being helped by them is a sinner. He is called ungrateful.

12. Expiation has been enjoined by learned men for a Brāhmaṇa-slayer, an imbiber of liquor, a thief, a rogue who violates solemn vows etc. But there is no rite of atonement for an ungrateful one.

13. Hence, O excellent Brāhmaṇas, be pleased with me and tell me something whereby I shall be free from indebtedness and my life will be a good one.

*The sages said:*

14. O highly esteemed one, it is indeed true that there is no rite of atonement for the ungrateful. But the defect is only there where the donor is one having some desire.

15. O leading king, if one who has no desire is the person who renders help, there is not the slighest defect.

16. Hence, do go and protect your kingdom according to Dharma, whereby there shall be happiness in this world as well as in the other world.

17. Thus a thousand times the Brāhmaṇas refused to accept anything from the king. He bowed down to them repeatedly and went to his abode with great difficulty.

18. With great delight, he installed a fascinating idol of Maheśvara after reaching his place. He performed adoration along with observance of Jāgaraṇa (keeping awake at night) with songs, dances and instrumental music. After duly destroying the enemies, he ruled the kingdom.

19. Day and night, he used to think about those Brāhmaṇas: 'How can I help in return those Brāhmaṇas who gave me this new, fresh body (free from illness)?'

20. All those excellent sages were endowed with the power of moving through the sky, due to their penance. They used to go to different Tīrthas with great devotion.

21. They used to perform the rites of holy bath, Japa and Tarpaṇa (libation unto the Pitṛs) in those places and later they came back to their hermitages and continued their earthly sustenance.

22-24. A few of those Brāhmaṇas carried on their daily rites there itself. Others went to far-off Tīrthas. After visiting those charming places and spending there a night or two they used to return home. A few others returned within three days. (They visited) Vārāṇasi, Prayāga, Puṣkara, Naimiṣa, Prabhāsa and Kedāra. They never desired to stay in any other holy place.

25-26. Once all those excellent Brāhmaṇas resolved to take their holy bath in the three Puṣkaras at the time of the Kārttikī festival day. They decided: "We shall stay there for five nights with mental concentration and purity. The protection of our wives shall be done by the sacred fires within our homes."

27. When those excellent Brāhmaṇas went thus with such a decision, the king came to know that no one stayed behind.

28-34. The king came to know that no one among those leading sages, the residents of the hermitages in the excellent Tīrtha, stayed behind.

There was a lady with the countenance resembling the disc of the moon. She was well-known as Damayantī (one of his queens evidently). He said to her thus in secret: "O lady of charming smiles, do go now at my bidding to the holy spot of Hāṭakeśvara. The wives of the sages of purified souls live there. Give them different kinds of ornaments as per their desire (and liking). O lady of excellent hips, though I attempted to tempt them many times, their husbands never accepted presents from us. Women always think much of the ornaments. They always cherish a fancy and temptation for ornaments. Even if an ornament is made of clay, wood, thread, wax or glass a woman eagerly wears it. This alone affords a possibility of helping them. O lady of eyes like the petals of a lotus, there is no other means at all."

35. She said "So be it" and joyously went to that holy place, taking with her different kinds of ornaments.

36-38. There were splendid earrings made of jewels and pearls; necklaces shining like the moon and big anklets studded with Indranīla and Mahānīla (blue sapphires) and lapis lazuli, rubies, diamonds etc., of great charm. There were bracelets, bangles of divine exquisiteness resembling splendid rainbows. There were gold threads and girdles of excellent quality.

39. On the auspicious day of Viṣṇu's waking up (i.e. eleventh day in the bright half of the month of Kārttika) she took her holy bath in a tank and observed fast.

40. The huge mountain-like heap of the great ornaments was placed on the bank. The lustre of those ornaments illuminated the entire firmament.

41. In the meantime wives of the sages came there in their eagerness to know how the queen looked like and what ornaments she wore.

42. They saw the beautiful queen adorned with divine ornaments engaged in meditation. They thought thus:

43. 'This queen is blessed. She is adorned with ornaments thus. She is Damayantī of excellent beauty, marked with all characteristic features.'

44. After concluding her meditation, Damayantī looked at the saintly ladies (women-sages) and duly bowed down to them.

45-46. She spoke these charming, sweet words with palms joined in reverence: "On this day of Hari, I have taken the holy bath and observed fast with the Garuḍa-emblemed Lord in view. I have set apart this collection of ornaments.

O saintly ladies, these ornaments of various kinds have been given to you joyously by me. May you be pleased to accept them. Let me be favoured thus."

*Then one of those ladies said:*

47. This pearl necklace is mine. Give this to me. O beloved wife of the king, I have no other desire.

48. The queen laughed loudly and washed her feet and gave her the pearl necklace along with divine garments. The pure pearls themselves weighed six Māṣas.

49. O excellent Brāhmaṇas, the pearls shone like stars in autumn.

Another Tāpasī lady urged by rivalry requested for a pure necklace of inestimable value and blameless lustre. It was highly pleasing to the mind.

50. The queen took the necklace in the hand and gave it to her. By that time, another lady eagerly longing for elegant embellishments caught hold of the necklace.

51. Then, O Brāhmaṇas, the remaining Tāpasīs too became eager to seize the ornaments. They vied with one another in seizing the ornaments themselves.

52. One lady seized the beautiful ornament in the hand of another with force and attacked her.

53. As the Tāpasīs were continuously honoured with ornaments, Damayantī's joy rose in her heart.

54. She threw at them hundreds and thousands of ornaments. Still, O excellent Brāhmaṇas, they were not satisfied.

55-56. The beloved queen of the king found the ornaments exhausted. She told all of them: "Be satisfied with this much today. I shall undoubtedly bring other ornaments of wonderful features and give them to you as you like."

57. Then all of them said: "O beloved wife of the king, do go. Come again taking more ornaments."

58. On being told thus, O excellent Brāhmaṇas, the beloved wife of the king bowed down to them and joyously went to her city quickly.

59. The Tāpasīs too went to their abodes and vied with one another in openly displaying and wearing the different kinds of clothes and ornaments on their bodies.

60. With the exception of four Tāpasīs of solemn vows and restraints, all the others accepted these embellishments and ornaments as they pleased.

61-63. Then the day dawned and the pure disc of the sun rose up. The queen brought further collections of ornaments and garments. She gave them to the Tāpasīs and they accepted them as before. Thus with great devotion she continued to offer the gifts daily for five days. The beloved wives of the sages became satisfied. Making the gifts with sincere devotion, the queen did not rest satisfied.

64. Then she heard that four lady sages (Tāpasīs) still continued to wear bark garments or antelope skins. They were without any desire and they did not come to her (for any sort of present). Nor did they appear to be jealous of the other Tāpasīs who were well-adorned.

65-66. Thereupon, the queen of blameless qualities took with her very valuable ornaments on the Pañcamī (fifth) day and hurriedly went to them. She said to them all: "May you be pleased. May these ornaments be received for the sake of adorning yourselves."

*The Tāpasīs said:*

67. We have nothing to do with the ornaments. We consider ourselves well adorned with our own bark garments. You may go back to your own mansion. Let everything be given to those who seek.

68. Even as they were talking to her thus, the excellent Brāhmaṇas, the four husbands, came there.

69. They were Śunaḥśepa, Śākreya, Bauddha and the fourth one Dānta. All these four came to their hermitage by the aerial path.

70-71. All the rest (of the sages) lost their capacity to move through the air and had to resort to the paths on the ground.

They found their hermitages were a mockery of their former ones, desecrated due to ornaments.

They said: "What is this? What is this? Our saintly wives have been deceived by the offer of garments and ornaments. Who is that sinner by whom this hermitage of ours has been made a mockery by offering ornaments and garments to the saintly wives?"

*Their wives said:*

72. That woman who is the wife of King Camatkāra was present here. Ornaments were given to everyone by her.

73. The beloved queen of the king was here in our houses also in order to give ornaments thus. But that was rejected by us.

*Sūta said:*

74. On hearing those words, all of them became extremely angry. By way of giving curses to the King's wife, they said thus repeatedly:

75-77. "O sinful woman, seventy-two of us went to Puṣkara for taking the holy bath on the Kārttikī day with the speed of mind and wind, by the aerial path."

Only four have come back, those whose wives did not accept the gifts at all, of the silly woman, the wife of the king.

Since this hermitage of the sages has beeen deceitfully desecrated you shall be transformed into the ugly shape of a rock."[1]

78. At the very instant, she was turned into a rock. Immediately, after the utterance of the sages, she became motionless.

79. Thereupon all her attendants became extremely distressed. With their eyes filled with tears in their wretched state, they set off towards their city.

80. O excellent Brāhmaṇas, they told the king the entire report about the curse of Queen Damayantī.

81. On hearing the details of the curse the king hurriedly went to the forest to pacify the Brāhmaṇas. He was in great distress.

1. The curse is not justifiable. Damayantī obeyed her husband who wanted to return the obligations of the sages.

82-83. On coming to know that the king had arrived there in order to pacify them in the matter concerning his wife, all those four sages quickly went to Kurukṣetra by the aerial path taking their wives and the Agnihotra requisites with them.

84. The king assiduously searched for the sages everywhere. He became tired and dejected in addition to his grief at the plight of his wife.

85. Thereafter he went to that place where his queen was present in the form of a rock. She was surrounded by the groups of the Tāpasīs.

86. On seeing her in such a state, the king who had been attended upon by all the servants repeatedly uttered "Alas! Alas!" Ultimately, he fell down on the ground and swooned.

87. Water was sprinkled on him. With very great difficulty he regained consciousness. Later he recollected the various good qualities of his beloved and began to lament.

88-90. "Alas! my beloved with eyes resembling those of a fawn! O lady of splendid countenance, by abandoning me, your dear lover, you have put an end to my very life. Where have you gone?

Hitherto you never took food until I had taken mine. You never went to sleep until I did. You have never transgressed my behests with misplaced haughtiness due to your conjugal felicity.

I don't remember that any evil utterance was made by you even in private, O lady of large eye. There is no question of your doing so publicly during dinner or in the assembly?"

*Sūta said:*

91. In the meantime the ministers of the king heard that he was in such a plight. They came to the place where the king was piteously lamenting.

92. They enlightened and consoled him with detailed accounts of ancient saintly kings facing calamities.

93. As the king heaved sighs like an elephant (or serpent) bereft of its splendour in an utterly wretched state with tears turning his eyes turbid, they took the king away.

94. He created a beautiful shrine for her all round. He embellished his wife in the form of a rock with camphor, agallochum incense, garments, saffron, sandalpaste etc.

## CHAPTER ONE HUNDRED TWELVE

# The Creation of Barren Land

*Sūta said:*

1-2. After the distressed and dejected king accompanied by his attendants had gone back to his abode, a few days elapsed. Then the sixty-eight excellent Brāhmaṇas reached the place utterly exhausted. They were emaciated in their limbs and had their faces turned greyish with dust. They had to come on foot.

3. They saw their wives bedecked in divine ornaments and dressed in divine garments as though they were queens.

4-6. They were very hungry. They asked them in great surprise, "O sinful ladies, what is this? What is this? Your bodies are rendered incongruous (as wives of asceties)?

How did you receive these costly ornaments and garments? Certainly, the loss of our ability of aerial movement could not have been caused by anything else.

O despicable women, excepting this aberration of yours, there can not be any other cause."

Thereupon the wives of those sages narrated all the events.

7. They told them how Damayantī, the beloved wife and queen of the king, came there. O Brāhmaṇas, they told them how the ornaments were distributed by her.

8. They told them how the noble-souled (four) Brāhmaṇas cursed her.

On hearing those censurable words, the sages became angry. The acceptance of the gift from the king was blameworthy especially to the sages.

9. With great anger they began to shake uncontrollably. They took up water to destroy the king and his kingdom.

10. "Our aerial movement has been destroyed by this evil king of sinful nature. He has tempted our simple and straight-

forward wives and brought his ornaments to them and therefore this adverse situation has occurred."

*Sūta said:*

11. While those sages were about to curse the king, the wives spoke to them angrily:

12. "O excellent Brāhmaṇas, no curse should be uttered against the king. Our words should be listened to unreservedly.

13. All of us were adorned by the wife of the leading king by means of excellent garments and divine ornaments with her mind sanctified with faith.

14. All along we have been staying in your houses along with the defect of poverty. We are emaciated and feeble. We never had any pleasure possible in human life.

15. To those who are engaged in penance there exists only the other world. They will not have even the slightest of human pleasure and benefit.

16. This world has been proclaimed for those others who are engrossed in worldly pleasures. They are base and wicked with their minds solely attached to the pleasures here.

17. In the case of those householders with the minds turned towards their duties this world as well as the other world are both assured. There is no doubt about it.

18. We shall undoubtedly resort to the excellent stage of the householders and thereby achieve the best of both the worlds.

19-20. That is why persons with cogent reasoning say that the household (i.e. householder's stage) is very beautiful.

As for you, do accept the gift of the plots of land from the king as well as all desired means of sustenance. Then look after your sons and grandsons and their welfare. See to the happiness of your daughters and kinsmen in particular.

21. If you are not inclined to do as we have suggested, we shall all give up our lives unhesitatingly.

22. Afflicted by the sin of murdering your wives you will fall into the grave hell of Raurva certainly."

23. On hearing their words, the sages let fall the water they had held in their hands for the purpose of cursing the king.

24. Thereupon, O excellent Brāhmaṇas, that portion of the ground became burnt by that water. It became an arid land. It is visible even today.

25. Seeds sown there do not grow at all. Further, a bird or worm that dies there is not reborn.

26-27. Not even grass nor an animal survives there. All the more so in the case of a devout man! One who faithfully performs a Śrāddha in the month of Phālguna on the Full-Moon day and on a Sunday will redeem his Pitṛs even if they had fallen into a terrible Naraka due to their own action.

## CHAPTER ONE HUNDRED THIRTEEN

## Greatness of Agnikuṇḍa

*Sūta said:*

1-3. Then all those Brāhmaṇas shed their anger and directed their minds to the sacrificial rites and householder's duties pertaining to sons and grandsons.

In the meantime, the king heard that the Brāhmaṇas had returned. On hearing it, he went to them for the purpose of making obeisance to them with devotion.

He also heard that they were angry at first but later became calmed down on hearing the words of their wives. Further they had accepted the life of householders as well.

4. He prostrated before them with eight parts of the body touching the ground. The king then stood humbly with palms joined in reverence and said:

5. "Thanks to the favour of you all, my ailments perished and I have attained the fruit of life. Tell me what I should do."

*The Brāhmaṇas said:*

6. By giving different kinds of jewels, O leading king, all of us, the residents of this place, have been rendered happy by your wife.

7. Hence build an excellent city here itself, in this splendid holy place and grant us the wherewithals of domestic life, whereby everything can become perfect.

8. We shall perform various kinds of Yajñas always with full complement of monetary gifts. Stationed here always, we shall achieve the benefits of this world as well as those of the other one.

9. On hearing it, the king became delighted. He said, "So be it." On an auspicious day, he summoned many craftsmen.

10. He got a very great city built. It had many ramparts. There was a moat all round and ornamental gateways embellished it.

11. The excellent king built sixty-eight big mansions in the middle for the sake of the sixty-eight Brāhmaṇas.

12. There were many ponds and parks all round as in the case of royal palaces. The houses had turrets and upper apartments.

13. After building them, he filled them with heaps of jewels and other things. Then he gifted them sixty-eight villages.

14. He called all of them and their sons and grandsons. In a loud voice he proclaimed thus before them:

15-19. "What I say may be listened to: This city has been given to these Brāhmaṇas with a mind sanctified by faith.

Hence protection should be accorded to them so that no loss, no pain, no discomfiture is caused to these leading Brāhmaṇas.

If anyone born of our race or any other king propitiates these, he will certainly attain the highest prosperity.

One who subjects them to criminal offence, leads them to distress, makes them suffer on various ways or adds to their discomfiture will be overwhelmed by enemies or oppressed by various kinds of ailments.

In this world, he will meet with terrible sufferings like bereavements and then will fall into horrible hells beginning with Raurava."

20. After saying thus, the king engaged himself day and night untiringly in carrying out their tasks himself.

21. Then, O excellent Brāhmaṇas, all the wives of the leading Brāhmaṇas lovingly went to the palace (shrine) of Damayantī.

22. They adored her image with saffron, agallochum and camphor as well as various kinds of flowers and scents everyday. The king also did likewise.

23. Standing before the image and creating great delight in the mind of the king, O excellent Brāhmaṇas, those Tāpasīs spoke to one another:

24-26. "Whenever there is an auspicious occasion in our house for the celebration of any prosperous event we shall adore Damayantī both before and after such an event. There is no doubt about it. In fact we shall do so always in the case of all holy rites.

A bride who sees her and then enters the marriage-pavilion shall undoubtedly be very dear to her husband like his very life breath.

Hence, when the Yajña-like sacred ceremony of a marriage is about to be performed, Damayantī should be visited and worshipped assiduously."

*Sūta said:*

27. Thus, in that city the sixty-eight Gotras (of Brāhmaṇas) were established and rendered delighted by that noble-souled king.

28. Of them four Gotras went away due to the fear of serpents to that place where the previous races were present so that only sixty-four Gotras of the Brāhmaṇas remained in the city.

*The sages said:*

29. O holy Sir, of what nature was that fear from serpents whereby they had to go away forsaking their own original position? Describe this to us in detail.

*Sūta said:*

30. There was, formerly, a king of Ānarta named Prabhañjana. He was conversant with Dharma and sacred rites. He was valorous and capable of destroying hosts of his enemies.

31. O excellent Brāhmaṇas, a son was born to him when he was very advanced in age. At that time the planets were in unfavourable positions.

32. He called together astrologers fully conversant with the scriptures and told them the time of the son's birth.

*The Daivajñas said:*

33. O king, this son of yours is born during an unfavourable and censurable hour. It is a terrible period when there are three Gaṇḍāntas (inauspicious positions of planets).

34. If somehow this boy survives, O king, he will destroy the country and the assets of the city of his parents.

*The king said:*

35. Is there any remedy here, divine or human, whereby there shall be all-round welfare of the son as well as the kingdom?

*The Brāhmaṇas said:*

36. Just as a mechanical device coming up is checked by another mechanical device, just as armour acts as a protection from the attack of arrows, so also the Śānti rite (pacificatory rite conducive to peace and prosperity) can be a check against the evil effects of the planets.

37-38a. Hence, O king, give up your dejection and perform Śānti (pacificatory) rites always. Thereby all the planets will become mild and auspicious. This is the remedy when planets become malefic and they are stationed in unfavourable houses.

38b. Thereupon, the king hurried to the city of Camatkāra.

39-42. There he summoned together the Brāhmaṇas and said to them respectfully: "It is with your favour that we always rule the kingdom. Just as rain-bearing cloud is the basis and support unto the crops so you are the redeemer to all the excellent kings who were born in our family and who are yet to be born.

My son was born when the planets were stationed in evil houses. *Śāntika* rites for (their) pacification have been recommended by Daivajñas.

Hence, O leading Brāhmaṇas perform the *Śāntika* rites as enjoined in the scriptures so that my son, kingdom and the royal prosperity may prosper."

43-45. Then those Brāhmaṇas consulted one another and said: " O King, we shall perform Śānti rites for your welfare. Sixteen of us, good, quiescent Brāhmaṇas of great restraint, shall perform them always. O king; presents should always be sent by you with great devotion. At the end of every month, the Abhiṣeka (water for ablution) should be received from the *Rudraghaṭas* (waterpots pertaining to the deity Rudra). If you continue to do thus your son will prosper, so also the kingdom, the treasury and everything else."

46. Then he bowed down to them and happily went to his abode. Urged by them he always celebrated the festival of the birth of his son.

47. Then he sent all the requisite things to the city of Camatkāra. At the end of every month, he duly received the water for ablution.

48. Those tiger-like Brāhmaṇas too strictly adhered to the practice of celibacy and performed the Śāntika rites in due order in groups (or units) of four.

49. Every month they did thus quiescently and with the sense-organs fully under control. At the end of the month another set of Brāhmaṇas performed the Śāntika rites.

50. The king came there at the end of every month with great devotion, honoured the excellent Brāhmaṇas and accepted the Abhiṣeka water.

51. He then used to propitiate them with garments, coronets and gifts of cows and plots of land. Similarly, the king propitiated the other Brāhmaṇas also and went to his abode.

52. As these Śānti rites continued to be performed on behalf of the king, a great deal of time elapsed according welfare, health and wealth.

53. After some time, once at the beginning itself of a month, when the Śāntika rites were to be begun, a major disease afflicted the king.

54. There was decline in health of his son in particular, of his women, of the entire kingdom and the vehicles.

55. Thereupon the king sent extra requisites for the Śānti rites to the city and also special monetary gifts.

56. As the Brāhmaṇas went on performing the rite of Homa in the fire, all types of diseases particularly went on spreading everywhere.

57. Horses began to die. So also elephants. Enemies appeared from all the quarters for waging war.

58. The king himself fell ill. In great excitement, he hastened to the city of Camatkārapura and said to all the Brāhmaṇas:

59-60. "O highly esteemed ones, even as you all remain in charge of these rites adversities assail me. Why? Why do my assets dwindle? The ailments increase along with groups of enemies. Hence some special Homa may be performed for suppressing the ailments. I shall make special gifts unto the Brāhmaṇas."

61. Then all those Brāhmaṇas performed the Śāntika rites with great mental concentration for the welfare and in the very presence of the king.

62. As at the conclusion of the Homas the ascetic Brāhmaṇas pronounced (blessings) with great concentration, the ailment of the king became all the more serious.

63. In the meantime, all those excellent Brāhmaṇas became greatly enraged. They decided to curse the Planets including the Sun.

*The Brāhmaṇas said:*

64. Although they have been worshipped with very good devotion and also in accordance with the injunctions, these Planets harass the city of the king along with his sons, kinsmen and wealth of cattle!

65. Thus they decided. They remained pure with mental concentration. They were about to curse the Planets in their fit of anger.

66-71. By then the Fire-god assumed a personal form and spoke to the excellent Brāhmaṇas: "O leading Brāhmaṇas, do not curse at any cost. Do not curse the Planets that are free from blemish. May my words be listened to. Sixteen Brāhmaṇas perform Homa every month. In their midst there is one Trijāta[1]. All the articles pertaining to the Homa have been defiled by him. The Planets including the Sun do not accept what is offered by me. Therefore, they cause greater harassment to the king. Hence exclude him and begin the Homa without delay so that all the Planets including the Sun will have the greatest happiness. The king will become free from ailment along with his son. His enemies will go away. Thanks to the power of my Śāntika rites, he will attain perpetual happiness."

72. After saying thus, Lord Vahni disappeared. Those Brāhmaṇas became dejected in appearance indicating how deeply they felt the sense of shame.

73-74. Thereupon they stayed on there and eulogized Pāvaka (Fire-god) again. They spoke to Vaiśvānara: "Tell us who is the Trijāta Brāhmaṇa here?

1. Thrice-born—This seems to be a derogatory term implying two persons responsible for the nativity and then the third birth i.e. sacred thread ceremony.

Thereat we can exclude him completely and resume our rite for the purpose of peace and suppression of the defects of the noble-souled king."

*Vahni said:*

75. I will never speak out the defect of the leading Brāhmaṇas even though I know. All the Brāhmaṇas on the earth are worthy of my veneration.

*The Brāhmaṇas said:*

76. O Vahni (Fire-god), if you do not proclaim to us who that Brāhmaṇa is, we will curse you. Hence hurry up and tell us.

*Sūta said:*

77-79. On hearing their words, Vahni became afraid and thought thus for a long time: 'What is the best thing I should do here? If I reveal the defect of the Brāhmaṇa, I shall incur that much of sin undoubtedly. There will also be a curse coming from him. If I don't proclaim the truth about the excellent Brāhmaṇa, these Brāhmaṇas comparable to serpents (in fury) will undoubtedly curse me.'

80. Even as he pondered thus, there was profuse perspiration on his physical form and that holy Kuṇḍa which was specially prepared for the purpose of Homa was filled with it (sweat).

81. Then the Fire-god came out of the Kuṇḍa. He was trembling with fear. He stood there with palms joined in reverence and said to the Brāhmaṇas:

82-84. "O Brāhmaṇas, I will never utter the defects of a Brāhmaṇa by means of my own tongue at any cost. Hence listen: All the sixteen Brāhmaṇas who are present here should take their bath in the pit of sweat drops for the sake of purifying themselves. When the person who is Trijāta takes his bath his body will have tumours and boils."

85. Then all those took their bath there in due order. All except one Brāhmaṇa attained purity.

86. On seeing that excellent Brāhmaṇa with tumours and boils all of a sudden, there was a great hue and cry among the people there.

87. That Brāhmaṇa became filled with shame. With the face hanging down he went out of the assembly of Brāhmaṇas.

*Vahni said:*

88. O excellent Brāhmaṇas, your (unprecedented) task has been accomplished by me. So I shall go to my abode with your permission.

89. But, O excellent Brāhmaṇas, viewing me even in a dream shall not go in vain. Hence the desire cherished in the heart may be requested for.

*The Brāhmaṇas said:*

90. O Vahni, may this water reservoir of your sweat drops be permanent here for the sake of the purification of Brāhmaṇas.

91. If a person born of illegal father takes his plunge here, you must mark his body with tumours and boils.

92. Saying "So it shall be" Pāvaka vanished from there and all the Brāhmaṇas held consultation together.

93. From today onwards the test of purity of all the Brāhmaṇas in regard to their fathers and mothers shall be conducted here.

94. A Brāhmaṇa said to be hailing from Camatkārapura should take his bath here. On being found pure, he will be considered a noble son.

95. A virgin should be given to him alone. He should be one deserving invitation to a Śrāddha rite. Only he should be entertained in all sacred rites.

96. All the members of the sixty-eight Gotras should gather together. He who proves to be pure in their presence should be regarded as deserving a place in the row of Brāhmaṇas for meals.

97-98. If any scandalous rumour spreads, if there is any suspicion as to the sin of Brāhmaṇa-slaughter or if there is any accusation from evil-minded persons casting aspersions on virtue—all these should be tested here and the purity established. All the calumny shall automatically drop down.

99. No one shall be clearly pronounced as a Brāhmaṇa until this bath is taken in the presence of all the Brāhmaṇas.

*Sūta said:*

100. Thus all the Brāhmaṇas hailing from Camatkārapura performed the Śāntika rites for the welfare of the king.

101. Then bath was taken by all the remaining noble-souled Brāhmaṇas also for the sake of purity, though at the outset they were afraid (naturally).

102a. Then, O Brāhmaṇas, the king became rid of all his ailments instantly.

102b-103a. O excellent Brāhmaṇas, even today one who takes his bath there on the Kārttikī day becomes rid of the sins of having intercourse with other men's wives.

103b. In three yugas the Brāhmaṇas had purity.

104. Of other sinners, even though they were devoid of nobility of birth and behaviour, in view of Kaliyuga as highly terrible with carnal connection with other men's wives in abundance the purity was proclaimed by Brāhmaṇas.

105. The declaration was made in front of Brahmā, the Lord of Devas, O excellent Brāhmaṇas, in order to proclaim the purity of the families of the fathers and the mothers. They were scrupulous in regard to this.

106. Even today, O excellent Brāhmaṇas, if a Trijāta takes his bath there he is scorched by fire undoubtedly.

## CHAPTER ONE HUNDRED FOURTEEN

# The Term 'Nāgara'

*Sūta said:*

1-3. O excellent Brāhmaṇas, that Brāhmaṇa who had boils all over the body was utterly ashamed. He went to a dense forest with utter disgust and engaged himself in a severe penance. He had renounced his house etc., and all affection for his wife and sons.

With all controls and restraints he dried up his body. He went near a water reservoir (a lake or a pond) and installed Maheśvara.

4. After a long time, Maheśvara was pleased with him. Appearing before him he said: "Request for anything you like."

*Trijāta said:*

5. On account of the default of my mother, O Lord, I have become extremely embarrassed in the midst of the chiefs of Brāhmaṇas and the king of Ānarta.

6. Though I am endowed with great learning, O Lord, I am unable to show my face to any one after knowing that I am 'thrice-born.'

7. O Lord of Devas, do something so as to enable me to become the best of all those Brāhmaṇas:

*Śrī Bhagavān said:*

8. Certainly you will become the best of all the Brāhmaṇas who stay in Camatkārapura, with my favour, O excellent Brāhmaṇa.

9. Hence, O excellent Brāhmaṇa, wait for some time. When the proper time arrives I shall take you there.

10. After saying thus, the Lord of Devas vanished from there. The Brāhmaṇa continued his penance, worshipping Hara.

11. O Brāhmaṇas, once thereafter a Brāhmaṇa named Devarāta was born of the family of Maudgalya in Camatkārapura.

12. His son named Kratha was very haughty when he was in the prime of youth. He was very manly but was always very proud.

13. Once, on the fifth lunar day in the dark half of the month of Śrāvaṇa that Brāhmaṇa went to Nāgatīrtha, O Brāhmaṇas, and was roaming in the forest.

14. He saw the highly refulgent son of the leading serpent. He was well-known as Rudramāla. He was accompanied by his mother.

15. The serpent child was very small. On seeing it he thought it was a water-snake and thrashed it with a stick.

16. On being hit by him he shouted very loudly: "Alas mother! Alas father! I am blameless yet I am in trouble."

17. On hearing a human voice from a serpent, the Brāhmaṇa became afraid and went home hurriedly.

18. Its mother came out of the water reservoir and saw her son felled down on the bank.

19. On seeing the son in such a plight with blood splashed all over his limbs shattered on being struck by a stick, she fell into a swoon.

20. After regaining consciousness, she began to lament piteously in various ways. Her eyes were filled with tears and she was tormented in the height of her grief.

21-27. "Alas! My son, where have you gone forsaking me? why have you gone to a place from where there is no return? Don't you have any affection for me?

By which sinful and wicked-minded one have you been killed? Though you are sinless, you have been slain. With whom is Yama angry today?

On this fifth lunar day, you have been killed and not adored and honoured. Hence, Yama shall be angry with that wicked-minded one along with his city, family and land of birth.

Today my clothes will not become soiled as before when you used to come back to me after playing in dust for a long time and sit on my lap as you pleased.

Excepting you who will be lisping faltering but delightful words that make people laugh, in front of me?

You being not present, O my son, who will accept the lap of your father and cause merriment by pulling your father's beard?

You were forbidden, O dear one, yet you closely followed me to this mortal world which is full of many defects!"

28. After lamenting thus that Nāga woman who had been angry as well as pained with grief took the dead son and went to the presence of Ananta.

29. Then she placed her dead child in front of him and began to lament like the female osprey wretched in her separation.

30. Even the king of serpents fell into a swoon on seeing the son thrown down. He was afflicted by the grief for his son.

31. On being sprinkled with cool water, he regained consciousness with great difficulty. Like an ordinary man, he began piteous lamentations.

32. In the meantime, all serpents assembled there. They cried miserably with the eyes bedimmed with tears.

33-35. The following Nāgas were present there: Vāsuki, Padmaja, Śaṅkha, the highly poisonous Takṣaka, Śaṅkhacūḍa with the diadem on the head, the terrible Puṇḍarīka, Añjana, Vāmana, the great Kumuda, Kambala, Aśvatara, the serpent

Karkoṭaka, Puṣpadanta, Mūṣaka the devourer of mice, Elāpatra, Supatra, Dīrghāsya and Puṣpavāhana.

36. On coming to know that the king of serpents was struck with grief for the son, these and thousands of other serpents came there.

37. Quoting earlier incidents and different kinds of similar instances, they consoled their Lord, the chief serpent.

38. The excellent serpent in his misery got consoled after a long time. Then he performed the cremation rites for his son.

39. When, at the time of offering water libation, all the serpents had assembled for the offering of libation, he spoke to them:

40-41. "Unless and until the utter annihilation of that wicked slayer of my son is brought about along with his wife, servants and sons, I will not at any cost offer the libation to my son, though urged by you all as well as other kinsmen."

42. After saying this Śeṣa formally proclaimed his retaliation against the sinful Brāhmaṇa who killed his son with a heavy wooden stick.

43-45 Then the Lord of serpents spoke to all those serpents who were near: "O my excellent friends, all of you, do go to the holy spot of Hāṭakeśvara.

After quickly killing the slayer of my son along with his attendants and members of the family the entire city of Camatkāra should be devoured by you all.

All the excellent serpents should put up their residence there. Manage in such a manner as to make the resettlement of that city impossible."

46. On being told thus by him, those of the serpents renowned as the most important ones hurriedly went to that excellent Brāhmaṇa at the outset.

47. After eating the sleeping son of Devarāta they ate the entire family with great fury.

48. All of them devoured furiously the others also, children, old people and youth and even the creatures and brutes there.

49. In the meantime, a terribly loud lamentation of the leading Brāhmaṇas rose up there on account of the devouring spree of the serpents.

50. Whatever else was seen on the ground was covered by the terrible serpents of dark-coloured bodies.

51. In the meantime, some who came there were subjected to death. Some who were trembling with the effects of poison fell on the ground.

52. A few others abandoned their children, houses and other things. Greatly afraid they ran far and wide towards the forest.

53. Other Brāhmaṇas conversant with the Mantras endeavoured (to cure the people) all round. Others accepting the medicinal herbs ran about in great fear.

54. Thus all the excellent serpents continued to proceed towards the city so that no Brāhmaṇa stayed behind there.

55. Then all those excellent serpents rendered that city desolate and freely roamed about in the Tīrthas and the shrines.

56. No serpent left the holy spot and went out. No other man dared to enter the holy spot.

57. Thus as a result of murder and devouring a kind of adjustment between the serpents and the human beings occurred based on the exterior and interior (of the holy spot).

58. In the meantime, Śeṣa set aside his grief for the son. In great delight, he offered the water libations along with the others of his class.

59-60. Some of those Brāhmaṇas who were grief-stricken and terribly afraid of the serpents collected together from all the quarters and came to that forest where Trijāta was present. He had been delightfully performing a great penance and had received boons from Hara.

61-62. On seeing all those people overwhelmed with grief on remembering their sons, wives etc., and crying piteously in various ways, he too became agitated. On seeing the persons, the leading Brāhmaṇas hailing from his own city, he also became miserable. He spoke to them with eyes turned turbid with tears:

63-65 "May all the Brāhmaṇas hear my statement now. As soon as I came out of that city, Hara was propitiated by me.

O excellent Brāhmaṇas, I have been granted the boon of accepting anything desired by me. Till today I have not accepted it. I shall now request for it.

I shall request for a boon whereby all the wicked-souled serpents will be destroyed. Those Nāgas of sinful activities have well nigh made our city utterly desolate."

66. After saying thus, the Brāhmaṇa Trijāta requested Parameśvara: "O Lord grant me that boon now."

67. Then the Lord of Devas said: "O Brāhmaṇa request for it; even if what is desired by you is very rare I shall grant it."

*Trijāta said:*

68-69. O Bull-vehicled One, the entire city of ours has become bereft of people due to the Nāgas. Hence, let them all be destroyed.

Thereby, O most excellent one among Suras, the city can once again be filled with Brāhmaṇas. I too can have the credit of having redeemed my own native land."

*Śrī Bhagavān said:*

70. O Brāhmaṇa nothing improper has been committed by those noble-souled serpents whose son free from any defect or crime, was killed by the Brāhmaṇas.

71. O excellent Brāhmaṇa, the murder was committed on the fifth lunar day in particular and that in the month of Śrāvaṇa when serpents are honoured.

72. Hence I shall tell you an excellent Siddha-Mantra at the mere utterance of which the poison of serpents is destroyed.

73. After going there accompanied by all those Brāhmaṇas, O highly esteemed one, do utter that Mantra in a loud voice that can be heard everywhere.

74. If the base serpents do not go to Pātāla after hearing it, they shall undoubtedly become poisonless at your instance.

*Trijāta said:*

75. O Śarva, tell me that great Mantra that destroys poison, so that I can go to my native land and eliminate the serpents.

*Śrī Bhagavān said:*

76-77. *Gara* means poison. That is not present there now. O excellent Brāhmaṇa, you utter "Nagaram, Nagaram" and you will have my favour. Nagaram Na-garam (there is no poison there is no poison). *Nagaram* is the Mantra. On hearing this if the base serpents still remain there they will be worthy of being killed easily.

78. From now onwards that spot shall be well-known all over the earth by the name "Nagara" and it will increase your reputation.

79-80. If any other Brāhmaṇa of pure race hailing from Nagara and called Nāgara repeats the Mantra named 'Nagara' and charges water thrice with it and pours that water into the mouth of any creature bitten by a black serpent and killed thereby, he can be restored to life.

81. A man staying elsewhere and remembering this three-syllabled Mantra (*na-ga-ra*) at the time of going to sleep cannot be harmed by a serpent.

82. If the poison comes from an immobile thing, or a mobile one or if it is artificial it becomes nectar-like when touched after uttering this Mantra.

83. Other stomach ailments caused by indigestion are entirely eradicated by the power of this Mantra.

84. After saying thus to that Brāhmaṇa the Bull-emblemed Lord went out of sight like a lamp without oil.

85. Along with the other Brāhmaṇas who survived the murderous attack Trijāta quickly and joyously went to the city of Camatkāra.

86. Thus all those Brāhmaṇas accompanied by Trijāta arrived there uttering loudly "Nagaram Nagaram".

87. They came to the holy spot of Hāṭakeśvara which was pervaded all round by the ruthless and terrible serpents obeying the command of Śeṣa.

88. On hearing the Siddha Mantra given by Śiva the serpents were deprived of their poison. Bereft of their vigour, they ran all round.

89. Some of the serpents took shelter in the anthills with diverse kinds of holes and others went to Pātāla.

90-91. Thousands of those serpents who were extremely terrified, who could not even crawl, who were overwhelmed by old age or who were in their infancy were struck with heavy sticks by the Brāhmaṇas who wanted to take revenge.

92. After exterminating all of them, the Brāhmaṇas were rid of their anguish. With that Trijāta at their head they performed the essential things for the holy spot.

93. Thus, O excellent Brāhmaṇas, with the favour of Bharga, the Lord of Devas, (the name of) that place became known as 'Nagara' thereafter.

94. If one reads this narrative concerning the 'Nagara' always (everyday) he will never have any fear from serpents anywhere.

## CHAPTER ONE HUNDRED FIFTEEN

# Gotras of Sages

*The sages said:*

1-2. O highly intelligent one, do proclaim to us the name of that Brāhmaṇa Trijāta. Whose son was he? What is his Gotra? What is his appellation? How is he, though a Trijāta, greater than those people of noble birth, having good qualities and radiant due to their brilliance and learning? It was by him that his land of nativity was lifted up (rehabilitated).

*Sūta said:*

3. That excellent Brāhmaṇa was born of the race of Sage Sāṅkṛtya. He was well known as Prabhāva. His appellation was Datta and he was son of Nimi.

4. After redeeming the native place he built an auspicious shrine of the Trident-bearing Lord of Devas by the name Trijāteśvara.

5. Then some time, thereafter, he propitiated that Lord day and night with great faith and went to heaven along with his physical body.

6. If one visits that Lord with true devotion and bathes him always on the Viṣuva (Equinox) day, never shall a Trijāta be born in his family.

*The sages said:*

7. O Sūtanandana, recount to us the names of those Gotras that became extinct and those that were re-established in that city.

*Sūta said:*

8-9. Like the four Gotras of those beginning with Śuka who disappeared (left permanently) due to the fear of serpents, the following excellent Brāhmaṇas did not come back: those of Upamanyu Gotra, those born of Krauñca Gotra, those hailing from Kaiśorya Gotra and also those of Traivaṇeya Gotra.

10. I shall mention to you the remaining Brāhmaṇas of different Gotras. Twenty-six are remembered as born of Kauśika family.

11. O excellent Brāhmaṇas, eighty-seven were born of Kaśyapa family; twenty-one families born of Lakṣmaṇa's family came back to that city.

12. Those who had vanished earlier came back again in great misery. Three of the Bhāradvāja family and fourteen of the Kauṇḍanīya family came back.

13. Raitikas were twenty and Pārāśaryas eight; Gargas twenty-two and Hārītas twenty-three.

14. The families of Aurvas and of Bhārgavas were cited as twenty-five; those of Gautamas twenty-six and those of Ālūbhāyanas (v.1. Ālūtāyana) were twenty.

15. The families of Māṇḍavyas were twenty-three, those of Bahvṛcas twenty-three, those of Sāṁkṛtyas and Viśiṣṭas (? splendid) (or those of distinguished Sāṅkṛtyas) were severally ten in number.

16. Further, Āṅgirasas were proclaimed as five in number; Ātreyas numbered ten and the same in the case of Śuklātreyas.

17. Vātsyas are reckoned as five and Kautsas sixteen (nine and seven). Śāṇḍilya sub-division of Bhārgavas are five and Mudgalyas are remembered as twenty.

18. Baudhāyanas and Kauśalas are proclaimed as thirty; Atharvas fifty-five and Maunasas seventy-seven.

19. Yājuṣas were thirty and the well known Cyāvanas were twenty-seven; Āgastyas thirty-three and Jaimineyas only ten.

20. Naivṛta Brāhmaṇas were fifty-five and Pāṭhīnas seventy. Gobhila Brāhmaṇas and Kākva Brāhmaṇas are remembered as five each.

21. Auśanasas and Dāśārhas are cited as three each. Further, there were sixty families of Lokākhyas and those of the Aiṇiśas seventy-two.

22. Kāpiṣṭhalas, those designated as Śārkaras and Dattas were seventy-seven, Śārkavas are mentioned as one hundred and Dārjyas seventy-seven.

23. Kātyāyanyas were three; Adhiṣṭhas and Vaidiśas are remembered as three. Kṛṣṇātreyas and Dattātreyas were five (each).

24. Nārāyaṇas, Śaunakeyas and Jābālas were one hundred in number. So also were Gopālas, Jāmadagnyas, Śālihotras and Karṇikas.

25. Further Bhāgurāyaṇakas, Mātṛkas and Traiṇavas were also similar.

O excellent Brāhmaṇas, all these were excellent Brāhmaṇas in due serial order.

26. It was for the consecration of all these that forty-eight excellent Brāhmaṇas were announced formerly by the Self-born Lord.

27. All of them were separately directed by the Lotus-born Lord. The enjoined rites were Sandhyā prayers, libations (Tarpaṇa to Pitṛs) and other things connected with Vaiśvadeva, Śrāddhas, the rites in the different Pakṣas (fortnights), balls of rice to be offered to the Pitṛs etc.

28. All the Pravaras connected with the rite of investing with the sacred threads, the particularly significant Mauñjis as well as the various styles of keeping hair-tuft were announced.

29. It was done by Trijāta after propitiating Pitāmaha, the Lord of Devas, for the sake of those leading Brāhmaṇas and for his own reputation.

*The sages said:*

30. How was Brahmā pleased by the noble-souled Trijāta? How was the Karmakāṇḍa (procedure of performing different religious rites) differentiated by that noble-souled one? Do mention everything. We are very much eager to know.

*Sūta said:*

31-33. For his sake, Prapitāmaha was propitiated by all the Brāhmaṇas: "O Lord, our native land was entirely redeemed (and rehabilitated) by this one alone.

Hence, O Lord, grant him the excellent knowledge of the Vedas so that the different special rites can function here, in this excellent city.

O Lotus-born One, do manage everything with due expedients so that he can have the status of preceptor with your favour, O Lord of Devas."

34. Then Brahmā granted to him the excellent collection of the Mantras whereby the meanings of the Vedas and (the procedure of) the Yajña rites were entirely understood.

35-39. Then with a highly delighted mind, he told them all: "This one will become richly endowed with the knowledge of the meaning of the Vedas. He will become famous.

He will become well-known as Bhartṛyajña and will be an expert in the rites of Yajña. Whatever he tells you in the matter of Karmakāṇḍa should be unhesitatingly carried out by you for the sake of heaven and salvation. As enlightened by my statements, he will explain the meanings of the Vedic passages to you.

It shall be due (applicable)to you all who had abandoned this land and gone to other lands and holy spots. O excellent Brāhmaṇas, this is the truth.

Whatever act he performs shall be with his intellect keenly rooted in the Vedas. His speech shall never be directed towards falsehood or sin."

40. After saying thus, Pitāmaha, the Lord of Devas, stopped. Bhartṛyajña performed all those auspicious Yajña rites.

41. For the sake of the welfare of the Brāhmaṇas alone he expounded the meaning of Śruti. All those excellent Brāhmaṇas were mentioned as having ten valid authorities (or extended to ten).

42. In this manner, excellent Brāhmaṇas belonging to all the sixty-four Gotras were brought together by the noble-souled Trijāta.

43. Thus, one thousand five hundred families collected there together in one place. Trijāta made them enjoy pleasures in common and attain salvation.

44. Formerly, the income and expenditure were reckoned in the Gotra in sixty-eight divisions or groups on the basis of the numbers of the men (i.e.members) thereof.

45-46. But ever since then, at the instance of Trijāta the matter became established in common pool.

Thereby, leading Brāhmaṇas used to come there from far-off lands and the city flourished. No one abandoned the city on account of sufferings or penury to go elsewhere, O Brāhmaṇas.

47. Then it became filled up with thousands of their sons, grandsons, great-grandsons, daughters' son, nephews etc. to a great deal.

48. That city is flourishing, O Brāhmaṇas, with innumerable citizens like the growth of the sprouts of Dūrvā grass, that grow from stem to stem.

*Sūta said:*

49. Thus the auspicious reckoning of the Gōtras of the sages has been narrated to you all. The recital thereof is destructive of all sins.

50. If anyone reads this daily or listens to it devoutly, he shall never have extinction of his family on the earth any time.

51. He is liberated from sins committed ever since his birth upto death. He never suffers separation from people near and dear.

## CHAPTER ONE HUNDRED SIXTEEN

## Greatness of Ambā-Revatī Tīrtha

*Sūta said:*

1-3. Further, there is another well-known deity Ambārevatī. The goddess fulfills cherished desires of men and accords happiness to children.

By visiting and worshipping her especially on the eighth lunar day in the bright half of Caitra, a men will seldom face calamity in the whole family anywhere.

*The sages said:*

O Sūtaputra, do narrate to us everything. By whom was that goddess Ambārevatī installed there? What is her nature? What is her power?

*Sūta said:*

4-5. When the different varieties of highly poisonous Nāgas, with eyes reddened through anger, were directed by Śeṣa for the destruction of the city, his beloved wife who was afflicted on account of her dead son, herself went ahead and swallowed along with the entire family that Brāhmaṇa by whom her son had been struck down.

6. Incidentally, there was a younger sister of the leading Brāhmaṇa. She was a child-widow but richly endowed with the power of penance. She strictly adhered to the practice of celibacy.

7. Her name was Bhaṭṭikā. On seeing that the entire family had been swallowed by the wife of the Nāga, she took some water in the hand and said:

8-10. "O two-tongued one, you have brought about the ruin of my family. You have caused much suffering to my kinsmen. Hence you will get the despicable human birth, you will marry a man and beget sons and grandsons. In that mortal life you will experience grief due to the death of those near and dear. I am uttering this curse to you even as you still continue to be a Nāga woman."

11. On hearing that imprecatory utterance of Bhaṭṭikā, Revatī (Nāga lady) was overwhelmed with anger and bit her quickly.

12. As soon as the poisonous fangs of the female Nāga came in contact with her (Bhaṭṭikā's) body they were shattered into hundred pieces and penetrated at no place on her body.

13. Thereupon, she became overcome with shame. Her own blood splashed her mouth (face). In her utter bewilderment, she sat quietly on the ground.

14-15. In the meanwhile, the Nāgas and others who had come there saw her frightened and in that condition. They asked: "O queen, what is this painful thing in your mouth? Or is this the power of a peculiar type of blood?"

*Revatī said:*

16. O excellent Nāgas, you see here a wicked woman-sage. This strange change (ailment) in my mouth has taken place due to her.

17. This is the wicked sister of that evil-minded one, the son of a Brāhmaṇa, by whom my son was killed.

18. Let her be eaten. Let her be swallowed. She is out for destroying me. O excellent serpents that is why there is blood in my mouth.

19. Those serpents became infuriated. All of them collectively bit that saintly woman all over her body as though she was an ordinary woman.

20. Thereupon, their fangs too fell down from their mouths and blood flowed out therefrom as in the case of the wife of the Nāga.

21. On becoming aware of the power of that saintly woman, the remaining Nāgas became terrified and they fled in all directions.

22. Bhaṭṭikā too was miserable. She hurried to her own hermitage even as the utterly terrified great serpents looked at her from all round.

23-24. That chaste lady perfectly engaged in the observance of holy vows became very sad on seeing the holy spot being scorched and harassed by the great serpents and therefore abandoned by her own people utterly miserable themselves. She, therefore, wandered all over the earth performing a pilgrimage.

25. When the place became deserted in this manner in that spot, Revatī became more miserable on recollecting the curse of Bhaṭṭikā.

26-29. 'What will be the nature of my stay within the womb of a human female as a result of the curse? How will the intercourse with a human lover take place?

The misery due to the death of my son does not give me so much pain in my heart as the thought of stay in a human womb and co-habitation with a human being.

Further, bereft of my fangs, how can I show my face to my husband. This is somewhat like sprinkling salt in a wound.

Hence I shall continue to worship in this holy spot itself restricting my movements to it. What will I do after reaching home, now that I have been rendered bereft of my son?'

30. Then she installed goddess Sureśvarī (Deity of the Suras). With perfect faith she propitiated the goddess Aṁbikā.

31. She adored the deity with offerings of scents and flowers, different kinds of food offerings and with charming songs, dances and instrumental music.

32. After a few days, Sureśvarī became pleased with her and said: "I shall grant the boon. Request for whatever is cherished in your heart."

*Revatī said:*

33-34. O goddess, formerly, for another reson I was cursed by a Brāhmaṇa lady: "You will become a human female and will associate with a human male. Then you will have sons and face the sad consequence of their destruction." I am already greatly miserable due to the death of the son. In addition, I have been cursed.

35. Moreover, O Sureśvarī, the fangs have been smashed in my mouth. How can they grow up again by your power?

36. Let sons be born to me making our family flourish. O goddess, this is desired by me. I do not wish to get anything else.

*The goddess said:*

37. O splendid lady, no fear need be entertained by you in this that you will have to stay in a human womb and that a man will be your husband.

38. Hence, O lady of excellent complexion, listen to my words which I shall utter now. In truth it is destructive of your misery.

39. There is no doubt that, for the sake of the fulfilment of the task of Devas, your husband will assume a human form and be born in these three worlds.

40. O splendid lady, the serpent named Takṣaka will be born in Saurāṣṭra due to the curse of a Brāhmaṇa. He will have the name Raivata.

41. Undoubtedly due to the curse of a Brāhmaṇa an excellent lady born of a noble Nāga family, named Kṣemakarī ('Causing welfare') shall be his wife.

42. You will be in her womb and will be born thereof. You will be the wife of Śeṣa again, who will be in the form of Rāma.

43. Hence, O fair lady, O splendid one, do not have any grief in this matter Therefore, your birth will take place in human womb.

44. The fact that you will see the destruction of your family there shall undoubtedly be for your good in that plight then.

45. Since thereafter there will be the advent of the sinful Kali Age, so all persons staying everywhere will be Mlecchas with the characteristics of human beings.

46. Then, for the purpose of stay in heaven, the Lord, the son of Devakī will destroy his own family entirely. There is no doubt about it.

47. Beautiful fangs will again grow in your mouth. So do go to Pātāla where your husband stays now.

48. O auspicious lady, do say if you have any other desire lurking in your mind. I have great pleasure.

*Revatī said:*

49. O Sureśvarī, you should stay here in this spot for ever by my name so that my reputation shall spread everywhere in the three worlds consisting of mobile and immobile creatures.

50-51. Further, on the eighth, ninth and especially on the fourteenth day of the bright half of Āśvina I shall come from the Nāga world accompanied by all the Nāgas and worship you. I shall perform the excellent worship with great faith.

52. If other men too perform your worship on that day, let them not witness the destruction of their beloved ones. Grant this favour.

*The Devī said:*

53. O fair lady, I shall thus stay here by your name. I shall always bestow welfare on the worshippers always, O lady of pure smiles, particularly so on the day of Mahānavamī.

*Sūta said:*

54. On being told thus by her (the goddess) Ravatī, the beloved of Śeṣa, went to her abode later with great delight.

55. Ever since then, that goddess became well established in that holy spot by her name. She bestows desired things on men and destroys all distresses.

56. Goddess Durgā is glorified as Aṁbā and that beloved wife of the serpent was Revatī. Hence the deity is glorified in the world as *Aṁbārevatī*.

57. One who remains pure and worships her with great faith on the ninth day in the bright half of the month of Āśvina will never witness any disaster in his family for the whole of that year.

58. By seeing a hole in front infested by a serpent one is rid of all evil arising from malefic planets, ghosts and spirits and also gets free from other troubles.

## CHAPTER ONE HUNDRED SEVENTEEN

# Emergence of Bhaṭṭikātīrtha

*The sages said:*

1-3. O Sūtanandana, the lady named Bhaṭṭikā was described by you earlier. How did the fangs of the Nāgas get broken when they came into contact with her body? O Sūtanandana, is it the power of her penance? Is it the power of magic spells? We are highly curious about this. How even in the body of a human being got shattered those poisonous fangs of the serpents in particular. Do describe everything.

*Sūta said:*

4. That Brāhmaṇa lady became a widow even when she was in her father's house during her childhood. That was a result of her previous Karmas.

5. Even in her childhood, she had the opportunity to listen to the various scriptural texts. She took part in religious pilgrimages. With great mental concentration and purity, she used to take holy bath in Tīrthas.

6. She used to go to the temple of Lord Kedāra with great mental concentration everyday. She used to get up early in the morning and sing devoutly before the deity.

7. Urged by the temptation to listen to her songs Takṣaka and Vāsuki assumed the form of two Brāhmaṇas and came there from Pātāla.

8-10. Her songs were exquisite with the Tānas and Mūrcchanās in the proper order. All the seven notes of the gamut embellished her songs. The *Yatis, Grāmas* and *Varṇagrāmas* were of different kinds. The four types of musical instruments viz. *Tata* (stringed ones), *Vitata* (drums etc.,), *Ghana* (cymbals etc.), *Suṣira* (flutes etc.) have their own Tālas (beating of the time), *Kālakriyā* (the process of timing) etc. The Brāhmaṇa lady was of course not an expert in those different aspects of music. Merely by the purity of the mellifluous voice of her throat, she delighted those two.

11. Getting up early in the morning with avidity (great attraction) for her music, all the citizens of that town eagerly assembled in the Kedāra shrine.

12. Once those two Nāgas forcibly took her to their city even as all the people were watching.

13. They had resumed their serpent form of terrible nature, causing great fright to the people and coiled their bodies around her. They then took her to Pātāla.

14. After taking her to their abode, those two serpents afflicted by lasciviousness said to her: "O lady of large eyes, become our faithful wife. It is for this that you have been brought here to Pātāla from the surface of the earth."

*Bhaṭṭikā said:*

15-16. O Takṣaka, I am a quiet woman born of the family of a Brāhmaṇa. I am indifferent to the gaiety of sexual activity. Still you had assumed the form of a Brāhmaṇa and abducted me. You have further touched me with your mind and soul swayed by lust. In view of these things you will become a human being.

17. O wicked one, if you ravish me per force your head will immediately shatter into a hundred pieces.

18. On hearing her terrible curse, he became extremely terrified and bewildered. He stood with palms joined in reverence and tried to pacify her:

19. "I admit that out of delusion you have been brought here by me overcome by passion. So be pleased to bring about the end of the curse."

*Sūta said:*

20. Thus the daughter of the Brāhmaṇa was propitiated by that Takṣaka. Then she said to him with her eyes dimmed with tears:

21. "O Takṣaka, if you take me again to the human world I shall undoubtedly bring about an end to the curse there."

22. In the meantime Takṣaka's wives[1] came to know that a human female had come to the abode; in fact she had been brought there by Takṣaka whose mind had been overcome by lust.

23. Overwhelmed with great jealousy, she came there apparently to destroy her. Her eyes were red due to anger.

24. Takṣaka understood her intention very well. Moreover, he was already frightened and he keenly desired the final dissolution of the curse from the lady (Brāhmaṇa).

25. He recollected the magical spell named *Vajra* and in order to protect her body cast the spell on her body. Presently, the serpent lady too came upon the scene.

26. She took the chaste daughter of the Brāhmaṇa for her co-wife and consequently became highly infuriated. She at once bit her only to get her fangs shattered thereby.

27. On seeing the serpent lady vitiated by jealousy and the feelings of animosity the daughter of the Brāhmaṇa became angry and cursed her also:

28. "I am without any fault. Still you consider me as full of defects. So, O sinful one, be born a human female experiencing misery."

29. Then Takṣaka, the most excellent one among Nāgas, carried her off and left her at the Kedāra shrine at midnight.

30. Standing there with his palms joined together in reverence, he spoke to that fair lady: "O chaste lady, bring about an end to my curse so that I can go to my abode."

*Bhaṭṭikā said:*

31. O serpent, you will become a king named Raivataka in the land of Saurāṣṭra on the earth. You will always enjoy worldly pleasures.

32. Then, by abandoning your body in the holy shrine in the middle of the hermitage in the holy place, you will regain your own original position by the power of the holy spot.

1. The plural form 'wives' is used to indicate the plural '*kalatrāṇi*' in the text. It is only one wife intended in the story.

*Takṣaka said:*

33. Let this beloved wife of mine whom also you have cursed be my wife even during the human life.

34. At least do this favour to this distressed soul of mine earnestly requesting you. Let there be no contact of another male person with her.

*Bhaṭṭikā said:*

35. She will be born as the splendid daughter of King Ānarta. Then after the marriage, she will become your wife.

36. She will be well-known as Kṣemaṁkarī. She will be equipped with beauty of form and prime of youth. After enjoying many pleasures on the surface of the earth, the splendid lady will follow you to the other world too.

*Sūta said:*

37. On being told thus by her, he became delighted. After respectfully bowing down to her and saying, "May you be pleased to forgive", he went to his own abode.

38. Even as a part of the night still remained, she stood before Lord Kedāra and began her songs highly delightful to the ears.

39. Thereafter, many hundreds of Brāhmaṇas endowed with devotion to Kedāra deity came there with a desire to see the deity.

40. On seeing the daughter of the Brāhmaṇa, the lady Bhaṭṭikā who had returned there, they were surprised and they began to question her:

41. "O highly splendid lady, who was this serpent who had come in the form of a Brāhmaṇa? Where were you taken to by him? Why? Do tell us."

42. Why were you set free again? Do mention everything in the manner it had occurred. A great curiosity has heen generated in us on account of you.

*Sūta said:*

43. She narrated everything concerning the story of Takṣaka, the curse and the subsequent pacification.

44. In the meantime all the members of her family came there. On hearing that she had returned, their misery increased and they were crying loudly.

45. With her eyes turned turbid, her mother embraced her. Her companions too with affectionate mind closely clasped her.

46. They took her to their abode listening to the narration of the events that happened in Nāgaloka. They were extremely surprised in their minds.

47-49. The citizens of the city met together and said to one another: "An improper act has been committed by this wicked-minded Brāhmaṇa. His youthful daughter who had stayed in the mansion of others has been brought back. Other Brāhmaṇas too here have many women to take care of, who are young, beautiful and unfortunately overtaken by the state of widowhood. This may set a bad precedent unto all of them resulting in promiscuous sexual relationships and mixture of castes. Hence she should be banished."

50. All those excellent Brāhmaṇas gathered together and spoke to him these words in a gentle manner conforming to scriptural texts:

51-53. "O Brāhmaṇa, this beautiful and youthful daughter of yours was carried off to Pātāla by a lustful Nāga.

Yet on being released by that lustful one she says, 'I am blemishless and pure'. People do not believe that she can be considered pure.

Hence, O excellent Brāhmaṇa, let her pass through a *Divya* (ordeal) to prove her purity to leading Brāhmaṇas. In this way, O wise one, the downfall of other young women can be prevented."

54-55. "So it shall be", he said and he asked his daughter privately away from the people: "If you have any blemish confess it out. Otherwise undergo the ordeal to satisfy the Brāhmaṇas and demonstrate your purity."

*Bhaṭṭikā said:*

56. Dear father, what is proper has been said by you as well as the other Brāhmaṇas. The purity of a woman can be called into question even on stepping out of the door.

57. All the more so in my case, who had been to an alien land with a lustful person. Hence, I shall take the holy bath in the morning and (enter) fire.

58. By entering fire I shall demonstrate my purity to all the Brāhmaṇas undoubtedly. Food or beverage whatever I have to take in, I shall take in only after getting the clearance through the fire-ordeal.

59. On being told thus by her, he was extremely pleased. Getting up early in the morning, he piled up logs of wood at the outskirts of the city.

60-61. Bhaṭṭikā took her bath and made herself pure. She wore white clothes and was accompanied by members of her family as well as by friends and attendants. With the face beaming with pleasure, she meditated upon Viṣṇu and went to that place where the huge pile of logs was made.

62. Then, O excellent Brāhmaṇas, she set it on fire herself. After circumambulating it three times, she said with palms joined in reverence.

63-64. "If there is an iota of blemish arising from lust in my body forcefully caused by that wicked-minded Takṣaka or by anyone else, or if such a blemish may arise later, let this well-kindled fire burn me quickly."

65. After saying thus, that chaste lady entered the burning fire as if it were her own mansion. The well-kindled fire turned into cool water.

66. She saw herself moving about in the middle of water. The splendid lady felt the coolness everywhere. A great shower of flowers fell from the sky.

67-72. A messenger of gods seated in an aerial chariot spoke these words: "O highly esteemed one, you are pure due to the chastity of the limbs.

No other woman will ever be equal to you. O highly esteemed one, in all the limbs together in a human body, there are altogether thirty-five million hairs.

Among them, O chaste lady, not a single one is sinful. Hence hasten back to your abode along with your kinsmen.

Do meritorious acts. Propitiate Keśava. This spot of the fire orderal filled now with water shall become a Tīrtha well-known after your name. Those who take their holy bath here at the time of Śayana and Bodhan of Hari (eleventh day in Āṣāḍha and Kārttika) will attain great Siddhis which even the immortal ones cannot."

After saying this, the messenger of gods stopped.

73-75. Bhaṭṭikā became highly delighted. She bowed down to her father and said: "I will not go home. What will I do in the house?

Here itself in my own Tīrtha I shall propitiate Acyuta always. Further I shall perform penance with the food received as alms as my sustenance.

Hence, O dear father, I shall stay here in this place of resort."

76. Then her father and those citizens went home with great delight, praising her individually.

77. Earlier an idol of Trivikrama was installed by her and later the Liṅga of Maheśvara after building the excellent palatial shrine.

78. Then she performed a great penance taking the alms received as her food. She was praised by all the people of Camatkāra city.

*Sūta said:*

79-80. Thus, O excellent Brāhmaṇas, everything whatever I was asked, has been narrated to you by me, I have told you how her body remained firm and unbreakable always to serpents and others such as weapons etc. One who reads this excellent narrative of Bhaṭṭikā, O execellent Brāhmaṇas, will never meet with calumny caused by wicked people.

## CHAPTER ONE HUNDRED EIGHTEEN

# Installation of Raivatakeśvara and Kṣemaṁkarī

*The sages said:*

1-4. O Sūtaja, it was mentioned by you that Takṣaka would be born in the land of Saurāṣṭra as a highly powerful king named Raivata and further that his beloved wife would be born as a beautiful lady in the palace of the overlord of Ānarta by the name Kṣemaṁkarī. O Sūtanandana, give a fully detailed information about those two. In this matter, we are rather curious since what you tell is wonderful.

Moreover, O Sūtaputra, we have heard that Kedāra is in Himācala. How did it happen to be there? Describe everything in full.

*Sūta said:*

5. In this connection, O excellent Brāhmaṇas, I shall speak unto you in the manner heard earlier by me from by own father.

6. Due to his earlier default and the curse thereof, Takṣaka was born in the mansion of the Lord of Saurāṣṭra by the name Raivata.

7-8. A daughter was born in the house of the Lord of Ānarta. Her name became well-known all over the earth as Kṣemaṁkarī. O leading Brāhmaṇas, (the significance of the name) became manifest through her activity.

Formerly the Lord of Ānarta was Prabhañjana.

9. His enmity with many kings cropped up. Thereupon, O excellent Brāhmaṇas, the land began to be rid of its citizens (due to exodus). Cattle were carried off forcibly. There was a battle with the enemies (which continued) during day and night.

10. After a few days his wife Priyaṁvadā who had her menstrual cycle, duly conceived a meritorious foetus in her womb.

11. Ever since the conception of the foetus in her womb, there was an overall state of welfare in the city as well as in the country.

12. A few invincible enemies were conquered by him in a battle. Others were killed and a few were taken over as allies.

13. A splendid girl with wide eyes resembling lotus-petals was born to her, when the lying-in-chamber shone even in darkness.

14. The king was highly delighted at her birth. He celebrated the birth with great festivities as though at the birth of a son, with the singing of songs and playing of musical instruments.

15. On the thirteenth day, O Brāhmaṇas, a befitting name was given to her by the king in the presence of Brāhmaṇas.

16. "O Brāhmaṇas, since there was Kṣema (welfare) even while she was in the womb, she shall be called Kṣemaṁkarī."

17. Thus duly consecrated and well reputed she grew up day by day like the digit of the moon in the firmament.

18. Then when she became one endowed with the prime of youth, the king, gave her to Raivata, the Lord of Saurāṣṭra, at a time very auspicious for marriage.

19-20. The celebrated wife of Śeṣa who had been wedded to the intelligent king of Nāgas in the form of Rāma and who had (was to have) sons and grandsons, became haughty on account of conjugal felicity. She was born as their daughter and was well-known as Revatī.

21. Even when the two had grown old, O leading Brāhmaṇas, no son was born of them to perpetuate their line. Therefore they suffered great misery.

22. Then they entrusted the group of ministers with the whole kingdom and came here for practising a penance to get a son.

23. They went to their hermitage and stayed there with great mental concentration. They installed goddess Kātyāyanī and engaged themselves in propitiating her.

24. (You may remember) that it was this goddess engaged in *Kaumāravrata* (vow of celibacy) on the Vindhya mountain who had killed the terrible Asura named Mahiṣa.

25. The goddess who was pleased granted them a son destined to perpetuate the line. He became well-known by the name Kṣemajit. He was a powerful warrior capable of destroying hosts of enemies.

26. The king went back to his kingdom with great delight and brought up his son with great pleasure.

27. When this son Kṣemajit became a young man, the elderly king crowned him (as king of) the kingdom and went back to his original holy spot.

28. That holy spot is this Hāṭakeśvara Kṣetra, O excellent Brāhmaṇas. He left all his attendants and came to this holy spot along with his wife.

29. There he installed the Liṅga of the Trident-bearing Lord. Then he constructed with great concentration a beautiful palace.

30. The deity is called Raivateśvara. It was simply through paying a visit to the Lord that it destroyed all the sins of all embodied beings, O excellent Brāhmaṇas.

31. With great faith Kṣemaṁkarī constructed the palace of the deity Durgā that had been earlier installed by the king in that holy spot.

32. Ever since then she is glorifed by the name Kṣemaṁkarī, the deity who was earlier called Kātyāyanī and Mahiṣāsuramardinī (suppressor of the demon Mahiṣa).

33. O excellent Brāhmaṇas, if a person visits her on the eighth day in the bright half on the month of Caitra, all his desires will allways be realized.

34. Thus everything regarding Raivateśvara and the sin-destroying power of Kṣemaṁkarī has been narrated to you.

## CHAPTER ONE HUNDRED NINETEEN

## Defeat of the Army of Gods[1]

*The sages said:*

1-2. O Sūtaja, it has been mentioned by you that Goddess Kātyāyanī destroyed Mahiṣa. How was it? Narrate it to us.

Of what nature was that heroic Dānava who had assumed

1 Chapters 119-121 deal with the story of the creation of Kātyāyanī and killing of Mahiṣāsura. Mbh, *Vana* 231-92 states that Skanda killed him.

the form of a buffalo? Why was he slain by the goddess. Tell it to us in detail.

*Sūta said:*

3. In this context I shall expound to you the excellent greatness of the goddess completely. Even if it is merely listened to, there shall be the destruction of the enemies of all mankind.

4. Formerly, there was a Dānava named Mahiṣa. He was son of Hiraṇyākṣa. Assuming the form of a buffalo, he enjoyed the three worlds.

*The sages said:*

5. O Sūtanandana, was he born along with the form of a buffalo? Or did he become so due to a curse as a result of a crime? Tell us.

*Sūta said:*

6. Indeed he was born with a fine form and features. His face resembled a lotus. His arms were long and his neck was thick. He was characterised by all excellent features. He was endowed with brilliance and vigour. He was called by the name Citrasama.

7. Ever since his childhood he generally avoided other vehicles like horses etc., and used to rouse the buffaloes (for the purpose of riding).

8. Once that son of Danu was seated on a buffalo and moved about near the banks of Gaṅgā killing aquatic birds.

9. It happened that the excellent sage Durvāsā was seated in the lotus pose on the bank of Gaṅgā, practising excellent meditation.

10. Since the Dānava was keenly looking for birds, his mind was no better than absent in regard to the leading sage. He was not at all noticed by him and the Brāhmaṇa was trampled upon by the buffalo under his hoofs in its mad rush.

11. Smeared with the blood from his wounds, the sage saw the Dānava before him. Further, the fellow did not bow down to him. This enraged him.

12-13. The sage then took up water in his hand and said angrily: "O sinful one, my body was trampled upon by the hoofs of your buffalo and you have caused disturbance to my meditation, so you shall become a buffalo. O evil-minded one, you will be aware of this perfectly as long as you live."

14. Thereupon, he became a huge buffalo of dark complexion. He was like another mountain of collyrium. His horns were very long.

15. With great humility he pacified the sage: "O Brāhmaṇa, I was too childish to observe things. Do put an end to the curse."

16-17. Then the sage said to him: "My words cannot go in vain. As long as you live, this will be like that. O highly evil-minded one, you will have this despicable form of a buffalo."

After saying so, the leading sage left the banks of Gaṅgā and went elsewhere. The demon went to Śukra and said thus:

18-19. "I have been cursed by Durvāsas for some reason and have been turned into a buffalo. Hence you should be my refuge. O leading Brāhmaṇa, do employ some means so that with your favour, the brutish form vanishes and I regain my original physical form."

*Śukra said:*

20. Excepting Lord Maheśvara, this curse cannot be altered by anyone else.

21. Hence hasten to the holy spot of Hāṭakeśvara that bestows all Siddhis and propitiate the excellent Liṅga.

22. O excellent Dānava, acquisition of perfection is very quick even in the sinful age of Kali. All the more so in the first yuga (called Kṛta).

23. On being told thus by Śukra, the Dānava immediately went to the holy spot of Hāṭakeśvara and performed a great penance.

24. With great devotion, he installed a great Liṅga of the Trident-bearing Lord and thereafter erected a palace comparable to a peak of Kailāsa.

25. The large-hearted Dānava continued the strenuous ordeal of the penance for a long period.

26. Then Mahādeva became pleased. He appeared before him and said: "O Dānava, I am pleased with you. Choose a boon."

*Mahiṣa said:*

27. I have been cursed by Durvāsas and have been turned into a buffalo. Hence with your favour, let this brutish form vanish.

*Śrī Bhagavān said:*

28. His utterance (curse) cannot be altered at any rate. Hence I shall suggest an easy means to you. Listen to it.

29. All types of sensual pleasures, human, divine and demoniac, will resort to your physical form.

30. It is for the sake of sensual pleasures that a human form is sought after by Suras and Asuras. Hence this body of yours will obtain all those pleasures.

*Mahiṣa said:*

31. If thus, O Lord of the chiefs of Devas, I will obtain sensual pleasures, let this physical form of mine be indestructible.

32. It may not be killed by the ten categories of divine beings and, all human beings, brutes, Nāgas and birds, O most excellent one among Suras.

*Śrī Bhagavān said:*

33. O Dānava, no embodied being can be indestructible on the surface of the earth. Hence, O leader of Daityas, except this one, seek other ones (boons).

34-36. Then he thought for a long time and spoke to the Bull-emblembed One: "Leaving womankind alone let there not be my destruction by others.

Further, O Śaṅkara, if a man takes his holy bath in my Tīrtha with great faith and unperturbedly visits you thereafter, let him have the fulfilment of all desires with your favour. May all calamities end in his case and may his splendour increase.

*Śrī Bhagavān said:*

37-38. If a person takes his holy bath in your Tīrtha on the fourteenth lunar day in the bright half of the month of Mārgaśīrṣa and lovingly visits my Liṅga thereafter, all troubles arising from ghosts, spirits, vampires etc. and all ailments like fever will finish.

39. After saying this the Lord of Devas vanished. Thereafter Mahiṣa went to his own abode.

40. After going there, he seated himself in the middle of the assembly and full of rage and vehemence of intolerance, summoned all the Dānavas and spoke to them:

41-42. "All the Dānavas such as my father, paternal uncle and other ancestors were killed by Devas with Vāsudeva as their leader. Hence, I will exterminate all those Devas in a great battle. Then I will seize the kingdom of all the three worlds."

43-44. Then those Dānavas said: "This is proper. This is excellent. The kingdom ruled by Śakra in heaven is our own realm. Therefore we shall go there now itself and immediately kill Indra in battlefield. We shall then stay happily in heaven enjoying divine pleasures."

45. After taking the general counsel thus, all the Dānavas went to the peak of Meru along with their servants, armies and vehicles.

46. On seeing the army of the Dānavas equipped with weapons and missiles descending upon them all of a sudden at the very threshold of their city for the purpose of fighting, Śakra and the other Devas too came out.

47. All these came out: Ādityas, Vasus, Rudras, the expert physicians Nāsatyas, Viśvedevas, Sādhyas, Siddhas and Vidyādharas.

48. Thereupon, a battle ensued between the Devas and Dānavas who reviled one another and dared death bravely.

49. Thus the battle dragged on for three years in heaven. Vast rivers of blood overflowed.

50. One day, he saw Śakra seated on Airāvata. A white umbrella was held above his head and he was surrounded by the Devas with divine missiles and weapons in their hands.

51. Thereupon, the infuriated Lord of the Dānavas, Mahiṣa, rushed against him with great speed.

52. With his sharp horns, he hit the elephant Airāvata in his chest. The elephant made a terribly tumultous trumpeting sound.

53. Then he reverted his face and began to flee. He ran speedly towards the city of Amarāvatī.

54. The elephant driver pierced his forehead by hitting it with the goad. Though he was checked thus, he never stopped at all.

55. On seeing very haughty Mahiṣa and the Daityas roaring gruffly and striking their arms and chest as wrestlers do with their hands, the Thousand-eyed One spoke:

56-57. "Of course, this elephant of mine is going away from the battlefield helplessly. But, O Daitya, do not think that the Lord of heaven has fled away. Hence wait for a while. Let me get into my excellent chariot. I shall hit you with my sharp arrows and destroy your arrogance."

58. In the meantime, Mātali, the charioteer of Śakra, came there with the chariot fitted with ten thousand horses with the speed of the wind.

59. Struck with the whip by Mātali, those horses ran speedily as though they were flying up into the sky.

60. Then Pākaśāsana (Indra) lifted up his bow and covered the Dānava with the arrows having serpentine shapes.

61. Thereupon, he became all the more infuriated and rushed with great speed to the place where the Lord of heaven was present.

62. He then furiously hit and pierced the excellent horses with his horns and tore them violently again and again.

63. The excellent horses with their chests wounded and bodies drenched and smeared with blood, followed the path of Airāvata.

64. The excellent Suras observed the chariot of Śakra turning away. They were all frightened and they too fled following its path.

65. On seeing all the Suras shattered in the battle, all those Dānavas roared like rumbling clouds and showered volleys of missiles.

66. In the meantime, night overtook them enveloping everything in darkness. Nothing became visible to the eyes of anyone.

67. All the Dānavas then retired from fighting. They resorted to the beautiful peak of Meru and decided to camp there.

68. Crowned with success in the battle, they became highly delighted. They recapitulated the incidents of the battle and began extolling how it took place.

69. The Devas lost all their enthusiasm on being utterly hit and wounded. They held discussion together in secret with Bṛhaspati as their leader:

70-71. "Now our army has been turned away (defeated) by the Dānavas. It has been annihilated and rendered demoralised and incapable of fighting further. No vestige of enthusiasm for fighting remains in it now. Hence we shall abandon the city of Amarāvatī and enter the abode of Brahmā where there is no fear from the Dānavas."

72. All the Devas including Vāsava decided thus, evacuated the city of Śakra and went to Brahmaloka.

73. The Dānavaṣ got up in the morning and seeing the city of Śakra vacant entered it gladly.

74. They installed the Daitya Mahiṣa in the post of Śakra. With great delight they bowed down to him and celebrated a great festival.

75. They partook of all the shares in the Yajñas that belonged to the heaven-dwellers. They occupied all the spots endearing to the Devas.

## CHAPTER ONE HUNDRED TWENTY

## The Origination of Kātyāyanī

*Sūta said:*

1-3. Thus Śakra and the Devas were defeated in the battle by Mahiṣa. Then he ruled all over the three worlds. Whatever he saw in all the three worlds as important and substantially good, such as elephants, horses, chariots etc., that Asura appropriated for himself.

Even as he went on doing so, the Devas including Vāsava became all the more miserable. Meeting together they began to discuss ways and means for bringing about his death.

4. In the meantime the excellent sage Nārada who had seen all the outrageous activities of Mahiṣa came there.

5. He described in all details to them all the acts of harassment of the three worlds on his part.

6. On hearing the words of Nārada regarding such atrocities of Mahiṣa inflicted on a universal scale, their anger which was already intense increased all the more.

7. The heat generated by their cumulative anger issued forth through their mouths and the quarters became defiled (darkened) instantly.

8. In the meantime Kārttikeya came there and asked: "O sage, what is the cause of the anger of the Devas? The entire range of the quarters has become dark and foul."

*Nārada said:*

9. O Skanda, I have just now conveyed to these the news how everything was carried off by the arrogant Dānavas in all the three worlds.

10. The demons are haughty and unthwartable. A jewel of a woman, a splendid house or anything fine in anyone's house falling within their vision is never left alone.

11. On hearng this, a spasm of rage issued forth from the mouth of Kārttikeya just as the fury of the Devas did.

12. In the meantime, from within that mass of rage a splendid virgin endowed with divine splendour and marked with all auspicious characteristic features arose.

13. Since this virgin was evolved out of the rage of Kārttikeya getting mingled with that of the heaven-dwellers, she was remembered as Kātyāyanī.

14. Then the Lord of the Devas gave her his weapon Vajra (thunderbolt), Skanda gave her the sharp pointed Śakti, and Lord Janārdana, the bow.

15. Mahādeva gave her the Triśūla (trident). Varuṇa gave his Pāśa (noose), Āditya sharp arrows and the Moon an excellent shield.

16. The delighted Nirṛti gave the Nistriṁśa (sword) and Hutāśana (Fire-god) gave the firebrand. Vāyu gave the sharp Churikā (dagger) and Dhanada gave the Parigha (iron club).

17. The Lord of Pretas (departed souls i. e. Yama) gave the Daṇḍa (baton) of terrific nature for the destruction of the enemies of the Suras. O excellent Brāhmaṇas, the virgin saw these twelve weapons.

18. Kātyāyanī saw these twelve excellent weapons of the heaven-dwellers and assumed twelve hands and grasped them immediately.

19-20. Then with evident delight as indicated by the rising hair, she spoke to them all: "O excellent Devas, tell me quickly why I have been created? I shall carry out all your tasks. There is no doubt about this."

*The Devas said:*

The terrifying Dānava named Mahiṣa has come up (born) now.

21. He cannot be killed by any living being and never indeed by human beings. Excepting a woman, none can kill him. Therefore, you have been created by us.

22. Hence do go to the excellent mountain named Vindhya and perform a severe penance there whereby your refulgence can increase.

23. After coming to know that you have become fully equipped with brilliance, we shall ourselves keep you in front and fight with that wicked-souled one.

24. Then, consumed by the fire of your weapons, he will meet his death. With the enemies killed we will regain the lost prosperity and glory of Devas.

## CHAPTER ONE HUNDRED TWENTYONE

# Mahiṣāsura Defeated

*Sūta said:*

1-2. On hearing the words of the Devas, that great goddess said: "May the Devas give me a vehicle immediately."

Thereupon, Gaurī gave her a hideous-faced lion as her vehicle. Then, riding on it she set off towards the Vindhya mountain.

3. She settled on one of its peaks. It was beautiful. It had excellent trees full of fruits and flowers. It appeared as though the peak was embellished with a pavilion of creepers.

4. Then the chaste lady observed severe vows and performed a penance. She controlled the group of her sense-organs and meditated upon Maheśvara.

5. As and when her penance grew steadily, O Brāhmaṇas, the beauty and refulgence of her body went on increasing.

6. In the meantime, the servants of the Lord of Daityas came there. On seeing a lady of wonderfully refulgent physical form engaged in the observance of Vratas, they went and reported it to their Lord, the wicked-souled Mahiṣa.

*The spies said:*

7. As we were roaming about on the surface of the earth we saw an extraordinary girl on the Vindhya mountain. She had twelve brilliant hands holding different kinds of weapons. She had covered her body with a hide.

8. No lady of (such) beautiful buttocks like hers having such an exquisite form has been seen by us before. She does not belong to the category of Devas, Gandharvas, Asuras, or Nāgas.

9. We do not know what she was performing the penance for. The lady of great reputation may be desirous of heaven, or she may be covetous of wealth or she may be desirous of a befitting husband, O Lord.

*Sūta said:*

10. On hearing their words, Mahiṣa, the Lord of Dānavas, was overwhelmed by Kāmadeva (god of Love) at the very moment he heard them.

11. Then, keeping them in front and accompanied by a great army he went to the place where the girl was present. He was very much swayed with eagerness.

12. It was as though for the sake of meeting sure death, a dull-witted jackal was approaching the beloved of a lion sleeping without any fear from any quarter quite complacently in a forest.

13. Merely at the very sight of that goddess the leader of Dānavas was struck with the arrows of Kāma instantaneously, O excellent Brāhmaṇas.

14. Then the demon who had become infatuated by her beauty and utterly deluded, kept the army at a distance and stood alone before her. He spoke to her sweetly:

15-19. "O lady of sweet smiles, this Vrata of yours is inconsistent with your youth. Hence, give this up and become the mistress of the three worlds.

I do not know whether you have heard about me. I am the Lord of Dānavas named Mahiṣa. It was by me that the thousand-eyed Lord Indra was defeated in a duel.

The entire area of the three worlds stays under my control now. Hence, O lady of excellent buttocks, become my extremely favourite wife..

I have already a thousand wives who are very splendid. All of them shall render menial service unto you now.

O lady of excellent lips, I shall hand over to you all my riches and shall behave like your very humble servant."

*Sūta said:*

20. On hearing his words the great goddess rebuked him and spoke thus with her eyes red due to anger:

21-22. "Fie upon you, fie upon you, O demon of sinful activities! Your mind is assailed by lust. Why do you speak like this to me observing the vow of virginity?

I have been created by the excellent Devas for the purpose of killing you. I shall hence destroy you. Remember the ardent desire lurking in your heart."

*Mahiṣa said:*

23. If it is so, O beautiful lady, it is but proper that a virgin should be sought after by all living beings.

24. O lady of excellent complexion, virtuous rites and penances are performed for the sake of heavenly pleasures, whereby people enjoy human as well as divine pleasures.

25. Therefore, O highly splendid one, surrender yourself to me through the Gāndharva form of marital alliance because it has been glorified as more important than other types of marriage alliance.

26. Even as he was saying thus the goddess became very furious and in an instant discharged an arrow aiming at his mouth.

27-30. In the manner of a serpent that enters an anthill the arrow pierced his mouth. On being hit with the arrows he cried aloud. Much blood flowed out of his mouth like the red chalk that flows from a mountain in liquid form. With anger overpowering him, he slowly receded and hurriedly resorted to the presence of his vast army. Completely under the control of Kāma he ordered thus to his soldiers: "May this wicked woman be captured. Although she may be shattered with blows see that the life does not leave her. If she does not fall dead due to the shower of arrows, she will certainly became my dear wife. There is no doubt about it."

31. On being told thus by him the Dānavas, foolishly arrogant of their ability to fight, rushed at her discharging sharp arrows.

32-33. In the meantime the goddess observed that they had arrived with a firm determination to fight. Consequently they were threatening and taunting her again and again. Thereupon the goddess discharged sharp arrows and struck them instantly in all their vulnerable joints.

34. Hit by those sharp arrows some of those Daityas and Dānavas died and others were made to flee in different directions.

35. On observing that his army has been shattered by her in the battle the Daitya became furious and himself rushed at her.

36. Rumbling and roaring frequently like and autumnal cloud he hit her hundreds and thousands of times with his horns.

37. In the meantime the goddess laughed boisterously making the entire space of the three worlds filled therewith.

38. Thus, when she laughed, Pulindas, Śabaras, Mlecchas and other forest-dwellers issued forth from her mouth.

39. Śakas and Yavanas too came out thus in their hundreds of physical forms (bodies) covered with armour. They appeared like messengers of Yama.

40. They spoke: "O fair lady, for what purpose have we been created? Do tell us, O lady of excellent countenance, so that it can be carried out quickly."

*Devī said:*

41. At our instance slay, as you please, these soldiers of this evil fellow. They are foolishly proud due to their inordinate strength. Slay them quickly.

42. On hearing her words, they danced and pranced holding their bows and swords. With great speed they rushed at the army of the Daityas.

43. Then a great and very terrible battle ensued between the two armies wherein the soldiers of the same side could not be distinguished from those of the others.

44. Then all those Dānavas were shattered and annihilated by the soldiers originating from the goddess. Others were wounded and disabled by their blows.

45. On seeing his army broken up, the infuriated Mahiṣa spoke angrily to the goddess these harsh words:

46. "O sinful woman, you were not killed by me in the battle solely on the consideration that you are a woman. So, see how I can strike. Otherwise you will not understand the reality."

47. After saying thus and reviling her frequently, he butted against her with special force with his horns.

48. On seeing the Dānava close by, the goddess rode on him from behind furiously.

49. Shattered at the hind quarters the Daitya was fully drenched with blood. He rose up into the sky and roared loudly.

50. In the meantime, a lion came out from her refulgence and seized the hind part (of his body) angrily with his curved fangs.

51. The Dānava became motionless as he was caught under the feet (of the lion). He could not even take a step ahead. He gave out terrific roars.

52. In the meantime, all the Devas, including Vāsava came there and stood in the sky. Joyously they spoke to the goddess:

53. "O goddess of Suras, cut off the head (of this demon) with this sharp-edged sword so that he cannot go elsewhere."

54. On hearing their words, the goddess became very angry. She wielded the sword and hit his stout neck.

55. On being struck with the sword the neck of the Daitya though stout and tough split into two causing the delight of the heaven-dwellers.

56. It had the splendour of twelve suns. The mouth held within it the shield as well as the sword. (The demon) began to revile the great goddess who had lifted up her hand with the sword. He then made the sword resembling the morning sun strike her body.

57. Then (the goddess) caught hold of his hair and was about to strike him to destroy his body. Then the Dānava said:

*The Dānava said:*

58. Be victorious, O goddess; be victorious, O omnipresent goddess of Suras, be victorious. Be victorious, O omnipresent goddess. Be victorious, O goddess, O favourite of all the people.

59. O bestower of desired things, be always victorious. Be victorious, O most beautiful lady in all the three worlds. Be victorious, O goddess endeavouring to protect all the three worlds. Be victorious, O goddess who have no fear from anywhere.

60. Be victorious, O goddess who cause delight. Be victorious, O destroyer of the Daityas. Be victorious, O lustrous one who destroy sufferings. Be victorious, O bestower of delusion on the non-devotees.

61. You are the creation. You are the excellent goddess. You are the goddess of fortune. You are Sarasvatī. You are Svāhā; you are Svadhā, Tuṣṭi (satisfaction), Puṣṭi (nourishment). You are Medhā (intellect). You are Dhṛti (fortitude). You are Kṣamā (forgiveness).

62. Hence accord favour unto me. Protect my life. Take pity on me as I have bowed down, as I am bereft of everything and extremely wretched too.

63. I am the powerful son of Hiraṇyākṣa. I have been cursed by Durvāsas and turned into a Mahiṣa (buffalo). But, O goddess, I have been liberated by you.

64. Hence the haughtiness due to being a Dānava has been got rid of today. I shall be your servant now, O goddess of Suras.

65. Be victorious, O goddess present in all, O destroyer of all wicked ones.

66. On hearing these piteous words of the Daitya, the goddess of Suras was overcome with compassion. She then addressed these words to the Suras who stood in the firmament:

67-68. "What shall I do, O Suras? I have been moved with pity for him. Hence I will not kill the Dānava who is prattling piteously. I will not kill an enemy in the battle even if he be the murderer of my father, should he turn his face (back), leave off swords and weapons and aver 'I am yours.'"

*The Devas said:*

69. O goddess of Devas, if you do not kill this base Dānava, he will surely destroy all the three worlds consisting of the mobile and immobile beings.

70. In that case all our efforts regarding your creation would be in vain. So also will be all your painful efforts.

*Devī said:*

71. O immortal ones, I will neither kill this one nor will I leave him off. I will catch hold of his hair and hold him always.

*The Devas said:*

72. O highly esteemed one! Excellent! Excellent! The proper word (decision) has been uttered by you. O goddess of Devas, indeed this alone is the proper thing to do on this occasion.

73. Do be in the mortal world now resorting to this terrible form with the weapons lifted up in the hands and seated on the buffalo. You will receive here highest adoration.

74. One who propitiates you present here in this form (will attain) fruits rarely achieved even by the immortals.

75. You shall be well-known as Vindhyavāsinī in association with this Demon. Of what avail is speaking too much! Listen to the words in brief.

76. Our words will be the truth and beneficial unto all the worlds. O goddess, the strength of kings shall depend on you.

77-78. Especially when a time of war comes, the kings who are your devotees shall gain strength through you. There is no doubt about this.

If any man undertakes any compaign or enters into any undertaking after recollecting you, bowing down to you and offering you special worship, he will always achieve success in every activity. Even a coward will have success. All the more so in the case of an excellent warrior.

79-80. If any man worships you on the eighth or ninth lunar day in the bright half of the month of Āśvina with excellent devotional fervour, O most beautiful lady of Suras, he will never meet defeat, fear or ailment for a full year thereafter. He will never have premature or accidental death nor the harassment and torment due to thefts.

*Sūta said:*

81. After saying thus to the goddess, those delighted Devas went to their city Amarāvatī on being permitted by her.

82. After going there and having regained his realm after a long time, Pākaśāsana joyously protected the three worlds after the eradication of all thorns (obstacles).

83. All the worlds were blessed with happiness thereafter. Devas once again became regular partakers of their shares in Yajñas in all the three worlds.

84. Thereafter, that goddess became well-known in all the three worlds, in all the holy spots and Tīrthas in particular.

85. In the meantime, Suratha, a king of Ānarta, was born. She was installed by him in this holy spot with great devotion.

86. A person who devoutly visits her on the eighth lunar day in the bright half of Caitra shall undoubtedly be blessed for the period of a full year.

## CHAPTER ONE HUNDRED TWENTYTWO

# Creation of Kedāra

*Sūta said:*

1-3. Thus, O excellent Brāhmaṇas, everything I was asked has been narrated to you all, as to how that excellent Dānava named Mahiṣa was killed by the goddess.

Now I shall tell the sin-destroying story concerning the meritorious Kedāra. Listen to it with great concentration and mental purity.

*The sages said:*

O Sūta, it is heard that Kedāra is in Gaṅgādvāra on the Himālaya mountain. How did it come to be here? Narrate everything in detail.

*Sūta said:*

4. It is true that the Self-born Lord is present on that mountain. But, O Brāhmaṇas, the Lord stays there only for eight months.

5. During summer and rainy season, the Lord stays there. But during winter, he is always stationed in this holy spot.

*The sages said:*

6. O Sūtaputra, what is that purpose for which the Lord stays in this holy spot for four months and on Himācala for eight months? Do tell us.

*Sūta said:*

7. Formerly, in the beginning of the Manvantara of the first Manu named Svāyaṁbhuva, there was Hiraṇyākṣa, a Daitya of inordinate strength. He was of great lustre and possessed the power of penance.

8. He (and his associates) encompassed the whole world. After ousting the overlord of Devas they appropriated the shares of Devas in Yajñas by means of their valour.

9. Thereupon, Śakra took refuge in Gaṅgādvāra along with the Suras. In his excessive distress due to the loss of royal glory, he performed a great penance.

10-11. Even as the noble-souled one performed the severe penance thus, Mahādeva himself assumed the form of a buffalo and came out of the surface of the earth. He then said to Śakra: "Whom should I tear off (*ke=kān, dārayāmi*)[1] from the entire hosts of the Daityas by means of this form? O Vāsava, O most excellent one among Suras, tell me quickly."

*Indra said:*

12. O Lord, tear asunder these five Dānavas, namely Hiraṇyākṣa the great Daitya, Subāhu, Vakrakandhara, Triśṛṅga and Lohitākṣa. If these are killed, undoubtedly all the Dānavas are annihilated.

13. Of what use is the destruction of the other men and wretched ones? Nothing can be achieved thereby.

On hearing those words, the Lord hastened to that place where the important Dānava, the extremely powerful Hiraṇyākṣa, was present.

14. All those Dānavas saw from a distance the buffalo comparable to a mountain coming on in a frightening form.

1. A popular etymology of *Kedāra*.

15. Some of them hit him with stones and others with sticks. Still others in the arrogance of their strength slapped and clapped their arms shouting battle cries.

16. The Lord disregarded them all. He sportingly advanced to that place where the leading Dānava was present along with his four ministers.

17. Even as he lifted up the weapon and rushed against him, the Lord despatched him to the abode of Yama[1] hitting him with his horns.

18. After killing him, the Lord killed the ministers, the most important one among whom was Subāhu. Of course the other Dānavas struck him from all sides.

19. The Dānavas struck with great effort and their aim was perfect. Yet none of the weapons had any serious effect at all on the body of the Lord.

20. After killing the five important Daityas thus, Maheśvara once again went to the place where Śakra was waiting. With great delight in his mind, he spoke to Śakra fully equipped with the power of penance:

21-22. "Those five Dānavas mentioned by you have been killed by me. Hence enjoy once again the kingdom of the three worlds. O Lord of Devas, do choose from me another boon too that is desired by you so that I can hurry back to the peak of Kailāsa."

*Indra said:*

23. O Śaṅkara, do stay here in this very form to accomplish protection to the three worlds and preservation of virtue and welfare.

*Śrī Bhagavān said:*

24. O Śakra, this form was assumed by me in order to slay him (Hiraṇyākṣa) since he could not be killed by other living beings. He has now been killed by me.

25. Hence, at your instance, O most excellent one among Suras, I shall stay here along with this very form accordingly, for giving salvation unto all embodied ones.

* * *

1. According to the Bhāgavata and other Purāṇas Viṣṇu assumed the form of a divine Boar and killed Hiraṇyākṣa also. Cp. Mbh, *Sabhā* 38.29 ff.

26. After saying thus, Lord Virūpākṣa (Śiva) made a great Kuṇḍa with water resembling pure crystal and pleasing and tasty like milk.

27. Then Lord Tripurāntaka spoke to Devendra in a voice majestic like the rumbling sound of cloud, even as all the Devas were listening:

28-30. "A person should remain pure and visit me and this Kuṇḍa. He should drink the water thereof first by the left hand, then by the right hand and again with both the hands. That man shall certainly redeem the entire family even if it be sinful in its activities or even if it has fallen into hell. He shall redeem the members of his mother's family by the act of drinking the water with the left hand, his father's family with the right and himself with both the hands. Everything shall be in accordance with my words."

*Indra said:*

31. O Bull-vehicled One, always (everyday) I shall come from heaven and worship you stationed here. I shall also drink the holy water.

32. Since you said when you were in the form of a buffalo, *"ke dārayāmī"* (vv 10, 11), you shall become well-known by the name *Kedāra*.

*Śrī Bhagavān said:*

33. O Śakra, if you do so, you will never have any fear from Daityas. A great lustre will envelop your body.

34. On being told thus, the Thousand-eyed One caused an excellent mansion to be built there. It was extremely beautiful to see and pleasing to the mind.

35. Then he bowed down to that Lord, took leave of him and went to his own abode stationed on the top of a peak of Meru.

36. Then he used to come there everyday from heaven. Endowed with great devotion to Kedāra he performed the adoration of the Trident-bearing Lord with great mental concentration.

37. He drank the holy water thrice and went away, O excellent Brāhmanas. After some time, he returned to the place.

38. At that time he saw the entire peak of the mountain covered with snow. The holy Kuṇḍa, the Lord and the entire palace too was covered with snow.

39. He was miserable. With great devotion, he simply bowed down (uttering salutation) in loud voice in that direction and went back to his abode.

40 Four months elapsed thus since his return. All along, his mind was eager with the desire to see, but he could not see (the Lord).

41. Then, O Brāhmaṇas, there was the advent of summer on Himācala. Then the Lord appeared again in the same form as before.

42. Then he performed the adoration with great eclat that had been held up for four months. He sang and played the musical instruments before the Lord with great faith.

43. The Lord noted the faith of the Lord of heaven. Lord Tripurāntaka appeared before him and said:

44. "O Lord of Devas, I am pleased with your exclusive devotion. Hence request for any desire lurking in your heart."

*Śakra said:*

45. With your favour, I already possess an excellent and prosperous glory. Whatever (valuable) is in the three worlds is present in my abode too.

46. Hence, O Bull-emblemed One, if you are favourable to me, if you are pleased and willing to grant me a boon, then kindly do as I say.

47. O Lord of Suras, I have heard that this mountain is accessible for eight months when the Sun occupies the zodiac of Pisces and proceeds ahead.

48. Thereafter, it becomes inaccessible because it will be covered with snow i.e. for four months till the Sun comes to Aquarius.

49. O Lord of Suras, O Tripurāntaka, if it becomes inaccessible even to me, then in the case of human beings and others of inferior power it is all the more so.

50. Hence, O Lord of Tridaśas, do stay in this form for four months either in Svarga or in Pātāla or in the mortal world, so that my vow need not be broken.

*Sūta said:*

51. Then the Lord thought for a long time and with great delight said to Balasūdana (Indra) in a voice like the rumbling of a cloud:

52-54. "O Thousand-eyed One, on the earth there is our holy spot named Hāṭakeśvara in the land of Ānarta.

At your instance I shall undoubtedly be present there, O Vāsava, during the period beginning with when the Sun is in Scorpio until when he is in Aquarius.

Hence, go there quickly, erect an excellent palace, install my form (image or Liṅga) and perform the suitable adoration so that I can invest my own refulgence there for your sake."

*Sūta said:*

55. On hearing these words the Trident-bearing Lord of Devas, the Thousand-eyed One went there and did everything as told by the Lord.

56. He built a palace, installed a form (Liṅga) of the Trident-bearing Lord and made a holy Kuṇḍa of the same form filled with clear water.

57. Then he propitiated the Lord with flowers, incense and unguents. He took his bath in the Kuṇḍa and drank water thrice as before.

58. Thus propitiated by Śakra, O leading Brāhmaṇas, the Lord came there from the beautiful Himācala.

59. A man who perfectly propitiates him for the period of the four months when there is snowfall, shall attain welfare.

60. A sensible man who worships with great devotion during the remaining period too shall wash off his sin acquired ever since birth and upto death (i.e. throughout his life):

61. Wise men conversant with all the scriptural texts speak in praise of music and dances of various kinds before the Lord.

62. In this connection there is a Śloka sung by Nārada, the celestial sage. O excellent Brāhmaṇas, I shall proclaim it for you. May it be heard:

63. "By drinking the holy water in Kedāra, by offering balls of rice in Gayā and by gaining the knowledge of Brahman, there cannot be rebirth."

64. Thus, everything connected with Kedāra has been

narrated to you. This narration is destructive of all sins, O excellent Brāhmaṇas.

65. O Brāhmaṇas, a man who listens to it perfectly, or reads before the deity or expounds to others, this sin-destroying description of Kedāra becomes liberated from clusters of sins instantly.

## CHAPTER ONE HUNDRED TWENTYTHREE

# Glory of Śukla Tīrtha[1]

*Sūta said:*

1-3. Further, there is another excellent Tīrtha there named Śuklatīrtha. It is known even today by means of the white Darbha grass, O excellent Brāhmaṇas.

Formerly, there was a washerman named Śuddhaka in Camatkārapura. He was an expert in the use of darts. He was accompanied by his sons and grandsons. He was chief of all washermen. He used to wash the garments of important Brāhmaṇas.

4. Once upon a time though he had mental concentration he put the garments of the leading Brāhmaṇas in the cauldron of indigo and became aware of it only later.

5. Moody in mind, the terrified washerman called his wife and sons and spoke to them in secret:

6-7. "Many costly garments of noble-souled Brāhmaṇas were put in the indigo cauldron by mistake. Undoubtedly, they may imprison or even kill us. Hence, we shall go elsewhere tonight itself."

8. After deciding thus, he took all essential things from the house, O excellent Brāhmaṇas, and prepared to set off along with his wife like fugitive.

9-10. In the meanwhile, his daughter went to a fisherman's daughter who was her friend and said: "O fair lady, if any

1. The Tīrtha (that is water in it) turned everything placed inside it white and hence is called 'Śukla Tīrtha.'

misdemeanour has been committed by me, let it be excused. While playing with you I might have committed some mistake knowingly or unknowingly. It might have been due to my childishness or over-friendliness. Or perhaps due to anger or keen jealousy."

11. On hearing these words all of a sudden, her eyes became dimmed with tears. She said: "What is this, O fair lady? Why do you tell me like this?"

*The friend said:*

12. O lady of excellent eyes, very costly garments of Brāhmaṇas were put in the indigo solution by my father by mistake.

13. On coming to know of this in the morning, they are sure to fine him or give him some other terrible punishment. Thinking about this, my father has set off now.

14. O uncensured (praise-worthy) one, I have come to you to meet you. I shall go away on being permitted by you. Hence I may be allowed to go.

15. On hearing her words, she spoke with a pleasant face: "If this is the case, O lotus-eyed one, you need not go anywhere.

16. Hurry up and prevent your father from going away. Tell him not to go. To the north-east of this place, there is a water-pond.

17. Once a net of very dark fibres and hair was cast into it by my father. Immediately it turned white.

18. He was surprised. Out of curiosity, he himself took his bath there. He was dark-complexioned before. He turned into a white-complexioned one.

19. His hairs too suddenly became white causing disgust to women onlookers. Ever since then no one consciously goes there.

20. So, let your father wash those clothes there itself soon. O splendid girl, they will become quite pure (white)."

21. The girl thereupon hurried back to her father and with the face beaming with pleasure and eagerness repeated those words:

22-23. "I have been informed by my friend that there is a water-pond not far off. Whatever is nonwhite and put therein becomes white. So go to that pond in the morning and wash these clothes, there. They will undoubtedly become white."

*The washerman said:*

24. Dear daughter, this is simply impossible that the indigo-colour of a cloth can disappear. It has been said by old people.

25. "There is only one tenacious grip: that of *Vajralepa* (hard cement-like adhesive), of a fool, of women, of a crab, of a fish, of blue indigo and of a drunkard."

*The girl said:*

26. Go there taking all the clothes with you. If they turn white come back.

27. You can come back home or go away to distant quarters from that place along with all of us. This is what I think.

28. On hearing her words, the kinsmen and servants repeatedly said: "Well said!" All of them went away during the night itself.

29. O excellent Brāhmaṇas, they still had a great doubt. Hence, they went away with all their valuables and possessions. They kept the fisherman's daughter in front of them as their guide.

30. The fisherman's girl showed them the water pond overgrown and densely covered with many creepers. It was impenetrable to all embodied beings.

31. The washerman entered the pond with all the garments, O Brāhmaṇas and washed them.

32. All those excellent garments originally dark-coloured turned entirely crystal-white instantly.

33. Then he became glad and exclaimed, "Excellent!" He embraced his daughter and respectfully said to the daughter:

34. "We shall return all the excellent garments to the leading Brāhmaṇas in due order."

35. Then, O excellent Brāhmaṇas, he went back to his abode joyously and gave back all those garments (to the respective Brāhmaṇas).

36. On seeing the whiteness of the garments and on finding that the washerman himself had been turned all white, the Brāhmaṇas became surprised.

37. They asked him, "What is this wonderful unprecedented change? What has happened to the garments and also (to you)? Speak out if you think (you know the cause)."

*The washerman said:*

38. O Brāhmaṇas, these garments were put in indigo solution by me by mistake. All the excellent garments were rendered useless.

39. Then, O excellent Brāhmaṇas, a great fear caught hold of me. As soon as night fell, I moved out into the wide world along with my family.

40. Then this daughter of ours went to her friend, the fisherman's daughter. She was extremely miserable and was eager to see her again.

41. She understood everything that caused sorrow (panic) to me. She stood as a guide and showed us the water-pond.

42. As soon as these garments were put in it, they turned into these bright colours causing surprise (to us).

43. Further my dark hair became white as soon as I took bath. Everything has thus been clearly explained by me.

44-45. On hearing this, the Brāhmaṇas became curious. They went there in order to test it themselves. Thousands of dark-coloured objects like hair etc. were put in it. Everything turned white losing its (original) dirty colour.

46. Then those who had their hair particularly white due to old age took bath with perfect faith. Young men of righteous behaviour too (took bath).

47. Then they attained purity and were equipped with refulgence and vigour. Thanks to its power, they attained the great goal.

48. Then Vāsava observed that the Śuklatīrtha was the bestower of salvation. Afraid of (its misuse by) human beings, he filled it up with dust particles.

49. Even today whatever grows there like grass etc. becomes bright (white), thanks to the power of that water.

50. One who is endowed with faith and performs Śrāddha with the white Kuśa grasses growing there, redeems all the Pitṛs even though they have fallen into Naraka.

51. An excellent man who applies over his body the mud taken out of the Tīrtha and takes the holy bath attains the benefit of all the Tīrthas.

52. O Brāhmaṇas, a man who offers libation devoutly by means of those Darbhas and gingelly seeds grown naturally in the forest propitiates grandfathers.

53. O excellent Brāhmaṇas, what could be attained by a horse-sacrifice, through Gayā Śrāddha or by loosening a blue bull is attained here also.

*The sages said:*

54. How did this Śuklatīrtha come into being here, O Sūtanandana? Explain it in detail. We are very eager.

*Sūta said:*

55-56. Śvetadvīpa was brought here by the powerful Viṣṇu. He was afraid of Kali and thought it would lose its whiteness. Śvetadvīpa will not attain dark colour though contacted by Kali Kāla. O excellent Brāhmaṇas, it was for that purpose that it was placed here.

## CHAPTER ONE HUNDRED TWENTYFOUR

# Creation of Mukhāra Tīrtha[1]

*Sūta said:*

1-2. Then there is another excellent Tīrtha named Mukhāra where excellent Brāhmaṇa-sages had contact with a thief.

That thief attained Siddhi, thanks to their power. Later he composed the epic Rāmāyaṇa and became well-known as Vālmīki.

3. Formerly, there was a Brāhmaṇa named Lohajaṅgha in Camatkārapura. He hailed from the family of Māṇḍavya. He was devoted to his father and mother.

4. He had a wife who was dearer to him than his own life. The chaste lady considered her husband as her very life. She was always engaged in what was pleasing and beneficial to her husband.

5. A great deal of time elapsed as he continued to pursue

1. Vālmīki was originally a highwayman Nārada reformed him with Rāma Mantra and he became the author of Rāmāyaṇa. Herein Saptarṣis reform him with a Sāma-mantra.

the profession fit for a Brāhmaṇa and be devoted to his father and mother.

6. Once Lord Śakra did not shower rain in the entire land of Ānarta on the earth for twelve years.

7. Then, O excellent Brāhmaṇas, that Lohajaṅgha underwent great sufferings. He did not get any alms or monetary gift.

8. On seeing his parents and wife afflicted with hunger, he was overcome by great sorrow and he thought thus:

9. 'What shall I do? Where shall I go? How can I continue to see these elderly people and particularly my wife in this miserable plight?'

10. In his great grief he went to a forest for the sake of (gathering) fruits. He could not get any. All the trees were dry and parched.

11. Then he saw an old lady going along with some quantity of vegetables. She was extremely tired thereby.

12. The merciless wretch snatched her vegetables and clothes and joyously went to his abode and offered the same to his parents.

13. Achieving his purpose thus, everyday by the acts of a thief, he maintained his family through thievery.

14. When the famine passed off and the time of plenty arrived, he never did any personal work. Forsaking his Brāhmaṇical pursuits, he continued the practice of a thief.

15. Once, O Brāhmaṇas, the seven sages, the chief of whom was Marīci, came there in the course of their pilgrimage.

16. On seeing them in an isolated place, he became furious and inimical. Raising forcibly his stick, he ordered: "Stop there."

17. He knitted his eyebrows and rushed at them. He rebuked them with harsh words as if he was about to beat them.

18. The sages saw him as one comparable to the messenger of Yama. They noticed that he had a sacred thread. Then they said to him with compassion:

*The sages said:*

19. Alas, you appear to be a Brāhmaṇa. How childish you are in pursuing this barbarous practice! Why do you carry on this despicable activity?

20. We are quiet and quiescent sages. We have given all our belongings. We have nothing with us which you can take away.

*Lohajaṅgha said:*

21. O Brāhmaṇas, hurry up and give me these white bark garments and antelope skins along with your shoes.

22. If not I will kill you all with my stick comparable to the thunderbolt. Undoubtedly, I will despatch you to the abode of Dharmarāja.

*The sages said:*

23. O robber, we shall give away everything to you but we would like to ask you something in general out of curiosity. Tell us.

24. You are a Brāhmaṇa. Why do you mercilessly commit theft? Have you became enslaved to terrible vices? Are you a hunter in the guise of a Brāhmaṇa?

*Lohajaṅgha said:*

25. This act of thievery on my part is not an indulgence in vice. It is for the sake of the maintenance of the family. Hence it is undoubtedly righteous.

26. My parents are in their advanced state of senility. My chaste wife is an adept in household chores.

27. What little I earn by means of this activity is entirely for their sake. I state this on a solemn oath.

28. Hence at the very outset, out with all your possessions. Why indulge in vain talk? My hands throb to hit you all.

*The sages said:*

29. If it is so, O thief, go home and ask everyone, "Are you willing to share a portion of my sins or not?"

30. If by their sharing, a part of your sin goes away, you do as you please; otherwise the sin will become unbearable (to you).

31. O extremely wicked one, you will fall into Raurava Naraka. We are saying this only out of the consideration that you are a Brāhmaṇa.

32. We are feeling compassionate towards you. It is good that you have met us. Auspicious indeed is the result of seeing sages of controlled minds.

33. One commits the sin. The other man enjoys the benefit. Those who enjoy escape punishment. It is the doer who is affected by the adverse result.

*Sūta said:*

34-36. On Hearing their words the thief became slightly afraid. He thought: 'There is no doubt about this that what these people say is true. So I shall go home and ask all the members of the family. If they are amenable to partake of a share in my sin I shall continue to do like this. If they do not take a share therein, I shall abandon this thievish activity. Now a great terror has entered my mind.' (Then he said to them:)

37-39. "O great sages, if you do not go elsewhere and flee from me I shall go home. I shall ask all my dependents what you said in particular. If the family accepts a share in my sin, I will take away whatever you possess. If they refuse to have anything to do with my sin, I shall undoubtedly let you (go) along with all your possessions."

40. Taking pity on him, they promised (not to leave the place) in order to make him believe and then sent him homewards.

41-43. After going home, he first asked his father: "Dear father, listen to my words and then reply:

Thousands of forbidden acts like thievery I do everyday and nourish you. Do you partake of any share (of sins) therein or not?

In this I entertain my own doubt. Tell me even as I ask "are you prepared to share the sin duly? Tell me quickly."

*The father said:*

44. Dear son, during your childhood I went through many worries and sufferings, committed many things good and bad with an affectionate heart and nursed you.

45. In view of this, when I am in advanced (old) age, you commit things good and bad and protect me.

46. O child, just as you had not the slightest share in the

auspicious or sinful acts then committed, the same is the case with me now.

47. The (fruit) of Karma committed by a person, whether meritorious or sinful, has to be experienced by him only. But the partakers of the beneficial results are others (not responsible for the *Karmas*).

48. I am not worried whether you bring me food by honest means or thievery. Nor do I care to think whether you cultivate the land or engage yourself in trading or commerce.

49. Hence this should not be entertained in the heart that we are all the partakers of shares in the despicable thing you commit (we are only the enjoyers). You alone are the person who have to share.

*Sūta said:*

50. On hearing these words he became greatly agitated in his mind. He then went to his mother and asked the same assiduously.

51. O excellent Brāhmaṇas, what was said by the father was repeated by her too, namely non-participation in his activity whether good or bad.

52. Then he went to his wife and asked the same. She too had the same stand in regard to the sin as the elders had.

53. Thereupon he got extremely distressed with regret. He despised himself; he went back to the place where the sages were present.

54. He bowed down to all of them standing there with palms joined in reverance. He said: "You all may go, O Brāhmaṇas. May my crime be forgiven.

55. I have been sinful and deluded. So I foolishly rebuked and threatened you. So you should forgive me.

56. O excellent Brāhmaṇas, your words came true in the utterance of my parents and wife. Hence I feel regret.

57. Hence, O excellent sages, be pleased ye all to impart some sound instruction to me so that I can eradicate my sins.

58. O excellent Brāhmaṇas, I have always been doing these despicable things. Women, eminent Brāhmaṇas and sages in particular (were attacked by me).

59. All those persons of weak nature, those who are incapable of fighting, have been robbed by me, never those who could fight.

60. All this I did for the sake of the family, deluded that I was, not having associated with good people (before). But something has entered my heart today as though I have been reading the scriptural texts.

61. O excellent persons, if I had not met you all today, I would have continued to perform other sinful acts too. There is no doubt about it."

62. There was a good sage among them named Pulaha, one of a jovial nature. He said to the excellent Brāhmaṇa just to bewilder him:

63-65. "I shall tell you a splendid Mantra. By repeating it and meditating you will attain permanent Siddhi. This Mantra namely Jāṭaghoṭa is the bestower of all Siddhis. O Brāhmaṇa, repeat this Mantra day and night untiringly. Thereby you will attain perfection rare in the case of even Devas."

66. After saying thus those Brāhmaṇas went on their pilgrimage. The thief on his part stayed there completely engrossed in the Japa.

67. The Japa was begun by him in all earnestness with his mind not turning to anything else. He maintained the mental absorption. He reached the climax thereof.

68. As the Brāhmaṇa continued the recitation of the Mantra, his body remained motionless and he was steady in the Japa.

69. After a great deal of time had elapsed an anthill enveloped the noble-souled one engaged in meditation, O excellent Brāhmaṇas.

70. His parents and his wife of lofty mind made a fruitless search for him and ultimately they died themselves.

71. The man engaged in the great Vrata had renounced everything. He was liberated from all worldly feelings, thanks to the association with those sages. He could not be found out even as he was there itself.

72. After some time, those sages came the same way in the course of their pilgrimage.

73. They said thus, O Brāhmaṇas: "This is the place where you had come into contact with that terrible thief who was in the guise of a Brāhmaṇa."

74. They heard from within an anthill the sound of the Mantra *Jāṭaghoṭa* from the same noble soul.

75. They heard the vibrations on the ground from all sides. They saw the anthill all round and the thief seated in the midst.

76. They saw that he had been repeating the Mantra jocularly imparted to him by Pulaha. O excellent Brāhmaṇas, they found out the Siddhi yielded by that Mantra.

77. What the preceptors whose eye is the scripture, say is true. Very little indeed is enough for the achievement of perfection (Siddhi). Hence the Siddhi was attained by him.

78. The Siddhi in the case of Mantra, Tīrtha, Brāhmaṇa, deity, astrologer, medicine and preceptor is always in proportion to the mental fervour and faith one has.

79. They were surprised to observe that the thief had become a great Siddha even through an insignificant sham Mantra. The Brāhmaṇas were overcome with compassion too all the more.

80-81. They massaged his body with things specific for recovering from Samādhi, such as oils and medicines. O Brāhmaṇas, you know that he had been in meditation for a long time. After regaining consciousness he stared at them frequently and said to them in utter surprise:

*Lohajaṅgha said:*

82. O excellent Brāhmaṇas, why did you not go away? I will not take anything belonging to you. You were let off by me. Since I do not want anything for the sake of the family, you can go away as you please.

*The sages said:*

83. We have been wandering in the forest. We have come here after a long time. The long period of time that has elapsed has not been noticed by you because you were in meditation.

84. Your aged parents whom you left have all died. With our favour, you have achieved great Siddhi.

85. Since you achieved great Siddhi seated within a *Valmīka* (an anthill), you will become well-known in the world as Vālmīki.

86. O Brāhmaṇa, you stayed here and robbed *(muṣṭaḥ)*

the world earlier. Hence this will become famous as a Tīrtha named Mukhāra.[1]

87. Those who faithfully take their holy bath here on Śrāvaṇī day, O Brāhmaṇas, will wash off their sin due to thievery.

*Sūta said:*

88-91. After saying thus, those Brāhmaṇas took leave of the sage. They were duly bowed down to by him and they went in the direction they desired. Engaged in his penance he was later remembered as Vālmīki. He became a leading sage. Even today that leading sage is present there in the form of an idol. One who worships him with great faith and devotion especially on the eighth lunar day will certainly become a poet.

## CHAPTER ONE HUNDRED TWENTYFIVE

## The Story of King Satyasandha[2]

*Sūta said:*

1-2. Beyond it there is the well-known splendid Tīrtha named Karṇotpalā. A man who takes his bath duly therein, will never get separated from his desired object, wealth or servant-folk. Nor will he be devoid of valour, virtue and a splendid wife.

3. Formerly, there was a king well-known as Satyasandha. He was born of the Ikṣvāku race and was endowed with handsome features and all good qualities.

4. He had many sons but only one daughter named Karṇotpalā. She was very splendid and endowed with all good features.

5. After repeated consultations with Brāhmaṇas, servants and ministers, her father gave her the name on the twelfth day.

6-7. "My daughter resembles a lotus-like ear-ornament. Hence the splendid girl shall be named Karṇotpalā."

1. A strange etymology?
2. This king Satyasandha is different from the three Satyasandhas mentioned in Mbh.

She is the only daughter among many sons. She is marked with all good features. Hence, O excellent Brāhmaṇas, let her be Karṇotpalā by name.

8. After the naming ceremony, the girl grew up day by day delighting everyone like the digit of the moon (in the bright half of a month).

9. O excellent Brāhmaṇas, as a child she went from hand to hand and was fondled by all the kinsmen. She grew up and attained youth.

10-11. On noticing that she had become endowed with the prime of youth, the king considered in his mind, "To whom shall I give her? Neither on the earth, nor in Svarga, nor in Pātāla, is there a bridegroom suitable to her. What should be done by me now?"

12-13. That king thought thus in various ways on her behalf and ultimately decided thus: "In this connection, Pitāmaha (Brahmā) should be asked. In this matter that Lord is to be consulted. He will guide me. I shall give my daughter to him, not at all to anyone else."

14. After deciding thus, he took her to the world of Brahmā in order to consult him about a bridegroom for her.

15. O excellent Brāhmaṇas, by the time the king reached Brahmaloka, the Brāhmī Sandhyā (the twilight of Brahmā) had set in.

16. In the meantime, Brahmā was eager to perform the evening rites. At that time, he was engaged in meditation.

17. On observing that Pitāmaha was engaged in meditation, Satyasandha sat near him waiting for the conclusion of the meditation.

18. In the eight-petalled lotus situated in the heart, that was blooming perfectly, Prapitāmaha saw the Ātman within the (higher) Ātman.

19. It was refulgent in the centre of the pericarp. On seeing the Ātman, Brahmā experienced horripilation and tears of joy drenched his face.

20. He then washed his feet and performed the *Ācamana* (ritualistic sipping of water) rite. Then he looked all round, when he was bowed to by all the residents of Brahmaloka.

21. In the meantime the king together with the splendid-faced girl bowed down and spoke respectfully:

22-24. "O Lord, I am King Satyasandha well-known in the land of Ānarta. I have come to you from the human world. This is my splendid daughter named Karṇotpalā. A husband suitable to her was not found by me anywhere on the earth.

Therefore, O excellent one among Suras, I have come to you. Hence, tell me who her husband should be, so that I can give her unto him."

25. On hearing his words, the Lotus-born One laughed, O excellent Brāhmaṇas, and spoke to him in the assembly of all the Devas:

26-33. "If you ask me concerning a righteous husband for this girl, O king, then she should not be given to anyone now. Listen to the reason.

For the purpose of virtue, fame and prosperous increase of the family, a girl should be given, O king, to one who is older than her in age and belongs to the same caste as oneself. This daughter of yours has attained very great seniority in the mortal world to all the kings. You do listen to the reason.

Since your arrival here in my presence, three yugas have passed off. Those men who were seen by you are not aware of these things (on the earth).

Devas do not take mortal women as their wives because they being the receptacles of phlegm, urine and faeces are despicable to them. Hence, O king, stay here itself along with your daughter. Whatever you had, elephants, horses etc. have perished. The sons, grandsons, servants and all your kinsmen have died. So also, all the others seen by you (earlier)."

34. "So it shall be", said the excellent king and stayed back But his extremely distressed daughter wept and said:

35-37. "O father, I will not stay here in the region of Brahmā, bereft of my girl companions and away from the groups of kinsmen. Hence I will go there where my mother is present as also my friends who delighted me and with whom I had played. I am not going to continue endlessly in time without a husband. So go quickly to that place where my mother is present."

38. On hearing her words, the excellent king had his heart filled with affectionate compassion. Taking her with him he reached his land.

39. He saw water-ponds in the place of dry lands. Impassable land regions had risen up in (former) water ponds.

40. Those areas were inhabited by different people with different customs and rites. Although he asked many, he could not come to know of any relationship with anyone.

41. The moment they came into contact with human atmosphere (touched by winds of the mortal world) the king and the girl were overcome with old age. Their hair turned grey.

42. O excellent Brāhmaṇas, all her limbs were covered with wrinkles. Her teeth dropped down and her breasts hung loose. With deformed limbs and flattened eyes, she became utterly ugly.

43. The king also became like that and faltered at every step. He asked the people, "Who is the king here? What is this land (called)? What is the name of this city?"

44-46. Then the people said: "This is the land of Ānarta. The king here is the well-known Bṛhadbala excellently conversant with virtue. This city is called Prāptipura. This is the river Sābhramatī. The Tīrtha here is meritorious and is glorified as Gartātīrtha. It is the place where these highly esteemed quiescent sages are engaged in penance. They possess the eight qualities and they are devoted to holy bath and Japa."

47. On hearing this, the king embraced his daughter with great sorrow. He lamented loudly.

48. On seeing these two old people cry all those persons felt sorry. They came near them and asked sympathetically:

49-51. "O old man, why are you miserable? Why do you cry continuously along with this old woman? Tell us the reason thereof. Is anyone dear to you lost or dead? Have you incurred loss of wealth? Or have you been humiliated by anyone? Tell us quickly. Our king Bṛhadbala is the destroyer of the wicked and is engaged in protecting the good. He is fully conversant with virtue and righteous conduct. He will accord happiness to you."

*Satyasandha said:*

52. I too was a Lord of Ānarta. I am remembered as Satyasandha. This is my daughter named Karṇotpalā who has always been my darling. She is dear to me always.

53. I had gone to Brahmaloka from here in connection with giving her in marriage. I wanted to consult Lord Pitāmaha and stayed there only for a short while.

54. Then immediately, I returned to the earth. What do I see? Everything has changed the wrong way. I do not know anything.

55. On hearing it, all the persons were surprised with eyes raised up and beaming with great delight they reported everything to Bṛhadbala.

56. On hearing everything, Bṛhadbala hurried on foot and reached the place where King Satyasandha was present.

57-58. He made obeisance with deep reverence to him and stood there with palms joined in veneration. He said: "Welcome unto you, O king, hearty welcome unto you again. Take back this kingdom of yours once again along with me as your respectful servant. Rule over it as you please, giving religious gifts of various kinds."

59. Thereupon, the other king embraced him and smelt the crown of his head frequently. With tears drenching his face, he said with words choked with emotions:

60-61. "Dear One, I have amply held sway over the kingdom. Different kinds of gifts had been made. I have also performed many Yajñas like house-sacrifices with the full complement of monetary gifts. So I shall perform penance along with this daughter of mine, so that she can regain her earlier splendid youth."

*Bṛhadbala said:*

62. O great king, this has been heard by me traditionally that King Satyasandha went away taking his daughter.

63. He had gone somewhere and never returned to his excellent city. O king, his (your) ministers waited for a long time and crowned his son well-known by the name Suhaya.

64. I am the seventy-seventh successor in your family. I have now become the king.

65. Hence in this meritorious spot in the sacred Gartā Tīrtha, O Lord, do perform the rites of your penance along with this lady.

66. May this favour be done to me, so that I can bow down at your feet thrice a day and attain the welfare doubtlessly.

*Satyasandha said:*

67. Formerly there, in Hāṭakeśvara Kṣetra, a Liṅga of the Lord of the bull (Vṛṣabhanātha) had been installed by me. O good son, I hope it is still there.

68. Hence I shall propitiate it day and night. So do take me there along with this daughter of mine.

69. Even as the two kings were conversing together thus, Brāhmaṇas from Gartātīrtha who had heard that the age-old splendid king had come, came out of curiosity.

70. Then the king offered them *Argha* and stood with palms joined in reverence. He said respectfully, "Be seated" and narrated to them the events of Svarga.

71-72. Then all those Brāhmaṇas who were wonder-struck sat comfortably all round the great king in the order of their seniority. They asked the king for detailed news about the abode of Brahmā as to how he went there earlier and came back from there and the way the various talks were held with the Lotus-born One.

73. Then at the close of the dialogue King Satyasandha came and told Bṛahadbala:

74. "I have performed various kinds of sacrifices with plenty of monetary gifts. Innumerable gifts were made by me.

75. Once, dear son, I went to the excellent city of Camatkāra. The entire city was full of Brāhmaṇas.

76. Those Brāhmaṇas were always engaged in regular practice of Japa and self-study of the Vedas. They were devoted to Agnihotra rites. They regularly performed all the rites of householders and they were fortunate enough to enjoy the benefit of the two (this and other) worlds.

77-78. Thereupon, I thought in my mind, 'That ancestor of mine is blessed. He has earned everlasting fame. Hence, I shall also create a great city like this and I shall give it over to Brāhmaṇas for increasing the reputation thereof.'

79-80. Even as I was always thinking thus, O king, the trip to Brahmaloka took place incidentally. This is the only matter and nothing else that causes regret to my mind. O king, I have fulfilled all my duties.

81. Hence, ask some of the leading Brāhmaṇas from among these noble-souled ones so that, with your permission, I shall make a good place for living and give it over to them.'

82-83. Thereafter, he requested the excellent Brāhmaṇas: "Have compassion on me and let this be accepted. Thanks to the good devotion of this king who has given an excellent city. I shall protect you all. So also all the persons born of my family."

84. Then Bṛhadbala brought some persons with great difficulty and submitted to the king, "Let it (the township) be given to these."

85. Then Satyasandha, the king, washed their feet and gave them excellent plot of land for the construction of the city.

86. He gave directions to Bṛhadbala: "O destroyer of the cities of enemies, this city should be made fit by you." Then he started.

87. Along with her (his daughter) he went to the holy place Hāṭakeśvara. Approaching that Liṅga he became delighted and then performed penance for a long time.

88. Karṇotpalā went to a sacred waterpond and installed Gaurī there with great faith. Then she too performed penance.

89. In the meantime, the king of Ānarta (i.e.Bṛhadbala) was killed in battle along with his sons.

90. Then all those Brāhmaṇas hailing form Gartātīrtha approached Satyasandha and told him with deep sorrow:

91-93. "O Lord of the earth, only we have formally accepted the gifts. But nothing has been done in regard to the city and our means of sustenance.

Hence, O excellent king, do the things necessary to augment your virtue by making arrangements for our sustenance. King Bṛhadbala who was pointed out to us by you for the purpose of our sustenance, has been killed in battle."

*Satyasndha said:*

94. O excellent Brāhmaṇas, I am a recluse. I have renounced the world. Hence I am not competent to create means of sustenance (for you). There could have been no doubt about it if there was a man in our family.

95. Hence be pleased to go home. Since you are unlucky, king Bṛhadbala has been killed.

96. On being told thus, those Brāhmaṇas thought it true. They considered his words based on facts. Then they went to their abode and the king continued his penance for a long time.

## CHAPTER ONE HUNDRED TWENTYSIX

# Greatness of Satyasandheśvara

*Sūta said:*

1. O excellent Brāhmaṇas, while he was engaged in penance along with his daughter (Karṇotpalā) all the Brāhmaṇas hailing from Camatkārapura came there.

*The Brāhmaṇas said:*

2. Loss (of justice) and confusion has arisen due to the absence of a leading king who could take decision in all doubtful cases, particularly in disputes.

3. Then the king who had renounced was requested by the excellent Brāhmaṇas for the protection of their kingdom. On another day, he stood with palms joined in reverence and asked:

*The king said:*

4. O excellent Brāhmaṇas, I am not competent to remove your doubts. I am particularly incapable of according protection as I have set aside all weapons now.

*The Brāhmaṇas said:*

5-6. O great king, since all of us are considered to be superior to king, since we have resorted to our place with selfishness and arrogance, no one has any doubt at any time in regard to the duty regarding rites to be performed at the holy spot and also sustenance.

7. Formerly, innumerable means of sustenance were assigned to us by the noble-souled one. Then increase was done in it by the later excellent kings.

8-9. Especially this has been said by you: "As long as King Bṛhadbala continues to be in Ānarta land and later whoever happens to be the king, he will assiduously offer sustenance to the householders." Now what can we say before you? For you know everything.

10. You know how sustenance was offered earlier and how

it was maintained by you. Hence, O leading king, think about the spot and also the means of sustenance whereby there shall be happiness and comfort. Everything shall be within bounds.

11. Thereupon, he thought for a long time and summoned those masters of the Vedas born of the family of Upamanyu, hailing from Gartātīrtha.

12-16. After making obeisance he respectfully told: "All the duties should be carried out humbly like servants, in regard to all the people residing in my holy spot particularly the Brāhmaṇas. Protection should always be accorded (to them).

They will strictly observe the bounds and limits of decorum in cases of doubts and especially in cases of all disputes (But the following is to be noted).

In administrative matters and other cases also these people will ultimately decide after listening to your words, good or bad.

These should be protected with favour. They should be nourished in accordance with your capacity. Jealousy should be eschewed. Everything should be done for the prosperity of my holy spot."

17. On being told by them, "So it shall be" the king once again respectfully said to the Brāhmaṇas hailing from Camatkārapura:

18-20. "For your sustenance in regard to all matters for ever, these Brāhmaṇas hailing from Gartātīrtha have been appointed by me. Everything concerning you shall be at the instance of these. The establishment of everything shall duly result as indicated by the four Vedas. Not otherwise, O excellent Brāhmaṇas, whether little or much is expressed by others hailing from your city numbering one hundred thousand."

*Sūta said:*

21. Thereupon, those Brāhmaṇas joyously took those excellent Brāhmaṇas and did everything forever in accordance with their advice.

22. Thereupon, there arose bounds of morality (Dharma) causing the increase of virtue in that city. In every affair everyone in the city flourished.

23. With their favour those Brāhmaṇas hailing from Gartātīrtha attained great riches and rejoiced happily.

24. Once thereafter that king arrived at the city and spoke respectfully to all those Brāhmaṇas:

25-27. "With your favour, a severe penance has been performed by me in the holy spot here. O excellent Brāhmaṇas, I shall now go to Svarga.

Now there is no king belonging to our family, O excellent Brāhmaṇas, to whom I can show this Liṅga, who could have used this for the purpose of adoration, livelihood or for enjoyment of pleasures. Hence this worship should be assiduously carried out by you alone. Taking pity on me, do these things and particularly the *Rathayāṭrā* (religious procession with the deity in a chariot)."

*The Brāhmaṇas said:*

28. Already twenty-seven Liṅgas are dear to the sons of Camatkārapura and are always worshipped by them.

29. Similarly your Liṅga shall be the twenty-eighth one. We shall worship it always. O king, be free from any anxiety (about it).

30. We shall perform the Yātrā always in the month of Kārttika and offer oblations, presents, adorations, songs and instrumental music within our capacity.

31. On being told thus, he became delighted. After going to the hermitage, he bathed the Liṅga and performed the worship with great devotion.

*Sūta said:*

32. Thus, the Liṅga of Hara was dedicated to all those leading Brāhmaṇas, O Brāhmaṇas, when the extinction of the family was about to happen.

33. A man who is endowed with perfect faith and who bathes and worships it during the whole of the month of Kārttika shall certainly attain salvation.

34. A devotee should wait patiently for a year and on a Monday the worship should be performed after duly bathing it. He also will attain salvation. I have heard this from my father.

## CHAPTER ONE HUNDRED TWENTYSEVEN

# Greatness of Karṇotpalā Tīrtha

*The sages said:*

1. The lady named Karṇotpalā was mentioned by you. She had gone to some water-pond and engaged herself in penance. Do tell us everything connected with her and also the details of her penance.

*Sūta said:*

2. She resorted to the feet of Gaurī and was endowed with great faith. Girijā, the beloved wife of Śaṅkara, became pleased.

3. Then she said: "Dear daughter, I have become pleased with you. Say what is desired by you, so that I can grant it to you even if it is extremely difficult to get."

*Karṇotpalā said:*

4. O goddess, my father had been very miserable in seeking a husband for me. He ceased to be a king, lost his happiness and had no kinsmen.

5. He became disgusted and detached, so performed a penance. I have become old, yet I continue to be a confirmed virgin.

6. Hence, O goddess of Suras, with your favour, let someone be my husband—someone who is most handsome among all the Devas and human beings.

7. Further, let me regain youth and beauty, with your favour, so that even as a sage my father should be happy.

*The Devī said:*

8. On the third lunar day in the month of Māgha, when the splendid day of Saturn coincides with the constellation Dhaniṣṭhā, you shall meditate upon beauty and youthful form.

9. Then you should take your holy bath in this meritorious water-pond. Thereby you will attain a divine physical form as well as the prime of youth. There is no doubt about it. It is the truth that is spoken by me.

10. O highly esteemed lady, any other woman who takes her bath on that day, shall also become endowed with beauty.

11. After saying thus, the goddess disappeared. She too began her quest for the third lunar day coinciding with a Saturday.

12. She wanted eagerly that day to coincide with the constellation Dhaniṣṭhā. She continued her meditation on the goddess, the bestower of all desires.

13. After a few days the third lunar day had such a combination as mentioned by the goddess earlier, O Brāhmaṇas.

14. Then she meditated upon exquisite beauty, prime of youth and a desirable husband. She entered the pond at midnight.

15. Thereby she attained the prime of youth as well as a divine physical form. She came out of water causing surprise unto all the people.

16-18. In the meantime, Lord Kāma who was enlightened in this respect by the words of Gaurī came there joyously to claim her as his wife. He said: "O highly esteemed lady, I am Kāma himself present before you. Hence, as commanded by Pārvatī, be my wife. Do not delay. O Lady of splendid nature, since I came near you with great Prīti (pleasure), you shall become my wife well-known by the name Prīti."

*Karṇotpalā said:*

19. If this be so, O Smara, go to my father and request him yourself since no girl can act independently as she pleases.

20. Yonder, not very far away, is seen a beautiful palace. My father is engaged in penance within it.

21. I shall go there before you and stand by my father. You will come there later and request him for me.

22-24. When Kāma said "So be it", she went (ahead) near her father. After bowing down to him, she said: "Dear father, fortunately exquisite prime of youth has been regained by me after propitiating the beloved of Hara. So perform my marriage and be satisfied in your heart. A very handsome husband has been sent by the goddess for my sake. The Flower-bowed One (god of Love) himself has come to you, dear father."

25-26. On seeing his daughter blessed with youthful form, extremely pleased in the company of her lover, he said: "Dear daughter, now my penance has become fruitful. O splendid lady, my life is blessed, since you have regained prime of youth and a covetable husband, the mind-born Kāma himself, bestowed, by the goddess."

27-28. In the meantime, Kāma came quickly to his presence and said: "O king, give me your daughter of beautiful smiles. O excellent king, I have been ordered by Gaurī herself in regard to this lady. I am well known as Kāmadeva by whom the three worlds have been enchanted."

29. Then, O excellent Brāhmaṇas, at the instance of Brāhmaṇas, the king offered his daughter to him keeping the Fire-god as witness.

30. Since the splendid-eyed lady became the object of his love, being second only to Rati, the auspicious fair lady became Prīti by name.

31. Since the lady had performed her penance in that holy pond, it became well-known all over the earth after her name.

32. A woman who performs holy ablution during the whole of the month of Māgha, or a man who gets up early in the morning and takes his bath, shall attain the benefit of (bath in) Prayāga.

33. In every birth he will be handsome and expert and efficient in everyting. Never will he be separated from his kinsmen.

## CHAPTER ONE HUNDRED TWENTYEIGHT

# Origin of Aṭeśvara

*Sūta said:*

1-3. On seeing his daughter happy after being united with her desired husband, Satyasandha became highly pleased in his heart and felt that he had done his duty.

He resorted to the southern phase (side?) of the same Liṅga and seated himself in lotus posture firmly. He began the meditation properly thereafter. He saw the Ātman within himself. With a sensation of horripilation, he released it through Brahmadvāra (cerebral aperture).

4. The Brāhmaṇas hailing from Camatkārapura came there for viewing the deity but saw his dead body.

5. It was dead, displeasing and lacking in lustre. It was not worthy of being touched. It was found not far from the Liṅga. They then prepared for the cremation thereof.

6. They prepared a large pyre and came in to take him out. Then they saw the corpse missing. It could not be seen anywhere.

7. They were overwhelmed with surprise. They repeatedly spoke about him in highly laudatory terms.

8. Then all of them reviewed the mode of worship of the Liṅga pertaining to him, in the middle of the twenty-seven (other Liṅgas).

9. Of all the Liṅgas, that Liṅga happened to be the bestower of desired things upon all devout creatures and the destroyer of all sins.

*The sages said:*

10. O highly intelligent one, when the line of the king of Camatkāra (pur) became extinct which other king became the overlord of Ānarta?

*Sūta said:*

11. O excellent Brāhmaṇas, when king Bṛhadbala was killed in battle, all the people accompanied by their sons and kinsmen came there.

12. They came to the place where King Satyasandha was engaged in penance. With great distress and sorrow they spoke to the King in his secret resort:

13-16. "This line of yours is extinct since none of your cousins and successors is present (alive). How shall the earth be sustained now?

In the state of anarchy, O excellent king, *Mātsya Nyāya* will prevail (i.e. a powerful one will prey upon weaker ones). Whether it is the whole country or a city or, more particularly, a village the same rule will hold good (everywhere).

Those who are enamoured of other men's wives, those who adopt thievery as the means of sustenance—all these keep to the bounds of morality and decorum only because they are afraid of the king.

Hence, do stop your penance and rule over the kingdom that has come to you by succession. Take a wife for the sake of begetting a son."

*The king said:*

17. O excellent Brāhmaṇas, I have renounced the world. I am not eager to rule over a kingdom. Nor do I want to marry or beget sons.

18. Therefore, I shall tell the means of getting a leader of you all and his son. Thereby, a king of Ānarta ruling over the people shall be obtained.

19-20. When the entire Kṣatriya race, even those in the womb, was exterminated by the furious son of Jamadagni, Paraśurāma, in his furious onslaught, the wives of those Kṣatriyas, before their menstrual bath, approached Brāhmaṇas for begetting sons and not out of lust.

21. Sons were born who were full of refulgence and virility. Being *Kṣetrajas* (born of the wives) of kings they duly became kings.

22-23. Hence, O people, there are the wives of Bṛhadbala. Let Brāhmaṇas approach them after their menstrual bath and get befitting sons, leading Kṣatriyas. They will rule over the earth and protect the people.

24. Further, here there is the splendid Kuṇḍa of Vasiṣṭha, which bestows sons. A woman in her menstrual cycle who takes her bath there, becomes pregnant immediately. The beautiful one becomes *Amogha-retā* (one in whose womb semen never becomes futile) by taking bath here.

25. Those Kṣatriyas who were earlier born to Brāhmaṇas from Kṣatriya women, were born by its power undoubtedly.

26. On being wooed by a Kṣatriya woman the Brāhmaṇa had his bath with due utterance of the Mantras, and then had union with her.

27. It was, due to the efficacy of the Tīrtha that by a single sexual contact male issues (sons) were born to all (those Kṣatriya women) and no daughter at all.

28. All Mantras possessing the power of bestowing sons, which were found (incorporated) in the Vedas were utilized by Vasiṣṭha who was desirous of (the continuity of) Kṣatriyas.

29. If the bath is taken by a wedded pair, a good son will be born. Hence this Kuṇḍa is called *Suputrada* ('Granter of a good son').

30. Hence, O people, all the wives of Bṛhadbala should take their bath here in accordance with the injunctions.

31. There is no untruth in this nor is it blameworthy. For, there is this Śloka cited by earlier Ācāryas (preceptors):

32. "Fire is produced from water, Kṣatriyas from Brāhmaṇas and steel from rocks. Their refulgence spreads everywhere and gets dissolved in their original causes."

33. On hearing those words of King Satyasandha the people informed the ministers about it.

34. All those wives of the king after their menstrual bath joyously courted and contacted very beautiful Brāhmaṇas.

35. They went to the Putrada Tīrtha created by Vasiṣṭha, had their bath therein and had intimate contact once only with Brāhmaṇas.

36. O excellent Brāhmaṇas, all of them gave birth to sons. The great king had one hundred five wives.

37. O Brāhmaṇas, one hundred five Brāhmaṇas had their sexual union with them.

38. Everyone of them begot excellent sons and increased the family. They caused prefect bliss to all the residents of the country.

39. The most excellent of those sons was well known all over the world by the name Aṭa and he became the Lord of Ānarta. He destroyed all enemies.

40. It was by him that the deity well-known as Aṭeśvara was installed with great devotion. If the deity is visited, the extinction of the family can be averted.

*The sages said:*

41-42. Why was he given this name Aṭa? This has been abandoned by the family. Do explain this, O Sūtaja. Was this name given by the ministers or Brāhmaṇas? Or by the mother? Tell this as we are very eager to hear it.

*Sūta said:*

43. That name was given neither by the mother, nor by

the Brāhmaṇas nor by the ministers. O excellent Brāhmaṇas, it was given by the messenger of Devas stationed in the firmament.

44. How it was given, I shall explain. Listen with attention. It was the daughter of the king of Daśārṇa who gave birth to that king.

45-46. The fawn-eyed lady blessed with beauty and prime of youth obtained an excellent Brāhmaṇa. Desirous of the holy bath in the *Putra Tīrtha* she set off along with the Brāhmaṇa resembling Kandarpa. At the (first) sight of each other, their love became very intense.

47. Their mutual attraction was so much that they reached *Sutaprada* Tīrtha with very great difficulty. (They were so eager for union that they felt the journey to the Tīrtha very long and difficult.)

48. While going along the path, they indulged in sexual intercourse. They were very delighted due to ardent desire. So they cast aside shame.

49. The people censured them with words urging them to separate. By that time the semen had been discharged and the Brāhmaṇa tried to get up.

50-52. By that time an aerial voice caused by Devas announced: "Since this son was eagerly begot by the Brāhmaṇa while going along the Highway, he will become a king well known by the name Aṭa. He will be long-lived. He will have many sons and he will conquer the enemies."

It was for this reason, O Brāhmaṇas, that he was called *Aṭa*.

53. He was a person who lifted up his family arising from it like the Moon. He gifted wealth to all suppliants. He came to this holy spot and installed an excellent Liṅga after his own name. O excellent Brāhmaṇas this Liṅga is the bestower of all desires of men.

54. One who worships it with great faith on the fourteenth lunar day in the month of Māgha will never have any sorrow regarding the continuity of his race.

55-56. A woman may be hundred years old but if she has great devotion to Śiva and takes her bath in Sutaprada Kuṇḍa and then visits Aṭeśvara, she will immediately attain a son who will increase the prosperity of the family. This is undoubtedly due to the favour of the deity. So says Kārttikeya.

## CHAPTER ONE HUNDRED TWENTYNINE

# Greatness of the Hermitage of Yājñavalkya

*Sūta said:*

1-4. Further, there is an Āśrama belonging to Yājñavalkya. It is well-known all over the world. It accords Siddhi even to dullards.

It was here that the intelligent Yājñavalkya performed a severe penance and regained all the Vedas that had been taken away by his preceptor.

*The sages said:*

5. There was a tiger among Brāhmaṇas well-known as Śākalya. He hailed from the family of Bhārgavas. He was master of the Vedas and Vedāṅgas.

6. Formerly, in the Bṛhat-kalpa, O Brāhmaṇas, he lived in the excellent city of Vardhamāna with a great number of disciples. He was eagerly engrossed in the study of the Vedas.

7. O excellent Brāhmaṇas, he always got up in the morning and imparted instructions to deserving disciples with great pleasure.

8. At that time, he was the royal priest of the noble-souled king Supriya born of the solar race, O Brāhmaṇas.

9. After performing all the holy rites (of the day), he used to return home everyday, honoured duly by the king.

10. For the performance of the Śānti rites of the king, he used to leave one disciple thereafter telling him the scope and procedure of the Homas.

11. The disciple used to perform all the rites with great concentration. After offering the blessings to the king, he used to return home.

12. Thus, O excellent Brāhmaṇas, the noble-souled Śākalya performed the priestly duties for a long time.

13-14. After seeing his (of Brahmā) aberration on the altar at the time of marriage, Śaṁbhu cursed him. He was then born as Yājñvalkya. Śākalya engaged Yājñavalkya in the royal palace for the performance of the Śānti rites.

15. In the pride of youth he also went shamelessly exposing

his body marked all over by the nails of courtesans without covering it.

16. Then he performed the Śānti rites. At the end of the Japa, he went to the king to offer the holy water of the Śānti rite. While going there, he was laughed at by the people.

17. On seeing the Brāhmaṇa in such a vicious form of a Viṭa (lustful person), the king did not accept the blessings uttered by him. He then spoke these words:

18. "I am *Ucchiṣṭa* (impure), O excellent Brāhmaṇa. Hence I am still in the bed. So pour this water on the pillar in the hall."

19. Yājñavalkya understood that the king showed contempt. Hence he became angry. With the pillar in view, he meditated upon the eternal Brahman.

20. He recited the Yajurveda Mantra beginning with *dyām tāmālikhya* etc., and poured the holy water of Śāntika rite quickly on its top.

21. As soon as the water fell on it, the pillar instantly became splendid with sprouts and was embellished with flowers and fruits.[1]

22. On seeing this, the eyes of the king beamed with wonder. He repented for his conduct and spoke these words:

23. " O excellent Brāhmaṇa, give me this holy water of ablution with (uttering) the same Mantra. I am not impure."

*Yājñavalkya said:*

24. O king, you are unworthy to receive the offer of the holy water of ablution from me. So I shall go immediately to the place where my preceptor is present.

*The king said:*

25. I shall give you ample wealth, vehicles and garments. Offer me this holy water of ablution now with the same Mantra.

*Yājñvalkya said:*

26. Before the conclusion of the Homa, O excellent king,

1. It shows wooden pillars were used in palaces then.

the Mantra cannot manifest (and function) the Mantra that was earlier uttered by the Lotus-born One in connection with the procedure of ablution. Hence I will not carry out what is present in your heart.

27. After saying thus to the king, Yājñavalkya, the Brāhmaṇa who strictly adhered to the principle of non-covetousness, went home immediately.

28. When Śākalya came (to the palace) next day, the king said to him humbly with palms joined in reverence:

29. "The excellent Brāhmaṇa, your disciple who was deputed by you yesterday, should be sent to my abode again for the purpose of Śānti rites."

30. He said, "So be it" and went to his abode. He called Yājñavalkya and told him earnestly:

31. "Today also you should go to the abode of the king for the Śānti rites. Dear son, you have been specially invited by the great king."

*Yājñavalkya said:*

32. Father, I will not go to his mansion for Śānti rites, because he is very arrogant and devoid of cleanliness.

33. The sacred water I proffered to him for the purpose of holy ablution was directed by that evil-minded one to be poured over the wood (i.e. pillar).

34. At the very instant the water was poured over the wood and it flourished instantly.

*Śākalya said:*

35. That is why, dear son, you have been specially summoned. So go there quickly. Kings should not be treated with contempt.

36. On being disrespected kings may become angry doubtlessly. One who makes them angry may not become a favourite.

37. The servants who piece together the matters of anger and favour, get the upper hand over the king who always tries to repulse them.

38. One who takes respect and disrespect equanimously, one who knows the mind (of the king), one who understands

the opportune time, one who endures everything and remains patient is wise. He shall be a favourite of the king.

39. Ignore the disrespect shown to you and go to the abode of the king. Further, you must not transgress my command. This is the eternal right conduct.

*Yājñavalkya said:*

40. If the convention is violated transgression of the command will surely follow. Should you alter the arrangement of your disciples who have been employed there by you?

41. Hence, if you forcibly employ me there, I will leave you and go elsewhere, since it has been said by great sages:

42. "Desertion is enjoined in the case of even a preceptor who is overbearing and arrogant, who does not discriminate between what should be done and what should not be done and who adhers to wrong path."

*Sūta said:*

43. On hearing his words Śākalya became farious. He said rebuking him repeatedly:

44-45. If a preceptor teaches but one syllable to a disciple, no sufficient wealth exists on the earth (is available) for giving it to the Guru and to get oneself free from debt.

Hence go to your abode after returning the lore received from me. Renounce the learning imparted by me. Otherwise I will curse you."

46. After saying thus, he charged the water by means of the Ātharvaṇic Mantras evolved from Nādabindu (Eternal Sound and Oṁkāra) and gave it to him to drink.

47. Instantly, he drank the water after which he experienced excessive exhaustion in all the sense-organs. He vomited all the contents of the bowels mixed with the spiritual knowledge.

48-49. Then he spoke to Śākalya with extreme anger manifest in his face: "There is not even a single syllable taught by you in my stomach. Hence I am no longer your disciple, nor are you my preceptor. I will now go elsewhere as I please. What can you do?"

50. After saying thus he went out of that age-old holy spot according Siddhi.

51. Then this holy spot was mentioned to him by learned men. It bestows Siddhi on all creatures. It cannot be fruitless at all.

52-53. "Leave aside Siddhi acquired by performing penance or observing Vratas and restraints. Siddhi is acquired by one who simply stays in the Hāṭakeśvara kṣetra.

The Siddhi of people shall be splendid or otherwise (auspicious or inauspicious) in accordance with the mental fervour and feeling of the people with which they stay there."

54-55. On hearing it, O excellent Brāhmaṇas, he hurried to this holy spot, installed an image of Bhānu and propitiated it. He observed celibacy. He assigned Gāyatrī Mantra to the various limbs (ritualistically as Nyāsa) and meditated with a mind cleared of all doubts.

56. At the end of a year, the Lord was pleased with him, restrained his terrifying refulgence, appeared before him and spoke to him:

57. "O Yājñavalkya, speak out whatever is in your mind. Take it as my boon. I will grant you everything. There is nothing that cannot be given to you."

*Yājñavalkya said:*

58. If you are pleased, O excellent one among Suras, be my preceptor in regard to the study of the Vedas. This is the desire of my heart.

*Bhāskara said:*

59. O Brāhmaṇa, out of compassion for you I have restrained my excessive refulgence and come here. Hence you are not burned.

60. Now I shall deposit here in this holy Kuṇḍa all the splendid Sārasvata Mantras mentioned in the Vedas myself, O excellent Brāhmaṇa.

61. Take your holy bath and be pure and clean. Whatever Vedic Mantra you may utter then once, it shall remain with you permanently.

62. The entire meaning and principles will be manifest to you with my favour. There is no doubt about it. It is the truth that has been spoken by me.

63. From now onwards, if a man takes his holy bath in the pool here in the morning and recites Sāvitra Sūkta facing me, O Brāhmaṇa, he shall undoubtedly have everything that has been mentioned in your case by me.

*Yājñavalkya said:*

64. Let it be so, O Lord of Devas; may all the words uttered by you be true. But what I wish to say is another thing. Listen. I shall tell you.

65. O Lord of the universe, be merciful to me. I will never have a human being as my preceptor.

66. Then with his inner self fully pleased Sūrya granted him the splendid Vidyā named *Laghimā* for augmenting his prowess.

67-68. He said to him: "Enter the ear of my horses and practise the recitation of the Vedic Mantras.

Learn the Vedas direct from my mouth, O excellent Brāhmaṇa, if that be your desire. You will not have any harm from my rays."

69. On being told thus by him (i.e. Sun) Yājñavalkya became very small and weightless. He resorted to the ear of the horse and learned the Vedas from the mouth of the Sun.[1]

70. Thus the excellent Brāhmaṇa Yājñavalkya attained Siddhi. He composed the Upaniṣad (Bṛhadāraṇyaka) in a fascinating manner incorporating all the meanings of the Vedas.

71. He explained it to king Janaka. He begot a son named Kātyāyana who composed the Vedic Sūtras (*Śrauta Sūtras*).

72. He cast off his body in the holy water made by Brahmā. He united his refulgence with the body of Brahmā in accordance with his capacity.

73. A man who takes his holy bath in the Tīrtha, visits the deity Divākara (Sun) and utters *Nāda-bindu* Mantra before him, shall attain salvation.

---

1. Mbh, *Śānti* 318. 6--12 states that Yājñavalkya got the Veda from the Sungod. But the story given here is special to this Purāṇa.

## CHAPTER ONE HUNDRED THIRTY

# Creation of Pañcapiṇḍā Cow

*The sages said:*

1. O Sūta, you have said about a son of Yājñavalkya. Who was his mother? Do speak everything in detail.

*Sūta said:*

2-3. He (Yājñavalkya) had two excellent wives endowed with all good qualities. One is gloriously mentioned as Maitreyī who had good qualities. She was the senior. The other one of good features (*Kalyāṇī*) was well known as Kātyāyanī. Kātyāyana, the expounder of the meaning of the Vedas, was her son.

4. There are two holy pits of splendid features pertaining to them there. Men who take their holy baths therein, attain those worlds of great glory.

5. The excellent Tīrtha of the chaste lady Śāṇḍilī is another Tīrtha near Kātyāyanī Tīrtha.

6. Kātyāyanī who was distressed due to the (rivalry) of her co-wife, had great detachment and she became enlightened by Śāṇḍilī at that place.

7. A woman who takes her holy bath there on the third lunar day in the bright half of the month of Mārgaśīrṣa shall enjoy conjugal felicity.

8. O excellent Brāhmaṇas, a one-eyed woman, an aged woman, a dwarfish woman, and one overcome by misfortune becomes a desirable one by its power.

*The sages said:*

9. What sort of distress due to her co-wife assailed Kātyāyanī? O Sūta, how did she get spiritual instructions from Sāṇḍilī? What was it?

10. Do mention how Kātyāyanī obtained the instruction, which couldn't have been ordinary as (it was) uttered by her (Śāṇḍilī).

*Sūta said:*

11. Once Kātyāyanī saw Yājñavalkya enamoured of and united with Maitreyī. Due to jealousy, she became very miserable and distressed.

12. She stopped taking bath and eating food. She never indulged in jokes and fun. She always heaved sighs and kept her eyes filled with tears.

13-14. Once she chanced to go out for gathering fruit. Then she saw Śāṇḍilī standing by the side of her husband. The chaste lady was standing very humbly with palms joined in reverence. The husband was lovingly looking at her face with eyes displaying pleasure.

15-16. He was eliciting facts regarding good and bad things and explaining them. On seeing the couple pleased with each other, she thought within herself, 'This saintly lady is blessed. Her husband always looks up to her and expounds matters good and bad. He is full of love. He never has anything to do with other women.'

17. Brooding over it frequently, O excellent Brāhmaṇas, she went back to her hermitage censuring her own physical form.

18-22. Then once, O Brāhmaṇas, when Śāṇḍilī was sitting alone as her husband had gone out on some business Kātyāyanī approached her and respectfully asked her: "O fair lady! Can I have some instruction from you, which will lead to great prosperity? Please tell me.

I am extremely afflicted by the miseries caused by my husband, especially those caused through the co-wife. So do tell me how a husband can be turned into one always looking at the face of his wife. He should not disrespect her by means of offensive words, nor associate with other women even mentally.

Do tell me how your husband has come to be under your control and how he always accords you what you desire, not thinking of another women even mentally."

*Śāṇḍilī said:*

23. Listen, O chaste lady, I shall tell you an excellent secret as to how my husband looks only at me and is subject to my control.

24-25. Śāṇḍilya, the excellent sage of Kurukṣetra, is my father. He was in the stage of Vānaprastha when I was born as the sole child and daughter of that noble-souled one. I grew up gradually in that very hermitage.

26. I used to render him befitting service at the time of Homa. I used to fetch Nīvāra (wild rice) and other grain everyday.

27. Once the excellent Sage Nārada came to my father's hermitage utterly tired.

28. At the behest of my father, I gave relief to him from weariness by fetching water for washing feet, toilet, bath etc., and by other services.

29. At the conclusion of meal, the sage was relaxing. Then, O lady of excellent complexion, he was asked politely by my mother.

30-32. "O tiger among sages, this is our only daughter born in our advanced age. She is dearer to us than our own very vital breath.

Therefore, quickly explain some easy means leading to her happy future, be it an observance (*Vrata*), regulation, Homa or some Mantra.

By resorting to that means, she should attain a husband of gentle manners and good features. He should speak pleasing words and always look at her only. He should be averse to other men's wives."

33. On hearing her words, the sage thought for a long time and spoke thus with a pleasant face:

*Nārada said:*

34. In the holy spot of Hāṭakeśvara, Gaurī has been installed as Pañcapiṇḍā (five lumps). The great goddess has been installed by Gaurī herself.

35. Let this (daughter of yours) worship her with great faith and devotion for a period of one year, particularly on the third lunar day.

36. At the conclusion of a year, she will attain a befitting husband. There is no doubt about it. He will be as handsome as she is beautiful.

37. O highly esteemed lady, formerly Gaurī had resorted to that place which, she knew, bestows success, after having

been distressed due to her jealousy of Gaṅgā and having deserted Maheśvara (for that reason).

38-39. Then she had thought, 'Which goddess should I worship? Other women of Suras worship me for the sake of conjugal felicity. Therefore, with great devotion and excessive enthusiasm I shall worship myself through my own self for achieving success.'

40. With great concentration, she joined together in one place five lumps of earth uttering the auspicious Atharvaveda Mantras referring to *Prāṇāgnihotra*.

41. She deposited in those lumps of earth the elements of *Pṛthvī, Apaḥ, Tejas, Vāyu* and *Ākāśa*.

42. Then the goddess observed the holy vow and worshipped these five elements with flowers, incense and unguents.

43. On coming to know that Girijā was engaged in penance there and his mind having been attracted by those Mantras, Bhava (Śiva) came there hurriedly.

44-45. He joyously said to her: "Why have you come here forsaking me, though I am free from faults and despite my being always devoted to you? I have been looking up at you always. Now be seated on the bull along with me and come to Kailāsa. Otherwise, if at all I have any fault tell me the reason for your coming away."

*Devī said:*

46. You are holding on your head Jāhnavī, the personified form of the water from the feet (of Viṣṇu). Hence I will never go to your place at all.

47-49. I am not inclined to return unless you clearly repudiate her occupying the position of my co-wife. Further, O Bull-emblemed One, even while I look on you bow down to Sandhyā everyday. You are not ashamed of it, hence give up these shameful acts. Thereafter, if you call me, I will respond approvingly. Otherwise, I will not come to your place at all. After hearing this, O Bull-emblemed One, do what pleases you.

*The Lord said:*

50. O goddess of Suras, it is not for my pleasure that I hold Gaṅgā.

51. After performing severe penance for a period of a thousand years according to the divine reckoning I had been requested by King Bhagīratha on behalf of his ancestors:

52. "O Lord, do hold on your head Jāhnavī, so that after falling from Svarga she may not flow towards Pātāla. Do this at my request."

53. I had promised to him, "I shall undoubtedly hold the rapid current of Jāhnavī falling on the earth from the firmament."

54. Otherwise, she would have gone to Pātāla which is the matter of concern here. So I shall mention something important in this connection which you do listen with attention.

55. O lady of exquisite features, this Gaṅgā came out of my head (tresses of hair) and breaking on the Himālaya mountain she split into two.

56. The part named Sindhu flowed into the western ocean, O Parameśvarī, taking nine hundred rivers along with her.

57. The other part named Gaṅgā flowed into the eastern ocean, O Daughter of the Mountain, taking as many rivers with her.

58. Thus, O Daughter of the Mountain, these eithteen hundred rivers flow into the ocean everyday. Thereby it stands sustained.

59-60. Though the Vāḍava fire (submarine fire) dries it up (evaporates it) day and night, it is never exhausted.

Clouds take up the waters of the ocean and shower them on the world of mortals (i.e. earth). Thereby vegetation grows up. The world is sustained by the vegetation. This enables the performance of Makhas (sacrifices). Through getting their share in the Makhas all the Suras become satisfied.

61. It is for this reason, O fair lady, that I hold Gaṅgā and not through affection or lust. On account of this the world goes on.

62. If for any reason I were to let her off from my head, it would pierce, through the earth in full force and flow into Rasātala.

63. Then the Ocean, the Lord of Rivers, would get dried up on being drunk by *Aurva* (submarine fire). There will no longer be any shower. Absence of rain will lead to the ruin of the world. It is the truth that is uttered by me.

64. Thus, O goddess of Suras, everything has been (explained) to you in regard to Gaṅgā. Listen to another explanation of mine as to why I bow down to Sandhyā.

## CHAPTER ONE HUNDRED THIRTYONE

# Kātyāyanī's Distress

*The Lord said:*

1-3. O goddess of Suras, this night has been assigned to Dānavas, Piśācas, Bhūtas and Rākṣasas in particular.

It has been granted by the Self-born Lord that whatever auspicious rite, such as ablution etc., is performed then, the benefit thereof accrues to them.

This agreement was made by Devas with them because being the sons of Kaśyapa, both of them deserved share in the Yajñas.

4. For this purpose ten thousand Dānavas assail Bhānu with raised bows. They are very irrepressible in battles and hold javelins and spears in their hands.

5. When water is poured down with the thousand-rayed Sun in view, uttering the Sāvitra Mantra, the result is manifest in them.

6. They are killed at the same instant by that water powerful like thunderbolt. Hence, O goddess of Suras, the Thousand-rayed One is let off everyday.

7. It is for this purpose that I pour down water in the form of a missile at the time of twilight with Bhānu in view and not Sandhyā.

8-9. Whatever the best and leading ones do, persists subsequently. The terrible ones restrain Ravi who proceeds to rise up. But, O goddess, they are killed through the water offerings during Sandhyā by me and also by excellent Brāhmaṇas. They swoon and fall down and let off the Sun.

10. It is for this reason, O goddess, that I and other Brāhmaṇas bow down to Divākara (Sun) during the two Sandhyās (dawn and dusk).

11. Hence eschew your jealousy, O daughter of the Mountain, and come home. Excepting you, the praiseworthy one there is no other woman in my heart.

*Devī said:*

12. O Lord, whether you are interested or disinterested (in Sandhyā), it causes to shower rain when you bow down to Sandhyā who has (even grammatically) feminine appellation.

13. Hence, O Lord, I will not be satisfied unless and until you abandon Gaṅgā and Sandhyā in particular.

14. Thus the goddess refused to comply with the request made by Mahādeva himself and resorted to a special vow.

15-16. Then he thought: 'What is the reason hereof? Though she is unattached, she does not destroy (eliminate) my eagerness about her.

The goddess is adopting the pretence of jealousy. Pārvatī will never be satisfied and agreeable with peaceful overtures. And this is an insignificant cause.'

17. Parameśvara knew the potency of Mantra. He meditated with this subtle realization on himself.

18. He worshipped his own self through himself. He uttered the selfsame Mantra along with ritualistic touching of the limbs (*Nyāsa*) in particular and perfected his propitiation.

19. In the manner, in which the goddess separated the Ārman from the five elements and worshipped them, the Lord also did so by being immanent in all of them.

20. By means of Samādhi, he separated them and worshipped them. Again he united them externally and performed the rite of adoration.

21. There is no one greater than he. He alone is worthy of the worship of those who themselves should be worshipped. Īśāna was thus created by him through the Aiśvarya (potency and glory) of all the Devas.

22. Even as the Lord propitiated Īśāna[1] the goddess who had been drawn by means of the Mantras came to the place where he was present.

---

1. The reading should be *īśānam* and not *īśānaḥ* as in the text.

23-24. Then she bowed down to the Lord with palms joined in reverence. She spoke to him: "O Lord, everything has been understood by me. Do not forsake me, your beloved one. Hence, do come. O Lord, let us go wherever you wish to go. The fact that I had not complied with your words may kindly be excused."

25. Mahādeva who was pleased, embraced her even as he smiled pleasantly. Then he said thus laughingly in words majestic like the rumble of clouds:

26. "A great physical form arising from the Ātman and the five elements has been created by you. If a woman in love devoutly worships this form in accordance with this procedure, she will get a husband.

27. Particularly, if she worships it on the third lunar day and continues it for a year, O splendid one, she will get a good husband who will accord her everything she desires and will bless her with sons.

28. Similarly, those men who worship my idol named Īśāna can make even their wicked (disobedient) beloved gentle.

29. Those who devoutly worship for the sake of a daughter, shall undoubtedly obtain a daughter of their mental choice.

30. Those men who are free from all desires and worship it always, will attain the greatest Siddhi devoid of old age and death."

31. After saying thus, Mahādeva made his beloved mount the Bull and then he himself mounted it. Afterwards, he went to the mountain Kailāsa.

*Nārada said:*

32. Hence, let this daughter of yours propitiate splendid Gaurī consisting of the five lumps for a year.

33. She should worship particularly on the third lunar day. Then she will get a good husband who will look up to her, will be very loving and will be endowed with handsome features and other good qualities.

*Śāṇḍilī said:*

34. After saying thus, Nārada, the excellent sage, proceeded ahead, in his pilgrimage. My mother lovingly bade farewell to him.

35. At his behest, I remained steadfast in the vow of virginity and worshipped the deity for a period of one year with a desire for husband.

36. I worshipped especially on the third lunar day in the month of Mārgaśīrṣa with various kinds of food offerings, gifts, scents, garlands and unguents, O splendid lady.

37. By its power, O Kātyāyanī, this excellent Brāhmaṇa named Jaimini was obtained by me. As you have seen him, why should there be further glorification?

38. Hence, O fair lady, worship the goddess with great concentration. You will attain good conjugal felicity, O splendid lady, on par with that of Maitreyī.

39-40. Earlier, the goddess was not worshipped by you in the prescribed way. You did not resort to the vow of celibacy. You did not continue it for a year. You did not make special adoration on the third lunar day. Hence, the pain due to a co-wife, although good fortune should have been unrestricted. The truth has been said by me.

*Sūta said:*

41. After hearing everything said by Śāṇḍilī Kātyāyanī bowed down to her. Then taking leave of her she went to her own house.

42. On the third lunar day in the bright half of the month of Mārgaśīrṣa, she propitiated the goddess. She continued the same on the same (third day) for a year.

43. She fed virgins with sweet food and tasty juices avoiding oil and salt. She offered them sweet scents and substances like saffron.

44-45. When the year was complete, Yājñavalkya went near her and said: "O lady of pure smiles, why do you undertake such a trouble? While I, your affectionate lover, am ready to give whatever you desire always, why should you worry? O splendid lady, come, let us go to our own house."

46. After saying thus to her, he grasped her right hand even as she experienced horripilation all over her body and went home.

47. Thereafter, he was as much delighted with her as with Maitreyī. He was always a smiling face without any change.

48. He begot of her a son of good qualities named Kātyāyana, an expert in the lore of Yajñas[1] (as the author of a *Śrautasūtra*).

49. His son was Vararuci, an ocean of good qualities. He was omniscient and expert in all rites. He was a master of the Vedas and Vedāṅgas.

50-54. For the good of pupils he installed Mahāgaṇapati the bestower of all lores, with great devotion, after duly worshipping him on the fourth lunar day on a Friday.

One who takes a flower garland and recites the Vedas in accordance with the injunctions, O excellent Brāhmaṇas, shall be an expounder of Vedānta in the course of every birth.

One who is incapable of reciting himself but makes others recite by offering cash reward shall become a Brāhmaṇa who masters the Vedas and Vedāṅgas.

He will always be born in the houses of Yājñikas (performers of Yajñas). He will never be born in the houses of fools or censured ones.

## CHAPTER ONE HUNDRED THIRTYTWO

# Creation of Vāstupada

*The sages said:*

1-3 O Sūtaja, you mentioned the Tīrtha of Yājñavalkya as situated there. The Tīrtha of Vararuci known as Vaināyakya is also there.

O highly intelligent one, no Tīrtha of Kātyāyana has been mentioned. Is it because no such Tīrtha was made by him or has it escaped your memory?

Now tell us quickly if any Tīrtha bestowing all the Siddhis was created in the holy spot here by the noble-souled one.

*Sūta said:*

4. A Tīrtha named Vāstupada was made by that Brāhmaṇa Kātyāyana. It gives all desired things unto men.

---

1. This Kātyāyana is different from the grammarian (Vārtikakāra) Kātyāyana. *Prācīna-caritra-kośa* (I. 217) states that Vararuci is another name of Kātyāyana.

5. At that place forty-eight deities are worshipped. On being worshipped, they bestow Siddhi instantly.

*The sages said:*

6. Why are those deities stationed there worshipped, O Sūta? Describe them by names separately.

*Sūta said:*

7-8. Formerly, a great Bhūta (Spirit) came out of the surface of the earth. It was unprecedented, highly frightening and formidable and had black teeth. It was spike-eared, lean-faced and had upraised hairs. It came out terrifyingly for destroying Devas and human beings in particular.

9. It was attracted and activated by the leading Dānava by means of Mantras indicated by Śukra. It could not be killed by any weapon or even missiles.

10. On seeing such a highly terrifying spirit, the Devas provoked by great anger struck it with sharp weapons of various kinds.

11. In spite of their effort, they were unable to strike its limbs. Hundreds and thousands were simply gobbled up by it.

12. With great effort then all the Devas including Vāsava, kept Brahmā at their head and rushed against that Bhūta.

13. Thereafter, they caught hold of it with great effort. They bound all his limbs five times with a rope (of five strands?) and felled it on the ground.

14. Then all of them sat around it and began to strike it but no blow had any effect on it.

15. Then a Bhūta originating from the Ātharvaṇa Sūkta named Amṛtabindu was hurled by the Daityas near it along with a shaven head (Muṇḍa Sūkta?)

16. Thus for a thousand years it remained there in that condition. They could not leave it due to fear nor could they strike it.

17. Brahmā stood on its belly and the furious Immortals beginning with Śakra stood in the four directions with great effort. Thereupon all the Dānavas began to have consultations together.

18. The destruction of the Devas was suggested as the sole aim of this formidable Bhūta created by Śukra instantly.

19. Then those mighty Dānavas discharged sharp weapons and shouted loudly. Thus they came there in thousands.

20. In the meantime, Viṣṇu came there at the same instant. Then Viṣṇu spoke to the Bhūta delighting it as it were by means of his words:

21-22. "Each of the Devas will propitiate you after getting the adoration in the respective limb pertaining to you wherein he is present. The type of worship mentioned by me in your case has never been adopted in the case of a Deva in the whole world."

23-24. Thereupon, the Bhūta promised with an unhesitating mind: "I shall carry out your words thus. But listen to my words: If any human being at any time does not adore me in any manner, he shall be my prey."

*Sūta said:*

25. The Discus-bearing Lord said, "Of course." Then the Bhūta became motionless with great delight.

26. Then the weapon-wielding Devas left it and got up. With their sharp arrows they struck down (the Dānavas) who were eager to flee and shameless. With the disappearance of their ire they began to utter piteous words:

27. With the Daityas struck down, Hari felt relieved. He spoke to the Lotus-born One: "Oh, give a name to this Bhūta."

*Brahmā said:*

28. In reply to your statement the words uttered by this (Bhūta), O Hari, were *"vā astu etad"* ("Or this may be so"). Hence, its name shall be "Vāstu."[1]

29. On being told thus, Hṛṣīkeśa summoned Viśvakarman and told him the detailed procedure of the adoration.

30-32. In the mean time, the intelligent son of Yājñvalkya summoned Viśvakarman, O excellent Brāhmaṇas, and said: "First make my hermitage at the holy spot of Hāṭakeśvara, O

1. A popular etymology of *Vāstu*.

highly intelligent one, in accordance with this procedure now explained. Thereafter, I shall understand everything and make it flourish on the earth so that children (ignorant persons) may learn and understand the same. Hence come quickly."

33. Then Brahmā, inclined to abide by what was beneficial to his son (Yājñavalkya being Brahmā's own incarnation) summoned Viśvakarman and sent him to him (son of Kātyāyanī).

34. Viśvakarman came there and fully performed the Vāstu adoration in the manner explained by Brahmā.

35. Kātyāyana observed everything and rendered it a thousand-fold for the benefit of the universe including *Śālākarman* etc. (method of building the hall).

36. It was thus, O excellent Brāhmaṇas, that the site of abode (*Vāstupada*) came to be in that holy spot. A man overwhelmed by sins will become released therefrom by means of holy rites performed in this holy spot.

37. He will not incur any sin due to any house, architecture, bad site or irregular activity of the site (rite).

38. It was on the third lunar day in the bright half of Vaiśākha, coinciding with Rohiṇī star, that the Vāstupada was placed there by that noble-souled one.

39. A man who performs its adoration on that day in accordance with the injunction shall attain the status of king.

40. A house may be defective or it may have structural slips but due to this association (with the Vāstu-adoration) it flourishes day by day.

## CHAPTER ONE HUNDRED THIRTYTHREE

# Origin of Ajāgṛhā[1]

*Sūta said:*

1. Further, O excellent Brāhmaṇas, there is another deity there well-known as Ajāgṛhā. It is destructive of all ailments.

2. When Ajāpāla who was engaged in what is beneficial to all the worlds, was the king, O Brahmaṇas, all the ailments used to go away in the form of goats. He used to bring them back during the night and place them at that holy spot.

3. The place being their (of the ailments) resort came to be remembered as *Ajāgṛha*. By visiting it once, people residing on the surface of the earth, get (their) ailments destroyed.

4. I shall recount unto you all, O excellent Brāhmaṇas, the Aiśvarya (lordly glory) that existed there formerly. It should be listened to with great concentration.

5. A certain Brāhmaṇa in the guise of a sage came to that holy spot in the course of his pilgrimage. He came there at night and he was awfully tired.

6. He saw that a flock of goats was kept there comfortably. They were chewing the cud in a carefree manner without any fear from any quarter.

7-9. He knew that undoubtedly some person must be present there. Cattle or beasts are not kept at night in a desolate forest. He repeatedly shouted at the sky but there was no response. He went to sleep thinking: 'Certainly for the protection of these animals some man should soon come from somewhere. So I shall stay here fearlessly.'

10. While he was asleep thus in utter exhaustion, O excellent Brāhmaṇas, the night passed off quickly.

11. In the morning when he looked all over his body, he found it covered by leprosy and other ailments.

---

1. For protecting his subjects against diseases, Aja converted them as goats and kept them confined in a fold. Once a Brāhmaṇa-pilgrim ignorantly slept there and contracted leprosy. King Aja performed penance and propitiated the Kṣetra Devatā. The Devatā advised the Brāhmaṇa to take a bath in the Candra Kūpikā nearby which cured his disease. Hence the Devatā came to be known as Ajāgṛhā.

12-13. He was unable to move even a step from that place. He became lustreless on account of the terrible ailments. He began to think: 'What is the cause? My body has become like this suddenly with this ailment. I am unable to move.'

14. Even as that Brāhmaṇa was thinking thus, a person resembling twelve suns in lustre came there instantly.

15. He called and grouped that flock naming them specifically. He had a stick in his left hand and he was separating them.

16. Then he saw that Brāhmaṇa completely overpowered by ailment and unable to move anywhere. Then he spoke to him respectfully.

17-19. "O excellent Brāhmaṇa, who are you and whence have you come to this spot in such a plight? In my kingdom clearly no one suffers from any disease anywhere. I am a king named Aja. Perhaps you have heard about me. For the sake of the people, I segregate the ailments in the form of goats. Hence, O excellent Brāhmaṇa, tell me what is the sickness that has overcome your body? Tell me so that I can control it."

*The Brāhmaṇa said:*

20. I am engaged in pilgrimage. I am wandering all over the earth. In due course, I have come to this holy place of Hāṭakeśvara.

21-22. O excellent king, I came here at nightfall. On seeing these animals, O King, I thought there should be human beings around and decided to stay here. O king, I went to sleep by the side of these animals.

23. When it dawned, I saw my body completely covered with leprosy and other ailments.

24. In fact I do not know of any other cause. Let it go, O excellent king. Why should we talk much? Do something so that my body shall be free from disease.

25. The Ailments were told by King Ajāpāla: "By whom was my command broken? Who should be killed by me?"

*The Ailments said:*

26. O king, do not be angry at all in this matter wherein this Brāhmaṇa has now been assailed by three Ailments.

27. The three Ailments, O excellent Brāhmaṇa, are consumptive disease, leprosy and scabies. All these three defects (diseases) are proclaimed till today as contagious.

28. The first two of these Ailments are remembered as irremediable either through medicines or through Mantras. The others can be destroyed.

29. There is curse of Brahmā on these two. Hence there is no question of their removal. O excellent king, do whatever is within your power in this matter.

30. O king, all these three have been touched by this Brāhmaṇa. Hence undoubtedly these have entered his body.

31. Further, O king, listen these words issuing from our mouths for the benefit of all creatures and for increasing your glory.

32. O king, a permanent spot had been made there on the ground where excreta have been dropped (by the goats). Therefore, the ground has been broken down and rendered uneven immediately.

33. Even on later occasions, those men who come to this region and touch the ground will become like this.

34-35. We, the remaining ailments, O great king, are amenable to Mantras and medicinal herbs. We should be set free by you, not these two uncontrollable ones cursed by Brahmā.

36-37. On hearing it the king too settled down in that place. He told the Brāhmaṇa again: "O Brāhmaṇa, you should not be afraid. I will protect you from this gruesome disease. At my behest, therefore, wait here for some time."

38. After saying thus he performed very great penance for that purpose, propitiating the presiding deity of the holy spot perfectly with great devotion.

39. O Brāhmaṇas, he untiringly recited the various Sūktas of Atharvaśīrṣa such as Muṇḍa, Kṣetrapālottha and Vāstusūkta.

40. The king performed Homa with white mustard and red flowers rendered well fragrant with incense. Then he (recited)the Nīlarudra Sūktas particularly.

41-42. The presiding deity of that holy spot, the goddess attracted by the Mantras, pierced the earth towards the close of the night at the conclusion of the Homa and came out. She spoke to the king:

43-44. "O king, by the power of this Homa of yours, I

have risen up from the surface of the earth. I am the only one remembered as the presiding deity of this holy spot. Hence, O highly esteemed one, tell me. What task of yours shall I carry out? I have attained the greatest pleasure. Hence, speak out what is desired by you."

*The king said:*

45. O goddess, you must stay particularly in this holy spot forever so that the defects of this land arising from the contact of the ailments, may disappear.

46-47. From now onwards, O goddess of Devas, let this policy be adopted. Otherwise men will become afflicted with diseases due to contagion, like this Brāhmaṇa seen in front. For a long time these diseases were contained by me here. Otherwise it would undoubtedly be a fault of mine.

48. Further, O goddess of Suras, let this Brāhmaṇa be rid of this disease, with your favour. You must stay in this place forever.

*The Kṣetra Devatā said:*

49. The entire spot has been rendered free from the blemish of disease by me. I shall stay here forever.

50. Whoever comes here afflicted with sickness and worships me devoutly, will become free from sickness.

51. Hence, let this leading Brāhmaṇa respectfully worship me today. He must possess great devotion. He must be clean. He must have great concentration and mental purity.

52. There is another quite well-known well in this holy spot named Candrakūpikā. O king, let him duly take his holy bath therein everyday.

53. It was formerly dug up by Candra cursed by Dakṣa. The noble-souled one afflicted with the consumptive disease wanted this for the sake of his own holy ablution.

54. There is another deity stationed there named Khaṇḍaśilā. Let the Brāhmaṇa take the holy bath in the Saubhāgyakūpikā and then visit the deity.

55. This well was dug formerly be Kāmadeva who was afflicted with leprosy. He did it with great respect for his own ablution as well as for the destruction of leprosy.

56. O excellent king, there is a Kuṇḍa (holy pit) of Apsarās also here. One who bathes therein on a Sunday gets rid of scabies.

*Sūta said:*

57. Then the Brāhmaṇa went to the very sacred Candrakūpikā, took his bath and worshipped that goddess with devotion for a period of one month. Then he was immediately relieved of the consumptive disease.

58. Then he visited Saubhāgyakūpikā made by Kāma. After taking his holy bath, he visited Khaṇḍaśilā.

59. As before, he did this for a month and was rid of leprosy, O excellent Brāhmaṇas, by the power of the goddess as well as of the Kūpikā in particular.

60. Then on a Sunday, he took bath in the Kuṇḍa of Apasrās. He was rid of scabies like one immersed in worldly pleasures (but) who is rid of them by means of knowledge and good sense.

61. Then that Brāhmaṇa gained a lustre like that of twelve suns. He became extremely pleased. He gave a blessing to the king.

62. He bowed repeatedly to those two deities. On being permitted by the king, he went to the land of his choice.

63. The king realized the defect of the diseases in the form of the goats. On seeing the Brāhmaṇa healthy he became glad.

64. He himself went to the place where the Lord of Hāṭakeśvara was present in his own body accompanied by his beloved.

65. Since the presiding deity of the holy spot was stationed in Ajāgṛha, O excellent Brāhmaṇas, she became well known everywhere as Ajāgṛhā.

66. Even today a consumptive patient who worships well that goddess in accordance with the injunction shall quickly become rid of the sickness.

## CHAPTER ONE HUNDRED THIRTYFOUR

# Origin of Tīrthas like Saubhāgyakūpikā

*The sages said:*

1-3. You have narrated the story of Somanātha as to how the Snow-rayed One was cursed by the furious Dakṣa.

Now tell us how Kāma suffered from leprosy and what was his fault. By whom was he cursed? Recount to us how goddess Śilākhaṇḍa (Khaṇḍaśila) and Saubhāgyakūpikā originated there.

*Sūta said:*

4. Formerly there was a Brāhmaṇa well-known by the name Hārīta. He performed his penance there in his Vānaprastha stage.

5. He had a chaste lady as his wife. She possessed beauty and other exquisite qualities. Like Lakṣmī, the wife of the enemy of Madhu (Viṣṇu) she was the most beautiful lady in all the three worlds.

6. She was well-known by the name Pūrṇakalā. She had well-developed good qualities. On seeing her even the Lotus-born One fell victim to the influence of Kāma.

7. Once, with a desire to see Kāmeśvara (i.e. Lord Śiva), Manobhava (Kāma) too came there along with (his wives) Rati and Prīti.

8. In the meantime, she too came there for her bath. She stripped herself of all her garments and entered the waterpond.

9. Then on seeing the lady of splendid countenance, Kāmadeva too was hit in his heart by his own flowery arrows.

10. Wounded by his own arrows, he left Rati and Prīti, reached a lonely spot beneath a tree and slept there.

11. All his limbs experienced horripilation. He repeatedly heaved hot sighs with fiery colour (*agni-varṇa*) and long puffs. his eyes were filled with tears.

12. He then stood in the range of her vision and looked at her with fixed stare like a Yogin in the midst of his mental absorption meditating on the steady established Brahman.

13. She too stared at Kāma who was standing lovingly in front of her, yawning and having various facial contortions. His whole body was trembling.

14. She was attracted by Kāma. She was fascinated by his extraordinary features. Her heart was pierced by the arrows of Kāma.

15. With great difficulty the lady of pure smiles came out of water and reached the bank. Then she stood within his view.

16. Then Kāma got up and came near her very slowly. With palms joined in reverence, he spoke to her respectfully:

17. "Who are you, O lady of large eyes? You have come to the water pond for bathing. But, O lady of beautiful limbs, you are out to ruin me. So listen to my word

18. O lady of beautiful smiles, I am famous in the world as the Flower-arrowed One. Even Devas have been subjected to mortification by me through my arrows.

19. On being struck down by my arrows, Rudra held his wife by means of half of his body, thereby casting off all shame.

20. Pierced by my arrows, Brahmā entertained lust for his own daughter and begot of her the Brāhmaṇas Vālakhilyas of such peculiar features.

21. Śakra was enamoured of Ahalyā, the beloved wife of Gautama. Because he was tormented by my arrows, he came down to the earth from heaven.

22. Thus, O lady of excellent eyebrows, even the Devas of superior status have been assailed by my arrows. What then about human beings, very fickle and almost like worms!

23. O lady of sweet smiles, the entire universe beginning with an insect and ending with Brahmā, has become mortified on account of my arrows.

24. Despite all those things, O splendid lady, O timid one, I have been reduced to this plight by you.

25. Hence, O highly esteemed one, give me the grand gift of sexual intimacy today lest my vital breaths should forsake my body.

*Sūta said:*

26. On hearing his words, she was in a great dilemma. On the one hand she was devoted to the vow of fidelity to her husband, but on the other hand, she was excessively assailed in the heart by his (Kāma's) arrows.

27. The poor chaste lady was stranger to the perversity of love-lorn activity. She had grown up in the midst of hermits. She knew none else, nothing else.

28. She did not know what to speak and how to speak as is usually the case with those who are tormented by Kāma. She stood thus for a long time looking down and scratching the ground with the big toe of her foot.

29-31. In the meantime, the sun arrived on the setting mountain (the western quarter). Hermit Hārīta who maintained the sacred fires came back at the time of the elaborate rituals. He waited for her for a long time without taking food. He began to worry: 'Why has she not come back? After taking her bath in the excellent Tīrtha, viewing that Candrakūpikā and visiting Kāmeśvara, the Lord of the Devas, the bestower of desired happiness on men (she should have come back by this time).'

32. Then in the company of his disciples, he looked for her here and there. Ultimately, he came to that place where both of them had been standing.

33. Being struck by his own arrows, Kāma was uttering many (overtures of love), but she was standing looking down with excessive bashfulness.

34. Concealed behind a hedge, he heard whatever was prattled by Kāma. He noticed her emotional fervour. Thereupon, he became furious and said:

35-37. "O sinner, you have afflicted my wife thus with the arrows. She has been an innocent chaste lady devoted loyally to her husband. She has been hit by you and made to stand with face down with excessive bashfulness. Hence you will be overcome with the fell disease of leprosy. You will be unpleasant to see. Even your wives will forsake you. On seeing you, she became enamoured of you. Thereby she transgressed her duty. She shall become senseless resembling a rock."

38. Thereupon, Kāma prostrated down to him and pacified him: "O Brāhmaṇa, this beautiful lady was not known to me as your wife.

39. Therefore, she was told by me various kinds of words not suited to her. It is not her fault that she was acutely afflicted by my arrows.

40. Very well, she became infatuated, O sage, but no word was uttered by her. Hence, it does not behove you to curse her at all.

41. Herein it is my fault. Hence do chastise me. But, O excellent Brāhmaṇa, the curse against her is unbearable.

42. O excellent Brāhmaṇa, even Devas beginning with Rudra are unable to bear my arrows. Hence could she have borne? Why should she be turned into a rock?

43. Further, learned men say that sin is of three kinds, mental, verbal and the third one, physical. O leading sage, I am guilty of two types of sins, whereas she is guilty of only one type.

44. Your beautiful wife may have committed only one sin, but you want to mete out the full punishment. Are you not afraid of the future world?

45. A mental sin can be wiped off by mental anguish and regret. A verbal sin can be eradicated by pacifying him against whom something foul has been uttered.

46. A physical sin will disappear through atonement as mentioned in the scriptures on ethical conduct. O great sage, all those scriptures do lay down these."

*Hārīta said:*

47. O Kāmadeva, her sin may be as you say if it refers to other matters. But in regard to your sphere of activity, the importance is that of the mind.

48-50. At the outset everything is mentally conceived. Then it is uttered by means of words. Then the physical act takes place. Hence it is the mind that is more important in regard to all matters always. For this reason I had to mete out a full punishment to her. Hence she will stay in this manner always, O mean fellow. You may do what constitutes your duty. I will not say anything.

*Sūta said:*

51. After saying thus, Hārīta, the excellent sage, went to his hermitage. Pūrṇakalā was turned into a rock at the same instant.

52. O Brāhmaṇas, Kāmadeva was seized by leprosy of

terrible proportions. His nose, hands and legs became withered and he became repulsive to the eyes of onlookers.

53. O excellent Brāhmaṇas, when Kāma was afflicted with the disease and consequently lost interest in his routine activities, the process of creation in the whole universe stopped.

54. The whole world dwindled and deteriorated. There was no growth at all. Even the sweat-born living organisms faced ruin and destruction.

55-56. In the meantime, all the Devas were agitated with anxiety: 'Why does the world including all aquatic and groundborn living beings decay? No child is seen at all anywhere. Nor is a pregnant lady visible. We hope Smara is all right.'

57. On coming to know that he was afflicted with a disease and had resorted to this holy spot all of them hurried to the place with mental agitation and worry.

58. They saw the Flower-weaponed One staying in Kāmeśvarapura meditating on Maheśvara. His features were hideous and ugly.

59. In their great distress, they said: "O Flower-weaponed One, what is this? You have become afflicted with the fell disease of leprosy! You have lost all enthusiasm."

60. Overcome with excessive shame, he stood with face turned downwards. He narrated the entire account regarding Hārīta's action and his curse.

61. Then the Devas said: "The sin perpetrated verbally shall undoubtedly perish in full by propitiating her.

62. So, Mind-born One, propitiate her in the form of a rock. Thereby your leprosy will perish and your refulgence will increase.

63. Since you have not incurred any sin except the verbal one (this atonement will be enough). Let there be the great activity of creation. Let the divine task be fulfilled.

64-65. If any other man afflicted with the disease of leprosy, though it may be a result of a sinful action of the body, takes his bath in your Kuṇḍa with great faith and touches this rock freed from sin, he will also be relieved from his sickness and the distress thereof .

66. This water pond shall become well-known in the world by the name Saubhāgyakūpa. It shall be destructive of all ailments. There is no doubt about it.

67. Itches of excessively putrid nature and scabies of the person taking bath here will disappear afrter viewing this rock."

68. After saying this, the Devas went to the heavenly adode. Kāmadeva stayed there and performed the adoration.

69. Then, even when only a month elapsed, O excellent Brāhmaṇas, Smara regained that form which he originally had.

70. Then he made a temple for her with great faith and went to the place of his choice in his endeavour for creation.

71. The lady who had been standing with face lowered down when being cursed, became a fragment of rock. Hence, she is remembered as Khaṇḍaśilā.

72. If anyone devoutly worships her on the thirteenth lunar day, he will never face scandals arising from association with other men's wives.

73. Kārttikeya, the son of Śaṅkara, has prescribed this rite in particular to a lustful woman. O excellent Brāhmaṇas, what has been said by me is the truth.

74. By propitiating the deity called Kāmeśvara installed by Kāmadeva, on the thirteenth lunar day, one shall attain all desired things.

75. Smara is in a personified form there along with Rati and Prīti, O tigers among Brāhmaṇas. He has an excellent palatial shrine as his resort.

76-79. One ugly in form and unlucky in his plight should worship him with flowers and saffron with great mental concentratrion on the thirteenth lunar day. That man is reborn as a handsome person endowed with conjugal felicity.

A woman abadoned by her husband and surrounded by cowives should worship that deity along with excellent wives on the thirteenth lunar day with filaments of lotuses and saffron, O excellent Brāhmaṇas. She will enjoy conjugal felicity, O Brāhmaṇas. She will beget sons. She will have flourishing wealth and foodgrain. She will be free from misery and grief. She will have no blemishes at all. She will be one praised all over the earth.

## CHAPTER ONE HUNDRED THIRTYFIVE

# Boon to a Chaste Lady: Dīrghikā[1]

*Sūta said:*

1-2. Further, there is another very splendid lake there named Dīrghikā. It is well-known all over the world and is destructive of all sins.

A man who takes his holy ablution there properly at the time of sunrise on the fourteenth lunar day in the bright half of the month of Jyeṣṭha is liberated from all sins.

3. Formerly, in the excellent city of Vardhamāna there was a well-renowned Brāhmaṇa named Vīraśarman. He was a very efficient scholar of the Vedic lore and holy vows connected therewith.

4. Once he had a daughter without good features. She was too tall, beyond the normal size. Thereby she caused popular derision.

5. In the same form, the girl attained youth. Remembering the scriptural injunction, no one came forward to marry her:

6-7. "A man who deluded by lust, marries a girl who is too tall, too short or with very short tresses of hairs, shall certainly meet death within six months." Such was the scriptural passage and for this reason, everyone avoided that girl.

8. All men avoided her on seeing her excessive height. Thereupon, she became dejected and performed a very severe penance.

---

1. The main object of this chapter is to describe the spiritual power of a chaste lady.
The object of Chapters 135 to 138 is to glorify the Dīghikā Tīrtha. Dīghikā, an old lady, marries an old leper. She carries him on her head to make him perform the pilgrimage of 68 Tīrthas. She reached Hāṭakeśvara at night. In the darkness she inadvertently dashed against sage Māṇḍavya who was impaled there. Due to excruciating pain, he cursed that her husband? ground and a spring of water appeared where they quenched their thirst. The next morning the Sun did not rise. Devas approached her. She allowed the Sun to rise. The Devas made her husband who died due to Māṇḍavya's curse, live again. They made both of them young. The spring of water created Dīrghikā became known as Dīrghika-Tīrtha and is still efficacious.

9. She performed the expiations named Cāndrāyaṇa, Kṛcchra, Parāka and Sāntapana as laid down in the scriptures.

10. Whatever Vrata there was, she observed it. So also Niyama, Saṁyama (control) and all other meritorious rites.

11. Even as she observed all these Vratas, old age overtook her. Still there was augmentation of refulgence caused by her penance.

12. Due to excessive curiosity, she always used to attend the court of Mahendra in order to listen to the opinions of the celestial sages and Devas in particular.

13. Whenever she vacated her seat and went homewards, Śakra's servants used to sprinkle it with water.

14. O excellent Brāhmaṇas, on a certain day she herself saw the seat being sprinkled upon.

15. Thereupon, the aged virgin Dīrghikā became furious. Knitting her eyebrows, she said to Indra:

16-17. "What fault did you notice, O Śakrā? Why was the seat sprinkled with water? Is it a defect caused by another or is it mine? Hence tell me my sin. Otherwise, I will pronounce a terrible curse. There is no doubt about it. On this solemn truth, I vouch myself."

*Indra said:*

18. O splendid lady Dīrghikā, except a single one you have no other fault. It is for this reason that the seat is sprinkled with water.

19. Though you are a virgin, you do experience the despicable monthly menstrual cycle. Hence, you incur the defect. There is no other reason.

20. Hence even now, if any sage is prepared to marry you take him on as your husband so that you will acquire purity.

21. That aged virgin Dīrghikā became ashamed thereby and hurriedly went to the excellent city Vardhamāna on the earth.

22. Wandering here and there, in places where four roads or three roads meet, with her right hand lifted up, she began to proclaim with a loud cry:

23. "If anyone, Brāhmaṇa by birth, comes forward to grasp my hand in marriage, I shall give a moiety of the accumulated benefits of my penance."

24. On hearing her blurting out thus day and night, the people thought her to be mad and cut jokes about her among themselves.

25. Thus Dīrghikā carried on for many days when a Brāhmaṇa afflicted with leprosy heard her.

26. He called the distressed woman and spoke to her slowly:

27. "If you carry out all my behests I shall grasp your hand and marry you."

*The virgin said:*

28. I shall carry out your instructions, O leading Brāhmaṇa. There is no doubt about it. Grasp my hand duly in accordance with the scriptural injunctions.

*Sūta said:*

29. Then he grasped the right hand of the virgin in the presence of Devas, fire and preceptor in accordance with the scriptural injunctions laid down in the Gṛhya Sūtras.

30. After the auspicious rite of marriage, she spoke again: "O my lord, command me, I shall carry it out now."

*The husband said:*

31. O beautiful lady, I wish to take the holy ablution in sixty-eight Tīrthas with your help. If you can, kindly do so.

32-33. She said, "So it shall be". Then the chaste lady made a beautiful small hut of bamboos befitting his size. She placed soft cotton pieces therein and then spoke to her husband with great delight, standing with palms joined in reverence:

34. "For your sake this beautiful hut of bamboos has been made ready, O my lord. Get into it quickly. I shall carry it on my head and take you to all splendid holy spots."

35. The leper was pleased in his heart. As she lifted him up, he slowly got up from the ground, went into the bamboo-structure and slept there.

36. She carried him comfortably on her head. She wandered over all the holy spots and made her husband bathe in all the Tīrthas.

37. As the leper performed the holy ablution in the Tīrthas, the refulgence in his limbs went on increasing.

38. In the course of her slow wandering over the earth, the chaste lady reached Hāṭakeśvara Kṣetra at nightfall.

39. Burdened with the weight the chaste lady became weak and tired. Overcome with blinding sleep and heaving deep sighs, she faltered at every step.

40. It was at that spot that the leading sage Māṇḍavya was kept pinned down to the spike in a miserable state.

41. The great chaste lady groaning under a heavy burden, was passing by the spike at night.

42. She dashed against the leading sage shaking him slightly. Experiencing great pain, the miserable sage said:

43. "Who is that sinful one by whom the spike within me is shaken? Already miserable, I have been forced to bear greater pain!"

*Dīrghikā said:*

44. O highly esteemed one, my eyes have been blinded by overwhelming slumber. Hence you were not noticed. You are the most sinful one and so cannot be even touched. But you were touched.

45. There is no other single soul on the earth like you. Though the stake has pierced through your head, you have not met death!

46. I am a chaste lady, O deluded one, I bear my beloved husband on my head for the sake of pilgrimage as he is disabled.

47. In spite of all these, you despise me cruelly. Human beings are likely to err unwittingly. Still you were foolish to despise me.

*Māṇḍavya said:*

48-49. O cruel lady, your husband caused me acute pain, very nearly killing me. If that husband of yours continues to live in the morning, then undoubtedly I am, what you say, a sinful soul, one of deluded intellect and unworthy of being touched by all embodied beings.

50. Hence this lover of yours has been cursed by me. On being touched by the rays of the Sun, he will give up his life.

*Dīrghikā said:*

51. If thus the death of my husband should take place in the morning, then the Sun will not rise at all.

52. After saying thus, she placed the bamboo structure along with her husband on the ground and sat there.

53. Then the leper said to her: "I am thirsty. Fetch me cool water to drink."

54-55. On hearing the command of her husband, she eagerly moved about for water, but could not see. Nor did she go very far because she did not want to leave her husband in that plight in the forest, because she was afraid of the beasts of prey. She, therefore, sat on the ground. Touching the feet of her husband the distressed Dīrghikā spoke these words in high pitch:

56. "If I am perfect in my adherence to chastity and fidelity to my husband, let splendid water come out from the ground on the basis of this truth."

57. After saying thus she stamped her foot on the ground, remembering her devotion to her husband and desiring his life.

58. In the meantime, even as Māṇḍavya was watching, pure and tasty water sprang up after stamping the foot.

59. Then she made her weary and sick husband bathe in the water. Thereafter, she made him drink the water. She herself had her bath and drank the water.

60. In the meantime, due to the fear of the chaste lady's vow of fidelity, the Sun did not rise up. Much time elapsed then.

61. On noticing the prolongation of the night, all lascivious men and immoral unchaste women became delighted.

62. The owls, Rākṣasas, thieves and paramours embraced one another joyously and said:

63. "Today the fate is pleased with us. So also Manmatha, for the night has been prolonged and the Sun is made to vanish."

64. But in the case of Brāhmaṇas, quiescent and devoted to the rites of Yajñas, all of them became miserable due to the absence of the Sun.

65. No excellent Brāhmaṇa performed Yajña himself or made others perform a Yajña. None of them performed Śrāddha rite, Saṅkalpa (ritualistic proclamation of intended rite) or Svādhyāya (self-study of the Vedas).

66. None took the holy ablution, none made a gift; no one got engaged especially in worldly business or dealings with others. None carried out virtuous and sacred rites.

67. In the meantime, all the Devas with Śakra at their head experienced great inconvenience and misery, because they were deprived of their shares of Yajñas.

68-70. Then they approached Bhāskara and said in great sorrow: "O Divākara, why don't you rise, O Lord? without you all this universe has become agitated. Hence, for the benefit of all the worlds rise up as usual, so that Yajñas including Agniṣṭoma can be performed on the earth."

*Sūrya (Sun) said:*

71. I have cancelled rising at the bidding of a chaste lady. Hence may all the Devas go to her and plead on my behalf.

72. Then at her behest I can resume my activity comfortably. Otherwise, the infuriated lady may curse me. Indeed she is a chaste lady loyal to her husband.

73. O excellent Suras, endowed with the power of penance, she possesses the great and extraordinary power of chastity.

74. So who is powerful enough to transgress her behest. I am afraid to rise up at all.

75. Those who worship by means of a thousand Kratus cannot even aspire to attain that merit which naturally accrues to a lady equipped with the power of chastity.

76. Then all those Devas went to that excellent holy spot, stood before the chaste lady Dīrghikā and spoke these soft words:

77-78. "O chaste lady, in forbidding the Sun to rise, you have not done anything auspicious, since all the splendid holy rites are doomed. Hence, O sensible lady, let the Fierce-rayed One rise at your behest whereby the rites of Yajñas can earnestly be carried out on the earth."

*The chaste lady Dīrghikā said:*

79. If the solar disc comes up, immediately my husband who is dearer to me than my own life, will meet his death, O Devas.

80. He (my husband) has been cursed by this wicked and sinful Māṇḍavya. He (my husband) has been unnecessarily pointed out for this dire end (death). So how can I tell Bhāskara (to rise)?

81. How can I urge Bhāskara to rise. Without my husband, I have nothing to do with Yajñas or other rites such as Śrāddha, Dāna etc.

*Sūta said:*

82. Thereupon all the Devas looked at one another for a long time with great sorrow. Then they said to her humbly:

83. "O fair lady, may Ravi (Sun) come up. Let your beloved husband meet his death. This leading sage shall be revived again.

84. Even if he meets death, we shall resuscitate him for your sake, O lady endearing to your husband.

85. You will see him as a young man of twenty-five years, another veritable Kāmadeva. His limbs will be shining. He will be marked with all good features.

86. You will become a lady with large eyes resembling the petals of a lotus. You will be one aged fiteen years. You will enjoy all worldly pleasures as you please.

87. O splendid lady, let this tiger among sages be freed from his sins. Let him be released from the torture at the stake. Let him be reasonably happy."

*Sūta said:*

88. O excellent Brāhmaṇas as soon as she said, "So be it", Lord Sun rose up speedily at the moment.

89. Touched by the rays of the Sun, the leper died. Touched by the hands of the Devas, he rose up alive.

90. He was a young man of twenty-five years. He stood like another Kāmadeva. He joyously remembered the previous birth entirely.

91. Touched by Lord Śaṁbhu himself, Dīrghikā became endowed with youth and divine features.

92. She was beautiful with eyes resembling petals of a lotus. She was slender at the waist. Her limbs were fair-complexioned. Her breasts were thick and protruding.

93. The excellent Devas got that tiger among sages down from the top of the stake and spoke to him with respect and great delight:

94-96. "O sage, the words uttered by you were made true. The leper, the Brāhmaṇa, died on being touched by the rays of the Sun. Of course, he was resuscitated by us and made a young man again along with his wife. So, go back to your hermitage. (The act of) seeing us cannot become fruitless at any cost. Hence, ask for whatever you have cherished in your heart always."

## CHAPTER ONE HUNDRED THIRTYSIX

# Origin of Dīrghikā

*Māṇḍavya said:*

1. O excellent Suras, I shall surely accept the boon granted by you. But let Dharmarāja make a decisive statement in my case.

2. O excellent Suras, this is also true that it is only the virtuous and non-virtuous acts that always follow all living beings and not otherwise.

3. (Then) what is that sin committed by me in this world or in the other, wherefore I am experiencing such a torture not leading to death at all.

*Dharmaraja said:*

4. In another body (birth), O Brāhmaṇa, while you were yet a boy, a crane was pierced by you with the tip of a spear on the ground.

5. You did not commit any other sin even in the least. Hence, O Brāhmaṇa, this pain had to be experienced.

*Sūta said:*

6. On hearing his words, Māṇḍavya was excessively angry. He spoke to Dharmarāja standing before him:

7-9. "For this slight offence, O highly wicked one of defiled intellect, you have meted out a disproportionately severe punishment. So take this curse from me.[1]

You will be born as a human being in the womb of a Śūdra woman. Then you will have ample experience of sorrow due to the loss of your kinsmen.

Further, this declaration is being made by me now in regard to all the embodied beings. A man or a woman will be adversely affected by a despicable deed only if it is committed after the eighth year."

10. After saying thus to Dharmarāja, Māṇḍavya got rid of his anger, O Brāhmaṇas, and he went to the place of his choice.

11. On seeing him preparing to leave the place, all the Heaven-dwellers who were worried about the fate of Dharmarāja after hearing such a curse, said to him:

*Devas said:*

12. O holy Sir, although Dharmarāja was guilty of a sinful deed, it does not behove you to make him a Śūdra by means of the curse.

13. Hence, O Brāhmaṇa, be pleased with this Dharmapati at our instance, and immediately request for a boon.

*Māṇḍavya said:*

14. O excellent Suras, my speech uttered once cannot be altered. Certainly this Dharmarāja will be born of a Śūdra womb.

15. But in that birth he will not beget any child. He will regain the excellent status of Dharmarāja.

16. Unperturbed, let him propitiate the Three-eyed One in this holy spot itself here. With the favour of that Lord, he will meet with an early death.

17. Further, O rulers of heaven, if a boon has to be granted

---

1. Dharmarāja became Vidura (cf Mbh) due to this curse. See ch. 138.

by you all to me, then let this spear (the stake) of course be one that accords excellent merit merely on being touched.

*Devas said:*

18. One who gets up early in the morning and touches this Śūla (stake) shall become rid of sins in this world.

19. After speaking thus to the sage, those Devas with Śakra as their leader told the chaste lady and her husband:

20. "O fair-complexioned lady, you too do request for anything desired from us. You may ask for whatever is in your mind. In your case, there is nothing that cannot be given by us."

*The Pativratā said:*

21. O Lord of Devas, let the holy pit made in this holy spot by me[1] be well-known in all the three worlds as Dīrghikā after my name.

*Devas said:*

22. O splendid lady, from now onwards this holy pit shall become well known in all the three worlds as Dīrghikā.

23. Those men who get up early in the morning and take their holy bath in this will be rid of all their sins at the very instant.

24-25. On the fifth lunar day, when the Sun is in the Zodiac Virgo, men with great faith shall take their holy bath here. If they have no sons they will beget sons and augment their family.

After saying thus to her, O excellent Brāhmaṇas, those Devas went to heaven.

26. The beautiful chaste lady enjoyed the pleasure of love along with her lover (husband).

27. They roamed about in beautiful mountains, banks of rivers, wonderful parks, forests and gardens.

28. After the efflux of time in their later advancing age, they eagerly resorted to their own excellent Tīrtha.

1. Vide supra Ch. 135.57-59.

29. On seeing her husband dead, the chaste lady cast off her body in the waters thereof and went to the world of Brahmā.

30. Thus the excellent story of Dīrghikā has been narrated to you all. By listening to this alone, a man becomes rid of sins.

## CHAPTER ONE HUNDRED THIRTYSEVEN

# Māṇḍavya Impaled

*The sages said:*

1-3. By whom was this tiger among sages, Māṇḍavya of excellent penance, placed on the stake? For what reason? Do tell us.

*Sūta said:*

That sage Māṇḍavya was performing his pilgrimage with great faith. He came to this holy spot. That sage of great vows came to the great and excellent Tīrtha of Viśvāmitra and offered libation to the ancestors and also to the Sun.

4-6. He repeated the excellent Sūkta beginning with *"vibhrāṭ"*, a great favourite of Bhāskara. In the meantime a thief who carried the stolen booty of some person came there, O Brāhmaṇas, along with the people closely pursuing him. On seeing the excellent sage in the vow of silence, the thief dropped down the booty in front of him and entered a cave. In the meantime, those persons reached that place for taking away the booty.

7-8. The sage was strictly adhering to the vow of silence. The wise sage knew that the thief was in the cave. Yet he did not say anything. Seeing the booty in front of him, they said to the leading sage: "A thief with the booty in his hand has come this way. O esteemed one, say quickly which way did he go out."

9-10. He was repeatedly asked. But he was thinking about the Supreme Being (or consideration for others). He saved the life of the thief. Thereupon they whispered: "Indeed this man is the thief. Closely pursued by us, he has taken the guise of a sage."

11. Without thinking anything further, those tribal people of wicked intention took him to a dense forest and staked him on the spike.

12. It was thus that the sage was staked on the spear, as a result of the terrible Karma of the previous birth, though he was wise and faultless.

## CHAPTER ONE HUNDRED THIRTYEIGHT

# Origin of Dharmarājeśvara

*The sages said:*

1. What penance, meditation etc. was performed by Dharmarāja in order to wipe out completely the curse of Māṇḍavya? Narrate it to us.

*Sūta said:*

2. On getting the curse of Māṇḍavya, Dharmarāja was extremely miserable. O excellent Brāhmaṇas, he settled in the same holy spot and performed a penance.

3. He constructed a palace unto Kapardin (Śiva), the Lord of Devas, and worshipped him unperturbedly with flowers, incense and unguents.

4. After the lapse of a great deal of time Maheśvara was pleased with him. He said, "I am the bestower of boons. Request for whatever is desired."

*Dharmarāja said:*

5. O Lord, earlier I was cursed by the noble-souled Māṇḍavya although I was faultless and strictly adhering to my duty.

6-7. He had told me angrily, "You will be born of the womb of a Śūdra woman. There too you will experience great sorrow due to the death of kinsmen. As a result of my curse, you will soon attain the adverse effects due to your caste."

8. Hence, O excellent one among Suras, save me from

that (Śūdra) womb. How can I be born of that womb after being like this all along?

9. There too, the great misery of the death of kinsmen is to be borne. It was for this purpose that you have been propitiated by me.

*Śrī Bhagavān said:*

10. The utterance of that sage cannot be altered or invalidated. Yet, although you will be born a Śūdra, you will not beget a son.

11. Although you will witness complete destruction of kinsmen, you will not become miserable. Although you may forbid them, they will not pay heed to your words.

12. For this reason, O Dharmarāja, you will not suffer the sorrow arising from the kinsmen. The truth alone has been mentioned by me.

13. O wise one, you will live for a hundred years as a pious Śūdra. With a desire for the benefit of the kinsmen, you will offer them many instructions, although they may not have credence therein and they may be always sinful.

14. When hundred years are completed, you will take out your soul through Brahmadvāra (cerebral aperture) and attain salvation.

15. After speaking thus, the Lord vanished. Dharmarāja had to bear the effect of the curse of Māṇḍavya.

16. He took incarnation on the earth in the form of Vidura. The highly intelligent one made the statement of Māṇḍavya true.

17. He was born of Vyāsa, the holy sage of unmeasurable refulgence, the son of Parāśara. He was born from the womb of a woman-slave.

18. Thus everything connected with the story of Dharmarāja has been told to you all as I was requested for. This story is destructive of all sins.

# CHAPTER ONE HUNDRED THIRTYNINE

## Greatness of Dharmarājeśvara[1]

*Sūta said:*

1-2. O excellent Brāhmaṇas, I shall narrate unto you all the greatness of Dharmarājeśvara that was heard by me earlier from my father. Listen to that meritorious narrative with great concentration. It is well known in all the three worlds. It is destructive of all sins.

3. Formerly, there was a Brāhmaṇa hailing from the family of Kaśyapa in that holy spot. He was well-known as Upadhyāya. He was devoted to the Vedic lore.

4. He begot a son later in his advancing age even as he strictly adhered to regular study of the Vedas. He acquired ample wealth.

5. When only five years old that son expired causing great sorrow to his father and mother.

6. On knowing that his son had gone to the abode of Dharmarāja, the Brāhmaṇa became angry with Vaivasvata (Dharmarāja).

7. In his height of grief, he took some water in his hand. With mental concentration and personal cleanliness, he then pronounced a terrible curse on Dharmarāja.

8-10. "Since I have been made a sonless person by that wicked-souled one, Yama, of defiled soul, he will also become sonless.

Further people in this world will not perform worship to him nor glorify his name as in the case of other heaven-dwellers.

If anyone gets up early in the morning and recalls his name, there shall be obstacle in his auspicious activity."

11. On hearing the highly terrible curse of the Brāhmaṇa, though he had been abiding by his duties, Yama became grief-stricken.

---

1. Chapter s 138-140 tell that Māṇḍavya cursed Yamadharma to be a sonless Śūdra for the disproportionate punishment given by him. Yamadharma became Vidura, Dharmarājeśvara blessed him with a son (Yudhiṣṭhira) from Pāṇḍu's wife.

12. In the meantime Yama went to the abode of Brahmā. With palms joined in reverence, Yama said to Pitāmaha:

13-15. "See, O Lord of Devas, although I am faultless and I have been abiding by my duty, I have been cursed by the twice-born one as though I am like any other vulgar person.

I have been frightened by the curse of the Brāhmaṇa, O Pitāmaha. I shall give up your assignment. I have told you the truth.

Formerly, O excellent one, I was made to be born in a Śūdra womb by the curse of Māṇḍavya. Now I have been rendered devoid of adoration and of any son!"

*Sūta said:*

16. On hearing these pitiable words of Vaivasvata, Śatakratu himself said these words befitting that occasion:

17-20. "O Lotus-born One, O Lord of Suras, quite reasonable word (appeal) has been uttered by this Dharmarāja who is working as per your command.

O Pitāmaha, there is no doubt about this that in the mortal world, men as per rule should be withdrawn in childhood, youth or old age, but never prematurely (when not due).

This excellent name Dharmarāja has been given by you to that noble-souled one who sees friends and foes alike.

Therefore, after due consideration let some means be resorted to whereby a person who carries out your order should be immune from fault or sin."

*Brahmā said:*

21. O Lord of Devas, I cannot alter the curse of a Brāhmaṇa. I shall employ some other remedy.

22. Then, for that purpose, in front of all the Devas, Brahmā, the grandfather of all the worlds, began to meditate.

23. Even as he was engaged in meditation the personified forms of one hundred eight ailments with *Vāta* (Wind), *Pitta* (Bile) and *Kapha* (phlegm) as their causes appeared before him and respectfully said to him:

*The Ailments said:*

24. O Lord of the chiefs of Devas, why have we been created? Let the order be given quickly. May this favour be done.

*Brahmā said:*

25. At my behest, go quickly to the earth. At the behest of Yama, You must move about unhesitatingly among human beings.

26. After saying thus to those Ailments, Pitāmaha spoke to Dharmarāja who was standing nearby with downcast face in his great distress:

27-30. "O Yama, all these Ailments have been employed by me. They will always render help to you in all matters. Now if anyone reaches the end of his life-span these should be sent always by you to take his life. Thereby, the ignominy arising from the death of people shall devolve upon these alone on the earth and not on you. Therefore, at my behest, go to your own abode and be engaged in your duty. Undoubtedly, you will never incur a fault (sin)."

31. Then the Son of Ravi took all those Ailments to his world and spoke to them respectfully:

32-34. "You shall regularly ask Citragupta and go to the earth for taking away the life of people when the proper time arrives.

But there is an excellent Liṅga installed by me there in Hāṭakeśvara Kṣetra. It is destructive of all sins.

A man who gets up early in the morning and visits it with good devotion, shall always be avoided by you from afar, at my behest:"

35. After saying thus to those Ailments, Vaivasvata assumed the guise of a Brāhmaṇa, took the (recently dead) son of the Brāhmaṇa and went to his beautiful abode.

36-37. On seeing his own son coming to the house along with the wise Dharmarāja in the form of a Brāhmaṇa he went to them face-to face with a delighted heart accompanied by his wife, saying "My son! My son!"

38. He embraced him repeatedly and sniffed at his head. With tears agitating his eyes he spoke these words:

*The Brāhmaṇa said:*

39. O my son, how have you come back from that abode of Yama, from where not even a powerful person can return after going?

40. Is this some sort of jugglery happening near me? Is this a dream? Is this a perversion of my vision?

41. Who is this Brāhmaṇa standing by your side, dear son. He is endowed with divine refulgence. O my son, bow down to him.

*The son said:*

42. This is Yama himself who has come in the form of a Brāhmaṇa. Knowing that you are grief-stricken, he has become sympathetic and he has come for taking me with him.

43. Hence, father, let him withdraw the curse of you consider me your darling. He has come to your house with great friendliness.

44. Then the excellent Brāhmaṇa bowed down to him and remained with face turned downwards due to shame. Then he spoke respectfully:

*The Brāhmaṇa said:*

45. Today my life has become fruitful. My life has become excellent, since I have regained my son who had gone to the abode of Yama.

*The son said:*

46. O father, you have become extremely glad on account of your son. Hence see that he also has a son.

*The Brāhmaṇa said:*

47. O my son, my utterance can never be untrue even if it is jokingly made. It is all the more so if uttered by a grief-stricken one.

48. Hence, O wise one, he will not get a son from the divine womb due to my curse.

49. He will have another son born of the womb of a human

female by means of Rājasūya and Aśvamedha. He will redeem him.

50. Of what avail is a son born to one if he is not capable of redeeming the members of his father's family by performing excellent rites on the earth?

51. As regards the curse uttered by me in regard to his worship earlier, O dear son, listen to what I say:

52. His worship with various kinds of Mantras mentioned in the Vedas will not find a place on the earth at all, dear son.

53. His worship shall be with Mantras composed by humans. It will be different from that of the other Devas. It is the truth that has been uttered by me.

*The son said:*

54. O excellent Brāhmaṇa, I shall install him on the earth and propitiate him perfectly. Of what avail are the other Devas to me?

55. Hence, O my ancestor (father), I shall adopt human Mantras and procedure for worship, with your favour.

56. Then he composed the Mantra beginning with *"sugaṁ naḥ panthāḥ"* and performed the worship even as Dharmarāja was listening.

57. On hearing it, Yama was pleased in his mind. He spoke loudly to the Brāhmaṇa in words choked with delight:

*Yama said:*

58. O leading Brāhmaṇa, my vision (Darśana) can never be in vain like that of Devas. So request for what is desired.

*The Brāhmaṇa said:*

59-60. If any Brāhmaṇa worships uttering this Mantra, the idol of yours which this son of mine has installed on the fifth lunar day, let him have the benefit for the period of a year. Let him not have the grief due to the loss of a son in this world on any account.

*Sūta said:*

61. He promised "Let it be so." Then Yama joyously went to his world and resumed his duty.

62. That son of the Brāhmaṇa erected an excellent palace. In the centre, he installed the idol with great devotion by means of the Mantra uttered by his father and duly propitiated Yama.

63. He begot sons and grandsons in plenty. He lived on the earth for a long time and then passed away.

64. Thus what was heard by me from the Purāṇa has been narrated to you. One who recites this on the fifth lunar day with devotion shall never die prematurely. He will never suffer grief due to the loss of a son.

## CHAPTER ONE HUNDRED FORTY

## The Son of Dharmarāja

*The sages said:*

1-2. O Sūtaja, it has been mentioned by you that Yama would beget a son in human form. Who was born so?

*Sūta said:*

A son was born to him in the wife of Pāṇḍu on the earth. He was well-known all over the world as Yudhiṣṭhira. He was a leader of all the Kṣatriyas.

3. After rendering all the kings as the payers of tribute (to him) by means of his valour, he performed Rājasūya Makha with the full complement of monetary gifts.

4. Further, he made a horse wander all over the earth and performed five Aśvamedhas with the full complement of monetary gifts. Afterwards he attained the highest goal.

5. Many sons should be sought after so that at least one of them may go to Gayā. Or one should perform Aśvamedha Yajña or release a blue bull ritualistically.

6. This noble-souled one requested of me that he should be one having a son who will perform great Aśvamedha scrifices.

7. Thanks to that son, the Lord of Dharma can consider himself contented as having fulfilled his tasks. Of what avail are hundreds of other sons who never redeem the race?

*Sūta said:*

8. Thus, O excellent Brāhmaṇas, everything concerning The birth of the son of Dharmarāja has been narrated to you all. This narrative a great augmenter of virtuousness.

## CHAPTER ONE HUNDRED FORTYONE

## Greatness of Miṣṭānnadeśvara

*Sūta said:*

1-3. Further, there is a deity that bestows sweet food. By visiting that deity, a man obtains sweet food.

Formerly, there was a king remembered as Vasusena. O excellent Brāhmaṇas, in Bṛhatkalpa he was well known as the over-lord of Ānarta.

He possessed a large amount of wealth. He was equipped with elephants, horses and chariots. As highly refulgent one, he conquered all the hosts of his enemies. He was a liberal donor. He enjoyed pleasures and had full control over his sense-organs.

4-5. During Saṅkrānti, Vyatīpāta, eclipses of the Sun and the Moon and other auspicious occasions, with great devotion he used to make to Brāhmaṇas, gifts of various kinds of gems such as lapis lazuli, sapphire, coral, diamonds etc.

6. He made gifts of rubies, pearls, very fine corals, horses, elephants, chariots and vehicles and garments of various kinds.

7. Thinking it to be very cheap and easily accessible, he did not give anyone foodgrains and vegetables and water.

8. He ruled over the kingdom for a long time and saw sons born to his sons. After the lapse of some time he passed away.

9. Thereupon, his son remembered as Satyasena who was endowed with heroism and nobility and generosity, was crowned in the kingdom by his ministers.

10. By the power of his liberal-mindedness and readiness to give, Vasusena attained heaven. He was adorned with divine robes.

11. He was attended upon by Apsarās. He rode in excellent aerial chariots. He could move about in all the worlds as he pleased. But he was always hungry.

12. His mouth was always dry. He was agitated with thirst. But he could not see anyone else in heaven taking food.

13. He could not see anyone eagerly drinking. In fact there was neither water nor any type of vegetation or foodgrain.

14. In this state of hunger and thirst, O excellent Brāhmaṇas, he went to the Thousand-eyed One. He stood near him with the face turned downwards and said to him:

15-18. "O most excellent one among Devas, excepting me, no one is seen here afflicted with hunger and thirst. Why is this so? Do tell me.

This has come to me like veritable Naraka though it has the form of Svarga. Of what avail are these ornaments, robes, aerial chariots and other things?

To a person like me afflicted with hunger, O Consort of Śacī, this Svarga is projected before my mind like fire.

Hence do me this favour. See that hunger does not bother me. If not, O excellent one among Suras, cast me quickly into Raurava Naraka."

*Indra said:*

19. O king, you don't deserve being thrown into Naraka. Numerous gifts have always been made by you.

20. But, O king, nothing like water or cooked food was given by you at any place thinking that this was easily accessible.

21. But, one who wishes for permanent contentment here in this world as well as in the other world, should make gift of water and food or of food with monetary gifts.

22. Hence, O king, you are afflicted with hunger in heaven, though you are adorned with ornaments and moving about in the excellent aerial chariot.

*The king said:*

23. Is there any remedy here, divine or human, whereby my hunger and thirst can be quenched?

*Indra said:*

24-25. If any son of yours offers always water and vegetable dish to Brāhmaṇas, it shall be to your contentment, not otherwise, O excellent king. Even if it is not offered a single day, you will not be contented. The truth has been mentioned by me.

26. That son of yours follows your path in not offering water to you and not gifting vegetable or food dish to Brāhmaṇas.

27. In the meantime, Nārada, the excellent sage, came from the world of Brahmā to the place where the king and Indra were present.

28. Then Śakra joyously got up, duly offered him Arghya and spoke thus respectfully:

29. "O great Brāhmaṇa, whence have you come here? Where do you intend to go now? What is your mission? If it is no secret, do tell us now."

*Nārada said:*

30. O Śakra, I have come here from the world of Brahmā. I am proceeding towards the earth for pilgrimage. There is no other purpose.

*Sūta said:*

31-34. On hearing it that king became delighted. He spoke to the great sage: "O great sage, I am in a wretched plight. A favour may be done to me. O holy sage, my son is a king on the earth. He is the overlord of Ānarta and is well known as Satyasena. He should be told by you: 'Your father was seen by me at the abode of Śakra. In the midst of the Devas, he remains a wretched one because he is oppressed by hunger and thirst. If you are my son, if you wish to safeguard Satya (Truth), make in my name loudly, gifts of waters and vegetable dishes.'"

35. Having promised "It shall be so", Nārada, the great sage, took permission of the Thousand-eyed One (Indra) and started towards the earth.

36. Wandering over the Tīrthas one by one, the excellent Brāhmaṇa came to the land of Ānarta and approached Satyasena.

37. That sage was properly honoured by the king. He conveyed the message from his father while there was no one around.

38. On hearing it, King Satyasena became distressed with grief. He made farewell to the excellent sage after honouring him duly.

39. Then with his father in view, he duly fed a thousand leading Brāhmaṇas devoutly with dainty sweet food.

40. He made provision for watersheds (on the wayside) particularly during summer season. He suspended all other virtuous sacred rites.

41. O Brāhmaṇas, as the king proceeded thus, a terrific drought-situation befell the land causing destruction to all types of vegetation.

42. The Lord of Devas did not let down showers of water on the earth for twelve years. All the people were distressed due to hunger.

43. Due to want of food, there was distress. Hence he did not give vegetable dishes to Brāhmaṇas with his father in view as before.

44. Therefore the father of the king became overcome with hunger. He appeared before him in dream clad in very dirty robes and spoke to the son:

45. "O son, thanks that you are my son. I am distressed with hunger and thirst even though I stay in heaven. Hence make gifts of food along with water in my name. Do this if you are born of me."

46. In view of the dream the king became grief-stricken. On account of absence of food, he consulted his ministers. He spoke to them thus:

47. "I shall propitiate the Bull-bannered Lord (Śiva) for the sake of vegetation and crops of foodgrain. All of you shall accord all round protection in the kingdom with devotion to duty."

48. Then he came here itself, installed Maheśvara and perfectly propitiated him duly observing Vratas and restraints.

49. Then, at the end of a year, Lord Śiva became pleased with him and said: "I am the bestower of boons. Request for whatever is desired."

*The king said:*

50. O Lord of the chiefs of Devas, this procedure (of penance) has been undertaken by me for the sake of food. Hence, O Bull-vehicled One, give unto me plenty of it quickly.

51. Let there be rainfall all over the earth so that plants can grow with plenty of water now.

52. O most excellent one among Suras, thanks to your favour, let my noble-souled father in heaven have everlasting contentment.

*Śrī Bhagavān said:*

53. Ere long there shall be plenty of rainfall all over the earth. Different kinds of food-crops will grow on the earth.

54. At my bidding this shall undoubtedly take place. Therefore, O leading king, do go back to your abode now.

55-56. O king, one who gets up in the morning and properly (with devotion) visits my Liṅga installed by you shall certainly get dainty food as sweet as nectar. O excellent king, this shall be in (his) every birth at my instance.

57. After saying thus the Lord vanished. The king came to his abode with great joy and ruled over the realm destroying all thorns (enemies).

*Sūta said:*

58-59. O Brāhmaṇas, even now when the terrible Kali Age has come, one who gets up early in the morning and with devotion visits Lord Miṣṭānnada shall obtain dainty food, if he so desires. If he is without desire he attains the abode of the Trident-bearing Lord.

## CHAPTER ONE HUNDRED FORTYTWO

# Greatness of the Trio of Gaṇapatis

*Sūta said:*

1-2. Further there is the trio of Gaṇapati deities, that accords heavenly and worldly pleasures. It is meritorious and keeps off Naraka.

It destroys all obstacles. It is worshipped by Suras and Dānavas. It bestows all cherished things and increases learning and reputation.

*The sages said:*

3. O Sūta, three types of people are born on the earth. They are: the best , the middling and the worst or basest.

4. The best ones seek only salvation, after attaining which they never return to the earth.

5. The middling seek the path to heaven and enjoyment of divine pleasures. They seek to sport with Apsarās caused (attained) by Yajñas and other rites.

6. The base ones divert themselves in the mortal world identifying themselves with the objects of the senses. It is as though they take great pleasure therein like a worm in poisonous fluid.

7. How does a mortal wish for that after discarding heavenly pleasures and salvation? And why is this *Martyada* (one that bestows human pleasures) Gaṇanāyaka prayed to by human beings?

8. By whom have those Gajānanas installed in that holy spot? At what time should they be visited? Explain everything in detail.

*Sūta said:*

9. Formerly in the mortal world, excellent Brāhmaṇas performed severe penance and went joyously to heaven as they pleased. Similarly others whose minds become open through meditation, take to the path of Mokṣa (liberation from Saṁsāra).

10. Therefore, Svarga was completely filled by excellent

men once. Thanks to their power, the Devas were ousted all round.

11. Then, accompanied by all the groups of Devas, the Thousand-eyed One himself went to Śaṅkara who was seated along with Gaurī occupying the same seat and said to them:

*Indra said:*

12. O supreme Lord, everything connected with our glory such as (the possession of) abodes etc. is pervaded by human beings who have attained perfection, thanks to the power of penance.

13. Hence do this favour to us now. Think about some means whereby we can stay happily here in Śivālaya (abode of śiva).

14. O Brāhmaṇas, on hearing their words, Virūpākṣa (Śiva) glanced at the moon-like face of Pārvatī sitting by his side.

15. Thereupon, the goddess massaged her own body very well repeatedly and gathered the dirt thereof entirely. She made an elephant-faced one out of that lump of body-dirt.

16. It had a huge body with four hands and protruding belly. It excited the curiosity and fancy of all the Heaven-dwellers.

17-18. The newly created one spoke humbly to the goddess staying on the peak (of the mount): "O mother, tell me the job for which I have been created. Do not delay. With your favour, there is nothing which I cannot accomplish in all the three worlds."

*The goddess said:*

19. Obstacles should be created by you in the auspicious rites of those men in the mortal world, who are desirous of the attainment of Svarga and Mokṣa (liberation).

20-21. The Lords of rivers are thirty Śaṅkus (ten billions) and seventy-seven. There are eighty Nikharvas (billions) of the Mahāsarojas. There are various other Gaṇas numbering one hundred million ten thousand ninety-five crore fifty-five lakh twentyfive thousand sixty-nine hundred.

22. Of these Nandin is proclaimed as the foremost and Mahākāla as the next. May all those excellent Gaṇas function under your control.

23. O dear one, the overlordship thereof has been given to you by me. Be established in the overlordship of all these groups of Gaṇas and administer them.

24-25. After saying thus, the goddess fetched highly auspicious gold pots filled with waters from excellent Tīrthas and containing medicinal herbs as well. The goddess of Suras sprinkled the sacred water over him to the accompaniment of music, playing of musical instruments and auspicious chantings of the Mantras along with dances.

26. There are thirty-three crores of Devas stationed in heaven. All of them came there and celebrated that auspicious rite for him.

27. The Bull-emblemed Lord who was pleased with him, gave him a sharp axe as his permanent excellent weapon.

28. O highly esteemed ones, Pārvatī was full of motherly love for him and gave him a vessel filled with perennial supply of Modakas (round-shaped sweets) for his food.

29. Kārttikeya joyously considered him his brother. Endowed with the affection of a kinsman he gave him a mouse as his vehicle.

30. With a delighted mind, Brahmā bestowed divine knowledge on him comprising everything past, present and future.

31. Viṣṇu granted him intellect. The Thousand-eyed One gave him the great and excellent fortune. Kāmadeva gave him conjugal felicity. Kubera gave him riches etc.

32. Lord Sūrya granted him valour. Moon granted him excellent lustre.

33. In the same way, in order to please the goddess and the Lord, all the other Devas gave him various things belonging to them, and desired by him.

34. O excellent Brāhmaṇas, having obtained excellent things by way of boon thus Gaṇanātha became interested in the work of Devas and therefore worked out obstacles on the earth.

35. He produced the obstacles in the way of those who endeavoured for piety, salvation and meritorious acts. Then he came down to the earth and was remembered there as Gaṇeśa.

36. O Brāhmaṇas, Vaimānikas (persons moving about in aerial chariots) came there and installed him so that people seeking Svarga adored him as the first in all the sacred rites, because they were desirous of extermination of obstacles.

37. At that very time, Brāhmaṇas hailing from Camatkārapura, who had great interest in the knowledge of Brahman with salvation as their aim, installed Īśāna there. He was cited as Mokṣada ('bestower of salvation').

38. Heramba, *Svargadvārapradа* (the bestower of the portals of Svarga), was installed there by those who desired heavenly pleasures. He was true to his name given.

39. Gaṇeśa named Martyada was installed by others. Thanks to him, even those who slip down from Svarga never go to Naraka etc., or attain the state of a brute, worm or immobile being.

40. For this reason, O excellent Brāhmaṇas, Heramba (Gaṇeśa) became *martyada* in that meritorious holy spot. He was always *martyada* unto heaven-dwellers.

41. Thus the meritorious story of Heramba has been completely narrated to you all. On being listened to, this story destroys all obstacles.

42. If a man worships this deity on the fourth lunar day in the bright half of the month of Māgha, he will never meet with any obstacle for the period of a year.

## CHAPTER ONE HUNDRED FORTYTHREE

# Provocation of Jābāli[1]

*Sūta said:*

1. Further, O Brāhmanas, there is another deity there named Citreśvara. It is situated in the middle of Citrapīṭha and grants diverse kinds of pleasures unto men.

2. By visiting that deity, adoring it or bathing it a man is rid of major and minor sins arising from close intimacy with other men's wives.

---

1. Chapters 143-146 describe the greatness of Amareśvara Liṅga and the Kuṇḍa in front of it.
Jābāli beats his daughter practically to death for her immoral act. She does not die due to the power of Amareśvara Liṅga before which she was beaten. Śiva elevated her to Yoginī-ship.
The spirited dialogue between Jābāli and his daughter, a feminist of that age, is worth reading in original (in Chapter 144).

3. One who ravishes the wife of the preceptor or a girl of one's own family, a girl of a low family or a woman who has adopted Vratas, with the mind overpowered by lust, gets rid of the sin.

4. A man who worships that deity on the fourteenth lunar day in the bright half of the month of Caitra eradicates the sin thereof and goes to Svarga quickly.

5-6. Further there is King Citrāṅgada accompanied by Sage Jābāli. He is also accompanied by a girl born of the sage, a naked girl who has not yet attained the age of menstruation (*Nagnikā*). He stands before him having been cursed by Jābāli already. One who offers libations to all the three (on that day) obtains a woman loved by him as well as Siddhi sought by him.

*The sages said:*

7-8. Why was the youth Citrāṅgada cursed formerly by Jābāli? Why does his daughter stand stripped of her clothes? Why has she adopted this contrary form causing derision of the people? O Sūta, describe this to us.

*Sūta said:*

9. Formerly there was a well-known sage named Jābāli. He performed penances always with celibacy, ever since his child-hood.

10. O excellent Brāhmaṇas, even in his childhood he came to the holy spot of Hāṭakeśvara and began a great penance.

11. He was gradually performing Parāka, Kṛcchra, Cāndrāyaṇa and other rites. Thereby he made Devas highly frightened.

12. Śakra and other Devas who were afraid met together on the peak of Meru and consulted one another for the purpose of causing obstacles to him.

13-15. "If there is to be increase of his penance everyday thus, he will certainly destabilize Śatakratu and make him fall from his heavenly kingdom. Therefore let the foremost among the Apsarās named Rambhā go to him to cause destruction of the celibacy of that sage of sanctified soul.

Celibacy is the root cause of penance. It has been glorified thus by Brāhmaṇas. The loss of it causes great difficulty. Simply there will not be any fruit resulting from the Vrata."

16. After deciding thus all the Devas together with Mahendra summoned Raṁbhā and spoke to her respectfully:

17-18. "O highly esteemed lady, go quickly to the place where Jābāli is present in the holy spot of Hāṭakeśvara for the purpose of disturbing his penance. All emotional coquetries and charmingly eloquent speechess and tales should be employed by you exciting unrestricted lust in his mind."

*Raṁbhā said:*

19. O Lord of Suras, that sage does not know the art of love-play. O Lord, how can I convert a man devoid of fascination and charm into one of lascivious proclivity?

*Indra said.*

20. At my bidding this Vasanta shall go near him. Merely by his sight, he will become swayed by love.

21. Hence, O lady of excellent countenance, go there quickly along with him so that there shall be quick accomplishment of the tasks of Devas.

22. Thereupon, she bowed down to him elaborately and went along with Vasanta to the place where Jābāli was staying.

23. Then, all of a sudden, Aśoka became fully blossomed; bunches of flowers appeared on Tilaka and mango trees.

24. Even in the winter lotuses bloomed. A fragrant southern wind blew satisfying all desires.

25. In the meantime, Raṁbhā, the excellent Apsarā, reached the bank of the water-pond where Jābāli was present.

26. After offering the desired (i.e. requisite) oblation to Pitṛs with faith, he was uttering Mantras many times with the rosary of beads held in his hand.

27. Then even as he was looking on, the excellent Apsarā stripped herself of all garments and entered the water for taking bath.

28. Seeing her in the prime of youth but stripped of her garments, and being swayed by the southern wind, he became a victim of Kāma, under his full control.

29. The excellent sage experienced a tremor at the instant. The rosary fell down on the ground from his hand.

30. There was horripilation in all his limbs. It had terrific result. Slightly warm tears fell down drenching the ground.

31. On knowing that he had become excited the excellent Apsarā conversant with the mental predilection came out of water and wore the garments again.

32. She went near him, bowed down with great respect and spoke these sweet words increasing his lovelorn state:

33. "O holy Sir, I hope everytinhg is quite good in your hermitage. O wise Sage, I hope your study of the Vedas goes on smoothly; O Sage, I hope your disciples and the birds and animals here are also quite all right."

*The sage said:*

34. O beautiful lady, everything everywhere is quite all right in regard to me. Particularly, since you have come—you who are marked with all the characteristics.

35. O highly esteemed one, tell me who you are. You enhance love in me. Are you a Devī or an Asura lady, a serpent lady or a human one?

36. Tell me, don't you notice a tremor in my body? There is unrestricted flow of tears from the eyes, and the bristling of the bairs all over the body.

*Raṁbhā said:*

37. I don't see any normalcy in the state of your body. Are these aberrations in your body natural to it? Or are they caused by ailments?

*The sage said:*

38. O lady of excellent eyes, this is neither natural to my body, nor is it caused by ailments. Listen to the whole cause whereby the body has come to this plight.

39. As long as I continue to set my eyes on you, this state of the body persists.

40. That means, O splendid lady, I have been overwhelmed with love (passion) on seeing you. Though I am devoted to celibacy, though I have adopted great vows, this is my present condition.

*Raṁbhā said:*

41. If that is so, O excellent Brāhmaṇa, do comfortably resort to me. No harm can result from it because I am only a common courtesan.

42. O Brāhmaṇa, we have been created by the Self-born Lord as common for all the people especially for twice-born ones.

43. On seeing you, O sage, I too have been struck by the sharp arrows of Kāma, since you are on a par with Kāma. I don't feel inclined to go elsewhere.

44. Earlier Suras, Yakṣas, Vidyādharas, Siddhas, Kinnaras, Nāgas, Guhyakas and even human beings have been seen by me.

45. But, O tiger among Brāhmaṇas, such an exquisite form as this has never been seen amongst them, Hence do resort to me, your devotee.

46. A foolish person who avoids a woman distressed by love, who herself approaches him, is cooked in terrible Naraka for all years to come (i.e.a pretty long period).

47. After saying thus, she embraced the great sage. He showed unwillingness in speech, though he was desirous of it in his heart.

48. She then took the sage to the bower of creepers and made him sport about with artificial and coquetish behaviour as laid down in erotic science.

49. Thus till the end of the day, he remained with her eagerly engaged in erotic activities. He discarded all other holy rites.

50. Thereby he satisfied his lustful desire (but) became ashamed thereafter. He dismissed Raṁbhā and then washed himself clean.

51. On being dismissed by him the contented lady of graceful charms became glad. She joyously went to the place where Devas including Vāsava were present.

CHAPTER ONE HUNDRED FORTYFOUR

# The Story of Citrāṅgadeśvara, Phalavatī and Jābāli

*Sūta said:*

1-2. She went to heaven and later told the Lotus-eyed One (Indra) along with the Devas: "Fortunately, O Lord, the great sage has been rendered agitated. The penance that he had accumulated with great difficulty has been entirely shattered. He has become deprived of refulgence. Hence relax and be happy."

3. On uttering these words, Raṁbhā was congratulated by all the Suras.

Since the sage was Amogharetas ('one whose semen never goes in vain') she conceived the foetus in her womb.

4. As for sage Jābāli, he regretted very much for what he did. But he resumed his penance once again in the hermitage where he stayed.

5. Ten months later, the Apsarā delivered a splendid daughter marked with divine characteristics with eyes like the petals of a lotus.

6. In view of the fact that she had origin from a human being, the mother of the girl went to his hermitage and left her there. She then told him directly:

7-8. "O tiger among sages, nurse and bring up this girl born from your semen, and conceived in my womb. Human beings cannot have a permanent stay in Svarga. For this reason, O Brāhmaṇa, she is being entrusted to you."

9. After saying this, Raṁbhā hastened back to the abode of Devas. On seeing his own daughter Jābāli was drawn to her by great affection.

10. He kept his child well-guarded in a creeper-hut and nurtured her day and night with the juice of sweet fruits.

11. Like the digit of the moon in the sky in the bright half of a month, the girl slowly grew up day by day.

12. As the lotus-eyed girl grew up, the filial affection of Jābāli too increased steadily.

13. In her childhood the splendid girl played with the deer and birds that remained calm and carefree. Thereby she enhanced the delight of the sage.

14. She grew up form the childish stage into a young maiden regularly clad in bark garments. She always helped the sage in all his holy rites.

15. She brought sacrificial twigs, Darbha grass etc. along with fruits and flowers from the forest and thereby heightened his pleasure.

16. After a few days, once, in the heat of summer, the fawn-eyed girl went far into the forest from her hermitage to collect fruits.

17. In the meantime Citrāṅgada, a Gandharva out of the celestial beings, came there riding in his aerial chariot.

18. In the desolate forest, the girl with the countenance resembling the full moon was seen by him, like the digit of the moon fallen on the ground.

19. He experienced the pangs of love all over the body. He descended to the earth from his aerial chariot. With palms joined in veneration, he spoke these sweet words:

20. "Who are you, O bright-eyed girl roaming about in the great desolate forest? Your complexion is like the tender inside of a lotus. Yet you move about alone."

*The girl said:*

21. I am the daughter of Sage Jābāli, named Phalavatī. I have come to this forest to gather fruits for him.

*Citrāṅgada said:*

22. O lady of beautiful thighs, it is reported that the excellent sage is a life-long celibate. How were you then born without a wife of his?

*The girl said:*

23. O highly esteemed one, it is true that the sage has not taken a wife unto himself. Listen then how I came to be born.

24. Formerly an Apsarā named Rambhā was seen by him. As he was overcome by love then the celestial lady was resorted to by him for pleasure.

25. I was born out of her womb in the exalted Devaloka. I was then entrusted to the sage by her.

26. It was in this manner that the excellent sage Jābāli came to be my father. Thereafter, I was brought up by him by means of juice extracted from various kinds of fruits.

27. Then I was given the name Phalavatī by that noble-souled one. Indeed this befits me. This is the story about which you have asked.

*Citrāṅgada said:*

28. O timid lady, after seeing your beautiful form I have become a slave unto Kāma. Hence do resort to me. Otherwise I shall be doomed (die).

29. I am a Gandharva out of the heaven-dwellers named Citrāṅgada. I have come to this holy spot with great faith, in the course of my pilgrimage.

*The girl said:*

30. I am still virgin and under the control of my father. O Citrāṅgada, I am not conversant with the nuances of love play.

31. Hence request my father. He will give me unto you. You are a young man fully qualified and so suitable to me, a girl of exalted mind.

32. Your excellent words appeal to me too. I will consider myself blessed if I can embrace your neck as I please.

*Citrāṅgada said:*

33. O highly esteemed maiden, I cannot wait so much time. The great fire of love arising out of my body burns me.

34. Hence, O splendid maiden, do me the favour of the gift of sexual intimacy. Who knows how his mind will react?

*The girl said:*

35. If you behave thus, there is no doubt about it that my father, out of anger, will burn you down giving you a terrible curse.

*Citrāṅgada said:*

36. O honour-bestowing maiden, your father will burn only after the lapse of some time. But this fire of love will reduce me to ashes immediately.

37. After saying thus to the timid, bashfully trembling maiden, he caught her right hand and entered the temple.

38. There the Gandharva being afflicted with love, sported with her who had become shameless at that time with her passion rendering her blind.

39. O excellent sages, even as she remained thus along with him, the day passed off like a minute. Then the day came to a close. The sun set.

40. In the meantime, the Brāhmaṇa Jābāli became extremely miserable, after having noticed that his daughter had not returned. He wandered here and there.

41-42. 'Alas, has my daughter been devoured by tigers? Has she fallen on the ground after climbing up a tree? Or did she enter some pond and get drowned because she could not gauge the depth? She might have entered it seeking water.'

43. Lamenting thus the Brāhmaṇa roamed about in the dense forest. He was himself agitated due to hunger and thirst. Thorns and Kuśa grass wounded his limbs.

44. At night whenever he heard some sound of a bird or animal, he became startled thinking that it was Phalavatī.

45. Slowly the excellent sage came to the temple of Hara where his daughter was present in close intimacy with Citrāṅgada.

46. She was speaking many words expressing love unhesitatingly but improper in the case of virgins especially if they hail from a Brāhmaṇa family.

47. Even from afar he had been hearing those words for a long time and was astonished. On seeing the activity of the girl, he became angry with reddened eyes.

48. He gathered together a bundle of sticks and rushed against them with the intention of killing both. He rebuked them repeatedly:

49-50. "Fie upon you, O girl of sinful behaviour! You have defiled your own virginity. A stigma has been brought on me. It is bound to be known in all the three worlds.

Certainly, O base girl, you have obtained a husband by means of this misdeed. I shall destroy you already defiled by this sin."

51. After saying thus the excellent sage was about to hurl the stick to strike when Citrāṅgada disappeared quickly through the path of the sky.

52. Stripped of her clothes and fatigued by love play (Phalavatī) could not get up from the ground and go somewhere else.

53. With a number of strokes of the stick he continuously thrashed the fallen maiden on the ground with excessive anger. He thought her dead (and ceased to beat).

54. On seeing the frightened Citrāṅgada passing through the sky, he uttered a curse on him:

55-56. "Let this sinful fellow who has ravished my daughter and who tries to flee fall down immediately like a bird whose wings have been clipped. Let him be afflicted with leprosy and be incapable of even moving." In the meantime, he did fall on the ground from the sky.

57. The young man Citrāṅgada was overtaken by the disease of leprosy. With a piece of wood raised up in his hand with anger, the sage said to him:

58. "Who are you, O fellow of sinful activities? Who are you by whom the virgin had been ravished? Hence I shall send you to the abode of Yama."

*Citrāṅgada said:*

59. I am a Gandharva, one of the (categories of) Heaven-dwellers. I am Citrāṅgada by name, I came to this holy spot in the course of my pilgrimage.

60. On seeing this girl, I wsas overcome by Kāma (sexual desire).

61. Therefore I resorted to her in this bower of creepers isolated from people. So do forgive me. I am distressed myself and I readily bow down to you.

62. With your favour, let this disease be eradicated. Let me have the freedom of movement in the sky. Indeed the anger in good men is meagre and short-lived.

*Jābāli said:*

63-65. Indeed, as per my utterance you will be in this form alone. This my sinful daughter shall always be nude like this. There is no doubt about it. If at all she comes back to life and if she were to wear any cloth, her head will burst undoubtedly.

After saying thus he got rid of his anger and went back to his hermitage.

66-67. Cirtāṅgada continued to be there along with her in that plight.

Once thereafter, on the fourteenth lunar day in the bright half of the month of Caitra, the Moon-crested Lord came to that holy spot in order to sport about in the Citreśvara Pīṭha. He was surrounded by his terrible attendants and the fierce Yoginīs. It was at nightfall that he came.

68. When it was midnight the extremely terrible Yoginīs began to clamour for food saying, "The great (human) meat! The great meat (of humans)!"

69. They began to dance before the Trident-bearing Lord of Devas. In their devilish dances they vied with the chiefs of the Gaṇas dancing all round.

70. He who at that time offers to them the great meat (human flesh) sanctified by Mantras shall attain desired Siddhi.

71. If one offers liquor, meat or other food offering such as fruits etc., his Siddhi has been mentioned as anything cherished in his own heart.

72. In the meantime the daughter of Jābāli and Citrāṅgada went there and spoke respectfully."

73. "May the delighted Yoginīs eat comfortably our flesh that we offer ourselves voluntarily."

74. On seeing the male being afflicted with leprosy and the girl stripped of her clothes, all of them were surprised.

75. All the Gaṇas of Rudra and the three-eyed Lord were surprised. The Lord prompted by curiosity asked Citrāṅgada:

76-77. "Who are you, O bold one having great courage and strength? You are offering your very life which is endearing even to an insect.

Who is this maiden without clothes, without anguish, who offers along with you her own body that should not be given to anyone else?"

*Sūta said:*

78. Then he recounted everything regarding his own act, how he had intercourse with the girl and how the good sage cursed.

79. On seeing Citrāṅgada, the Gandharva (one) among the Heaven-dwellers, in that form, Śaṅkara became sympathetic and said to him:

80. "After seeing me no one meets death. Nor can my vision be futile. Hence request (for a boon) respectfully."

*Citrāṅgada said:*

81. O Śaṅkara, I have become greatly affected due to this ailment. Hence, O Lord, I came here so that along with the destruction of the body there can be the eradication of the ailment too.

82. Hence do destroy the disease. If you grant me any boon, give me back my ability to go freely through the sky so that I can go to Svarga.

*Śrī Śaṅkara said:*

83. Install my Liṅga on the sacred pedestal (Pīṭha) here, O most excellent one among Gandharvas. Then propitiate it with love and devotion for the period of a year.

84. As you go on performing the excellent adoration of my Liṅga everyday, so your ailment will be getting eradicated.

85. Then you will attain the ability to go through the sky and will go to Svarga with my favour. There is no doubt about it. It is the truth that I have uttered.

86. Since this maiden entered the area of the pedestal, she will become a Yoginī named Phalavatī.

87. She will become installed in this same naked form. She will be the chief object of worship. She will grant things cherished in the heart of those who worship. She will even grant the same a hundred-fold.

88. A man should worship her and thereafter the pedestal. If he worships so, he will attain the desired Siddhi.

89. On being told thus she became extremely delighted. Standing in the centre of the group of Yoginīs, she began to dance.

90. It was thus that the excellent maiden became a Yoginī. She danced well and Maheśvara was pleased with it.

91-93. On being delighted the Lord said to her in the presence of all the Yoginīs: "O dear maiden, I am pleased with this dance of yours as well as with the song sung. Hence listen to my words.On this day at mid-night, if a devotee worships you with the offerings of liquor, meat and cooked food uttering the Mantras taken from Āgamas, he will become at that very time one having the power to curse and bless."

94. There is no doubt about it that he will have the following powers against his enemies: *Bandhana* (bondage), *Mohana* (fascination, enchanting), *Uccāṭana* (exorcising) and *Vaśīkanaṇa* (keeping under one's control).

95. Occupying the triangular Kuṇḍa, he shall adore the Guardians of the Quarters, the Kṣetrapāla and all those deities of the firmament.

96-97. He should then duly perform the worship of *Catvara* (the levelled ground kept ready for Yajña); then he should worship you and perform Homa with *Guggula* (fragrant gum resin) mixed with the dust of the left foot of the enemy. The devotee thereby attains the power of *Staṁbhana* (benumbing, stupefying) of a thousand (persons).

98. The devotee thinks about the enemy in his heart and mixes the unguents, the bodily dirt and *Dhātrī* fruits (embylic myrobalan) (for the Homa). He will be able to enchant people or the enemy (*Mohana*).

99-100. Further, the devotee should collect the water wherein the enemy has bathed. It is then to be mixed with mud and Śivanirmālya (Remnants of the worship of Śiva) to be consigned to the sacred fire by way of Homa. The entire worship is to be performed before you and certainly the man outwits the enemy. This lover of yours, Citrāṅgada will get due worship by virtue of your contact.[1]

*Phalavatī said:*

101-104. If, O Lord, you are pleased with me, do grant me another excellent boon whereby the pleasure cherished in my heart can be realized fully. Let[2] this father of mine, Jābāli, also be stripped of his clothes always. Let him stand day and night in the manner that I stand.

1. This *vidhi* described in vv. 95-100. is really atrocious.
2. The boon sought is inhuman.

Let him thereby become more distressed on seeing my acts involving use of liquor and meat contrary to the conventions of Brāhmaṇa families.

He should smell the (odour)of liquor and see meat consecrated. He shall also witness me engaged in free love play. Thereby he shall undergo misery day by day.

*Śrī Bhagavān said:*

105. O splendid lady, this shall become as mentioned. It has already happened now. I shall go to Kailāsa. Do remain here as you are told.

*Sūta said:*

106. After saying thus, Lord Hara vanished. All those Yoginīs remained settled in their respective abodes.

107. Citrāṅgada made an excellent palace there and installed the Liṅga of the Trident-bearing Lord of Devas.

108. Then he propitiated it alertly without lassitude day and night.

109. Then at the end of a year he was rid of his disease and he regained excellent form. Riding on an excellent aerial chariot, he went to the abode of Devas. The sage named Jābāli remained naked.

110. He caused derisive laughter among the people and remained thus always ruefully observing the aberrations of his daughter.

111. The great sage having come near the Pīṭha (pedestal) became extremely distressed and censured the life and activities of women.

112-114. "Alas, such women come across sinful men, as have conduct like this although they are born of Brāhmaṇa families!

Only for once did I have close intimacy with a woman, but a sin like this extending from birth till death has been incurred.

On the other hand, there are base men who are enamoured of them always. What will be their destiny? Although I ponder over it, I do not understand."

115. Even as he was prattling thus, the infuriated Yoginīs surrounded the Brāhmaṇa with contempt and spoke thus:

*Yoginīs said:*

116. O deluded soul, you may have practiced yoga but do not censure women because this entire universe consisting of the mobile and immobile beings is sustained by women.

117. It is by them that Śeṣa and Kūrma were given birth to. These two, Śeṣa and Kūrma, sustain and stabilize the earth and it is the earth whereon the universe is established.

118. O deluded fool, blessed indeed is your daughter who has acquired the excellent yoga in the course of a very few days.

119. You are foolish enough and cling to the path of the Chandas (Vedas). You are associated with Avidyā (ignorance) and roam about in the world.

*The sage said:*

120. All the women deserve to be censured in all conditions. They give only misery. Neither in this world nor in the other world can pleasure be derived from them.

121. It is on account of them (women) that the great Asuras, Śuṁbha, Niśuṁbha, Rāvaṇa and Daṇḍabhūpa (King Daṇḍa) and thousands of others have been killed.

122. Despite the fact that she had such a brilliant husband as Brāhmaṇa Gautama, Ahalyā devoid of the conventional decorum, loved and resorted to Śakra.

*The girl said:*

123. O deluded one, you are going on censuring and trying to establish that young women are worthy of being censured. Well, speak with me so that I can make you sensible.

124. O sage, there is neither intellect nor shame nor mercy in your heart. Does even a base-born Śūdra commit the deed perpetrated by you?

125. O base one, I was killed by you when you struck me with the piece of wood (stick). You never worried about the sin arising from the murder of a woman.

126. Your sin is all the more, because it was your own daughter that you murdered in the height of your anger. Of course, a few sins get dissolved through different kinds of expiation.

127. But that arising from the murder of a woman? Say if there is any means whereby it will disappear. O mean Brāhmaṇa, I do not at all feel miserable for having been struck by you.

128. O highly evil-minded one, even at the end of a Kalpa, this sin of yours will not vanish—this sin caused by your curse whereby I was rendered nude forever.

129. Stay here itself along with me. Continue your misery and reap the fruit thereof. You will not dare to censure and you will not commit another murder.

130. All young maidens are not to be deemed censurable. They are not at all defiled. The monthly menstrual cycle takes away their sins.

*The sage said:*

131. Women are sinful in their conduct. They cannot be purified at all. Their attachment to another woman's husband gives them the status of a Śūdra.

*The girl said:*

132. O deluded one, do not say that young midens are impure. In this connection there is a verse sung by Manu earlier. Know it from me.

133. "Brāhmaṇas are pure in their feet. Cows are pure in their hind parts. Goats and horses are pure in their mouths. Women are pure all over their person."

*The sage said:*

134. Brāhmaṇas are pure everywhere. Cows are pure everywhere. Goats and horses are pure in their mouths. Women are not pure anywhere.

*The girl said:*

135. He who has a loving woman in his house has the Philosopher's Stone (Cintāmaṇi) in his hand, and the wish-yielding Kalpa tree in his house. Kubera is a servant unto him.

*The sage said:*

136. He who has a lustful woman in his house has all the

adversities. Everything in his house is miserable. Naraka is all round him.

*The girl said:*

137. It is from women that all these originate: wherever things are pleasurable, whatever things yield enjoyment, everything yielded by virtue, wealth and love.

*The sage said:*

138. It is from women that all these originate: whatever yields misery and pain unto embodied beings, whatever is desagreeable and undesirable.

*The girl said:*

139. Through the four circumambulations of fire at the time of marriage a woman displays the four Puruṣārthas (aims in life), viz. Dharma, wealth, love and salvation.

*The sage said:*

140. At the very first close contact under the pretext of the (religious rite of) circumambulations of fire, a woman makes the roaming (cycle of coming and going) in the worldly existence manifest.

*The girl said:*

141. Who among even the wise men, becomes disinterested on seeing a woman of plump breasts and wide eyes extending upto the ears?

*The sage said:*

142. What (that is all) people of deluded wisdom who approach a big-buttocked woman thinking her to be beautiful, do not get perished like fire-flies in flames? (All perish.)

*The girl said:*

143. Only a blessed man resorts to the breasts of a woman that are *Nirmukha* (having no face, no prominent nipple),

*Kaṭhora* (hard), *Proddhata* (haughty, protruding) and *manorama* (charming to the mind) and specially one who also resorts to liquor and meat.

*The sage said:*

144. It is better to touch two serpents rather than the two breasts of the wife though both are *Ābhogins* (having big body and expanded hood yielding pleasures), *Maṇḍalis* (circular in coils), *Muktakañcuka* (have bodice stripped; having shed the slough) at that time.

*The girl said:*

145. Not only the structure of the limbs of women is beautiful but their embrace also gives pleasure and causes horripilation.

*The sage said:*

146. The structure of the limbs of these is not merely beautiful but accords sin to the eyes. The body of women, if touched, is conducive to ruin and to Naraka after death.

*The girl said:*

147. If womenfolk begin to love one, who is not happy in the world, who is not meritorious and who is not covetable?

*The sage said:*

148. If one does not take interest in womenfolk, who does not attain salvation, who is not praiseworthy, who is not happy and well-off.

*The girl said:*

149. The female body appeals exceedingly even to an insect sleeping in the world, and to a discriminating man still more so.

*The sage said:*

150. The appeal of the female body to a lustful man in the world is like that (appeal) to a worm arising from rubbish.

*The girl said:*

151. The creator was thinking of (creating) a permanent and pleasing spot unto men. Not being able to see anything else, Strīratna (jewel of a woman) was brought (created).

*The sage said:*

152. A noose in the form of a woman was made by the creator who could not see anything else that could bind the world.

*Sūta said:*

153. Thus the tiger among sages was rendered incapable of making any reply by her. Then he said to his daughter:

*The sage said:*

154. Now I should not hold further conversation with you. Though a girl you have negated (refuted) me in every respect.

155. I consider myself highly blessed because I have a daughter like you, an able exponent of the scriptural texts.

156. Hence, O highly esteemed woman, I have not even the vestige of anger in me. So engage yourself in sports as you please in the midst of the Yoginīs.

157. On seeing her father so very affectionate she became bashful. Standing amongst the Yoginīs she bowed to him and spoke again:

158-159. "Whether through knowledge or ignorance, O holy Sir, if you have been negated by me, may it be forgiven especially because I am only a girl.

After coming to this *Pīṭha*, all the excellent Brāhmaṇas will perform your worship at the outset and only later the adoration of all the other deities in the Pīṭha. Devout men thus will attain the greatest goal."

160. It was thus that the daughter of Jābāli, the sage, happen to be there . So also the excellent sage Jābāli and Citrāṅgadeśvara.

161-164. A man who performs the worship of all the three everyday shall attain Siddhi. There is nothing here on the earth which cannot be achieved. Thus the narrative that accords all cherished desires has been told to you. It yields all benefits to those who read and listen both in this world and in the other world.

## CHAPTER ONE HUNDRED FORTYFIVE

## Greatness of Amarakeśvara Kṣetra

*The sages said:*

1-2. O sūta, it has been said by you that the girl did not die though she was killed with terrible blows. Here we have become very curious: How did she survive as the Yoginī giving delight to Hara? Describe the whole thing and the wonderful reason.

*Sūta said:*

3. Along with him (i.e. Citrāṅgada) she entered the highly meritorious Amareśvara on the fourteenth lunar day in the dark half of Māgha. There is no question of meeting death therein.

4. O Brāhmaṇas, there is no death even when there remain no span of life. There is no question of premature death. Therefore, although she was struck terribly, she did not meet death.

*The sages said:*

5. You have mentioned a deity name Amareśvara, the bestower of immortality. By whom was the deity installed there? What is its power? Do narrate.

*Sūta said:*

6. There were two splendid daughters of Prajāpati. They were extremely beautiful. They were Aditi and Diti. They were married to the noble-souled Kaśyapa.

7. Devas were born of Aditi and Daityas of Diti. Being sons of rival cowives, they become great enemies.

8. Some of the Suras were killed by the Daityas. Other were driven away with faces averted. Those who were frightened and those whose limbs were wounded fled to all the quarters.

9. So the mother of Devas settled here with great sorrow. Devoted to the meditation of Śiva, she performed penance day and night.

10. Four Yugas passed by even as she was engaged in her austere penance. Then a Śivaliṅga pierced through the surface of the earth and rose up.

11. The delighted lady eulogized the Lord with various kinds of prayers and made obeisance to him with great concentration falling at the feet with Aṣṭāṅgas (eight limbs) touching the ground.

12. In the meantime a divine voice arose in the firmament without a body. It had the rumbling majestic sound of clouds.

13. "I am the Moon-crested Lord. I am pleased with you. Request for a boon cherished in the heart. I shall grant it to you."

*Aditi said:*

14. O most excellent one among Suras, my sons are being killed in battle by Dānavas. Render them free from sufferings. Let them not be killed in battle.

*Śrī Bhagavān said:*

15. O splendid lady, those who touch this Liṅga and go to the battle front cannot be killed in the course of a year.

16-18. Any other man with great concentration who keeps awake in the night of the fourteenth lunar day in the dark half of the month of Māgha, shall be free from ailments for the period of a year. If a man comes to this splendid shrine on the day he is destined to die, the god of Death will avoid him from afar.

After saying thus, the voice ceased.

19. Aditi too was pleased. She summoned the surviving sons and showed the Liṅga to them. She told them everything that the voice had said while granting the boon.

20. Then all the Devas bowed down to that Liṅga and taking all the weapons with them, joyously marched against them (Daityas).

21. They went to the place where the Dānavas were present in the auspicious region of Śakra stationing themselves in the Nandana garden. There they were enjoying the pleasures of Svarga.

22. The Dānavas saw many Heaven-dwellers arriving suddenly with various kinds of weapons for the sake of fighting.

23. They equipped themselves with weapons and coats of mail and got into the excellent chariots. Like roaring and rumbling clouds, they marched ahead for the battle.

24. A big battle ensued between the Devas and the Dānavas. Incited by anger in their minds, they were not afraid of death (They made god of Death to recede).

25. Then all those Devas who had obtained the boon from Hara killed innumerable Daityas with many sharp weapons.

26. Those who survived among them abandoned the abode of Devas. Fleeing with great effort they entered the sea.

27. Then Śakra regained his kingdom that had been taken by the Dānavas. He got the entire dominion intact. He ruled over it after destroying all the thorns (enemies).

28. The remaining Dānavas came to know of the greatness of that Liṅga and the origin of the holy shrine of the Bull-emblemed Lord.

29-31. Everything was told by Śukra: "If any devotee remains pure on the fourteenth lunar day in the dark half of Māgha and worships that Liṅga, he shall never become bereft of his life even though grasped by Kāla.

Hence, O highly esteemed ones, ye all resort to that Liṅga at night on that day and worship duly. Thereby you shall be devoid of death.

Just like those groups of Devas you too do worship till the end of the year. By the power thereof, you shall be free from death. There is no doubt about it. It is the truth that has been spoken by me."

32. From Nārada, the son of Brahmā, the Lord of Suras came to know of the secret plan of the leading Dānavas. Thereby he became greatly frightened in his mind.

33. He had consultation with the Devas for devising the means of guarding the deity that day. Their endeavour (to protect) should be perfect for that purpose.

34. All the thirty-three crores of Devas with their weapons settled in that holy spot for protecting that deity on the fourteenth lunar day in the dark half of the month of Māgha. They prepared themselves for the purpose of striking.

35. On seeing the Devas already established there the Dānavas became extremely frightened.They fled in all directions.

36. When the day dawned fully and the solar disc rose up, the Suras took counsel with one another again:

37-39. "If we are to go to Svarga leaving the holy spot, the Dānavas will approach the Liṅga and worship it.

They will be free from being killed like us. Hence we all the thirty-three chiefs shall stay here. All the remaining ones of the crores of Devas may go back along with the Thousand-eyed One and remain as the protectors of heaven from the enemies."

40-41. Thereupon, eight Vasus, twelve Arkas, eleven Rudras and the two handsome Nāsatyas (Aśvins) remained in the holy spot for protecting that Liṅga. The others went to the abode of Devas along with Śakra.

*Sūta said:*

42. The Liṅga of the trident-bearing Lord of Devas which had been installed formerly by Aditi, has such a power. It was about this that you have asked me.

43. The Liṅga has become well known by the name of *Amara* in all the three worlds, because if it is visited, embodied beings will never meet death.

44-45. It was on the fourteenth lunar day in the dark half of Māgha, that the girl was struck by the infuriated Brāhmaṇa Jābāli. The place was the same. Therefore the poor girl did not meet death though hit with force.

46. Thus, O excellent Brāhmaṇas, the origin and greatness of that Liṅga has been narrated to you. It is destructive of all sins.

47. If a person reads this with devotion in the presence of that Liṅga, he will never have the danger of premature death at any cost.

48. In front of it, there is the splendid Kuṇḍa filled with clear water. It was made by the fair lady Aditi for the purpose of her own bath.

49. Even today the same effect continues. A man who takes his holy bath therein, visits that Liṅga and keeps awake there itself everyday, shall not have premature death for the period of a year.

## CHAPTER ONE HUNDRED FORTYSIX

# Greatness of Amareśvara Kuṇḍa[1]

*The sages said:*

1-3. O highly intelligent one, enumerate separately the names of all the Ādityas, Vasus, Rudras and Aśvins.

*Sūta said:*

The eleven Rudras are: Vṛṣadhvaja, Śarva, Mṛgavyādha (the third), Ajaikapāt, Ahirbudhnya, Pinākin (the sixth), Dahana, Īśvara, Kapālin (the ninth), Vṛṣākapi (the tenth) and Tryaṁbaka.

4. The following are glorified as the eight Vasus: Dhura, Dhruva, Soma, Makha, Anila, Anala, Pratyūṣa and Prabhāsa.

5-6. The following twelve are Bhāskaras (Ādityas): Varuṇa Sūrya, Bhānu, Tāpana, Indra, Aryaman. Dhātṛ, Bhaga, Gabhasti, Dharmarāja, Svarṇaretas, Divākara, Mitra and Vāsudeva.

7. Nāsatya and Dasra are the well known Aśvins. They are the highly esteemed physicians of Devas. They were born of the daughter of Tvaṣṭṛ.

8. These leaders of Suras are the thirty-three well-known ones settled in the holy spot for the purpose of destroying the Dānavas.

9. A man with well-controlled sense-organs who devoutly worships them on the said day will not meet with premature death.

10. The Rudras should be worshipped on the eighth and foruteenth lunar days by knowers who desire the greatest position. They shall perform special adorations in that holy spot.

11. Vasus should be worshipped on the eighth lunar day in particular and on the tenth lunar day by those who desire Svarga along with different kinds of graceful charms.

12. Ādityas should be worshipped on the sixth and seventh lunar days by men who desire strength (to be) devoid of enemies.

1. This chapter enumerates (by names) the thirty-three Devas protecting the Kuṇḍa and mentions the days on which these should be propitiated.

13. The physicians of Devas should be worshipped on the twelfth lunar day by those men who desire the destruction of ailments. They become rid of their ailments.

## CHAPTER ONE HUNDRED FORTYSEVEN

# Dialogue between Vyāsa and Śuka

*Sūta said:*

1. Further there is another deity there who is the bestower of sons on men. It is Śiva named Vaṭikeśvara and he dispels all sins.

2. O excellent Brāhmaṇas, there Vaṭikā performed a penance formerly, and obtained from Vyāsa a son, Kapiñjala, when Śuka went to the forest.

*The sages said:*

3-4. Whose daughter was Vaṭikā? Why did she perform penance there? Why did Śuka abandon his father and seek refuge in the forest? How did the lady of pure smiles obtain Kapiñjala as son from Vyāsa?

*Sūta said:*

5. O leading Brāhmaṇas, once Vyāsa was inclined to take a wife unto himself though he was devoid of lust. The noble-souled one was omniscient and quiescent.

6-7. Once the Kuru race became extinct ending with King Vicitravīrya, O excellent Brāhmaṇas.

Thereupon, at the bidding of Satyavatī, he begot three heroic sons including Pāṇḍu in the wives of Vicitravīrya.

8. Thus while he was in the stage of Vānaprastha, he had a desire for sexual intercourse once. Therefrom the race of Kuru was revived through the sons born of Kṣetra (wives of the dead king Vicitravīrya).

9. Then he thought thus, 'I shall take a wife unto me. Through the rites of a householder, I shall attain excellent goal.'

10 . Then he requested Jābāli[1] for his splendid daughter. he immediately gave him his splendid daughter named Vaṭikā.

11. Then he began his residence in the forest in her company. Continuing to abide by the Vānaprastha stage, he became inclined to have sexual intercourse.

12. Then Piñjalā (Vaṭikā) became pregnant, thanks to him. During the prescribed days of the menstrual cycle, she received the semen from Vyāsa, the son of Satyavatī.

13. The foetus developed gradually in the womb of Vyāsa's wife like the moon in the bright half of month.

14. The foetus thus attained development and twelve years passed by. But no delivery took pace.

15. The child in the womb was endowed with great intellect. Staying there whatever word he happened to hear, he immediately committed to memory.

16. Even while staying in the womb, the Vedas, the Aṅgas, Smṛtis, Purāṇas and the scriptural texts on liberation were entirely burnt by him.

17. Stationed there in the womb itself, day and night he regularly recited Vedic texts but he never thought of coming out as a child.

18. Even as he went on developing while staying there (in the womb), the mother experienced excruciating pain and was extremely agitated.

19-20. Suprised thereat Vyāsa spoke these words: "Who are you that have entered the womb of my wife assuming the form of a foetus? Why do you not come out? Will you kill her?"

*The foetus said:*

I am a Rākṣasa. I am a Piśāca, I am a Deva. I am also a man.

21. I am an elephant, a horse, a cock, a goat also. There are eighty-four thousand different types of species taking up nativity.

22. I have wandered over all these forms. Hence how can I say I am this or that? Now I have become a human being and am settled in a womb.

23. I will not at all come out as a human being in order to roam about in the terrible worldly existence.

1. This Jābāli is different from the father of Phalavatī (chs. 143-44).

24. Staying here itself, I will be perpetually engaged in the practice of Yoga and shall get rid of mundane existence. I will follow the path of salvation and undoubtedly attain salvation.

25. O Excellent Brāhmaṇa, all the creatures as long as they are in the womb, will have perfect knowledge, detachment and non-affection for all worldly objects and the memory of previous births.

26. As soon as it comes out of the womb and is touched by Viṣṇumāyā all this stops undoubtedly.

27. Hence, O excellent Brāhmaṇa, I will not at all come out of this womb. I shall attain salvation from this very spot.

*Vyāsa said:*

28-29. The Vaiṣṇavī Māyā will not affect you at all. Come out of this extremely terrible and despicable Naraka in the form of the stay in the womb.

Practice Yoga thereafter and resort to Śiva. So, you do show mc your face so that I shall get freedom from the indebtedness to the people of Pitṛloka.

*The foetus said:*

30. You must now itself offer Vāsudeva as the guarantor and surety. Then my birth may be possible. Not otherwise.

*Sūta said:*

31. Then, Vyāsa in his great distress hastened to Dvārakā. He narrated everything to the Discus-bearing Lord in detail.

32. Later he returned to his house along with him. Vyāsa wanted to offer Viṣṇu, the unsullied, as guarantor and surety.

*Śrī Kṛṣṇa said:*

33. I am the gurantor unto you for the destruction of Māyā when you come out. At my instance do come out and attain the excellent salvation.

34. Then at the instance of Viṣṇu, O Brāhmaṇas, he hurriedly came out as a person nearing youth, a person twelve years old.

35. Instantly, the son of Vyāsa bowed down to Daityāri (Kṛṣṇa), Vyāsa and his mother started for residence in the forest.

36. Then the sage said to him: "Dear son, stay in your own abode so that I can perform the post-natal consecratory rites unto you."

*The child said:*

37. Hundreds of consecratory rites have been performed on me in the course of the different births. These have worked as bonds whereby I have been thrown into the ocean of worldly existence.

*Śrī Bhagavān said:*

38. O sage, this son of yours who is expert in the yogic lore is prattling like a Śuka (parrot). So let him be named Śuka.

39. He is bereft of delusion and ignorance. He will not stay in your abode. Let him go. Do not exhibit much of affection for him.

40. I shall go home. You are freed from the indebtedness to the Pitṛs merely by the perception of your son. It is the truth that has been uttered by me.

41. After saying thus, Hṛṣīkeśa took leave of Vyāsa. Riding on the King of Birds, he started for Dvārakā.

42. After Hṛṣīkeśa had gone, Vyāsa said to his son who was at the point of starting forestwards and who was devoid of any desire for his own home:

*Vyāsa said:*

43. In the case of those who do not observe the householder's rites, a statement of father comes to nought. He who does not, due to delusion, strictly abide by the statement of his father falls into Naraka. Hence, O son, do not go. Desist from going at my instance.

*Śuka said:*

44. Just as today I am born as your son so also in another birth you were born as my son, O excellent sage. Therefore, I am your father.

45. Hence you must carry out my order. If this is the position of Dharma, I should not be denied permission to go to penance grove.

*Vyāsa said:*

46. It is through merits that men attain birth in the family of a Brāhmaṇa. There as a Brāhmaṇa, he gets the Vedic consecratory rites (and attains salvation).

*Śuka said:*

47. If without auspicious Karmas, salvation is attained, then heretics too will attain salvation by mcrely observing vows.

*Vyāsa said:*

48. One shall at first be a celibate student. Then he shall be a householder. He then becomes a Vānaprastha and recluse. Thereafter one shall attain salvation.

*Śuka said:*

49-51. If through celibacy salvation can be attained, then impotent eunuchs will always have it. If householders get it, then entire universe can get released. Or if the resident of forest were to get salvation, then (forest) animals can attain it. Or, if those having ascetic virtues attain salvation, all the poverty-stricken shall attain liberation at the first instance.

*Vyāsa said:*

52. It has been gloriously proclaimed by Manu that this world and the next one can be attained by men devoted to the pious activities of the householder following the path of the righteous.

*Śrī Śuka said:*

53. Whence can those who are well-concealed in domestic protection, and are well bound by the bonds of kinship follow the path of the righteous, since delusion and passion have adverse effect on them?

*Vyāsa said:*

54. In the case of a man residing in forest always, suffering is not caused by his body alone but also by supernatural beings and ancestors, because he does not fulfill the duties towards the deity and ancestors. Hence welfare of the soul should be considered seriously by one staying in the householder's stage.

*Śrī Śuka said:*

55. All the benefits of penance abide in the case of sages with great austerities sanctified by mental purity. This itself is the height of happiness that persons who seek refuge in their close proximity never see faces of bad people.

*Vyāsa said:*

56. In the house, the spouse accords permanent happiness in this world as well as in the other world to men following the practices of the householder stage.

*Śrī Śuka said:*

57. At the intercession of fate chillness may exude from fire and scorching heat from the moon. But the occurrence of happiness from a spouse is neither a thing of the past nor of the present nor of the future in the human world.

*Vyāsa said:*

58. Human birth is a rare thing. It is obtained with great difficulty through excellent merits. If that is acquired, what is it that has not been acquired if one is conversant with the practices and virtues of the householder's stage?

*Śrī Śuka said:*

59. If a man is endowed with knowledge at the time of birth, that knowledge itself will get lost on perceiving one's own plight.

*Vyāsa said:*

60. To the world, as fickle as ashes, the sound of a delighted son and of the young one of a donkey is conducive to joy.

*Śrī Śuka said:*

61. O sage, if the world gets satisfied and delighted with an impure child that cries and crawls in dust, then it is also childish.

*Vyāsa said:*

62. There is an exceedingly terrible Naraka named Pum in the palace of Yama. One not having a son goes there. Hence *Putra* (son) is honoured.

63. O great sage, if heavenly pleasure is attained through a son then all including pigs, dogs and locusts too should attain it.

*Vyāsa said:*

64. By seeing a son a man becomes free from indebtedness to Pitṛs; by seeing a grandson he becomes free from indebtedness to Devas and by seeing a great-grandson a man becomes a heaven-dweller.

*Śuka said:*

65. A vulture is long-lived and it sees a series of its generations (progeny). Why does it not attain salvation?

*Sūta said:*

66. After saying thus, he went to the forest abandoning his father and the exceedingly miserable mother who lamented in various ways.

67. On seeing him Vyāsa lost hope of seeing his son further and so became miserable. He became distressed due to the separation from the son and he stayed in the company of his wife.

## CHAPTER ONE HUNDRED FORTYEIGHT

# Greatness of Vaṭikeśvara

*Sūta said:*

1-2. On realizing that her son had no desire for householder's life, Piṅgalā (i.e.Vaṭikā) became miserable and spoke to Vyāsa thus: "O excellent Brāhmaṇa, I will perform a penance for the sake of a son. Do grant me permission so that I can propitiate Maheśvara. Thereby a son causing the family to flourish shall be born of me."

3. After deciding thus and getting the permission of the sage the chaste lady reached this holy spot and performed penance.

4. She installed Lord Śaṅkara and made a large tank of pure water. It was destructive of sins through bath.

5. Then Lord Tripurāntaka became pleased with her. With a delighted heart he spoke to her: "I am the bestower of boons."

*Śrī Mahādeva said:*

6. O fair lady, I am pleased with you. O lady of excellent Vratas, choose your boon whatever may be cherished in the heart. There is nothing which cannot be given.

*Vaṭikā said:*

7. O excellent one among Suras, give me a son who will make the family flourish, who will always delight my mind, is well-behaved and endowed with humility.

*Śrī Mahādeva said:*

8. O splendid lady, O highly esteemed one, there is no doubt about it that a son will be born to you as requested. In fact, he will be better qualified.

9-11. Any other woman who with great concentration takes her bath in this tank on the fifth lunar day in the bright half for a year and also worships this Liṅga installed by you today, will attain a good son by offering an excellent fruit. If one who suffers due to ill-luck takes her bath on the third lunar day in this tank and afterwards worships my Liṅga, she will be blessed with conjugal felicity by the end of the year.

12-14. A man who bathes here and worships me shall obtain his desires if he has desires, or salvation if he has no desire.

After saying thus Mahādeva vanished. She also conceived a son from Vyāsa. He was well known as Kapiñjala as was said by the Trident-bearing Lord of Devas earlier. By him Goddess Kelīśvarī was installed here. On being propitiated she bestows all Siddhis in the world.

## CHAPTER ONE HUNDRED FORTYNINE

# Manifestation of Kelīśvarī[1]

*The sages said:*

1-5. O Sūtanandana, a goddess is heard about as Kelīśvarī. Tell us her origin and greatness in detail.

At what time did she originate? What benefit results from her adoration and obeisance?

Kātyāyanī was described by you and also Cāmuṇḍā, the goddess of Suras. Śrīmātā, is also born as goddess of Suras. Śrīmātā and goddess Tārā, the destroyer of enemies, have been described. Keliśvarī was not described. Hence, extol her now.

Great curiosity and interest has been created in us, O Sūtanandana.

*Sūta said:*

6. The primordial single goddess established herself in many forms for the welfare of Devas and destruction of Daityas.

7-11. Whenever any distress occurs anywhere unto Devas, that great Śakti which pervades the entire universe incarnates on the earth.

1. Chapters 149-150 describe how demon Andhaka defeated Devas. Lord Śiva created Goddess Kelīśvarī for killing Andhaka. Śukra also propitiated the same Devī by oblating his own flesh in the Homa.

For the destrucion of Mahiṣāsura she descended to the earth as Kātyāyanī. The great form of the goddess extended all over the three worlds.

When the two Dānavas, Śuṁbha and Niśuṁbha became haughty on account of their strength, she hereself incarnated assuming the form of Cāmuṇḍā.

When Kālayavana striking terror into the Devas rose up, she was born on the earth in the form of Śrīmātā.

For the destruction of Andhāsura, Goddess Kelīśvarī was created by Śaṁbhu who occupied her mind and the entire universe was pervaded by her.

12. Then by her power, all the Daityas were killed entirely. Afterwards, Andhaka who caused great distress to all the three worlds was killed.

*The sages said:*

13. Whose son was Andhaka? What was his power? How was he killed? Why was he killed in battle? Do narrate everything in detail.

*Sūta said.*

14. There was a daughter of Dakṣa named Diti. She was the abode of all good qualities. She had a son named Hiraṇyakaśipu.

15. Śakra and other Devas were conquered by him in battle. The great soul ruled over the kingdom of Svarga himself.

16. Afraid of him, all the Devas made various kinds of weapons of great importance along with coats of mail and shields.

17. Viṣṇu, the powerful Lord, angrily placed him on his back on the knees and tore him up with his claws.

18. Two sons of great vigour and exalted virtues were born to him. The elder one is called Prahlāda and the second one was Andhaka.

19. When Hiraṇyakaśipu entered the world of the god of death, the groups of his friends and ministers humbly requested Prahlāda:

20. "Take up this hereditary kingdom and rule. Bear the weight of administration of the dominion. Strike down Devas in battle."

*Prahlāda said:*

21. I will not rule over the earth at any cost. Why? Listen to my words and understand now.

22. The Devas with Śakra as their leader never like the rule of Daityas. Viṣṇu, the Lord, is himself their protector always.

23. I would rather give up my life. I shall forsake all my possessions without any doubt. I am incapable of fighting with Hari.

24. This Lord of Suras has been bowed to and adored always by me. I will not engage myself in war against him on any account.

*Sūta said:*

25. When the kingship which was devolved on him from his father was refused by Prahlāda, Andhaka was established there by the ministers after having mutual consultation.

26-27. This son of Hiraṇyakaśipu could destroy the arrogance of Devas as well as of Dānavas. He entrusted the kingdom to the care of the ministers and performed penance for a long time meditating on Pitāmaha. He eschewed lust, anger, hypocrisy and rivalry.

28. He kept his soul quiescent and the sense-organs well controlled. He was impartial to all the creatures. With a calm and delighted mind, he resorted to the root of a tree.

29. For a period of a thousand years, his diet consisted of fruits alone. Then for another thousand years, he ate only withered and decayed leaves.

30. Day and night he meditated on Pitāmaha, the Lord of Devas. Then, O excellent Brāhmaṇas, his diet consisted of air only, for an equal time.

31. Then at the close of the fourth set of thousand years, Brahmā himself joyously approached him and said:

*Brahmā said:*

32. O dear one, I am pleased with you. O devotee of excellent Vratas, choose your boon. I am pleased. I shall grant you even the rarest of objects.

*Andhaka said:*

33. O Brahmā, if you wish to give the boon cherished in the mind then, O most excellent one among Suras, grant me the cessation of old age and cause of death.

*Śrī Brahmā said:*

34. Nobody devoid of old age exists on the surface of the earth. There is no one who is born on the earth and is without death.

35. Still, I shall grant it unto you devoted as you are to many pious rites. Hence, O highly fortunate one, go back to your abode and rule over the kingdom.

36. The kingdom shall be rich with many good things even if it is like a cremation ground overgrown with thorns and persons of ruthless activities (it will turn out into a home of happiness).

*Sūta said:*

37. After saying thus the Four-faced One vanished. Once thereafter, urged as if by the activities of Kāla, he recollected the enmity of his father and spoke to the ministers:

*Andhaka said:*

38. Our father as well as our mighty uncle were killed by Devas by fraud and not heroic fight. Hence I will kill them.

39. Of what purpose is a son born, who does not show himself at the forefront everywhere by means of well-prised activities like the banner at the top of the flagstaff!

*The Misisters said:*

40. O highly esteemed one, what has been said by you is but proper. Devas who are our enemies should all be killed.

41. All these worlds are ours. Who are these Devas? Who are the Brāhmaṇas? After killing Suras including Śakra, we shall take away our share in the Yajñas.

42. After resolving thus, they, accompanied with a powerful army, hurried to the place where Śakra was present.

43. On seeing the army of the Dānavas and noticing that they had launched a surprise attack Śakra rode on the elephant Airāvata and set out for the battle.

44-47. He was accompanied by all the groups of Devas including Vasus, Rudras and Ádityas. In the meantime Śakra,the destroyer of enemies, aimed at Andhaka and discharged his extremely terrible Vajra. On being struck by it, the excellent Danuja laughed and said to Śakra in a loud voice with great delight: "O Śakra, after a long time, the might of your arm has been seen by me in this battle. Now, O destroyer of Bala, you yourself see ours."

*Sūta said:*

48-49. After saying thus, he hurled with great force a huge mace that was made by Viśvakarman. It produced the loud sound of a hundred bells. It was fully made of iron and very huge as though it was another tongue of Yama. It extended to a hundred *Hastas* (hands) and increased the fright of all living beings.

50. On being struck by it Śakra fell into a swoon with all his sense-organs disorganized. With the support of the flag-staff, he fell on the head of the elephant.

51. On seeing Śakra unconscious in a swoon, Skanda became furious. He discharged his Śakti that was never ineffective and resmebled the thunderbolt.

52. On seeing it coming, the Dānava made it turn back with sharp arrows. The mighty one did this sportingly.

53. Then Skanda took up his bow and discharged arrows against him resembling furious serpents whose very breath was poisonous. By this he displayed how easily he could wield missiles.

54. In the meantime, all the Devas showered volleys of weapons and covered the army of the Dānavas all round.

55. All the Dānavas thereafter inflicted pain on the army of the Devas by a series of blows. The Heaven-dwellers fled then.

56. Then the Bull-vehicled Lord with his Gaṇas saw the Suras shattered. So he revealed himself thereby consoling the Devas as it were:

57-58. "O ye Devas, do not be afraid. See my act." Saying thus Lord Śaṁbhu invoked the excellent Parāśakti (the great power), the goddess of the universe, reciting Ātharvaṇa Mantras. On Being summoned thus, the greatest Śakti went near Hara.

59. On seeing that she had come before him, Lord Śambhu bowed down along with all the Devas and eulogized her devoutly by means of his prayer:

*Śrī Bhagavān said:*

60. Obeisance unto you, O goddess of the chiefs of Devas. Obeisance to you, O goddess endeared by devotion. O omnipresent one, O bestower of everything, O goddess, O sustainer of the Universe, obeisnace to you.

61. Obeisance to you who are the cause of creation and dissolution in the form of Śakti. Obeisance to you, O refulgent one one with earrings shining like lightning.

62. You are Svāhā; you are Svadhā, O goddess; you are the creation. You are purity. You are fortitude (Dhṛti). You are Arundhatī and Indrāṇī. You are Lakṣmī. You are Pārvatī.

63. This is the conclusion of all the scriptures that all those things in all the three worlds which are in female form are your forms.

*Śrī Devī said:*

64-65. Explain to me: why did you invite me with terrible Mantras from the Atharvaveda, O Bull-vehicled One, so that I shall carry out that entirely as per what you say.

*Śrī Bhagavān said:*

66. All the Devas including Śakra have heen expelled from Svarga, O highly esteemed one, by Andhaka, the overlord of Daityas.

67. Listen. I am proceeding ahead to kill him. Render assistance unto me. I shall kill him in the battle.

68. All these groups of Mothers are given unto you now. Emaciated with hunger, they will kill the Dānavas who are standing in front.

69. You have assumed a sportive form with various hideous forms in thousands. You have been invoked in this from the middle of fire.

70. Hence, you will be known all over the three worlds by the name Kelīśvarī. A devotee should worship you in this form alone with devotion.

71. He should worship you on the eighth and fourteenth lunar days. He shall attain what has been desired.

When the time of battle arrives, a devotee should eulogize you by means of his prayer.

72. A king who eulogizes with this hymn shall be victorious in battle even if this army is small and he has only a small cavalry.

73. Undoubtedly, with your favour he will be certainly victorious.

Thus goddess Kelīśvarī was addressed by the Lord of Devas then.

74. On being told thus by the Lord, the goddess Kelīśvarī went ahead of the army of Bhava joyously. She was accompanied by all the groups of Mātṛs whose shouts were extremely terrible.

75. They went along with the groups of Rudras keenly enthusiastic in fighting and striking with many kinds of weapons.

The Dānavas saw the army of women coming in this manner.

76. They were hideous in forms and features. They cried hideously with weapons lifted up in their hands. They were eager for fighting.

77. Some of the Dānavas laughed boisterously. Some rebuked them. Others knowing that they were women did not stoop to hit them.

78. On being hit by them, in return they felt bashful as they were conscious of their manliness (and did not retaliate).

In the meantime Nārada, the excellent sage, came there.

79-84. He told Andhaka the fact entirely: "O excellent Dānava these are not mere women. They have come for fighting."

This woman who is seated on a lion and has notably a discus in hand is the Kṛtyā (ogress of black magic) created by Rudra for killing you. Her name is Kelīśvarī. She come out of the fire pit when Homa was performed by means of his own blood by Śaṁbhu, the Lord of Devas. By resorting to the efficacy of the Mantras, she came out along with these Rudras (terrible ones created by Rudra). Here comes the furious Lord himself near you.

In front of Parameṣṭhin he has declared that you will be killed. He has kept all the excellent Suras in his own palace for the purpose of battle. Understand this, O highly esteemed one, and do what is proper.

*Andhaka said:*

85. I am not afraid of Rudra or anyone else. But I will not strike a woman. I will maintain the vow of manliness.

*Sūta said:*

86. Even as the noble-souled Dānava firmly said thus, there arose a loud cry all round in that place.

87. Some Dānavas were eaten. Others were killed. Others perished even as their bodies were partially eaten.

88. Other fighting Dānavas though themselves powerful, were being eaten along with their weapons and vehicles by the Mātṛs.

89. On hearing that loud tumult, Andhaka became highly furious. He seized his sword and rose up saying, "What is this? What is this?"

90. He saw those Dānavas who were very proud on account of their might, killed. Others were being eaten and still others were bent on fleeing.

91. He saw the beloved wives of others killed. They were standing near them and crying in the height of their misery.

92. On seeing that havoc, Andhaka was at the zenith of his anger. He rebuked all those Yoginīs engaged in battle.

93. They were not at all afraid of that Daitya. They simply continued the slaughter and ate up the Dānavas.

94. That Dānava noticed their activity angrily. Frightened much, he tried to guard his own body.

95. He terrifically yelled and discharged the missile of *Tamas* (Darkness). In an instant in the meantime all the three worlds were enveloped in darkness.

96. Nothing similar or dissimilar was seen anywhere there. Only the leading Dānava could see everything. None else.

97. With sharp arrows he killed those Yoginīs. Other women of the same form immediately cropped up.

98. On seeing the inordinate increase in the number of the Yoginīs, that Dānava withdrew that missile in great agitation due to fear.

99. He approached Śukra in a wretched condition with palms joined in reverence. He said: "O foremost one among the descendants of Bhṛgu, see the havoc perpetrated by the women in my case.

100. Though I am a Rākṣasa, these women cannot be killed by my weapons on account of the power of Mantras. They have cropped up in plenty and all my armies are killed.

101. Hence, O highly intelligent one, you also employ the same Vidyā if you wish my good; otherwise there is no hope of victory in the battle."

## CHAPTER ONE HUNDRED FIFTY

# Greatness of Kelīśvarī

*Sūta said:*

1-2. On hearing his words, Śukra took pity on him. He went to the holy spot of Hāṭakeśvara that yields Siddhis and duly performed the Homa in fire by means of his own flesh in the triangular Kuṇḍa made by himself. He recited the Ātharvaṇa and Rudra Mantras while performing the Homa.

3. While he performed the Homa with the same procedure as employed by Rudra, Goddess Keliśvarī became pleased.

4-5. She quickly approached Śukra, the priest of Daityas, and said: "O tiger among the scions of the family of Bhṛgu, do not waste your flesh. I have been created and sanctified by the Three-eyed Lord. Tell me what I need do unto you."

*Śukra said:*

6. O auspicious goddess, just as you rendered assistance to Rudra in the battle, today extend the same assistance to Andhaka. That is the boon I seek.

7. Those Dānavas of his army who were killed or swallowed should become alive quickly.

*The Devī said:*

8. O Brāhmaṇa, I shall resuscitate all those Dānavas killed in battle and recently swallowed, those who entered the mouths of the Yoginīs.

9. After saying thus the goddess delighted in her face gave him the Vidyā named Amṛtavatī by which the dead could regain life.

10-13. Then, delighted within himself Śukra went to Andhaka and said: "Goddess Kelīśvarī has been won over by me as in the case of Śambhu. An auspicious Vidyā has been granted to me by her. By its power, I shall resuscitate all those Daityas who died.

O most excellent one among the Dānavas, you must have devotion to this goddess always. On the eighth lunar day especially and on the fourteenth always she should be worshipped.

She is that great Śakti by whom this universe has been pervaded. She could be propitiated only through devotion and not at all by means of force."

14. On being told thus by Śukra, the overlord of the Dānavas adored that goddess with devotion and emotional fervour.

15. After eulogizing her and all the Mātṛs by means of various kinds of prayers, he spoke to her paying respects to the Mothers in due order of seniority:

16. "O goddess, I was angry with you due to ignorance. That should be excused. I am wretched. I have bowed down to you."

*Śrī Devī said:*

17. O dear one, I am pleased with you and the power of Bhārgava. Hence choose your boon. My sight cannot go in vain.

*Andhaka said:*

18. If embodied beings install your image in this form and meditate upon you with great devotion, a Siddhi desired by them in their heart should be granted by you.

*The Devī said:*

19. If any man, even if he be a sinner, installs my image in this form, I shall grant him salvation. There is no doubt about it.

20. O most excellent one among the Dānavas, if a man performs my adoration on the eighth or fourteenth lunar day, I will grant him Svarga even if he is a sinner.

21. If anyone simply visits me or meditates on me, I will grant him kingdom and all human pleasures.

22. After saying thus, the goddess vanished along with the groups of the Mātṛs in an instant even as he remained watching.

23. By means of the Vidyā achieved by him, Śukra brought to life all the dead and the recently swallowed Dānavas and Daityas.

24. Joining them with delighted mind, the leader of the Daityas went to the city of Śakra and ruled the kingdom day and night.

25. The highly powerful Dānava meditated on and adored the goddess day and night particularly on the eighth and fourteenth lunar days.

26. Knowing the power of the goddess Vyāsa's son (Kapiñjala) installed the goddess in this holy spot and attained perfection.

*Sūta said:*

27. Thus goddess Kelīśvarī, the great goddess, originated. Hence, she should be installed, worshipped and meditated upon.

28. A man who reads the story of the goddess or listens to it when it is read shall be rid of great distress.

29. If a king ousted from his kingdom, listens to this on the eighth (lunar) day he gets back the entire kingdom again with all the enemies destroyed.

30. When war is imminent, if a man listens to this, he will kill all the enemies and attain victory.

# CHAPTER ONE HUNDRED FIFTYONE

## Greatness of Bhairava Kṣetra[1]

*Sūta said:*

1-2. On coming to know that the great Vidyā has been acquired by Śukra, that Kelīśvarī has been pleased with devotion, that the Vidyā bestowed increased strength, and recollecting that he had been rendered difficult to be killed as a result of the boon of Pitāmaha, Andhaka became furious with Maheśvara.

3-5. He sent a messenger to Kailāsa mountain instructing him: "O messenger, go and tell Hara these words of mine now:

'Leave the side of Śakra and stay comfortably here on this mountain. Otherwise, I will come there quickly and kill you in battle along with your wife and Gaṇas. Then I will stay happily in the Nandana garden. I will destroy you. This is the solemn oath I take.'"

6. On being told thus by the Daitya, the messenger hurried there and told Śaṅkara those harsh words.

7. Thereupon, the Bull-emblemed Lord became very furious and he despatched the Gaṇas to kill that wicked fellow.

8-9. The leaders were Vīrabhadra, Mahākāla, Nandin, Hastimukha, Aghora, Ghoranāda and the mighty Ghoraghaṇṭa. Each of these had ten million followers under him. The Lord sent them all to kill that wicked one.

10. On being despatched thus by him, the Gaṇas of hideous faces became extremely delighted. They roared like rumbling clouds.

11. Holding up the weapons for the battle, all of them went to that city of Śakra which the powerful Dānava had occupied.

12. On seeing that the Gaṇas had come, the Dānavas too seized their weapons arrogantly and rushed out at once with the intention of giving a tough fight.

13. Then a battle ensued between the Gaṇas and the Dānavas. The mutual fight was extremely violent. They kept back death

1. The Purāṇa author used the Andhaka legend to glorify this Tīrtha. As against the version given here in Mbh, *Anuśāsana* 14.214-215 and VR 6. 43.6 Śaṅkara killed Andhaka.

reversed (regarded retreat as death). They were not afraid of death.

14. Then in the battle, all the Gaṇas of Hara were defeated by the Dānavas. They fled to the various quarters in their fright. They became eager to see Hara.

15. On seeing his Gaṇas shattered, Hara came out angrily. On seeing Hara, the Daityas fled in all the ten directions.

16. On seeing Hara, Andhaka came face to face with him for the sake of fighting. Thereupon, the fight between Andhaka and Hara started even as the great battle between Vṛtra and Vāsava had occurred earlier.

17. (Hara fought with) various weapons like discus, shafts, arrows, Tomaras, swords and hammers. But that Dānava could not be killed by these various weapons.

18. Then they ceased to fight with weapons. They resorted to (wrestling) a hand-to-hand fight. Each grasped the other by the hand and began to hit with fist.

19. The Lord of Devas was kept bound by the Dānava and great pain was inflicted on him. He remained motionless and fell in a swoon.

20. Coming to know that he had fallen in a swoon Andhaka went out of the abode (?) In an instant Sthāṇu (Śiva) regained consciousness and took up his bow.

21. The Lord then lifted an iron rod weighing a thousand Bhāras, approached the leader of the Dānavas and struck him on his head.

22. He struck the Lord of the Devas quickly and forcibly with a sword. Then the Lord remembered the missile of Kubera in the great battle.

23. With the missile he struck the Dānava in his chest. Being struck therewith he vomited blood.

24. With the face turned downwards he fell down. Then he was pierced with the trident. Perched on the top of the trident, the sinful (Andhaka) began to whirl like a wheel.

25. Finding himself in that plight, Andhaka eulogized Lord Maheśvara with richly worded prayer:

*Andhaka said:*

26. Obeisance to you, to Śarva, O creator of the worlds, having the three Guṇas within. O Lord with the moon (worn)

as an ornament, obeisance to the Lord stationed on (riding) the bull.

27. Obeisance to the Lord holding the Khaṭvāṅga in the hand, to the holder of the trident. Obeisance to the Lord holding Ḍamaru drum, Kodaṇḍa (bow), skull and fire.

28. Obeisance to the destroyer of the body of Smara, to the supreme soul with eight cosmic bodies. Obeisance to the Lord with his handsome body, to the Lord devoid of form, to the multiformed one.

29. Obeisance to the destroyer of the head of Viriñci (Brahmā), to the cause of creation, to the permanent resident of cremation ground. Obeisance to the Lord of Bhairava (terrible) form.

30. You are present everywhere; you are the creator of all. You alone are the destroyer and none else. You are the earth; you are the Rajas; you are the light as well as the darkness.

31. O Maheśvara, you constitute the body of all living beings; you are the soul of every individual.

Thus the leading Dānava eulogized even as he was held perched on the tip of the trident.

*Sūta said:*

32. On hearing his eulogy thus, Maheśvara was delighted. He joyously told the excellent Danuja held on the tip of the trident:

*Śrī Bhagavān said:*

33. O Daitya, this is not the established practice of heroes, especially of one born as a Daitya, to utter conciliatory words at the time of being afflicted at the hands of an enemy.

*Andhaka said:*

34. O most excellent one among Suras, I have become disgusted and dejected on remaining held up on the tip of the trident. Hence do slay me quickly so that my pain can be reduced.

*Śrī Bhagavān said:*

35. Your death has never been intended by me. Hence, you have been pierced in the chest by the trident and held thus.

36. Giving up your demoniac nature and behaviour you will be freed from sin. Attain the state of a Gaṇa and be equipped with great faith.

*Andhaka said:*

37. My Dānava state has disappeared. Now I shall be your servant undoubtedly. I solemnly take this oath.

*Śaṅkara said:*

38. O dear one, I am pleased with you. Tell me what is desired by you. Request. I shall grant it even if it is difficult to obtain.

*Andhaka said:*

39-40. If a man makes an image of yours with my body as it is now fixed at the tip of the trident, and places it on the ground, O most excellent one among Suras, salvation should be granted to him by you at my instance.

Saying "So it shall be" Maheśa freed him from the tip of the trident. O Brāhmaṇas, he was a skeleton of bones, very lean and resembling Cāmuṇḍā.

41. Then he attained the status of a Gaṇa. He sang a melodious song before the Lord of Devas and Pārvatī too.

42. His Raṭana (voice) was pleasing to the ears like the humming sound of a black bee. So he was called Bhṛṅgīrīṭa by the Slayer of the Tripuras.

43. It was thus that he attained the status of a Gaṇa of the Trident-bearing Lord of Devas. Later on, he became highly trustworthy and prompt in all his duties.

44. Ever since then, Maheśvara, the Lord of Devas, is installed by people on the earth in such a form.

45-46. Great *Siddhi* of super-worldly nature is obtained here with his favour.

Once upon a time, a famous king named Suratha hailing from the solar race, had been ousted from his kingdom. He approached Vasiṣṭha, his own preceptor and he bowed down to him and spoke with eyes dimmed by tears:

47-48. "O holy Sir, in spite of the fact that you were staying as my guide and master, the enemies have taken away my realm now. I am really unfortunate.

Hence do me this favour so that I may regain my dominion. I have none else to turn to."

*Vasiṣṭha said:*

49. O great king, if it is so, hurry up and go at my bidding to the holy place of Hāṭakeśvara that accords all Siddhis.

50. There you shall install Maheśvara in the form of Bhairava with the boby of Andhaka that is pieced with the tip of trident and raised up in his arms.

51. Then, O king, worship it uttering the Narasiṁha Mantra and offering red flowers, incense and red unguents.

52. Then after attaining excellent virility and becoming equipped with refulgence and heroism undoubtedly, thanks to his favour, you will kill all the enemies.

53. The Lord should be worshipped by you with great purity; otherwise you will meet with obstacles. It is the truth that has been uttered by me.

54. On hearing his words, the king hurried quickly to the holy place and installed Lord Bhairava.

55. Then reciting the Narasiṁha Mantra with devotion, he maintained purity and celibacy and worshipped the Lord.

56. When the Mantra had been repeated ten thousand times, Bhairava became pleased and spoke to him:

*Śrī Bhairava said:*

57. O king, by being worshipped with this Mantra I am pleased with you. Hence do request for what is desired, so that I can grant you everything.

*Suratha said:*

58. My kingdom has been captured by enemies. May it be mine again, thanks to your grace. It should be free from enemies.

59-60. If another man comes here and worships you with this Mantra, O Lord, you should grant him *Siddhi* at the end of a thousand recitations as in my case, O Sureśvara.

After promising him, "So it shall be," Hara vanished thereafter.

61. After killing the enemies in battle, Suratha regained his realm.

## CHAPTER ONE HUNDRED FIFTYTWO

## Greatness of Cakrapāṇi

*The sages said:*

1-2. O Sūtaputra, you have enumerated innumerable Tīrthas and shrines installed by Devas, human beings, monkeys and Rākṣasas.

Tell us what of all of those Tīrthas and shrines, when visited and touched, will facilitate the full acquisition of desired benefit.

*Sūta said:*

3. O highly esteemed ones, it is true that there is no limit to the number of Tīrthas, Liṅgas and Āśramas (hermitages).

4. One who takes his holy bath with great concentration in Śaṅkha Tīrtha especially on the eleventh lunar day, obtains the benefit of all.

5. If a man devoutly visits the eleven Rudras there including Siddheśvara, it is as good as all the Maheśvaras have been seen by him.

6. If anyone visits Vaṭāditya especially on the sixth lunar day in the month of Caitra, it is as though all the Bhāskaras stationed there have been seen by him.

7. If anyone endowed with perfect faith visits Goddess Māhitthā, it is undoubtedly as though all the Durgās have been seen.

8. If anyone visits Gaṇeśa, the bestower of the heavenly gate (*Svargadvāra-prada*) on men, it is undoubtedly as though all the Vināyakas have been seen by him.

9. O excellent Brāhmaṇas, if anyone visits Jyeṣṭhā Gaurī there, installed by Śarmiṣṭhā, it is as though all the Gaurīs have been seen by him.

10. If a man gets up early in the morning and visits Cakrapāṇi, it is as though all theVāsudevas have been seen by him.

*The sages said:*

11. O Sūta, how is it that Cakrapāṇi who is stationed there has not been mentioned to us. Has he been forgotten? Do narrate to us. At what time is he to be seen particularly by learned men?

*Sūta said:*

12-13. O leading Brāhmaṇas, the Lord was installed here, in this holy spot, by Arjuna. He is to be visited by devotees after getting up early in the morning on *Śayana* (eleventh day of the bright half of Āṣāḍha) and *Bodhana* (eleventh day of the bright half of Kārttika) days after devoutly taking the holy bath. If he visits Cakrapāṇi, the sins of Brāhmaṇa-slaughter and the like perish instantaneously.

14. O Brāhmaṇas, the two deities Nara and Nārāyaṇa were made to incarnate by Brahmā for the purpose of dispelling the burden of the earth and establishing virtue (Dharma).

15. At the close of Dvāpara, these Nara-Nārāyaṇa took incarnation as Kṛṣṇa and Arjuna, O excellent Brāhmaṇas. They took birth on the earth and they were mutually affectionate.

16. Just as Rāma, the son of Daśaratha, took the incarnation on the earth for the destruction of Rākṣasas, so also Kṛṣṇa was another incarnation.

17-18. Arjuna installed the Lord during pilgrimage. When Arjuna happened to see his brother (Yudhiṣṭhira) in their (intimate) privacy with Draupadī, he undertook a pilgrimage from the excellent city of Śakraprastha (Indraprastha) at the instance of Yudhiṣṭhira. He bowed down and humbly submitted:

*Arjuna said:*

19. O excellent king, I have now come here for taking my weapons to get the cows of the Brāhmaṇa released. O king, grant me permission.

*Yudhiṣṭhira said:*

20. O Arjuna, go there quickly to the place where the cows of the excellent Brāhmaṇa are being taken by the thieves. O Dhananjaya, get them released.
21. Thereafter undertake a pilgrimage for twelve years. Then, rid of the sins, you will come back to me.
22. Even a sensible man will become highly sinful if he looks at a man in union with his wife in a secluded spot. It is still more so, if the man happens to be one's own brother.
23. Hence one who wishes for his own welfare should not look at anyone in union with his wife in a secluded spot and particularly at a brother.

24. Thereafter, he promised "So it shall be", hurriedly got into his chariot seizing the bow and the arrows and went away.
25. O Brāhmaṇas, he went on that path on which the cows were being taken forcibly by the thieves holding sharp weapons, after warding off all the Brāhmaṇas.
26. He quickly killed the thieves and brought back all the cows himself and returned them to the noble-souled Brāhmaṇas.
27. Then the son of Pāṇḍu visited many Tīrthas and shrines and came here to this holy spot for the purpose of a holy ablution.
28. That holy spot had already been visited by him earlier when he was there in the company of Duryodhana.
29. Then with flowers, incense and unguents he worshipped the Liṅga name Arjuneśvara which had been installed earlier (by him).
30. Similarly (he worshipped) Liṅgas which had been installed by other Pāṇḍavas and leading Kauravas also.
31-33. Then the son of Pāṇḍu began to think in his mind: 'I am Nara himself. Hence I shall install here Cakrapāṇi, the Lord of Suras, and also build a palace a like of which no human being has as yet built on the earth.

Even at the close of the Kalpa, this holy spot will not perish at all. The palace too shall be so in this holy spot.'
34. O excellent Brāhmaṇas, this holy spot will not perish at all. The palace too shall be so in this holy spot.
35. Then he invited the Brāhmaṇas hailing from Camatkārapura and abiding by their views, he made them install the image.

36. He made various gifts to them and offered many grants of lands. He gave them later other things which gave them satisfaction.

37. Then with palms joined in reverence, he spoke: "I am Nara (in that birth) born of Brāhmaṇa (but now) begot of the wife of Pāṇḍu.

38. I left the auspicious Badarī and assumed a human form. This palace has been built by me here for the sake of reputation. I have built it with a mind sanctified by faith. The palace has been named after my name Nara.

39-40. Hence, O Brāhmaṇas, this deity should be glorified always as Cakrapāṇi so that my name could be echoed in the Viṣṇuloka as long as the Moon and the Sun shine.

41. Further a grand festival should be held on days of Viṣṇu's going to sleep (*Śayana*, on the eleventh day in the bright half of Āṣāḍha) and on that of waking up (*Bodhana*, eleventh day in the bright half of Kārttika) and in Caitra on the day of Viṣṇu (the eleventh lunar day in the bright half of Caitra).

42. On these three days, O excellent Brāhmaṇas, I leave Badarī and perform the worship of Viṣṇu personally.

43. A man who worships this deity on that day shall be rid of all sins and go to Viṣṇuloka.

44. Further all those who are settled in the holy spot of Vāsudeva should be seen by him and welfare will be acquired by him."

*Sūta said:*

45. They said: "So it shall be". The son of Pāṇḍu belonging to the family of Dāśārha (Yādava—from his mother's side?) entrusted all the responsibility to them. With a calm and peaceful mind, he went to the other Tīrthas. He felt contented.

46. Thus, Hṛṣīkeśa himself, the destroyer of the sins of all the creatures, stationed himself there in the form of Cakrapāṇi.

47. Even today, on the three Ekādaśī days the Lord's digit (part) thus manifests himself. Hence, he should be worshipped always by persons endowed with faith in accordance with the injunctions laid down before. He should be specially honoured and adored.

## CHPAPTER ONE HUNDRED FIFTYTHREE

# Origin of Apsarā Kuṇḍa

*Sūta said:*

1-3. Further, there is another excellent Tīrtha there called Rūpatīrtha. A man who properly takes his holy bath there becomes handsome even if he is ugly.

Formerly, Lord Brahmā, the creator of the world, brought into being the vast creation of the four types as mentioned.

Thereafter he thought: 'I shall create a divine Apsarā, Devamāyā, endowed with all the characteristics of beauty.'

4-5. He took a *Tila* (a gingelly seed, minute part) from all the Devas and created a highly wonderful female being,[1] on seeing whom Pitāmaha himself became excited.

6. Then, the Lotus-born One sent her to Kailāsa: "O fair lady of pure smiles, go and bow down to Mahādeva."

7. Then, she hurriedly went to the excellent mountain Kailāsa. There she saw Śaṅkara seated along with Pārvatī.

8 . On seeing her, even Śaṅkara was extremely surprised. Seeing that Pārvatī was by his side, he did not openly look at her because he was afraid.

9. Endowed with great faith and keeping the palms joined in reverence, she bowed down to Maheśvara and (began to) circumambulate him.

10. When she came to the southern side, Mahādeva whose eyes were attracted by her, created a southern face of his.

11. As the splendid lady came to the west in the course of her circumambulation, the western face was created by him.

12. In this manner, when she came to be in the north, the northern face was created by Lord Śaṁbhu who was afraid of Gaurī. (Hence) O Brāhmaṇas, he did not move his neck even a bit.

13. In the meantime, Nārada the leading sage (came there) and bowed down to Pārvatī and Maheśvara. Then he spoke to Pārvatī:

1. Hence named 'Tilottamā'.

*Nārada said:*

14. See the misdemeanour of your husband. On seeing a beautiful lady, four faces have been evolved by him.

15. O goddess of Suras, I know this. All men know this that there is no woman like you.

16. But, O Pārvatī, on their coming to know that Lord Śaṅkara is attached to another woman, you will be the object of derision of all the wives of all Devas.

17-18. O goddess, do you know how Śiva's mind works? He broods over this harlot censured by intelligent people. He will bring her and settle her in his own palace. But, O splendid lady, overwhelmed by shame, he does not express it in words.

*Sūta said:*

19. On hearing the words of Nārada, she found that her dear Lord had four faces. Realizing that Hara had become deformed, she was overwhelmed with anger.

20. Adopting the practice of chief of queens, the Daughter of the Mountain quickly closed all the eyes of the Lord.

21. In the meantime, all the mountains all round began to shatter. All the oceans transgressed their limits.

22. Pralaya appeared there, O excellent Brāhmaṇas. Then the next day of Brahmā dawned with the re-appearance of creation.

23. Because of the closing (of the eyes) there was Pralaya. It is called the night of Brahmā, the Prajāpati. Everything becomes flooded with water.

24. Then all the Gaṇas with Bhṛṅgī and Nandin as leaders came there. The celestial sage (Nārada) became afraid and he spoke to the Goddess of Suras:

25. "O seniormost lady of Suras, leave off the eyes of the Lord. Otherwise there will be the utter annihilation of this world."

26-27. Though requested thus, the goddess did not take away her hands.

Then another eye in the forehead was created by the Lord who was moved with pity, so that the worlds could be preserved. He could not prevent the goddess dearer to his own life.

28. Devas said to Aṁbikā, O Brāhmaṇas: "Since he has three eyes, the Lord of Suras is glorified as Tryaṁbaka."

29. Then the goddess, the Daughter of the Mountain, left the Lord. With the eyes turned red due to anger she spoke to Tilottamā who was standing in front:

30. "O sinful woman, my lover has been deceived by you through your beauty and converted into one with four faces. So be hideous and ugly quickly."

31. Then instantaneously her nose became flattened, her hair withered and her teeth elongated. Her eyes were rendered sunken within and her belly protruding.

32. On observing her body transformed thus, the excellent Apsarā trembled. With palms joined together in veneration, she spoke:

33-34. "O goddess, I have been sent by Brahmā for the sake of paying obeisance to the Trident-bearing Lord and to you all as well. So I have come here. Hence, it does not behove you to curse me because I am not blameworthy. Nor am I attached. It behoves you to do a favour unto me."

35. On hearing her piteous but truthful words, Pārvatī regretted (her action) and said to her lovingly:

36-39. "It is due to the innate nature of women that I got angry with you. Hence I got enraged with you all of a sudden. But now let us go to the earth. You do come with me.

There is a Tīrtha there created by me myself for the sake of holy ablution on the third lunar day in the bright half of the month on Māgha. Its waters are green from impurities and it bestows beauty. A woman who gets up early in the morning before the solar disc is visible and takes her holy bath (therein) shall certainly become beautiful.

I take my holy bath there on the third lunar day in the month of Māgha always. Today, it is the same day. I have decided to take my bath. I shall go there."

*Sūta said:*

40. After saying thus, the goddess took Tilottamā to the Rūpa Tīrtha in the holy spot of Hāṭakeśvara.

41. There the goddess of Suras took her bath herself as per injunctions and after her, Tilottamā also bathed with great devotion.

42. Thereupon the lady became very lustrous, in fact more lustrous than what she was formerly in complexion.

43. Then she was highly satisfied. Overwhelmed with surprise, she bowed down to the goddess of Devas. She spoke in vioce choked with delight:

44. "O great goddess, I have regained my beauty permanently with your favour. I shall now go to the world of Brahmā. It behoves you to permit me."

*Gaurī said:*

45. O my daughter, your visit to me cannot be futile. I shall grant you a boon. Hence do pray for whatever is cherished in your heart without hesitation.

*Tilottamā said:*

46. O splendid goddess, I shall also make my own Tīrtha in this holy spot. Let it attain renown all over the earth with your favour.

47. At the end of every year, you too should take your holy bath there for the sake of the benefit of all women. It should bestows beauty and conjugal felicity.

*Gaurī said:*

48. O splendid lady, for your sake, I will always take my ablution at the Tīrtha made by you, on the third day of the bright half of Caitra at mid-day.

49-50. Undoubtedly I do so at your instance and for the sake of the benefit of all women. A woman who takes her bath there on that day, will become happy. She will be one loved and liked by all the women on the earth.

51. Even a man who takes his bath there with great devotion will become very handsome for seven births and also enjoy conjugal felicity.

*Sūta said:*

52. O excellent Brāhmaṇas, on being told thus by the goddess, the celestial damsel made a big Kuṇḍa filled with pure water.

53. Near it Tilottamā installed Pārvatī and then joyously went to the world of Brahmā.

54. Then that Kuṇḍa made by the Apsarā came into being, O Brāhmaṇas. Merely by taking bath there, conjugal felicity is obtained.

55. Excellent sons are obtained by women. So also other desires cherished in their hearts.

## CHAPTER ONE HUNDRED FIFTYFOUR

# Greatness of Citreśvara Pīṭha

*Sūta said:*

1-2. A woman who takes her bath in that excellent Kuṇḍa, sees Pārvatī, takes bath again in the splendid Rūpamaya Tīrtha and finally visits Pārvatī with great faith shall be immediately rid of all sins committed from birth till death.

3. There itself, O Brāhmaṇas, near Gaurī Kuṇḍa is the Kuṇḍa made by the servant maid of Pārvatī named Jayā.

4. A woman who takes her holy ablution there on the third lunar day shall become a great favourite of her husband and be richly endowed with conjugal felicity, and happiness due to birth of sons.

5. Further, there is another excellent Kuṇḍa named Vijayākuṇḍa there itself. A barren woman who takes her holy bath therein becomes blessed with sons.

6. She does not see even in dreams any calamity befalling her sons, nor separation from them nor any other type of grief.

7. A Kākavandhyā (i.e. a woman with only one child) who takes her holy bath there shall beget many sons and become honoured in the heavenly world.

*The sages said:*

8. O Sūta, among these Tīrthas, is there any Tīrtha that bestows excellent bodily Siddhi if the bath is taken there?

*Sūta said:*

9-10a. There are twenty-seven Liṅgas. Complete Siddhi will be obtained out of anyone of them by a devotee who is endowed with the Sattva quality and has adopted Vīravrata.

10b-11. O excellent Brāhmaṇas, he who, at mid-night on the fourteenth day of the dark half of Āśvina, adores them (those Liṅgas) as per prescribed procedure and in due course devoutly mutters the previously mentioned Mantra is the best of the aspirants.

12-13. After performing *Aṅganyāsa* (ritualistic touching of the limbs) a devotee should loudly recite the *Kṣurikā Sūkta*. Then in front of them he should perfectly worship Śaṅkara and devoutly worship the Guardians of the quarters severally.

14-17. (*The text is obscure*) It is possible that Vighneśa may put obstacles. He may assume hideous and terrific form with protruding belly. He may be nude and he may have black teeth. With the sword in his hand he may say. "Fight with me if you are a hero of Sāttvika type, leave off this (Kapaṭa)[1] (Karpaṭa?) fraudulent practice on the ground." The devotee may be dragged and beaten, but he is ultimately taken to the highest region along with his own body—the highest region where there is never death or grief. So this Siddhi of one is glorified in the Citreśvarī Pīṭha.

18-23. (The worship of the goddess in the way of the vulgar Tāmasa people ).[2] The Devotee should worship the Pīṭha on the fourteenth lunar day in the dark half of the month of Māgha in accordance with the injunctions in Āgamas. He shall have perfect faith.

Then he takes up a Kapāla (potsherd, skull?) filled with Mahāmāṁsa (human flesh) and declares: "I am selling this Mahāmāṁsa now with Siddhi as the price thereof. If there is any Sāttvika let him take it."

O excellent Brāhmaṇas, he who begs, takes it and goes out to the Hāṭakeśvara Kṣetra where Lord Maheśvara is present in the form of a Liṅga installed by Citraśarman.

---

1. Probably *karpaṭa*, 'old garment', rag indicating old human body.
2. This Tāmasa type of worship is of the left-handed cult of Śakti (Vāma Mārga).

The devotee should seat himself in the centre of that place and worship it on Śivarātri day at midnight with devotion by means of flowers. He shall attain Siddhi with the body at the same instant.

O excellent Brāhmaṇas, all the Siddhisthānas are present in that holy spot. They are for men who have adopted Vīravrata (the vow of the heroes).

*The sages said:*

24. O highly intelligent one, this path of perfection is Tāmasa (that of barbarous and outlandish ones) that has been mentioned by you. This is not worthy of acceptance for great Brāhmaṇas and specially for those who are well-versed in the Vedas.

25-26. O Sūta, O highly esteemed one, tell us the path of salvation for Brāhmaṇas, the way whereby salvation is attained by Brāhmaṇas of pure mental predilection, who eschew injury to all living beings even if it may be a delayed process.

*Sūta said:*

27-28a. There is Ānandeśvaraka associated with ten Rudras. A devotee then should take his holy bath in the Kuṇḍa in front of him in accordance with the rules found in the scriptural texts.

28b-29. The man should take his holy bath in the Viśvāmitra Hrada in the month of Māgha. He should take the bath early in the morning and make the gift of a pot of gingelly seeds to a Brāhmaṇa. He shall be rid of all sins and be honoured in the world of Brahmā.

30-31. That shall be the result even if he be one with evil conduct, an indiscriminate eater and seller of anything and everything. A man endowed with faith should undertake fast and perform Prāyopaveśa (fast unto death) in front of the Lord named Suparṇa. One who forsakes his life thus is never reborn.

32. Thus three different methods of attaining Siddhi have been mentioned. They are beneficial to Brāhmaṇas. O excellent Brāhmaṇas, They are Sāttvika means praised even by Devas.

33. There are other Tīrthas and holy shrines. Sages of well praised holy vows say that they bestow heavenly pleasures.

34. Thus the greatness of the holy place of Hāṭakeśvara has been fully narrated to you all. It is destructive of all sins.

35. Even a sinner who takes his holy bath in all the Tīrthas and devoutly visits all the shrines, becomes liberated.

36. This Khaṇḍa is declared as the first one of this Purāṇa composed by Kārttikeya. It is (both) auspicious and destructive of all sins.[1]

37. He who devoutly reads this or listens to this with concentration shall enjoy all pleasures here and go to heaven.

38. One who listens with great faith (this Khaṇḍa) attains all the benefits obtained (by pilgrimage to) all Tīrthas and by giving all Dānas.

39. By listening to this Purāṇa one is rid of all the sins arising from millions of births. One redeems a hundred members of his family.

40. Then Vyāsa (the expounder of the Purāṇas) should be honoured by means of the gifts of garments, etc., cows, plots of lands, food offerings etc. of various kinds.

41. If the expounder of the Purāṇas is duly honoured then the original Vyāsa Kṛṣṇadvaipāyana, the son of Satyavatī, becomes honoured by him.

42. The preceptor may impart to the disciple only a single syllable. Even then there is nothing on the earth by giving of which the disciple can be free from the indebtedness.

43. This is sacred. This is conducive to longevity and wealth. This results in and leads to welfare. On nearing this great text one is liberated from all miseries. There is no doubt about it.

1. These verses show that this is the end of the first khaṇḍa of this Purāṇa.

## CHAPTER ONE HUNDRED FIFTYFIVE

# A Kṣatriya Addresses His Wife[1]

*Sūta said:*

1-4a. Further, there are other deities also there, O excellent Brāhmaṇas, (such as) the eight Vasus who have resorted to one spot. They are always worshipped by all Devas.

There are also eleven Rudras, twelve Ādityas and two Aśvins, the physicians of Devas.

The Devas who are leaders of crores and crores are stationed there, O excellent Brāhmaṇas. Everyone of them is overcome with fear of the Kali age.

4b-5. A man (devotee) should take his holy bath on the eighth lunar day in the bright half of the month of Caitra. He should wear newly washed clothes and remain pure. After propitiating excellent Brāhmaṇas, the devotee should begin his adoration (of Vasus).

6. He shall devoutly utter the Mantra, *vasavas tvā kṛṇvan*. Then he should make the food offering while reciting the Mantra, *vasavaśchandasau*.

7. The devotee with great concentration should offer incense and sweet scents and utter this Mantra, *vasavas tvāṁ jetu*.

8. O excellent Brāhmaṇas, the devotee then offers Ārārtika (waving of lighted lamps) reciting the Mantra, *vasavas tvāṁ jetu*. Now let it be heard what the benefit that accrues, is:

9. If the eight Vasus are adored, one gets the benefit of worshipping crores of virgins.

10. In the same manner, the devotee should install and worship those twelve Ādityas who are already settled in that holy place, on the day when the seventh lunar day coincides with a Sunday. He should worship them with flowers, sweet scents and unguents properly with full faith.

11. Thereafter, before them he performs twenty-one Vratas called Ādityavratas. Listen to the benefit thereof:

---

1. Though the printed text does not mention it, the Second Part (Khaṇḍa) begins here. There is duplication of many legends of the First Khaṇḍa in this (Second) Part.

12. One who worships here shall undoubtedly obtain the benefit of worshipping twelve crores of Ādityas.

13. Similarly, O excellent Brāhmaṇas, listen to the benefit of the worship of the eleven Rudras stationed in one spot in this holy Kṣetra.

14. The devotee should install the gods of Suras and devoutly worship them on the fourteenth lunar day in the bright half of the month of Caitra. He should repeat the Śatarudriya Mantra.

15. The Śatarudriya Mantra is to be recited eleven times. It will be as good as though eleven crore (Rudras) have been worshipped by him. There is no doubt about it. It is the truth that has been stated by me.

16-17. Further, the Aśvins, the physicians of Devas, are also stationed there. The devotee should worship them on the full-moon day in the month of Āśvina with the constellation Aśvinī coinciding. He should recite the *Aśvinī Sūkta*: The benefit acquired thereby shall be twenty million times more.

18. Thus the greatness of the Vasus, Ādityas, Rudras and Aśvins has been spoken to you all, O excellent Brāhmaṇas.

*Sūta said:*

19. Further, there is another deity there installed by Yājñavalkya. It is well-known by the name Puṣpāditya, the bestower of all cherished desires on men.

20. A man may think of any desired object before worshipping. He will obtain it completely even if it is difficult of access.

21. One without a son gets sons; a seeker of wealth shall get wealth; one with many enemies will get the enemies destroyed, and a seeker of learning shall become an expert in the scriptural texts.

22. O excellent Brāhmaṇas, a man who visits it on the seventh lunar day coinciding with a Sunday shall be rid of the sins which are accrued on that day even if they happen to be great.

23. By the adoration sins accumulated over a year will perish. There is no doubt about it that it will perish like darkness at the time of sunrise.

24. He who circumambulates one hundred eight times with fruits in his hand, shall be rid of sins accrued from birth to death.

25. A person who circumambulates shall obtain whatever he desires undoubtedly. One without desires shall attain salvation.

26. One who performs the rite of bathing (the deity) at the time of Meṣa (Aries) and Tulā (Libra) transit coinciding with a Sunday realizes (his) desires.

27. On that occasion, those who desire the benefit of their choice shall visit and adore the Lord with all efforts.

28. The benefit obtained on the visit shall be on a par with the benefit accruing from the visit to all the Devas stationed in Camatkārapura.

*The sages said:*

29. If, as you say, the Lord was installed by Yājñavalkya, why is the deity called Puṣpāditya? it behoves you to explain this.[1]

*Sūta said:*

30. In this connection I shall narrate an ancient legend as to how the deity installed by Yājñavalkya became Puṣpāditya.

31. Here on the earth there is an excellent great city named Vaidiśā. (Vidiśā). There are many mansions there. It is embellished with many excellent remparts and wells.

32. Hundreds of parks and lakes adorn it. There was an excellent king there well known as Citravarmā.

33. While that king who was a knower of Dharma (piety) and who loved virtue always, was ruling over the kingdom, there was no fear from thieves, no ailment and no famine.

34. In that city there was a person, a Kṣatriya by caste. He

---

1. The episode of Brāhmaṇa Puṣpa who through the boon of the Sun-god, misappropriated the wife and property of Maṇibhadra is given in this and the following chapters (upto 163-164). Though Puṣpa succeeded in giving his name to Yājñavalkya's Āditya, the immorality of the whole affair led Puṣpa to expiate (as Puraścaraṇa Saptamī) and the excommunication of Caṇḍa Śarman.

is remembered by the name Maṇibhadra. He had plenty of wealth inherited from father and grandfather.

35. Whenever necessity arises, the king along with his ministers, nay the entire city, sustained itself through loan taken from him on interest.

36. This Maṇibhadra was an old man of graying hair and wrinkled body (limbs). He was extremely ugly in appearance.

37. He was miserly despite ample wealth. He was a sinner who never gave anything to anyone. He remained thirsty and hungry. He never ate anything (to his fill).

38-41. Though that wicked man was like this, and ugly, he happended to see a beautiful girl of his caste. He wanted to marry the girl who had lips like a Bimba fruit. Her body was beautiful and fascinating. She had a slender belly that could be grasped within one's fist. Her eyes were large like the petals of a lotus. Her hair was glossy. Her ankles were not visible (because of ample flesh). She was red (in complexion)in seven limbs and deep in three. She was charming and endowed fully with all characteristics. But, O tigers among Brāhmaṇas, he requested for the girl from a Kṣatriya (her father) who was afflicted with dire poverty. He (the father) mentioned everything about this to his wife.

42. On hearing that she fell into a swoon due to sorrow. Thereafter, he enlightened her with suitable words with suitable (relevant) examples.

*The Kṣatriya said:*

43. There is no learning, no art or craft, and no object which is not given to rich people by persons seeking wealth.

44. In this world even a stranger becomes a kinsman in the case of rich people. In the case of poor people even a kinsman becomes wicked.

45. From increased riches collected from here and there, all activities spring up like rivers from mountains.

46. One unworthy of being approached is approached and one not deserving to be saluted is bowed down to. It is the consequence of wealth.

47. As sense-organs get activised through eating (food), so all the functions through their causes. Wealth is called the cause of all.

48. This world of living beings may resort to even the cremation ground while seeking wealth. A man without wealth abandons even his father and goes far away.

## CHAPTER ONE HUNDRED FIFTYSIX

# Maṇibhadra Cheats a Brāhmaṇa Named Puṣpa

*Sūta said:*

1-4a. On being addressed thus by him in a secluded spot, the wife evinced her keenness for the offer of the virgin (daughter). Then he washed the feet of Maṇibhadra at once and offered water along with raw rice grain in his hand as a prelude to the offer of the virgin.

As soon as the water was offered in the hand, he insisted to the Kṣatriya: "Perform the rite of marriage with the virgin today itself. For, I wish to set up my household. Hence I have come to your house."

*The Kṣatriya said:*

4b. The star is not favourable now. It is not Pūrvā Phalgunī.

5-6. There is no auspicious time for marriage when Viṣṇu is asleep (i.e.between Āṣāḍha and Kārttika). The girl who is married during this period will certainly become a widow within a year. I have heard prominent astrologers say thus.

7. Hence, after the advent of the auspicious constellation of Pūrvā Phalgunī, when Lord Viṣṇu gets up from his sleep, do marry my daughter. She will then bring welfare unto you and will be blessed with sons and grandsons.

*Maṇibhadra said:*

8. The constellation is Kṛttikā and Viṣṇu is asleep.

9. Now it will take a year to celebrate the marriage, but the fire of love has risen up and torments me.

10. Hence, do me the favour of giving the girl in marriage. I will give you ample wealth and you will be happy and comfortable.

*Sūta said:*

11. So, O excellent Brāhmaṇas, the Kṣatriya got the marriage celebrated at that very time due to his avariciousness for the money.

12. He gave the daughter in marrige, although her eyes were filled with tears and she was very unhappy. In the presence of the Brāhmaṇas and the holy fire, she was taken by him as his wife.

13. Later, he took her to his house and engaged her in loveplay. Though she did not like it, he indulged in it unfettered.

14. After the lust got subsided, he began to rebuke her repeatedly. He used many threatening words and made the maiden sad and distressed.

15. When it was about the daybreak, she was pacified a little. All the servants were then dismissed by him from the house.

16. It was a case of sheer jealousy, O excellent Brāhmaṇas. Only a single servant, an eunuch, was retained as the gatekeeper.

17. He told him: "You must not let into my house any servant or beggar, even an old man observing Vratas."

18. After making all these arrangements, he began his daily business activities with thousands and hundred thousands in cash.

19. Nothing was given by that wicked fellow even to his father-in-law, and to his own wife nothing except white clothes.

20. When two *Yāmaṣ* (six hours) of the day time passed off (after twelve noon) he came home. He then used to give her some measured quantity of foodstuff to eat.

21. She was given only enough for eating and while she took her food, he used to take his own food along with a single Brāhmaṇa. After taking food, he used to go out for his business activity.

22. Then he used to return home at dusk. That wife of this wicked fellow remained throughout within the house.

23. She was invariably dejected and overcome with sorrow and misery. She was as miserable as a fish that had slipped onto the ground from the water.

24. She could be compared to a female Cakravākī that is separated from her mate when the day comes to a close, or

to a female swan separated from her mate and to a hind taken away from her deer.

25. O Brāhmaṇas, he used to give food to a single Brāhmaṇa everyday, but invariably, he stipulated in a conciliatory tone the following pre-condition beforehand:

26. "O Brāhmaṇa, you must always keep your face down when you take your food. If you dare to look at my wife you will meet with mortification."

27. Thus many who dared to look up and stare had been subjected to mortification by him. Others who were quite frightened never came to his house.

28. Once thereafter an excellent Brāhmaṇa named Puṣpa came to that city in the course of his pilgrimage.

29-30. He was in the prime of his youth and was very handsome to look at. But on this occasion at midday, he was extremely hungry and weary. He wandered among the house of the people around. Someone told him that Maṇibhadra would give him food.

31. O Brāhmaṇas, he (Puṣpa) went to him and begged for food. The Brāhmaṇa was told thus:

32-33. "You must eat your food with the face kept down. My beloved should not be stared at by you. Otherwise, O Brāhmaṇa, you will undoubtedly meet with unpleasant vexation. Keeping this in mind, O highly esteemed one, do what is conducive to your welfare."

*Puṣpa said:*

34. I am now hungry, emaciated with hunger. What do I gain by staring at other men's wives? I am a student of the Vedas and am now engaged in pilgrimage.

*Maṇibhadra said:*

35. Then come to my abode along with me now. I shall serve unto you a special food with a monetary gift.

36. O excellent Brāhmaṇas, they made this settlement and proceeded homewards along the market path. They came to the place where the eunuch was standing guard.

37. Asking the Brāhmaṇa to wait by his side (i.e. that of

the eunuch) he entered the house. A measured quantity of cereal (was given to his wife and) she was asked to cook it.

38-40. At the close of the worship of the deity and Vaiśvadeva Yajña, Puṣpa was summoned and his feet were washed. He was made to sit and was duly honoured. Well-cooked food was served then, O Brāhmaṇas, Puṣpa sat down for his meal and (in front of him) he saw the lotus-like feet of the woman. The more the Brāhmaṇa in his youth gazed at the feet, the more out of curiosity he looked at her face.

41. This enraged Maṇibhadra. He immediately called the eunuch and said: "Punish this wretched adulterer."

42. Thereupon, O excellent Brāhmaṇas, Puṣpa was hit on his head by him.

43. He fell down on the ground stained and smeared with blood. The servant caught hold of his feet, dragged him away and left him on the highway.

44. When he was brought thus to the main thoroughfare where people moved up and down, there arose a long hue and cry in the excellent city.

45. On seeing him in that plight, all the citizens made a lot of noise. Some people compassionately sprinkled cold water over him.

46. The crowd was made to stand aside and there was open air. He was enabled to regain consciousness. After coming to consciousness with very great diffculty by the use of water, he spoke to them:

47-49. "No theft, no adultery has been committed by me. See ye men, how Maṇibhadra has tortured me.

I am a Brāhmaṇa engaged in pilgrimage. I am under the vow of celibacy. I was invited for food but reduced to this plight.

O men, is there no king here? How is this bad treatment with an innocent Brāhmaṇa allowed to happen?"

*The people said:*

50. Many Brāhmaṇas have been tormented by him earlier. He is blessed with the favour of the king. He is always jealous of other embodied beings (persons).

51. In view of his favour at the king's place, no one says anything directly to him. Now get up. We shall give you food.

## CHAPTER ONE HUNDRED FIFTYSEVEN

# Boons to Puṣpa by the Sun-god

*Sūta said:*

1-3. O Brāhmaṇas! Though Puṣpa was thus enlightened (and invited for food) by the people, he who was enraged, replied to them: "I will not take food till I do not avenge myself of this sinful fellow. Hence tell me, O fortunate ones, if there is a god or a goddess or (persons who mastered) Mantras which have immediate effect. They should, on being propitiated, confer good boons on human beings immediately."

*The people said:*

4. There is one Lord stationed here who will immediately bring about credence. Further a goddess is also spoken about on the earth.

*Puṣpa said:*

5. Who is that Lord? How far away is he? At what spot is he stationed? So also tell me about the goddess.

*The people said:*

6. O Brāhmaṇa, there is Lord Sūrya installed in Camatkārapura by Yājñavalkya. We have heard that he commands instant credence.

7-8a. O Brāhmaṇa! A person who, on the seventh lunar day coinciding with Sunday, circumambulated the deity one hundred eight times with a fruit in his hand, attains excellent Siddhī and obtains whatever he desires in his mind.

8b-9a There is also another deity called Śāradā, originally installed in Kaśmīr. She bestows Siddhis on being adored when one is observing fast.

9b-11. O excellent Brāhmaṇas, on hearing the words of those people, he proceeded towards Camatkārapura from that place. He reached Camatkārapura on the seventh lunar day coinciding with a Sunday. He took his holy bath and remained clean. With mental concentration and purity, he reached the place where the Sun-god installed by Yājñavalkya was stationed.

12. Holding coconuts in his hand, he performed one hundred eight circumambulations with perfect faith.

13. Then braving hunger, parched throat and great weariness, he sat in front of the deity reciting the prayers liked by the Sun-god.

14-15. The Mantras were those beginning with *yad etan maṇḍalam tapatī, sapta yuñjanti ratham ekacakram* (RV.I. 164.2), *agnireva* etc. He recited them in high pitch with great devotion. With devout fervour he recited the Sāman verses called Ādityavrata and the Ātharvaṇa Mantras such as Kṣurikā Mantras etc.

16. He continued this till the next Sunday. When Lord Sun did not become pleased even on the full-moon day, he became extremely dejected.

17. Then Puṣpa took his bath and wore washed cloth. Remaining pure, O excellent Brāhmaṇas, he consecrated a piece of land uttering the name of the earth, for the purpose of preparing a sacrificial altar.

18. The altar was made a *Hasta* (hand) high. He repeated the Mantra *agnimīle* (RV I.I.I) and placed the sacrificial fire there.

19. He performed the Upastaraṇa (ritualistic covering) rite repeating the Mantra, *tṛṇaiḥ paristṛnāmi*. He offered seat unto Brahmā uttering "*ā brahman*" etc. (VS 22.22)

20. Uttering the Mantra *sutrāmāṇam* (RV X. 63.10) he placed the Samit (sacrificial twigs). He went near the Prokṣaṇī vessel and sprinkled the water.

21. The Sruvā (ladle) and other utensils were kept in the usual order. In the place of *Havis* (food offering) he kept his own body.

22. He placed Nyāya in the place of the deity and considered himself Ācārya (Preceptor) in accordance with the injunctions. Uttering the Mantras *sūryāya tvā juṣṭam nirvapāmi sūryāya tvā juṣṭam prokṣāmi,* he performed the rites of *Grahaṇa* (reception) and *Prokṣaṇa* (sprinkling).

23. Uttering the Mantra *ayam ta idhma ātmā* he placed the Samit uttering the Mantras *agnaye svāhā somāya svāhā* he performed two offerings of *Ājya* (Ghee).

24. He performed the Vyāhṛti Homa by uttering *bhūrbhuvaḥ svaḥ,* O Brāhmaṇas. He then performed Dāruṇa (terrible) Homa, with the Mantra beginning with *yete śata* etc.

25. He invoked the Fire-god saying "O Lord be visible to me." Thus he made the fire appear in front.

26-27. He then invoked the seven tongues (flames of fire), Kālī, Karālikā etc. and when the fire blazed, he chopped off his flesh in pieces. He offered them to the quarters and interceding directions uttering the Mantra *lomabhyaḥ svāhā*.

28. He was then about to offer himself uttering the Mantra *agnaye sviṣṭakṛte* (Tait. Br. 3.12.2.3.). Immediately he was stopped and held by the Sun-god with his own hand.

29-30. He was eagerly held and addressed thus: "O Brāhmaṇa, do not do anything rash and reckless. Such a Homa as this has never been performed by anyone anywhere.

O highly esteemed one, I am pleased. Tell me what shall I do? I shall give you whatever is in your mind even if it cannot be ordinarily given."

*Puṣpa said:*

31. O Lord of Devas, if you are pleased, if a boon has to be granted to me, then a pair of pills should be given. It is for this that I request.

32. O Lord, in the city of Vaidiśā there is a great rich Kṣatriya named Maṇibhadra. He is short in his limbs, overcome by old age and wrinkles.

33-35. He is very mean and miserly. He is against Brāhmaṇas and is always rebuked by the people. Of the two pills let one be of this nature. Whenever I put it in my mouth let my form be exactly like his. When I take the other one and put it in my mouth, O Lord of Suras,let me have the natural form. This Maṇibhadra is in the city of Vaidiśā.

36. Another thing, whatever he possesses in his house, cash, grain etc., should be known to me.

37. Why should I say much? Let his friends, kinsmen and all business deals be clearly manifest unto me.

38. In all my activities at all times, no one should find out any difference between me and that base fellow.

*Bhāskara said:*

39. O highly esteemed one,take these two excellent pills. They are black and white in colour. When kept in the mouth they cause a great deal of difference.

40. O great Brāhmaṇa, through the white pill your form will be certainly turned into his. Through the black one you will get back your own form.

*Puṣpa said:*

41. There is another query, O Lord. Clear the doubt in my mind. O Lord of Devas, I shall ask you. I shall be conducive to increase in your reputation.

42. O most excellent one of Suras, I have heard this. If any one takes one hundred eight circumambulations around you with a fruit in his hand you bestow Siddhi on him instantaneously.

43-44. This you are ready to grant even to a fool and a sinner and one with all defects. On the other hand, I have mastered all the four Vedas and am regularly engaged in pilgrimage. Still you became pleased only after seven days and after such a Homa was performed.

*Śrī Sūrya said:*

45. You have performed all these with a Tāmasa (violent) feeling. So whatever has been performed by you has become useless.

46. Don't you know this, O Brāhmaṇa, that whatever is done by people of Tāmasa feeling becomes futile?

47. After saying thus, Sūrya touched him with his own hand. All the wounds became healed.

48-50. He said to Puṣpa once again with a pleased face: "If a person adopts gentleness and performs this *Kuśaṇḍikā* Homa in accordance with this same procedure, I will grant him much benefit. He shall use the sacrificial twigs made of Arka, tree or with gingelly seeds and raw rice grain. The Chanda and the sage invoked shall be the same. He shall offer a thousand Homas. I shall grant him more than what he wishes in his heart."

51. After saying thus the Thousand-rayed One vanished there itself like a lamp. It could not be seen which way he went away.

# CHAPTER ONE HUNDRED FIFTYEIGHT

## Maṇibhadra's Death

*Sūta said:*

1-3. Having received the two pills from the Sun, the stealer (evaporator) of waters, he took food after a long delay. Puṣpa then proceeded towards Vaidiśā.

O excellent Brāhmaṇas, Puṣpa was highly pleased in his mind when he reached Vaidiśā. He put the white pill in this mouth. Immediately, the Brāhmaṇa was transformed into one identical with Maṇibhadra.

With a highly delighted mind he entered his house which was on the main road leading to the market.

4. Then he called the eunuch stationed at the threshold. After presenting him with garments, he spoke to the eunuch:

5-6ab. "O Ṣaṇḍha (eunuch), an impostor, very clever in disguising himself, is moving about in the entire city in my guise. Now in his artificial guise, he is sure to come to our house to tempt the inmates. He should be refused entry." He (Ṣaṇḍha) nodded assent saying, "It shall be so" and stood (alert) at the entrance.

7-8. Thereafter, Puṣpa spoke to his (Maṇibhadra's) wife named Māhikā: "O Māhikā, today I saw my father Vīrabhadra standing before me clad in dirty rags and feeling highly distressed. He spoke in harsh words thus to me:

9-17a 'Fie upon you! Fie upon you! O sinful one, a very beautiful girl of excellent middle has been married by you after deceiving her father.

O my son, nothing has been given to her or to her father by you. You are keeping her like a widow always clad in white garments.

With sin lurking within you hold her back; you do not give her food to eat. So, give by all means ten thousand pieces of gold to her father.

Whatever ornament she likes, let your wife wear it and become highly delighted.

A woman without inner happiness, it is quite obvious, will not conceive. Since the line of family that is not perpetuated by a child will fall on the earth from heaven, our family will undoubtedly fall due to you, the cause of the ruin of the family.' So he said.

Now bring those excellent clothes from within the house, given by the king and the five articles of present gained by my business deals and wear these yourself. And cook our tasty dish quickly. I shall take food with you. We shall take food from the same pot. It is undoubtedly his command."

17b-18. The girl was delighted by what he said. She also did everything accordingly. She prepared the food unhesitatingly and wore the excellent garments. Then the impatiently lustful Puṣpa began the preparation for sexual intercourse.

19-20. In the meantime, Maṇibhadra came there with great earnestness. Due to his greediness and the consequent business engagement, he had become very hungry and thirsty. When he entered the house in all eagerness, he was stopped by the eunuch who repeatedly rebuked him.

21. When he forced his entry into his own house, he was hit on his head with a heavy srick.

22. Thereupon, he fell on the ground and was overcome with unconsciousness. Afflicted by the hitting (blow) he did not know what to do.

23. A great tumult arose at the gate of that house when people who flocked there also raised a hue and cry.

24-25. Some people asked him: "Fie upon you! O sinner, what have you done? By this action you have deprived yourself of the means of sustenance. Or have you been possessed by the devil? This fellow has been brought to this plight. Surely the king will hang you.

*The Ṣaṇḍha said:*

26. I have not abused my means of sustenance by this action. Nor have I been possessed by the devil. This is not Maṇibhadra. He is an imposter, other man in his guise.

27. He poses himself as Maṇibhadra. He has come here to request for money. When he forced his entry he was struck on his head by me.

28. Maṇibhadra is in fact within the house. He has taken food and is resting on his bed. He is not aware of this incident that has occurred.

* * *

29. Then Puṣpa also heard the tumultuons noise outside. He came to the door in the form of Maṇibhadra.

30-31. "Some base fellow poses like myself and comes here everyday begging for money.

Of course, this Ṣaṇḍha has not done the right thing by having struck this crooked fellow on his head for having come here to beg for money."

32-33. In the meantime, the other fellow (real Maṇibhadra) regained complete consciousness. When he looked ahead he saw a man exactly like himself. After fully surveying him he spoke these words:

34-35. "A thief has entered my house in my own form. He has bribed the eunuch with clothes to betray me. It is better you run away before I go to the king's place and get you along with this eunuch executed."

*Puṣpa said:*

36. You have come to my house in my guise thinking that the house is unoccupied. Then you come to know that I am in the house.

37. Therefore, I shall take you to the king for getting you done to death without any doubt. Or, if you wish to live, O sinful man, run away.

*Sūta said:*

38. After saying this to each other they began to fight dual. With great difficulty they were restrained by other people.

39. The kinsmen of Maṇibhadra who came there could not differentiate between the two and establish the identity of real Maṇibhadra.

40. With their large eyes blazing like heated copper due to anger, they argued and quarrelled like Bāli and Sugrīva who fought with each other over Tārā.

41. They went to the palace entrance and stood there in the midst of their own kinsmen. The king was informed by the doorman and they came to the Assembly Hall.

42. O excellent Brāhmaṇas, they appeared to be eager to slay each other and they shouted, "Oh you thief! Oh you thief!" The king glanced at both the twice-borns.

43-44. There was no bodily difference distinguishing between them. After the royal affairs at the court were over, they were asked in regard to all well-known and secret matters. They readily answered everything duly.

45. Then the kinsmen asked each of them away from the presence of the other, the details of the family and the lineage.

46. To these questions too, they gave the correct replies. Then king Bṛhatsena spoke to them all:

47. "Let the wife of Maṇibhadra be brought from his house. She shall be the real authority in identification of her husband."

48. The officers of the king went and told her, "Come on please. Find out your husband. You alone shall be the deciding authority."

49-50. Bashfully she stood before the king with the head covered and was asked: "Identify your dear husband. We do not know decisively. Nor these kinsmen of yourṣ"

51-54. Then the excellent lady thought in her mind: 'I have been scorched continuously by this Maṇibhadra in the fire of his jealousy. He orally offered plenty of cash and deceived my father. Thus he took me away but nothing was given by the sinful fellow. But this second man presented me with diverse kinds of garments and ornaments. He gave me the worldly pleasure too. He will also give my father the gold promised. So I shall grasp the second Maṇibhadra with my hand.'

55. After deciding thus mentally, she saw that the first Maṇibhadra was fully smeared with blood. So she grasped the second one.

56-57. She spoke these words when all the people listened to them: "In the presence of the sacred fire I was given in marriage to this man. This other one is an impostor of evil conduct. He has come here seeking me well-guarded by different kinds of conventions."

58. Thereupon, O excellent Brāhmaṇas, the king became furious and commanded the hanging, from the branch of a tree, of the evil-minded Maṇibhadra.

59. In the meantime, he was handed over to the hangman. As he was being led to the tree he recited these verses:

60. "These are the innate faults and defects of women: Want of mercy, hatred, crippledness, want of cleanliness and ruthlessness.

61. Women always resemble a Guñjāphala (red-black berry) poisonous within but having charming external features only.

62. The scriptural knowledge of Uśanas, the Vedic scholarship of Bṛhaspati and the wisdom of Manu and others are nothing in comparison to the wisdom of women.

63. Nectar resides in the lips of a woman and Halāhala poison in the heart. Hence the lips are kissed and tasted while the heart (chest) is pressed hard.

64. Lac juice is *Rakta* (red); so also a lustful man is *Rakta* (attached, loving). After the essence has been taken, he too is kept beneath the soles of the feet.

65. The poisonous tree of worldly existence has evil actions as the blossom and distress in hell as the fruit. Its root however is a woman of ample buttocks.

66. Who is not terribly frightened by seeing a woman from a distance?

67. Even at the first formal union, a woman makes the whirl of the mundane existence manifest under the pretext of the customary circumambulation of the sacred fire.

68. These women defile three generations of the family (or three families) through ruthlessness, want of mercy and a perpetual sluggishness in particular.

69. The abode of the three families spotlessly clean due to its reputation, is blackened by a woman with her misdeeds, like the flame of a lamp.

70. God Brahmā has created woman who upsets virtue and piety like a violent gust of wind uprooting a tree; who bedevils the minds like moonlight that destroys lotuses; who is like an alligator in the ocean of love and who is a bolt that closes the door to salvation.

71. Woman has been created by Brahmā in regard to men like a prison-house for a group of children, a net in the forest of worldly existence and an abysmal depth in the pathway to heaven.

72. Vedhas (Brahmā) could not find any other means of binding men. Hence, he made the firm noose in the form of woman."

73. Thus in the height of his sorrow he lamented much. Worried over his wife in various ways, he censured himself:

74. "I have been evil-minded and unwise. No benefit has been obtained by me from the worldy life. Nothing was given as gift by me at any time, because my mind was agitated by Tṛṣṇā (greed, thirst).

75. Although I had adequte wealth and prosperity no meritorious action has been done by me. I never performed a Japa or a Homa in the sacred fire.

76. As it has been truly expressed by a certain noble-souled man, 'Like a miser there never was a great donor nor will there ever be, because without even touching his own wealth himself, he gives it to others.'

77. Riches do kill like a poison those who seek refuge therein. They are neither given away nor enjoyed by the miser.

78. There are three states (ways of being spent) to which wealth is destined: gift, enjoyment and ruin. That which is neither given nor enjoyed meets with the third (i.e.ruin).

79. Even wealthy men also who do not give are considered as extreme type of the poor. Since the ocean does not quench the thirst, it is no better than a desert.

80. Riches are fully utilized by good people where they are at ease with to and fro movements. By coming near miserly persons, they go to sleep forever.

81. Miserly persons do not get the opportunity of enjoying pleasures because of their own Karmas. When it comes to the enjoyment of grapes, crows eating oblations suffer from inflammation of the mouth.

82. When one has adequate wealth, one should make a gift of it or enjoy it fully. One shall not hoard it. Look here: Others take away what is stored by honey-bees.

83. The well-guarded wealth of the miser that has been begged for but not distributed to excellent Brāhmaṇas, that has been hoarded but not employed in an excellent Yajña, is (finally) used up in the abodes of thieves and kings.

84. Munificence is a virtue of the wealthy; wealthiness is a virtue of the munificent; separation of wealth and munificence is a mockery.

85. What can be done with that wealth which is no exclusive possession like a bride nor a common property enjoyed even by travellers like a harlot?

86. Life is sustained by the warmth of wealth. Even without foodstuff man can have it. That by which the earth is sustained is the warmth from the miser.

87. Śeṣa (the serpent) supports the earth, thanks to the favour of the misers, because they keep their wealth under the ground and the warmth therefrom (gives comfort to Śeṣa)"

88. Thus Maṇibhadra went on prattling much. Even as he continued the prattle thus he was scolded by the men of the king with harsh words and they hanged him.

## CHAPTER ONE HUNDRED FIFTYNINE

# Puṣpa Acquires Prosperity

*Sūta said:*

1-3. Taking the excellent lady named Māhikā Puṣpa joyously went to the abode of Maṇibhadra together with all the kinsmen to the accompaniment of conches and other musical instruments.

None of them there had any doubt about him. Thanks to the favour of Bhāskara or others, he reached that abode as though it were his ancestral home.

4-6. He sat in the centre and summoned all the kinsmen. He said: "Today my fortune has hung in the balance. Though it oscillated it stood steady by the words of this excellent wife. So long extreme miserliness had overpowered me.

Today I have become aware that fortune is unsteady. In fact I have abandoned it. Hence I shall share it entirely with kinsmen, Brāhmaṇas and deities. I take a solemn oath myself."

7. After saying thus he called them severally uttering their names and gave them clothes and ornaments befittingly.

8. Then he invited Brāhmaṇas conversant with the Vedas individually by their names. With faith he gave each of them cash and clothes.

9. Then, O excellent Brāhmaṇas, he gave good food with delicacies and clothes to dancers, blind beggars and wretched people.

10. After dismissing the kinsmen along with the Brāhmaṇas, he himself took food in the company of his wife.

11. Thus another man's wealth was acquired by him which he enjoyed for long as he pleased along with his wife.

## CHAPTER ONE HUNDRED SIXTY

## Brāhmaṇas Invited for Puraścaraṇa

*Sūta said:*

1-5. On another day at night when he lay by her side, the wife massaged his feet and said to him in full confidence: "Undoubtedly you are my husband as long as I live. So, my Lord, do tell me. The other one has been forsaken by me for your sake. Is there any jugglery on your part? Or have you practised any sacred Mantra? Or is this the favour of the deities? How is it that you have come to be like this? Even on the very first day I had become aware of you when I was adorned and presented with clothes and ornaments. Oh! Were I to disclose your fraud entirely to the other one? No, no it shall not be. I touch your feet."

*Sūta said:*

6. On being told thus, O excellent Brāhmaṇas, he (Puṣpa) embraced her and spoke to her in sweet words:

7-8. "Oh my beloved! You have correctly understood all my activities. Oh fair lady! I am that Brāhmaṇa who was made to suffer by Maṇibhadra for looking at your moon-like face. I went to Camatkārapura and propitiated Ravi (Sun-god). This form and knowledge (of the details of Maṇibhadra) was granted to me by the delighted Sun-god."

*Māhikā (the wife) said:*

9-11. Merely at your sight, I was overwhelmed by Lord Kāma. Hence I shall also go and propitiate the Sun-god so that he will grant you joyously once again that original form of yours. O my Lord, of what use are my beauty and youth! I am worshipping your original form day and night.

*Sūta said:*

12. On hearing it, Puṣpa took out the other pill and placed it within his mouth. He regained that form in which she had seen him earlier.

13. Then the delighted Māhī (Māhikā) experienced horripilation. She embraced him closely and spoke these words:

14-16. "Today my birth, youth and beauty have become fruitful since you, fully comparable to Madana and desired heartily, have been obtained by me.

All these days I have been serving you in the form of the old fellow and hence only the least pleasure of love was attained by me. Now enjoy me fully, O Brāhmaṇa, to your heart's content. I am at your service, your very slave."

*Puṣpa said:*

17. Oh my beloved! I have obtained you after a long time. I do not know what to do. Shall I squeeze myself into you? Shall I merge my limbs into yours?

18. After this conversation, they indulged in close physical intimacy, O excellent Brāhmaṇas, as they got the opportunity and were fully under the control of Lord Kāma.

19. Then, as the night came to a close and the Sun's disc rose up, Puṣpa put the pill into the mouth and assumed the form similar to that of Maṇibhadra.

20. In this way, they spent a long time. Sons, daughters and grandsons were born.

21-23. When he became old and rather feeble due to senility, he thought: 'A great sin has been committed by me. The poor Maṇibhadra was treacherously made to meet his death. His wife was snatched away by me and forced to bear children. Hence I shall go to the holy spot of Hāṭakeśvara and perform the expiatory rite of *Puraścaraṇa* so that I can regain purity.'

24. After coming to this decision in his mind, Puṣpa took plenty of cash with him and went to Camtkārapura.

25. He gave to his sons severally the due share of their inheritance. Then he got a splendid palace of the Sun-god built.

26-27. The deity had been installed by Yājñavalkya and there he attained Siddhi.

Then he called his middle son. When he bowed down and made obeisance he said: "Bring a Brāhmaṇa well-versed in all the four Vedas. I shall perform the rite of expiation named *Puraścaraṇa* for the sake of purity and I shall duly pray."

## CHAPTER ONE HUNDRED SIXTYONE

# Greatness of Puṣpāditya

*Sūta said:*

1-4a. Then all the Brāhmaṇas were placed by him in the place allotted to Brahmā. Then those designated as *Cātuścaraṇas* were also placed.

Then Puṣpa shaved off hair all over his body. Accompanied by his wife, he bowed down to the excellent Brāhmaṇas. With palms joined in reverence, he spoke these words: "O Brāhmaṇas, this palace has been got built by me for the Sun-god. Let it be well-known in all the three worlds as Puṣpāditya.

*The Brāhmaṇas said:*

4b-5. We will not make the reputation of Yājñavalkya decrease and disppear. We shall grant you the expiation to your heart's content.

Some other Brāhmaṇas in the capacity of middlemen said:

6. "In connection with the Homa here, let a hundred thousand (coins) be set apart for the maintenance of this deity and another hundred thousand for the Brāhmaṇas so that the expiatory rite can be rendered clean."

*Puṣpa said:*

7. Let all the excellent Brāhmaṇas call this deity after my name and glorify this always.

8. Earlier, my wife had installed the honoured Durgā. Let it be well-known here in the excellent city after her name.

*The Brāhmaṇas said:*

9. Formerly, the palace of Hara was erected by Duśśīla. That of the deity installed by Durvāsas has been built by you with joyous minds.

10. Yet, let this palace of this distressed one be erected, O Brāhmaṇas.

11. Formerly Duśśīla propitiated the Lord merely by uttering the names. But by this (Puṣpa) the Sun-god Bhāskara had been propitiated earlier by means of his own flesh.

12. Hence there is no harm in giving the deity his name. What has been earlier installed by Māhikā shall be Māhī.

*Sūta said:*

13. When the requisite Dāna was made by Puṣpa with the approval of the Brāhmaṇas, the name well known as Puṣpāditya was given by the middle ones.

14. Goddess Durgā who was formerly installed by his wife named Māhikā, came to be known as Māhī.

*Sūta said:*

15. O excellent Brāhmaṇas, everything I was asked has been thus told, i.e. how the deity installed by Yājñavalkya became Puṣpāditya.

16. Even now in Kali age, that Lord of Suras, if visited devoutly, shall destroy the sin of men caused that day. There is no doubt about it.

17. Further, if a devotee holds a fruit and circumambulates one hundred eight times on a Sunday coinciding with the seventh lunar day, O excellent Brāhmaṇas, he shall obtain the desired benefits.

18. He who visits Durgā Māhikā everyday, will never meet with difficulties at all on that day.

19. If a man worships her on the fourteenth lunar day in the bright half of Caitra, no disaster shall befall him for the whole of that year.

## CHAPTER ONE HUNDRED SIXTYTWO

## Procedure of Puraścaraṇa Saptamī

*Sūta said:*

1-5. When the name was thus assigned unto Bhāskara of many rays, Puṣpa confessed all his misdeeds before the Brāhmaṇas, such as how Maṇibhadra was got executed and how his wife was fraudulently made his own wife.

On hearing it, the Brāhmaṇas became highly furious. Expressing strong protest they said: "O sinner, fie upon you! Go away with your gold and all; you cannot be sanctified. You are in fact a *Brahmaghna* (Brāhmaṇa-slayer) because all the three castes, Brāhmaṇas, Kṣatriyas and Vaiśyas are *Dvijottamas* (excellent twice-borns) as declared by the writers of the Smṛtis and scriptural texts."

*Sūta said:*

6. Thereupon, Puṣpa was grief-stricken. His eyes were filled with tears. He came out of the space allotted to the Brāhmaṇas and cried in great sorrow.

7. On seeing him lamenting continuously, those Nāgara Brāhmaṇas felt compassion for him and spoke to one another.

8-11. "The scriptural texts are of various kinds. The Smṛtis are diverse. With great concentration pore through all the Purāṇas. See whether some means of his purification somewhere (in some texts) is found. There cannot be any scriptural text that is not available in this holy spot.

O excellent Brāhmaṇas, the same is the case with Smṛti, Purāṇa and Vedānta. Further there is no Brāhmaṇa here who is not on a par with the ommiscient (Śiva). Hence, ponder over this quickly as to what can accord him purity. Taking that as an authority, the purificatory rite of this Puṣpa can be performed."

12-14. Then a Brāhmaṇa well known as Caṇḍa Śarman said: "In this Skanda Purāṇa,[1] I have read about Puraścaraṇa Saptamī. A sin committed shall vanish through this Puraścaraṇa. O leading Brāhmaṇas, there is no doubt about it. Hence let him perform this rite of Puraścaraṇa Saptamī."

15. Another thing: Maṇibhadra was executed by the hangmen at the behest of the king. If at all there is a sin, it is his (the king's).

16. In the capacity of judge, if the king does not carefully examine the plaintiff, the terrible sin devolves only on the king.

17. Now coming to the sin of his wife: She knowingly said, 'Earlier, it was this (Puṣpa) to whom I was given by my father and the Brāhmaṇas in the presence of fire.'

18-19. Through this deceptive means what has been committed is tit for tat. Hence there is no fault because leading sages have said: 'One should do in return what has been done to one. If one is injured one can injure in return. If one commits a michief or wickedness towards a mischievous or wicked fellow there is no fault (sin)'."

*The Brāhmaṇas said:*

20. O Brāhmaṇas, if it so, prescribe this procedure of Puraścaraṇa Saptamī for the sake of this poor Brāhmaṇa's purity today.

21. O excellent Brāhmaṇas, the Brāhmaṇa named Caṇḍa Śarman took pity on him and explained the Saptamī rite.

22. The rite was performed by him in the manner it was heard from him directly (orally). Then at the close of the year, he became free from sins.

*The sages said:*

23. O Sūtaja, expound the rite called *Puraścaraṇa Saptamī*. What is the procedure by which it should be carried out? What is the time? Where should it be performed?

---

1. It seems that another *Skanda Purāṇa* existed when this chapter of the present text was written.

*Sūta said:*

24. I shall narrate to you all that was said to King Rohitāśva by Mārkaṇḍeya formerly, on being devoutly asked by him.

25. O Brāhmaṇas, the great sage named Mārkaṇḍeya was one who could remember (the events of) seven Kalpas. He was asked by Rohitāśva, the son of Hariścandra:

*Rohitāśva said:*

26. O excellent sage, tell me some means to get rid of a sin that a man commits knowingly or unknowingly.

*Mārkaṇḍeya said:*

27. Sins of men occur in the world in three differentt ways viz. mental, verbal and physical.

28. Means for their eradication have been duly expounded. O excellent king, listen, I shall describe them.

29. In regard to mental sin that men commit, it perishes instantly when they repent for it.

30. A verbal sin does not perish before the fruit is reaped except in a case where Puraścaraṇa rite is performed. It is the truth that has been uttered by me.

31. After confessing it to eminent Brāhmaṇas one should perform the expiatory rite as (may be) instructed by them. Then he shall regain purity.

32. Or, if the king comes to know of it and he metes out the suitable punishment, then he regains purity even if he is sinful.

33. If out of shame, he does not at all confess before eminent Brāhmaṇas nor the king comes to know of it and the fellow dies even as the sin clings to his body, then Yama, the son of Vivasvān, will himself give him adequate punishment.

34. Hence, a person who commits a sin knowingly should assiduously perform the expiatory rite as instructed by the Brāhmaṇas.

*Rohitāśva said:*

35. O great sage, mention some Vrata, Dāna or Homa for the eradication of all the sins committed so that the person can be rid of sins without *Puraścaraṇa*.

36. A man commits very subtle sins everyday. How can he have the capacity to perform expiatory rite for all of them?

*Mārkaṇḍeya said:*

37. O king, there is a pious Vrata called Puraścaraṇa. The rite of *Puraścaraṇa Saptamī* is a favourite with the Sun-god.

38. O king, if this rite is performed, Yama's personal clerk Vivitra (Citragupta) shall wipe off the sins committed and accumulated in the course of a birth.

39. Hence, O great king, carry out my instruction immediately so that you can be rid of all the sins clinging to the body.

*Rohitāśva said:*

40. O excellent sage, by what procedure and at what time should the rite of Puraścaraṇa Saptamī be performed? Tell me.

*Mārkaṇḍeya said:*

41. One should perform this Vrata on the seventh lunar day in the bright half of the month of Māgha when the Sun is in Capricorn and it (the day) coincides with a Sunday.

42. On that day a devotee should not talk with heretics and hypocritical persons, O excellent king. Early in the morning the devotee chews a twig for cleaning the teeth. Afterwards, the Niyama (restraint) is to be observed by uttering this Mantra:

43. "O Lord of day, I shall observe fast as a part of the rite of Puraścaraṇa Saptamī. Today you are my refuge."

44. Then in the afternoon he takes bath and remains pure wearing washed clothes. He shall then worship with devotion the image of the Lord of Day.

45.[1] O great hero, the devotee worships the foot etc. with red flowers. The feet of the Sun-god are to be worshipped by saying "Obeisance to Pataṅga." It is in this way that the different parts of the person of the Sun-god are to be

1. These verses state the particular Mantra to be recited at the time of worshipping the particular part of the Sun-god's idol.

worshipped with flowers. The knees (of the Sun-god) shall be worshipped with the Mantra "Obeisance to Mārtaṇḍa."

46. "Obeisance to the Lord of Day" (privy). "Obeisance to one of twelve forms" (navel). "Obeisance to the Lord with lotus in hand" (arms). "O fiery-rayed one" (chest).

47. "Obeisance to the one having the lustre of lotus petals" (the neck). "Obeisance to the resplendent one" (the head)."

After worshipping duly the form, one should offer camphor.

48. Cooked rice mixed with jaggery should be the food offering. It should be covered with a red cloth. O king, the Dīpa (lamp) and Ārārtika (waving of lights) shall be with red thread.

49. The devotee then takes water in a conch and puts red sandalpaste therein. After placing a fruit thereon he offers the *Arghya*.

50. (Mantra) "O Lord, expiatory rite has been performed for the misdeed that has been committed knowingly or unknowingly. Let my *Arghya* be received."

51. Then the devotee honours the Brāhmaṇa with scents, flowers and unguents. After serving him food and giving him Dakṣiṇā according to one's capacity the devotee should eat *pañcagavya* (five products of a cow) for the purification of the body.

52. With palms joined in reverence, looking up towards the Sun and meditating on the Sun the devotee should recite this Mantra:

53. "O Lord Bhāskara, this Vrata is observed by me in front of you. With the favour of Your Lordship, let it reach perfection (completion) without obstacles."

54. Then, at the advent of the month of Phālguna, O excellent sage, the devotee should worship the Lord with Kunda flowers in accordance with the same procedure (explained previously).

55. For the purpose of purification of all sins the devotee offers *Guggulu* incense and cooked food (rice) as Naivedya. Then he eats Gomaya (i.e. *Pañcagavya*).

56-57a. In the month of Caitra, the devotee worships Hari with Surabhi (fragrance). "Guṇikās" are cited as the food offering and the resin of Sarja constitutes the incense. The devotee gains the purity of the body by imbibing Kuśa water.

57b. In the month of Vaiśākha, the worship (of the Sun-god) is done with Kiṁśuka flowers and drinkiing of Ghee (for purification).

58. The Naivedya is meat and liquor. Incense is to be offered. Drinking of curd should be done for the purification of the body.

59-60a. (In Jyeṣṭha) O king, the worship of Ravi is to be performed by means of Pāṭala flowers. *Saktu* (barley flour?) is recommended for food offering.

Ghee prepared from the milk of a tawny-coloured cow should be imbibed for the eradication of sins, O great hero.

60b-61. In the month of Āṣāḍha, O king, one should worship Bhāskara with Muni flowers. Ghārikās (small cakes of flour, jaggery and fruit boiled in ghee) are prescribed as the Naivedya (food offering to the deity).

62. The worship of the Fiery-rayed One (the Sun) in Śrāvaṇa is to be performed with Kadamba flowers. Modakas (sweetmeat) are offered as Naivedya and Tagara is to be used for incense.

63-64a. By taking in the water from Gośṛṅga (cow's horn) the devotee is rid of sins immediately.

The adoration in Bhādrapada is by means of Jāti flowers. Milk is offered as Naivedya.

The incense arises from claws (of certain animals). Milk is used for imbibing.

64b-65. In the month of Āśvina the worship is performed with lotus flowers. *Ghṛtapūrikā* (Puris fried in ghee) is to be offered as Naivedya.

The incense is from saffron and Karpūra water (flavoured with camphor) is to be imbibed.

66. O king, in the month of Kārttika the worship of Bhāskara is done by means of Tulasī. Khaṇḍa (sugar candy) is offered as Naivedya and the incense is from Kusuṁbha.

67. Laviṅga (clove) is to be taken in as destructive of all sins.

In the month of Saumya (Mārgaśīrṣa) one should perform the worship by means of Bhṛṅgarāja.

68. Pheṇikā (a kind of sweetmeat) is to be offered as Naivedya.

The incense comes from jaggery. For the satisfaction of Bhāskara, Kaṅkola should be taken in.

69. It is ordained in the Smṛti that the worship of Ravi in the month of Pauṣa should be done by means of Śatapatrikā (hundred-petalled lotus). Something natural (easily available) is offered as incense and *Śaṣkuli* (fried flour-coils) has to be offered as Naivedya.

70. As for imbibing, one can have all the things mentioned before. At the conclusion of the adoration one-sixth of the income of the household is to be given as Dakṣiṇā.

71. O excellent one among kings, the above-mentioned Dakṣiṇā is to be given to a Brāhmaṇa for the eradication of all sins. Thereafter friends and persons of one's choice are to be fed in accordance with one's capacity.

72. He who performs the Saptamī rite unto Bhāskara in this manner shall become pure after being rid of all sins.

*The Brāhmaṇas said:*

73. Thus the procedure was formerly described to the intelligent Rohitāśva by Mārkaṇḍeya. O highly esteemed one, do this yourself too.

74. Thereby the *Puraścaraṇa* rite will be perfected in your case.

*Sūta said:*

75. On hearing his words, O excellent Brāhmaṇas, Puṣpa too joyously performed that Saptamī rite in the manner described by him.

76. To that noble-souled Brāhmaṇa, he gave a sixth of all his wealth as a householder in the form of costly gems or ordinary metals.

77. He too accepted with a delighted mind that wealth in the form of innumerable gifts of gold and gems.

## CHAPTER ONE HUNDRED SIXTYTHREE

# Creation of Brāhma Nāgara [Community][1]

*Sūta said:*

1. On seeing that pot of wealth, all the Nāgaras (citizens with that appellation) came to the agreement that the pot should not be accepted by anyone.

2. They abandoned all their desires (for money). They made an agreement (within themselves) and appointed a "middleman" (umpire-like decision-maker). Stationed in the place assigned to Brahmā, they announced through the oral declaration of the middleman:

3-7. "The greedy one (i.e.Caṇḍaśarman) has ignored and dishonoured excellent Brāhmaṇas, accepted cash from Puṣpa and performed the expiatory rite.

A sixth of his (Puṣpa's) riches was received by him. So he will be excluded by all of us, the leading Brāhmaṇas of Nāgara (community). He will be on a par with a low-caste one. From now onwards, he who associates with this fellow shall also be excommunicated from the society of all the Nāgaras. He who accepts food or beverage from his house shall also become a fallen one in this manner."

8. After saying this, he clapped thrice from the place (post) of Brahmā and made him (Caṇḍaśarman) like a stale flower (that is thrown away).

9. Then all those Brāhmaṇas, went to their respective abodes. Caṇḍaśarman became highly distressed and went near Puṣpa.

10-11. (He said:) "It is with the consent of all these (Brāhmaṇas) that expiatory rite for you was performed by me. Still I have been declared as fallen from grace. I shall, therefore, fall into the well-kindled fire. I do not wish to remain alone after being forsaken by my people."

*Puṣpa said:*

12. O excellent Brāhmaṇa, do not be distressed in this

1. The legend in this chapter explains the formation of 'Brāhma Nāgara' as a subcommunity of Nāgaras (vide vv 35-37).

matter, as you have been slighted by the excellent Brāhmaṇas for the sake of money.

13-14. In order to get your person purified, I shall make those Nāgaras delighted by means of different kinds of wealth. I shall give them as much as they request for. For your sake I shall give them that much.

After saying this, he hurriedly came back to Brahmasthāna.

15-16. He caused the Cātuścaraṇa to be brought. Through the mouth of the middleman he said: "For my sake, the Brāhmaṇa Caṇḍaśarman has been rendered fallen from grace by you all due to your greed for money. I shall give you all the wealth that is in my house. Let this request be accepted by the Brāhmaṇas."

17. Then those angry Brāhmaṇas made different kinds of gruff sounds. With the eyes reddened due to anger they said:

18-22. "Fie upon you! Fie upon you! Oh sinful one. How is it that your tongue does not get split into a hundred pieces though you prattle this despicable thing!

This Brāhmaṇa has not been excommunicated and rendered fallen from grace for the sake of money. It is because the expiatory rite was performed by this wicked soul single-handed.

By performing this rite thus, Smṛtis have been defiled (by transgressing them). Purāṇas have been slighted and further this holy spot of ours has been rendered unholy.

Expiatory rite is to be performed after consulations with four others. O excellent Brāhmaṇas, this has been said by Manu.

Your sin has today clung to his body because the rite has been performed by him single-handedly. Therefore, he has fallen from grace."

*Sūta said:*

23. After saying this, all the Brāhmaṇas went to their respective abodes. Puṣpa too was much distressed and utterly confused.

24. He returned to his residence heaving sighs like a hissing serpent.

25-27. Then he thought, 'Human beings cannot attain Siddhi unless they take risks. Therefore, I shall perform something great for the sake of Caṇḍaśarman lest there should be ungratefulness. Wise men have declared thus:

"Rites of redemption have been laid down by good people in the case of a slayer of a Brāhmaṇa, an imbiber of liquor, a thief and one who breaks his vows. But there is no rite of redemption in the case of the ungrateful."

28-29. After resolving thus, O excellent Brāhmaṇas, when Sunday coincided with the seventh lunar day, he made one hundred eight circumambulations of Puṣpāditya. That sensible (Brāhmaṇa) took up a sharp weapon. As before he cut off pieces from his limbs and consigned them to the sacred fire.

30. When he wanted to offer the remaining part of his body as Pūrṇāhuti, the Sun-god himself appeared and said to him:

31. "O Puṣpa, O sinless one, do not be rash. I am pleased with you again. O highly esteemed one, what shall I give you?"

*Puṣpa said:*

32. O Lord, this leading Brāhmaṇa Caṇḍaśarman has been rendered fallen on account of me by all the Nāgaras. Do make him equal to them.

33. It was after going through the scriptural texts that the noble-souled one performed the expiation rite. Still all the mean fellows who were intolerant (and jealous) censured (rendered fallen) him.

*The Lord said:*

34. O excellent Brāhmaṇa, it is impossible to alter the words of even a single Nāgara. Still more so the joint declaration of all the Nāgaras.

35. But this Caṇḍaśarman shall become purified. He will be well-known all over the earth as Brāhmanāgara.

36. All his sons and descendants will become well-known all over the world. They will be honoured and esteemed by kings.

37. All the kinsmen and friends who associate with him shall also become splendid.

38. You too shall get back your entire physical body by my grace.

39. After saying this the Thousand-rayed One vanished. Puṣpa instantly regained his wounded limbs intact.

## CHAPTER ONE HUNDRED SIXTYFOUR

# Installation of Nāgeśvara etc.

*Sūta said:*

1-2. In the meantime, Puṣpa went to the abode of Caṇḍaśarman with a delighted heart. He saw him with pallid face and eyes filled with tears in the company of all kinsmen, wife, sons and servants. He exclaimed "Thank God! Thank God!" and said thus:

*Puṣpa said:*

3. For your sake the Sun-god has been propitiated by me by sacrificing my own body. Due to his favour, the state of being a fallen fellow shall not befall you.

4. Your sons, grandsons and all your successors yet to be born shall surpass the Nāgaras in good qualities and features.

5. Hence get ready. We shall go to the holy river Sarasvatī[1] in order to settle on her banks, O Brāhmaṇa, after building a hermitage there.

6-9. Definitely I too shall stay with you. There is no doubt about it. I have ample wealth. I shall maintain all your followers too. Leave all of your mental worries and anguish.

On hearing it, Caṇḍaśarman set off from Nagara[2] towards Sarasvatī accompanied by his sons and kinsmen.

With great grief and tears filling the eyes, he bowed down and circumambulated the holy spot. Accompanied by Puṣpa and repeatedly enlightened by him, he went towards the North.

10. They reached the meritorious river Sarasvatī of cool waters, tremulous with garland-like waves and ripples and served by groups of sages.

11. Relying on the suggestion of Puṣpa, he then set up his residence on her southern banks along with all his kinsmen.

12. While staying in Nagara, Caṇḍaśarman had taken the vow that he would take food only after visiting twenty-seven Liṅgas.

---

1. This is Prācī Sarasvatī on the bank of which there was a settlement of this branch of Nāgara Brāhmaṇas.
2. Modern Vadnagar, Dist. Ahmedabad, Gujarat.

13. Constantly remembering the vow taken earlier, O excellent Brāhmaṇas, his heart continued to burn day and night.

14. He took his bath in Sarasvatī with great concentration and regained cleanliness. Then he performed the Japa of the six-lettered Mantra severally (for every Liṅga).

15. He uttered the name of the particular Liṅga and made it end with *namaḥ*. O excellent Brāhmaṇas, he made the Liṅgas five hundred Aṅgulas long out of mud.

16. After installing them he devoutly adored them with flowers, incense and unguents. Thereafter, with great faith he performed the japa of Prāṇa Rudra Mantras.

17. One should not remove or dislodge a Liṅga whether it is firmly installed or remains unsteady. With this in view, the leading Brāhmaṇa did not perform the ritualistic *Visarjana* (dismissal).

18. Everyday he made twenty-seven Liṅgas out of mud and all these were heaped up, O excellent Brāhmaṇas.

19. In the course of a long time a huge mountain of clay piled up there.

20. Mahādeva became pleased with the excess of his devotion. Breaking open the surface of the earth he appeared and showed him a Liṅga.

21-23. He spoke courteously to him in words majestic like the rumbling of a cloud: "O Brāhmaṇa Caṇḍaśarman, I am pleased with this devotion of yours. So with great devotion do worship this Liṅga. Thereby you will get the benefit of worshipping twenty-seven Liṅgas. Another man too who happens to worship this will derive the benefit of worshipping all the twenty-seven Liṅgas."

24. After saying thus, the Lord vanished therefrom. Caṇḍaśarman joyously and truthfully as per prescribed procedure worshipped it.

25. He caused a splendid palace constructed for the Liṅga. He pondered over the matter frequently and arrived at a name to be given to it.

26. He happened to remember the Liṅgas stationed in Nagara. Hence he decided: "This shall be named Nāgareśvara."

*Sūta said:*

27. Thus, O excellent Brāhmaṇas, Caṇḍaśarman installed that Liṅga and propitiated it with flowers, incense and unguents.

28. Thus, O excellent Brāhmaṇas, he obtained the benefit of worshipping all the twenty-seven Liṅgas that were in Nagara.

29. After a long time, Nāgareśvara having been gratified, he sitting in the centre of a vehicle went directly to Śivaloka.

30. Puṣpa installed another Puṣpāditya on the banks of Sarasvatī and then became engaged in its worship.

31-32. He (Śiva) appeared before him and spoke these words with pleasure: "O Puṣpa, welfare unto you. O devotee of good holy vows, I am pleased with you. Request for a boon. I shall grant it to you even if it happens to be one that should not be granted. Hence do not delay. Request for it."

*Puṣpa said:*

33. If you are pleased, O Lord, with me, if a boon has to be granted to me, then even as I beg, grant to me what is in my heart.

34. O Lord, you have twelve Mūrtis (forms) stationed in Camatkārapura. They are worthy of being worshipped by all the Heaven-dwellers.

35. A man on the earth who worships your form that has been installed by me here, should get the entire benefit of all of them.

36. Let this form that has been installed on the banks of Sarasvatī in a palace be well-known all over the world as Nāgarāditya.

*Sūta said:*

37. Lord Ravi (Sun-god) promised, "Let it be so" and vanished like a lamp. It was all miraculous, O excellent Brāhmaṇas.

38. Then after a long time, O excellent Brāhmaṇas, Puṣpa attained the world of Sun-god by means of an aerial chariot of great refulgence.

39. Caṇḍaśarman had a wife well-known by the name Śākambharī. Durgā was installed by her on the excellent banks of Sarasvatī.

40. O excellent Brāhmaṇas, she was propitiated day and night with great devotion. Thereafter, she became pleased and granted her a boon:

41. "O dear daughter, I am pleased with you. Welfare unto you, O Śākambharī, let what has been always cherished by you in your heart be received as the boon, with my favour undoubtedly".

*Śākambharī said:*

42-43. O goddess, there are sixty-four groups of the Mothers settled in Camatkārapura. It is well-known that they become satisfied by laughter indulged in by one at night. The offer of oblations at the time of prosperity also satisfied them. Let all those merits accrue to one who worships your idol.

44. The idol has been installed by me after coming to the banks of the river.

*Śrī Devī said:*

45-46. In the bright half of Āśvina on the ninth day called Mahānavamī, if a devotee comes before me and worships devoutly, he will have the entire fruit immediately. There is no doubt about it. Particularly in the case of a Nāgara it is so. It is the truth that has been uttered by me.

47. After saying thus, the goddess vanished. That goddess is called on the earth after her name Śakambharī.

48. After Vṛddhi (prosperity) if a man worships her, there shall never be any impediment to his prosperity, O excellent Brāhmaṇas.

## CHAPTER ONE HUNDRED SIXTYFIVE

# Origin of Aśva Tīrtha

*Sūta said:*

1-5. Ever since then on the splendid and auspicious banks of Sarasvatī, a great holy spot of persons outside Nāgaras took shape, O excellent Brāhmaṇas.

They flourished with sons, daughters and grandsons ahead of Camatkārapura and it became well-known through learning and riches.

Once upon a time Sarasvatī was angrily cursed by the intelligent Viśvāmitra and was made to flow with blood.

Thenceforth, it is resorted to by delighted Rākṣasas day and night, and also by Bhūtas, Pretas and Piśācas engaged in singing and dancing.

*The sages said:*

6. Why was Sarasvatī cursed by the intelligent Viśvāmitra? What offence was committed against him by the great river?

*Sūta said:*[1]

7-8. Formerly, there arose a great enmity between Viśvāmitra and Vasiṣṭha for the sake of Brāhmaṇahood, O Brāhmaṇas. The great enmity was deadly.

Viśvāmitra, the great sage, was called a Brāhmaṇa by all though he was a Kṣatriya. This they did keeping Pitāmaha, the Lord of Devas, at the head. Vasiṣṭha alone did not do so. Hence this enmity grew up.

*The sages said:*

9-10. O highly intelligent one, how was Viśvāmitra a Brāhmaṇa, though he was really a Kṣatriya? How was it that he was not (called so by Vasiṣṭha, though he was called so by Brahmā himself?) Narrate this entirely to us. We have great curiosity.

1. The story of the curse of Sarasvatī is taken from Mbh, *Śalya*. 42. 38-39. But it was not Prācī Sarasvatī but Sarasvatī in Kurukṣetra area which was cursed.

*Sūta said:*

11. Formerly, there was a great sage named Ṛcīka. He was son of Bhṛgu. He was a regular observer of holy vows and engaged in regular study of the Vedas. He was highly renowned as an excellent ascetic.

12. By way of pilgrimage that leading sage once reached the holy spot named Bhojakaṭa.[1] It was in the dominion of King Gādhi. It was there that the river named Kauśikī flowed. It is well known in all the three worlds.

13. The excellent Brāhmaṇa took his holy bath there. He offered oblations to the Pitṛs and Devatās. Then he stationed himself on its banks performing Japa and meditating.

14. By that time the splendid princess came there. She was fully endowed with all characteristic features and all good qualities.

15. Hardly had he espied that girl, splendid in every limb, when he was fully overwhelmed by the arrows of Kāma. He was at a loss to know what he should do.

16-17. Regaining his balance of mind with very great difficulty, he asked the people: "Whose daughter is this excellent maiden? Why has she come here? Where will this exquisite girl go? Let everything be told to me, O people."

*The people said:*

18. This is the daughter of Gādhi, well-known by the name Trailokyasundarī.[2] Desirous of performing the worship of Gaurī, she has come here from the palace.

19. She covets an excellent husband having the full complement of all good qualities. Yonder you see a very huge palace situated on the banks of the river.

20. Umā is present here and is adored by all the Suras. This maiden has bathed the image of the goddess and has concluded the adoration duly.

21. After making different kinds of food offerings she will

---

1. The author seems confused. Bhojakata is in Vidarbha while Kosī (Kauśikī) is not in Vidarbha. Gādhi was the king of Kānyakubja (Kanauj), Uttar Pradesh.
2. Satyavatī according to Mbh, *Śānti* 49.7.

amuse herself of playing on the lute delighting the ears (of the listeners).

22. Thereafter, she will go back to the palace when the sun becomes less bright.

Ṛcīka was moved much on hearing the words of the people.

23. He was afflicted by the arrows of Kāma and so hastened to the abode of Gādhi. On noticing that Ṛcīka, the most excellent one among the descendants of Bhṛgu, had come all of a sudden, Gādhi, the most excellent one among kings, hurried to him to receive him directly.

24. After paying him obeisance in accordance with the injunctions laid down in the Gṛhya Sūtras, he stood with palms joined in reverence and spoke these words:

25. "O Brāhmaṇa, it is certain that you are free from desires. What may be the purpose of your visit? Do tell me entirely so that I shall give you everything."

*Ṛcīka said:*

26. O eminent king, haven't you a daughter of excellent complexion, befitting a good bridegroom? O king, do give her to me in accordance with the Brāhma mode of marriage.

27. It is for this purpose that I have come to your abode. I am tormented by Smara (god of Love). O king, I have already seen her when she came out for the sake of the adoration of Gaurī.

*Sūta said:*

28. On hearing those words, the excellent king hesitated in view of his belonging to a different caste. Besides he was very old and poor. In openly refusing him he was afraid of being cursed by him and so spoke thus trying to make an excuse.

29. "O excellent Brāhmaṇa, among us there is the practice of offering a fee when asking for a girl in marriage. If you are able to offer the requisite fee I shall undoubtedly give her to you."

*Ṛcīka said:*

30. O tiger among kings, tell me quickly what you intend

to have, by way of the requisite dowry so that I can readily offer it to you even if it happens to be very rare.

*Gādhi said:*

31-32. O eminent Brāhmaṇa, I demand seven hundred horses having the speed of wind. They shall be white in colour but the ears on one side shall be black. Whoever brings them and gives them to me, I shall give the daughter unto him.

*Sūta said:*

33. The excellent sage Ṛcīka promised, "It shall be so". He went to Kānyakubja and settled on the banks of Gaṅgā.

34. Thereafter he performed the Japa of the Sūkta among the famous sixty-four Sūktas beginning with *aśvo voḍha* (RV IX.112.4) proclaiming the Chandas, the names of the deities and the sages.

35. The application was for the sake of horses as demanded by Gādhi. Thereupon, O Brāhmaṇas, those horses rose up from the water.

36. They were completely white. They had great speed. One of the ears was black. There were seven hundred of them with as many men incharge of them.

37. Ever since then it became well-known all over the world as Aśvatīrtha. It is on the sacred and splendid banks of Gaṅgā, very near Kānyakubja. A man who takes his holy bath there shall obtain the benefit of a horse-sacrifice.

## CHAPTER ONE HUNDRED SIXTYSIX

# Birth of Paraśurāma

*Sūta said:*

1-5. Ṛcīka took those horses along with the obedient men incharge and went to the place where Gādhi was present.

He offered those excellent horses to the king for the sake of the maiden. Gādhi took them as they were worthy of horse-sacrifice. Each of them surpassed the other and the king derived great pleasure.

Thereupon, he gave his daughter Trailokyasundarī to him in accordance with the injunctions laid down in the Gṛhyasūtras. He gave the daughter in marriage in which the Fire-god and Brāhmaṇas were the witnesses.

But after the formal rite of marriage had been concluded, Ṛcīka, the excellent sage, became uninterested in cohabitation with her.

The sage without passionate attachment spoke to his wife:

6. "O lady of excellent buttocks, I am going to the forest for performing penance. Do request for some boon, so that I can give you what is desired by you."

7. On hearing the words uttered without any sexual attachment, she became distressed. With eyes filled with tears, she went to her mother.

8. O excellent Brāhmaṇas! She told her about the words of her husband who had no sexual desire but who offered her a boon.

9. O excellent Brāhmaṇas, on hearing the words uttered by her daughter, the mother spoke these words:

10-11. "O my daughter, if this husband of yours is giving whatever is desired by you as boon unto you, then request for a son endowed with Brāhmaṇical virtues.

O splendid girl, on my behalf also request for a son full of the refulgence of a Kṣatriya, since I have been without a son so long."

12. On hearing the words of her mother, the maiden of excellent holy vows went to Ṛcīka and told him what had been mentioned by her mother in full details.

13. On hearing her words, he duly performed Putreṣṭi sacrifice, bowed down to the Self-born Lord and prepared two Carus.

14. One of the Carus (Consecrated food offering) he charged with all Brāhmaṇical radiance in one and the other with the refulgence pertaining to Kṣatriyas, O excellent Brāhmaṇas.

15-16. He gave the former, the excellent Brāhmaṇical Caru, to his wife and told her, "Take this in and embrace an Aśvattha tree. Thereby you will get an excellent son endowed with Brāhmaṇical radiance. Give unto your mother this second Caru."

17-18. Then the excellent sage Ṛcīka spoke to her (the

mother): "Do eat this Caru and embrace a Nyagrodha tree. Thereby you will get an excellent son endowed with the entire radiance of Kṣatriya, O highly esteemed one, my words cannot be futile."

19. After saying thus, Ṛcīka joyously charged with two types of refulgence. The excellent Brāhmaṇa was in a happy (euphoric) mood.

20. They returned home in a highly delighted mood. They spoke to each other, "It will certainly take place."

21-24. Then the mother said to the daughter: "When the work on hand is common, it is the practice of all people to do something special.

O lady of excellent eyes, he would have certainly charged a group of Mantras into the Caru that was prepared for you. O highly esteemed one, it is the truth that has been uttered by me.

Hence, O lady of splendid smiles, take my Caru and give yours to me. Let there be alteration in the matter of embracing the trees too. O highly esteemed lady, thereby an excellent son will be born to me.

He will be an expert in the administration of the kingdom. He will be a hero capable of suppressing the army of enemies. Your son shall certainly delight you though he may be only a Brāhmaṇa[1]."

25. On being told thus in secret by her mother, the lady of great renown interchanged the Carus and the trees, O excellent Brāhmaṇas.

26. In the course of the Puṁsavana rite both the ladies of charming eyes had their holy baths and conceived instantly by the intimate contact with the husband.

27. After the conception Trailokyasundarī (Satyavatī) became instantly endowed with the refulgence special to Kṣatriyas. She began to think mentally of kingdoms, riding on elephants and horses and the like.

28. Stories regarding the battles between the hosts of Devas and Asuras were discussed and listened to and the mind was directed towards enjoyment. She put into practice many of her mental plans.

1. These two verses are irrelevant. Actually, the change was accidental, not premeditated (Mbh, *Śānti* 49. 18-28).

29. She caused excellent horses and elephants to be fetched from her father's house. Red garments and (saffron) unguents from Kāśmīra and other things too were brought.

30. Ṛcīka noticed the various activities of his wife befitting regal status and the enjoyment of diverse kinds of pleasures. She totally eschewed activities and behaviour worthy of Brāhmaṇas.

31-38. Thereupon, he angrily spoke: "O sinful lady, fie upon you! What has been committed ? Certainly interchange of the Carus and the trees has been committed by you.

O sinful lady, I do see that your activities are like these due to that. These activities suit Kṣatriyas. They are avoided in all the activities of Brāhmaṇas.

Bark garments are abandoned. You perform neither holy bath nor Japa. Various kinds of scents such as musk are used (by you). On the other hand your mother is tranquil and quiescent. She is devoted to Japa and Homa and is inclined towards pilgrimage and listening to Vedic Chants. Hence, there is no doubt about it that your son will be a Kṣatriya.

From the characteristic features of the pregnancy, it is certain that an excellent Brāhmaṇa devoted to propagation and practice of celibacy will be born to your mother.

Formerly this was said by the expounders of scriptural texts: 'The innate quality of the sons of young women in pregnancy will be in conformity with their longings and inclinations (of the mother) at that time.'

On being told thus, she trembled much in her great fright. She remained standing with palms joined in reverence.

39-40. With tears filling her eyes, the distressed maiden spoke these words: "O holy lord, the words spoken by you are true. Without the help of (telltale) signs, you can (directly) know the past and future. Hence, do me this favour of making my son a Brāhmaṇa. A Kṣatriya son does not befit you."

*Ṛcīka said:*

41. Whatever Brāhmaṇical refulgence there was had been deposited by me in the Caru intended for you and the regal refulgence in that intended for your mother. If I were to cause any change in this, I will be transgressing the scriptural injunction.

*The wife said:*

42-43. If it is so, O tiger among the descendants of Bhṛgu, let there be the entire Kṣatriya refulgence caused by you manifested in my grandson to be. Let the son be an excellent Brāhmaṇa even excelling you.

*Ṛcīka said:*

44. O splendid lady, let it be so. At my instance, your son will be a Brāhmaṇa and the grandson, an irresistible one in battle. He will be equipped with the radiance special to Kṣatriyas.

45. On obtaining the truthful boon, the chaste lady was delighted with the face beaming fully. She told her mother what was stated by her husband.

46. Then, in the tenth month, in the constellation Puṣya (the constellation with Bṛahspati as the deity) she gave birth to a son on a par with the rising Sun.

47. He was endowed with the Brāhmaṇical glory. He was clean, a storehouse of austerities. He was well-known in all the three worlds as Jamadagni. His son became well known by the name Rāma.

48. It was by him that the earth was rid of Kṣatriyas twentyone times, thanks to the favour of Pitāmaha and the power of the radiance pertaining to Kṣatriyas.

## CHAPTER ONE HUNDRED SIXTYSEVEN

# Viśvāmitra Renounces Kingdom

*Sūta said:*

1-3. By taking in the Caru and as a result of the Mantras, Gādhi's auspicious wife conceived during those days.

O excellent Brāhmaṇas, when the splendid lady became pregnant she became interested in pilgrimage. The chaste lady was highly devoted to holy Vratas.

Whereever the sound of Vedic chanting arose she became delighted and experienced horripilation in all her limbs. She always listened to it eagerly even ignoring all the ornaments and embellishments pertaining to the royal status and the happiness therefrom.

4. O excellent Brāhmaṇas, when the tenth month arrived she gave birth to a lustrous son endowed with Brāhmaṇical glory and radiance.

5. He became well-known as Viśvāmitra[1] in all the three worlds consisting of mobile and immobile beings. That highly esteemed one grew up day by day surpassing all men.

6. He grew up like the moon in the bright half of a month in the sky and attained the prime of youth, O excellent Brāhmaṇas.

7. He was considered capable of looking after the kingdom and was appointed to rule over the realm of his ancestors but he was unwilling.

8. He proceeded ahead in the path that befitted Brāhmaṇas. He showed much inclination for Vedic study and he recited the Vedas everyday:

9. Gādhi crowned his son in the kingdom and went to the fores t. The highly esteemed one entered the stage of life of a forest-dweller along with his wife.

10. Though crowned as king, Viśvāmitra was more devoted to the adoration of Brāhmaṇas. He moved about in the company of Brāhmaṇas and engaged himself in holy ablution and performance of Japas.

11. Once he became inclined for Pāpardhi (hunting wild animals) and entered a terrible forest infested with different kinds of beasts.

12-13. He was urged by a desire to chase, O excellent Brāhmaṇas, in the course of his wandering in the great forest, and killed boars, Saṁbara deer, elephants, bears, Ruru deer, rhinoceros, wild buffalos, lions, tigers, huge pythons and Śarabhas.

14-15. The sun was in the zodiac Taurus and the time was mid-day, O excellent Brāhmaṇas, Viśvāmitra became utterly weary due to hunger and thirst. He reached the sacred hermitage of the noble-souled Vasiṣṭha who received the excellent king Viśvāmitra.[2]

1. The birth of Viśvāmitra due to change of *Carus* is described in Mbh, *Śānti* ch 49 and again in *Anuśāsana Parva* ch. 4.
2. This story of Vasiṣṭha's hospitality with the help of his cow Nandinī, Viśvāmitra's attempt to take her away by force and defeat, is found in Mbh, *Ādi* ch. 174.

16. With great joy, he met the king directly (lit. face to face). As he entered the hermitage the sage offered him *Arghya* and *Madhuparka*.

17. He spoke: "Welcome unto you, O king. Do tell me what I can do unto you who have come to my abode."

*Viśvāmitra said:*

18. O great sage, I became too tired after hunting. All my sense-organs are upset due to thirst. I came to your hermitage for the sake of drinking water.

19. Cool water has been drunk and I have quenched my thirst. O holy Brāhmaṇa, permit me to go back to the palace.

*Vasiṣṭha said:*

20. O king, this is the terrible time of midday. The sun is greatly scorching. Take your food and go back to your residence in the afternoon. Do take in food (cooked rice) in my hermitage.

*The king said:*

21-23. I have come for hunting with the full complement of the four divisions of my army. They are left at the entrance of your penance-grove. If the master takes food even as the servants are hungry, he soon falls into terrible hell bereft of all good qualities. Hence, O sage, allow me to go back home.

*Vasiṣṭha said:*

24. If your attendants are at the gateway and are hungry, summon them all quickly hither. I shall make them satisfied.

25. O excellent king, I have a splendid cow named Nandinī acquired by means of my penance. It gives me whatever I desire.

26. O excellent King, it will satisfy the entire army of yours. Let them be fetched here and you can witness the gift of my cow.

27-28. On hearing it, the king summoned the entire host. He took his bath and offered libations to the Pitṛs and Devatās. Then he performed Japa. After making the Brāhmaṇas chant the Vedic passages, he took his rest on a throne-like seat. In the meantime the cow Nandinī was called in.

29. On being summoned by Vasiṣṭha, she came and stood before Viśvāmitra. Then she spoke these words to Vasiṣṭha, the excellent sage.

30. "May I be commanded. What shall I do? Order me."

*Vasiṣṭha said:*

31. At my instance carry out everything pertaining to the washing of the feet and the like in regard to the saintly king Viśvāmitra. Do manage everything including the preparation of the food.

32. Fully satisfy the king and the army with all types of food—lambatives, drinks of diverse kinds and things that can be sucked. Let the horses and elephants be rendered satisfied with grass etc. duly.

*Sūta said:*

33. "Yes as per your order", said the cow and in a moment created whatever was called for by the sage to cater food to the ten thousand (soldiers of the king).

34. Those attendants served the food to each of the guests severally, with great solicitude.

35. Thus the cow rendered the king and his attendants fully satisfied, along with the soldiers, elephants, camels, horses and bullocks.

36. On watching such goings-on creating wonder and curiosity. King Viśvāmitra and his ministers were surprised, O Brāhmaṇas. They whispered to one another:

37. "Oh, how wonderful it is! How marvellous! Our entire army was overwhelmed with hunger and thirst! Now every member of it has been rendered satisfied by this cow.

38. Hence let this excellent cow be taken to our hometown. What can this Brāhmaṇa do? He is isolated in the forest. He has no servants of his own."

39-40. Then he called Vasiṣṭha and spoke these words: "Let this Nandinī be given no me. What will you do with her? You are alone. You stay in forest. You are free from the mutually opposed passions. You don't require any possessions. Or, O excellent sage, if you have any expenses of your own I shall hand over to you excellent villages, elephants, houses and other desired things."

*Vasiṣṭha said:*

41-42. O king, this cow is an adjunct to the Homa rites. Whatever we desire can be milked out of her. Further, O great king, even an ordinary cow cannot be given away by the twice-born ones. It is all the more so in the case of Nandinī who accords to me all that I desire? Listen to one thing more, O great king. There is this excellent statement in the Smṛti text.

43-44. It is laid down by Manu himself in the context of the sale of cows:

"An excellent Brāhmaṇa who accepts cash proceeding from the sale of cows, should be considered an *Antyaja* (Śūdra). He is no better than the seller of his own mother."

Hence, O king, I will not give you the cow Nandinī."

45. Neither through conciliatory pleadings, nor by threats, neither as an exchange for some gift nor by the punishment (i.e.force) meted out, will I give you the cow. Hence, do go back to your own abode.

*Viśvāmitra said:*

46. O Brāhmaṇa, persons conversant with monetary transactions are of this view that every jewel, excellent and valuable, that is on the earth belongs to the king.

47. This cow Nandinī is present here as a jewel belonging to me. If you do not part with her at my earnest request I will seize her meting out punishment to you.

48. After saying thus to Vasiṣṭha, King Viśvāmitra commanded his servants. "Let this Nandinī be seized."

49. The group of servants led Nandinī away. They even hit her with stones and sticks.

50. The blows shattered the poor cow. Tears filled her eyes. With great difficulty she rushed towards Vasiṣṭha, the excellent sage and said:

51. "O excellent sage, have I been transferred to this king? His men dare to handle me like my masters."

*Vasiṣṭha said:*

52. O my dear cow, I will not give you away even if my death is imminent. So protect yourself, by my own power.

* * *

53. On being told thus by the noble-souled Vasiṣṭha, the cow became furious. She made gruff and dreadful hissing sounds.

54. At the gruffing sound of the cow innumerable men, Śabaras, Mlecchas, Pulindas all equipped with arms came out.

55. All the servants of King Viśvāmitra were killed by them. Thereupon King Viśvāmitra was overcome with anger.

56. With great fury he got his army of four divisions ready to fight with them. He resolved even to die if needed.

57. Even as he kept on watching them his soldiers, elephants and horses were killed in no time by the men created by the cow.

58-60. Barring Viśvāmitra everything else was struck. On noticing that though the king continued to fight he was pretty well surrounded by Mlecchas, Vasiṣṭha took pity on him and spoke to Nandinī thus: "O Nandinī, save the king encircled by these Mlecchas. The king should be assiduously protected. It is due to his favour that these all (people) abide by the path of the good and all desist from following the wrong path."

61. Thereupon, Nandinī came there to dissuade (the Mlecchas etc.) when Viśvāmitra raised his sword and tried to strike (Nandinī) with it.

62. On seeing the cow about to be killed, Vasiṣṭha rendered the hand and the sword of the king motionless and benumbed.

63. Thereat King Viśvāmitra found himself discomfited. Overcome with shame, he spoke to Vasiṣṭha, the best of sages:

64-66. "O excellent sage, save me who am about to be killed by the dreaded Mlecchas. Render my hand free from the benumbed state.

It is my fault (offence) that caused the destruction of my vast army. Hence I go back to my place. I have nothing to do with the battle.

A rude and impolite fellow cannot stand the rigour of a battle for long, though he may have won glory, learning and prosperity like me who have become haughty and arrogant."

*Sūta said:*

67. On being appealed to thus by King Viśvāmitra, Vasiṣṭha relieved that hand from the defect of numbness.

68-69. After making the hand excellent (free) he laughingly spoke these words: "O king, go alone. I have rid you of the fault of stupefaction. Do not come into clash and rivalry again with Brāhmaṇas." Thus Viśvāmitra, the king, was allowed to go by him.

70. O excellent Brāhmaṇas, he went to the palace bashfully on foot alone and reached the gate of his capital at nightfall when everything was shrouded in darkness.

71-73. There he lamented with the eyes dimmed with tears: "Fie upon the strength of Kṣatriyas! Fie upon their vigour! Fie upon their very life! Praiseworthy is the power of Brāhmaṇas alone, their radiance alone. I have to do that whereby I will have the Brāhmaṇical power. Abandoning my kingdom, I will perform great penance."

74. After resolving thus, he crowned his son named Viśvāsaha as the king and went to the penance grove.

## CHAPTER ONE HUNDRED SIXTYEIGHT

## Greatness of the Source of Dhārotpatti

*Sūta said:*

1-4. Thus abdicating kingdom, O excellent Brāhmaṇas, Viśvāmitra went to the Himālaya mountain and performed a severe penance.

During rainy reason he lay under the open sky and during winter he lay in water. During summer he performed the austerity amidst five fires and continued thus for three hundred years.

Then for three hundred years, his diet was fruits and roots. Then, O excellent Brāhmaṇas, he remained meditating upon the supreme Absolute. Then for a long time he subsisted on scattered dry leaves thereafter.

Then for the same period, he remained on water alone for sustenance. Then for ten thousand years he remained with the sole intake of air.

*Sūta said:*

5. On seeing the power of penance of Viśvāmitra, the

Lord of Devas thought thus: 'Certainly this excellent king will drag me down from my position.'

6. Actuated by great fright, he came to the excellent king Viśvāmitra and spoke to him these sweet words in conciliatory terms.

*Indra said:*

7. O Viśvāmitra, I am very much pleased by this penance. Welfare unto you, O king, choose your boon, whatever may be the desire in your heart.

*Viśvāmitra said:*

8. O Śakra, if you are pleased now, grant me Brāhmaṇical status. O Purandara, know that my austerity is aimed at this.

*Indra said:*

9. How can a Kṣatriya become a Brāhmaṇa with the selfsame boby? A Brāhmaṇa is made by the performance of the double of twenty-four Saṁskāras (i.e. forty-eight rites). Hence request immediately for something else which is more covetable.

*Viśvāmitra siad:*

10. O Lord of Suras, I don't wish to request for anything else than Brāhmaṇical status.

11. I don't request even for your dominion of all the three worlds. Then, how can there be even the talk of other objectives! Hence, O most excellent one among Suras, do go away and rule over your realm.

12a. This is my resolve. Either I will attain Brāhmaṇical status or I will cast off my life.

12b-13a. On hearing his words and knowing his resolve, the king of Devas surrounded by gods went to heaven.

13b. Viśvāmitra then resumed the performance of the harsh penance as before.

14. O excellent Brāhmaṇas, another period of a thousand years passed by, through which King Viśvāmitra continued his austerity sustaining himself only on intake of air.

15. Brahmā himself came there along with the holy celestial sages. He spoke to the king who had got all his sins burned by means of his penance.

*Śrī Brahmā said:*

16. O Viśvāmitra, O most excellent one, I am very much pleased with this penance. Welfare unto you. Choose a boon. I shall grant it to you even if it is difficult to obtain.

*Viśvāmitra said:*

17. O Lord, if you are pleased with me, if a boon has to be granted to me, then grant Brāhmaṇical status to me. Nothing else is eagerly sought after by me.

*Brahmā said:*

18. How can Brāhmaṇical status be granted to one begotten by a Kṣatriya? Why do you express such a desire as is opposed to the injunction of the Śruti and Smṛti?

19. This is what has never occurred on the surface of the earth and will never occur at all.

*Viśvāmitra said:*

20. Go away, O Lord of the chiefs of Devas, to the excellent Brahmaloka. I will either attain the Brāhmaṇical status or cast off my life.

21-24. Then Ṛcīka who was in the middle of the celestial sages spoke these words: "O Lord, for the birth of this king Caru was prepared by me with Brāhmya Mantras. All round thereof, *Brahma-Sarvasva* (everything Brāhmaṇical) was used by me. So indeed, O Four-faced One, he is a Brāhmaṇa though born of a Kṣatriya.

Hence, O Pitāmaha, proclaim him a Brāhmaṇical sage; though he was in the administrative post of a realm, he used to perform excellent rites befittting a Brāhmaṇa.

It is the power of the Brāhma Mantras. Hence, call him a Brahmarṣi so that all of us can glorify Viśvāmitra as the most excellent Brāhmaṇa."

25-26a. Then Brahmā meditated for a long time. He thought

of him as born of Brāhmya Mantras and refulgence. He then said: "You have been transformed into a Brāhmaṇa by me. At my instance leave off this terrible penance very difficult to perform."

26b-27. When he was proclaimed by Brahmā, "You are a Brahmarṣi", he was proclaimed so by Ṛcīka and other celestial sages.

28-29. Vasiṣṭha, the excellent sage, was also among them. He angrily announced, "I will not at all proclaim him thus. Knowing (full well) that he was begotten by a Kṣatriya, O Grandfather, out of courtesy to Ṛcīka, you proclaim him to be so (a Brāhmaṇa)."

30. Though importuned in diverse ways by Pitāmaha, and the sages including Nārada, Vas iṣṭha, the excellent sage, did not relent. He left all those excellent Brāhmaṇas and went away.

31. The excellent sage arrived in the land called Ānarta at Hāṭakeśvara Kṣetra near Śaṅkha Tīrtha.

32. The meritorious Brahmaśilā and the Śvetadvīpa are there. The splendid river Sarasvatī that dispels sins is also present there.

33. He built a penance-grove there and performed an elaborate penance. The revengeful Viśvāmitra also came there with an intention of killing him.

34. Far from Vasiṣṭh's hermitage in the southern quarter he set up his penance-grove and began to think about finding his vulnerable points.

35. Though he waited thus for a long time, he could not discover any. Thereupon, black magic began to be practised by him against Vasiṣṭha.

36. What has been laid down in the Sāmaveda as a means of killing by means of employing Sāman Mantras, he performed Homas in the sacred fire by uttering those deadly Mantras.

37. A terrible Śakti arose from the sacred fire. She was hideous-looking with hair dishevelled. She was riding on the shoulders of a monkey and making *Kiḷkila* (chattering) sounds.

38-39. She had various weapons. She appeared like another *Yamajihvā* (Yama's tongue). She said: "Tell, O leading Brāhmaṇa, what job on your behalf shall I carry out? At your bidding I shall destroy the entire group of the three worlds."

*Viśvāmitra said:*

40. I have a formidable foe here. He is a base sage named Vasiṣṭha. Do go there and kill him quickly. You have been created for that purpose.

41. On being told thus by the intelligent Viśvāmitra, she set off facing the northern quarter towards the hermitage of Vasiṣṭha.

42. In the meantime, O Brāhmaṇas, there occurred many great evil omens in the hermitage of Vasiṣṭha.

43. A great comet fell down hitting against the solar disc. A shower of blood with bones mixed fell there.

44. A vixen howled coming up to the illuminated spot. Vasiṣṭha, the great sage, saw her as well as the great ill omens.

45. When he closely scrutinized the form shrouded in wreaths of flames, he understood everything by means of the divine vision.

46. (He said to himself:) 'This is the Śakti employed by Viśvāmitra for killing me. She is in the form of a *Kṛtyā* (Evil Spirit) caused by the excellent Mantras of the Sāmaveda.'

47. She was addressed, "Stop! Stop!" by him (Vasiṣṭha). Suddenly she stood motionless. By means of his own Mantras taken from the Atharva Veda, she was rendered immobile and paralysed.

48-49. She then assumed the form of a woman and said to the great sage: "It is the Sāmaveda that is the most important of all the Vedas. The intelligent sage Viśvāmitra created me on the basis of the injunctions therein. Do not make my blow ineffective, O sage. Do endure it. Through a gentle touch I shall avoid death unto you."

*Vasiṣṭha said:*

50. If it be so, do not touch my vulnerable points. Make a gentle touch, O splendid one. Out of pity for you I have withdrawn the Atharva Mantras.

51. Then the terrible Śakti employed by Viśvāmitra gently touched a part of his body and fell on the ground.

52-54. Vasiṣṭha who was pleased thereby spoke these sweet words to her: "From now onwards, people with great concentration will perform your adoration, O highly esteemed one. They will be endowed with great devotion. Those who have great faith and worship you on the eighth lunar day in the bright half of the month of Caitra, shall be free from ailments for a year thereafter. Hence at my instance you must stay here always."

*Sūta said:*

55-56. On being told thus by the noble-souled Vasiṣṭha the goddess stays there itself at his instance from the same moment. She regularly gets the adoration performed specially by the Nāgaras. She is well known by the name Dhārā. She accords happiness unto the devoted folk.

## CHAPTER ONE HUNDRED SIXTYNINE

## Greatness of Dhārā Devī

*The sages said:*

1-5. Why is she well-known all over the earth by the name Dhārā? Why is she said to be the deity specially delighting the Nāgaras?

*Sūta said:*

Formerly, there was an ascetic woman well-known by the name Dhārā in Camatkārapura. She was an excellent Brāhmaṇa lady, a chaste Nāgara woman. Formerly, she was a close friend of the highly intelligent Arundhatī.

When she (Arundhatī) came at the outset to the splendid Camatkārapura along with Vasiṣṭha in order to take her holy bath in Śaṅkhatīrtha, she had met the lady who eschewing all food was performing a penance with the sole intake of air. The lady endowed with a divine physical form was standing on the tip of her big toe.

The chaste lady was asked by Arundhatī: "Who are you? O splendid lady, whose daughter are you? Why are you practising this severe penance? O splendid lady, do tell me."

*Dhārā said:*

6. I am daughter of a Nāgara Brāhmaṇa named Devaśarman. I became a widow during even childhood.

7. On hearing the greatness of Śaṅkha Tirtha and that of Śaṅkheśvara, I permanently settled here engaged in propitiating the same deity.

*Arundhatī said:*

8. Merely at your sight I am having a great affection for you. Hence, do come. Let us go to my splendid penance-grove.

9. On the splendid banks of Sarasvatī that is destructive of all sins, stay there with me devoted to the discussion of the scriptural topics.

10. After taking the permission of her father, mother and kinsmen, the ascetic lady started along with her (Arundhatī).

11. Their friendship continued for a long time. Once that Śakti too came there.

12. (You may remember that) she had been created by Viśvāmitra for killing Vasiṣṭha. She was rendered paralysed by Vasiṣṭha and turned into a goddess worthy of being adored by Devas and human beings. The splendid deity accorded protection unto all.

13. A palace (-like shrine) comparable to the peak of Kailāsa was built by Dhārā unto the deity, O Brāhmaṇas. It was wonderfully inlaid with different kinds of Jewels.

14. Then the ascetic lady eulogized the goddess:

15. "O supreme Brāhmī, obeisance to you. O Dhārā Yoga (Yoga of continuous flow), obeisance, obeisance. O greatest void! O half of a Mātrā! O Supreme Śūnya! A moiety of half thereof! Obeisance to you.

16. Obeisance to you, O basic support of the universe. Obeisance to you, O support of all living beings. Obeisance to you, O deity with eyes resembling lotus petals Obeisance to you, O deity lustrous like gold.

17. Obeisance to you, O deity having the Leonine vehicle. Obeisance to you, O deity of great arms. Obeisance to you, O deity granting the desire of Devas. Obeisance to you, O destroyer of the Daityas.

18. Obeisance to you, O deity with a shattered head and a body assailed by Mahiṣa. Obeisance, O deity liking to stay in Vindhya to whom liquor and meat are the favourite oblations.

19. You are Lakṣmī; you are Śacī; you are Gaurī; you are Siddhi (perfect achievement). You are Vibhāvarī (night, excellent in lustre). You are Svāhā. Your are Svadhā. You are Tuṣṭi (Satisfaction) You are Puṣṭi (Nourishment). You are the goddess of Suras.

20. O goddess, you are in the from of Śakti. You are the cause of creation and dissolution. All these, the entire group of the three worlds consisting of mobile and immobile beings, are seen in you.

21-22. Just as oil latent in gingelly seed, ghee present in curd and fire present in wood are all well concealed and cannot be seen, so also, O goddess of Devas, you cannot be perceived though you are omnipresent."

*Sūta said:*

23. She continued her adoration day after day for many years, remembering the great goddess through this important prayer.

24. Once, on the eighth lunar day in the bright half of the month of Caitra, the deity was bathed in the river and adored.

25. After offering the oblations and performing the worship she eulogized the goddess by means of the prayer quoted above. Thereupon, the deity manifested herself and she spoke to the ascetic woman:

26. "Dear daughter, welfare unto you. I am pleased at this eulogy, O sinless one, choose a boon. I shall give you the desired thing."

*Dhārā said:*

27. O goddess, if you are pleased with me, if a boon has to be granted to me, then let my name be yours too only in this palace.

28-29. Another thing: If a Nāgara devotee circumambulates you three times, offers you three fruits, eulogizes you with this prayer and bows to you on that particular day, then for the period of the whole of that year, all his ailments should be prevented by you.

30. A barren woman-devotee should be blessed with sons. An unfortunate woman shall become a woman enjoying conjugal felicity; an ugly one should become beautiful; and a sick woman should be rid of her ailments. She must have every happiness.

*The Devī said:*

31. For the sake of enhancing your reputation I shall become well-known as Dhārā in the palace built by you. There is no doubt about it.

32-33. O ascetic lady, if a Nāgara comes here, makes three circumambulations and offers me three fruits, he shall be rid of all ailments for the period of a year.

After saying thus the goddess vanished.

34. Dhārā stayed there permanently accompanied by Arundhatī. Even today she is visible in the sky very near her (Arundhatī).

35. O excellent Brāhmaṇas, one who glorifies this story of the origin of Dhārā or listens to it shall be rid of the sins of that day.

36. Hence, it should be read with all efforts and listened to with great devotion by every one, especially by the Nāgaras.

## CHAPTER ONE HUNDRED SEVENTY

## Creation of Dhārā Tīrtha

*Sūta said:*

1-4. Further, O Brāhmaṇas, another wonderful incident occurred there. That Śakti was discharged towards Vasiṣṭha by Viśvāmitra for the purpose of killing that saintly Brāhmaṇa. It was rendered motionless and steady by the intelligent Vasiṣṭha through the Atharvaṇa Mantras. Then he began to perspire profusely.

The sweat flowed down as cool water. When it flowed out of the feet it appeared visible like a cool stream of water that had broken through the ground. It was devoid of impurities. It flowed like the crystalline clean Gaṅgā water.

5. Gaṅgā herself appeared accompanied by all the Tīrthas. The Kuṇḍa was filled with water. It was auspicious and cool.

6. Even in the terrible Kaliyuga, O Brāhmaṇas, a barren woman who takes her holy bath therein shall immediately be blessed with a son.

7. Anyone else who takes his bath there shall obtain the benefit of all the Tīrthas.

8. A man who takes the bath and then duly visits the goddess, shall obtain wealth, foodgrain, sons and the happiness arising from a kingdom.

9. Even an unfortunate barren woman shall become endowed with sons. On the eighth lunar day in the bright half of Caitra she should offer a ball (Piṇḍikā) of oblations with great devotion at the time of Mahāniśā (between its second and third watches).

10. She may offer it herself or through a joyous virgin. A woman who grasps the Piṇḍikā of oblations also gets the benefit.

11. If a woman of advanced age of even a hundred years eats the Piṇḍikā she shall become endowed with sons.

12. This is all the more so in the case of youthful women enjoying conjugal felicity? Any woman merely by means of the sight (Darśana) of the goddess gets the happiness of having sons.

13. She is the hereditary deity of the fifty-two and eight Gotras of all Nāgaras. She is the deity remembered through devotional fervour.

14. For this reason the religious procession (Yātrā) performed by Nāgaras is more effective. Without the Yātrā performed by Nāgaras, the goddess of Suras does not become pleased.

## CHAPTER ONE HUNDRED SEVENTYONE

# Battle between Vasiṣṭha and Viśvāmitra[1]

*Sūta said:*

1-4. In the meantime, the great sage Viśvāmitra came to know that the Śakti had become futile and hence was very angry thereby.

He then discharged Brahmāstra for killing him after invoking the requisite Mantras. Even when it was only combined (with the Mantra) its sound was very loud. Then a great number of meteors started to fall down from the sky. Various weapons like Kuntas, Śaktis, Tomaras, Parighas, Bhindipālas, clubs, swords, axes, arrows, spears and Śataghnīs came down in hundreds and thousands.

5-7. Vasiṣṭha came to know that the Brahmāstra was discharged by the son of Gādhi to bring about his death. So he remained pure and clean, took an Iṣīkā reed and charged it with the power of Brahmāstra. Then he told Gādhi's son, "May it be well unto you. Let this missile be hit at sides at my instance without doubt." Then Vasiṣṭha struck down the Brahmāstra discharged by him.

8-9. Then Vajrāstra was discharged by Viśvāmitra and it was destroyed by another Vajrāstra (by Vasiṣṭha). Thanks to the power of his Mantras, Vasiṣṭha struck down every missile that the furious Viśvāmitra discharged. In the meantime, the ocean became agitated.

10. Peaks of mountains crumbled down. There was a tremendous shower of blood. Signs like those at the time of Pralaya (ultimate dissolution) were seen cropping up all over the earth. Devas wondered, "Why should there be an untimely Pralaya?"

11. All the Devas including Vāsava went to Pitāmaha and told him that the signs of Pralaya had been seen on the earth.

12-14. Thereupon, Brahmā meditated for some time and said to the Heaven-dwellers: "A fight between Viśvāmitra and Vasiṣṭha has ensued. O Devas, they are fighting with divine

1. Vide Mbh, *Ādi* ch. 174.

weapons. Hence, the entire universe is in throes (of this agitation). So we shall go there before all the living beings are destroyed due to the power of the divine missiles."

15. He then went to that place where the excellent sages Viśvāmitra and Vasiṣṭha were fighting with each other.

16. Brahmā spoke to them in gentle and sweet tones: "May this fight with divine missiles be withdrawn lest there should be a wide-spread Pralaya on the entire earth."

*Vasiṣṭha said:*

17. O Lord, I am not employing the missiles with a desire to kill Viśvāmitra. As a means of self-defence I am subduing his missiles by means of counter-missiles.

18. This ruthless fellow discharges the missiles solely with the intention of killing me. O Brahmā, restrain him now.

*Brahmā said:*

19-20. O Viśvāmitra, O most excellent one among the sages, protect (keep off from) Vasiṣṭha, the excellent Brāhmaṇa at my instance. So save the entire universe. O Brāhmaṇa-sage, quickly stop discharging the missiles.

*Viśvāmitra said:*

21. O Prapitāmaha, he does not at all call (recognize) me a Brāhmaṇa. Hence my anger has been provoked with the intention of killing him.

22. Hence, O Lord of Devas, let him presently call me a Brāhmaṇa, upon which I shall withdraw the missile aimed at him.

*Brahmā said:*

23. O Vasiṣṭha, it is my behest that you now call Viśvāmitra a Brāhmaṇa. Thereby your life can be saved.

*Vasiṣṭha said:*

24. O Lotus-born One, I shall never call by the name Brāhmaṇa, someone begotten by a Kṣatriya. He, born of a Kṣatriya, is incapable to kill me at all.

25. The Brāhmaṇical radiance will not get destroyed through the Kṣatriya refulgence. Fully comprehending thus, O Four-faced One, do what is befitting.

*Brahmā said:*

26. O Viśvāmitra, O most excellent one among the twice-borns, proceed ahead with your fight with Vasiṣṭha eschewing the use of divine missiles. Or I may have to curse you.

*Viśvāmitra said:*

27. Even after stopping the divine missiles, this evil-intentioned fellow can be done away with by attacking some vulnerable point. You may go to your abode.

*Sūta said:*

28. "Of course", said Vidhi (Brahmā) and went to Brahmaloka. Viśvāmitra and Vasiṣṭha stayed behind on the banks of Sarasvatī.

## CHAPTER ONE HUNDRED SEVENTYTWO

# Sarasvatī Cursed[1]

*Sūta said:*

1-3. Ever since then, O excellent Brāhmaṇas, Viśvāmitra stayed there looking for vulnerable points of Vasiṣṭha for the purpose of slaying him, thanks to the power, like a mosquito (would do) against an elephant.

On another day the river was summoned by Viśvāmitra. Immediately she assumed the form of a woman and appeared before him. With palms joined in reverence she said: "O saintly Brāhmaṇa, let the command be given as to the purpose for which I have been called now."

1. It was Sarasvatī in Kurukṣetra which was cursed in Mbh, vide Mbh, *Śalya Parva* ch. 42, 38-39 for the curse, or release from the curse Mbh, *Śalya* 43.16. Here that episode is used in connection with Prācī Sarasvatī.

*Viśvāmitra said:*

4. O great river, when he (Vasiṣṭha) plunges (while bathing) into your waters, bring him near me with great rapidity.

5. Let his ears be filled with waters. Let his limbs be shaken and exhausted. This will enable me to kill him. I don't see any other vulnerable point.

6. On being told thus by Viśvāmitra, that river became frightened. She was afraid of his curse and spoke these words:

7-11. "I will not do anything atrocious in regard to Vasiṣṭha, the noble-souled one. Nor, O Brahmarṣi, is it proper on your part to kill a Brāhmaṇa.

If you have been called a Brahmarṣi by Brahmā himself and it does not please Vasiṣṭha to do so, what is the harm? Hence give up your anger.

If someone even thinks of killing a Brāhmaṇa he can be rid of the sin by the rite of Taptakṛcchra. So says Manu, the son of the Self-born Lord.

The Lord has said that if a man says that he will kill a Brāhmaṇa, his purity can be brought about by Cāndrāyaṇa rite.

Hence, I will not carry out your bidding concerning Vasiṣṭha. You may do whatever you like."

12. On hearing it, O Brāhmaṇas, Viśvāmitra got angry. He cursed that excellent river. I shall tell you. Let it be heard what that curse is:

13. "O sinful bad river, since my behest has not been carried out, your watery stream shall become bloody."

14. After saying this with eyes turned red due to anger, he took some water in his hand. He charged it with Mantra seven times and poured it down into the water of the river.

15. Thereupon, the highly meritorious water of River Sarasvatī which was formerly white like a conch, turned into blood that very moment.

16. In the meantime, ghosts, goblins and night-stalkers came there. Drinking the blood they began to laugh, sing and dance about.

17. A few sages who had settled on her banks abandoned her in a body and went to some far-off land.

18. Caṇḍaśarman and others, the Nāgaras, who had settled there as external residents, went away.

19. Vasiṣṭha, the excellent sage, went to Arbuda (Abu) mountain. Viśvāmitra, the Brāhmaṇ-sage went to Camatkārapura.

20. There was a spot abounding in Brāhmaṇas at Hāṭakeśvara Kṣetra. He built a hermitage there and performed a severe penance.

21-22. Thereby Viśvāmitra became capable of creating the world and (could) compete with god Brahmā (in the matter of world creation).

Thus everything has been narrated to you as to how the waters of Sarasvatī turned into blood as a result of the curse of Viśvāmitra and how Caṇḍaśarman and other Brāhmaṇas went away to other lands.

## CHAPTER ONE HUNDRED SEVENTYTHREE

## Sarasvatī Gets Rid of the Curse

*The sages said:*

1-2. Oh, how miraculous and wonderful indeed is this! Thanks to the power of the Mantras of Viśvāmitra, the good sage, the waters thereof got turned into blood.

Now do narrate, O highly esteemed one, how the waters of Sarasvatī were re-eṣtablished (on purity). Narrate everything in detail.

*Sūta Said:*

3. O excellent Brāhmaṇas, for a pretty long time the stream of Sarasvatī was full of blood and it was resorted to by goblins, ghosts and Rākṣasas.

4. Once the excellent sage Vasiṣṭha who was staying in Arbuda was appealed by the River who was distressed and miserable:

5-7. "O sage, it was for your sake that I have been cursed angrily by Viśvāmitra whereby blood began to flow in my bed and I was deserted by the community of sages.

Hence O great Brāhmaṇa, do me this favour. Let there be flow of water once again in my bed and let the blood then disappear.

O lord of all sages! You are not deficient in the ability of creation, sustenance or destruction of the three worlds."

*Vasiṣṭha said:*

8. O fair one, I shall do that whereby water will flow once again in your bed and the blood gets eliminated.

9. After saying thus, the saintly Brāhmaṇa descended to the ground and went to the Plakṣa tree from which Sarasvatī flowed.

10. He went into *Samādhi* (trance) there and squattedon the ground. He was full of *Saṁbhrama* (fury) against Viśvāmitra.

11. Looking down at the ground he repeated the Varuṇa Mantra. Thereupon, a great stream burst open the earth and flowed out.

12. It flowed through two openings as Vasiṣṭha was looking at the ground with both of his eyes. From one flowed out water quickly which became the source of Sarasvatī.

13. The blood which completely filled the great river was flushed out forcibly at (its very source at) the Plakṣa tree.

14. The second current that had flowed out of his *Saṁbhrama* (fury) became river Sābhramatī (Sabaramati) on the earth.

15. Thus Sarasvatī attained her normal state once agtain. O highly esteemed ones, (this is what) I had been asked regarding Sarasvatī.

16. This narrative called Sārasvata gives great intellect. One who reads or listens to it has his intellect bettered, thanks to the favour of Sarasvatī. It is the truth that I mentioned.

## CHAPTER ONE HUNDRED SEVENTYFOUR

# Birth of Pippalāda[1]

*Sūta said:*

1. Further I shall describe unto you another Liṅga established there. This Liṅga was installed by Pippalāda and is called Kaṁsāreśvara.

2. If it is visited sins of people committed on that day are dispelled; if it is bowed down to, sins of six months are eradicated and if it is adored, of the whole year (are destroyed).

*The Ṛṣis Said:*

3-4. O Sūtanandana, you said that the Liṅga installed by Pippalāda is called Kaṁsāreśvara. Kindly tell us why it is so. Who is this Pippalāda? Whose son was he? Tell us for what purpose was the Liṅga installed there in that holy place by the noble-souled one.

*Sūta said:*

5. A great burden of questions has been placed upon me by you all. I shall, however, answer after paying obeisance to the Self-born Lord.

6. Yājñavalkya had a sister well-known as Kaṁsārī. Observing celibacy even in childhood, she performed a severe penance.

7-8. She stayed in the meritorious hermitage of Yājñavalkya in the company of kinsmen. Once, O Brāhmaṇas, Yājñavalkya had an emission of semen at the end of a dream when he saw an excellent Apsarā. Although he was endowed with the power of penance, O excellent Brāhmaṇas, he was after all in the prime of his youth.

9. His cloth got drenched with the powerful semen. Of course, at dawn he discarded that cloth.

1. An ancient teacher, the editor of the Atharva Veda, is mentioned in *Praśnopaniṣad.* He subsisted on Pippala leaves and hence came to be known as Pippalāda. The derogatory Puranic account is untraceable in the Upaniṣad and in Mbh.

10. But, O excellent Brāhmaṇas, Kaṁsārikā did not know that the cloṭh had been wetted by semen of never-failing efficacy. She took the cloth at the time of her bath.

11. It so happened that she was in her menstrual period then. While she was taking her plunge the water mingled with the semen entered her vagina.

12. As a result of that she conceived a foetus in her womb. It grew up daily like the Moon in the bright half of a month.

13. Realizing that a child had been conceived in her womb the poor woman was extremely distressed and overcome by shame.

14. She pondered over this for a long time. She was perplexed and wondered how it had happened. Perforce she concealed herself from men and never came within their view.

15. Under the pretext of the observance of holy vows, she always isolated herself. On the completion of ten months, at midnight, on a certain day, a boy was born to her. He had a lustre reṣembling that of the morning Sun.

16. She covered the child with a nice cloth and took it to a forest devoid of human traffic. All the while, she was crying to herself in great wretchedness. Her eyes welled up with tears.

17. In the desolate region, she came to the foot of a great Aśvattha tree and left the child there speaking these words:

18-19. "O Aśvattha, you are Viṣṇu in visible form. You have a pre-eminent position among Devas. Hence, O Vanaspati (Tree), protect my son from all sides.

This child, my son, is seeking refuge in you, though I may seem to be ruthless and sinful. Do protect him."

20. After saying thus, the poor ascetic woman cried for a long time and later started towards her hermitage with her eyes dimmed by profuse tears.

21. While the distressed mother was lamenting beneath that tree, an aerial voice arose resemblinġ a rumbling cloud:

22-28. "O splendid lady, do not grieve over this boy. He is the incarnation of Bṛhaspati who was cursed by his elḍer brother Utathya. He will occupy an honoured place on the earth. He will condense the Atharva Veda that has a hundred Śākhās and Kalpas into one of nine Śākhās and five Kalpas.

He will imbibe the juice of Pippala tree and therefore will be well-known as Pippalāda.[1]

You were wondering how a full-fledged child was born to you without (contact with) a man. Listen to the cause thereof.

The bath-towel of your brother which was drenched with his seminal discharge was worn by you during the menstrual period, O fair lady.

At the time of your bath the waters got mingled with the seminal fluid. This son of yours is the product of that never-failing seminal fluid. Now that you have understood everything, O highly esteemed lady, do what is proper in this respect."

*Sūta said:*

29. On hearing the thunderbolt-like words originating from the divine region, she cried loudly and fell on the ground.

30. That pitiable lady fell down like a creeper cut off from a tree.

31. On coming to know that the hermitage was vacant and her sister was late in returning, Yājñavalkya, the great sage, asked the other sages:

32. "Where has my sister Kaṁsārī, the excellent ascetic woman, gone? Without her the entire penance grove has become void."

33-34. A certain sage announced: "Your younger sister has fallen down on the ground near the Aśvattha tree without any movement of the limbs. I saw her, O excellent sage. Save her. Do not delay."

Thereupon he (Yājñavalkya) hastened there in bewilderment.

35. He went to the place where the ascetic had said she was lying. He saw her gasping for breath at that place.

36. He sprinkled her with cold water frequently and fanned her. By the time she regained consciousness Kātyāyanī and Maitreyī reached the place with great excitement.

37-38. "What has befallen you, O sister-in-law? Tell us quickly. Were you bitten by a serpent or are you afflicted with the derangement of the three humours (*Vāta*, *Pitta* and *Kapha*)?

1. A popular etymology from Pippala + *ad* - to eat.

Are you posessed by spirits? Or are you in the grip of the Māhendra fever?"

39. Though she had regained consciousness, she was overcome with bashfulness seeing Yājñavalkya standing in front in the company of his wives. She gave up her life.

40. On seeing her dead, O Brāhmaṇas, Yājñavalkya and his wives lamented much. They cremated her and offered libations. Eventually, they returned to their hermitage.

41. At the foot of the Aśvattha, the boy grew slowly sustaining himself by the tasty Pippala juice.

42. Once Nārada, the excellent sage, came that way in the course of his pilgrimage.

43-45. On seeing the boy with the refulgence of twelve Suns engaged in regularly tasting the Pippala all by himself in that desolate forest, he asked in great surprise: 'Who may you be, O lonely fellow? This is a extremely terrible desolate forest infested by lions and tigers. Why do you stay here alone? Where are your mother and fathe r? How do you manage to live? Tell me in detail.'"

*Pippalāda said:*

46. I do not know my father and mother or any kinsman. Nor do I know you who came near me now.

*Sūta said:*

47. On hearing his words the leading sage meditated for some time. When he understood everything by means of his divine vision, he laughingly said:

*Nārada said:*

48. O dear boy, I have understood who you are. The seminal fluid of Yājñavalkya gained entry into the womb of his sister entirely by chance at the time of the menstrual period. You are born thus.

49. You are the incarnation of Bṛhaspati, the preceptor of Devas (born), as a result of the curse of Utathya. It is for the accomplishment of a divine task. Listen to it.

50-51. The Atharvaveda of a hundred Śākhās and a hundred Kalpas has been composed for the accomplishment of various tasks of kings. Its meaning is incomprehensible. It should be condensed within nine Śākhās and five Kalpas so that there will be facility thereby.

52-54. O highly esteemed one, your mother, the sister of Yājñavalkya, was a woman with geat ascetic virtues. By mistake and due to no desire at all, she took the bath towel of Yājñavalkya and wore it. Earlier, that cloth had been drenched with his own seminal fluid which got mingled with water and gained entry into her vagina. It was never ineffective. You are born on the earth due to that. After realizing this, your mother became ashamed resulting in her ultimate death.

55. O highly esteemed one, your progenitor as well as maternal uncle is present at Camatkārapura now. Do go to him now.

56. This is your eighth year. It is time for religious Vratas and rites.

On hearing these words of Nārada, the boy bashfully stood with face turned down.

57-5 8. After a long time, he spoke to the sage these piteous words: "O excellent sage, tell me what sin was committed by me in my previous birth as a result of which this birth has been so deplorable. I am also separated from my mother. I will forsake my life on account of this misery."

*Nārada said:*

59. No sin was committed by you in the previous birth. Then why this mishap? Listen.

60. You are born with Saturn in the house of nativity. There is no doubt about it. Hence you fell into this miserable plight. There is no other cause.

61. On hearing these words his eyes became red with anger. He looked up towards Śanaiścara (Saturn).

62. As his glance fell on him, the son of Ravi (i.e.Saturn), fell down from his aerial chariot like Yayāti, the son of Nahuṣa.

63. He fell with face down, O excellent Brāhmaṇas, as per the command of his father. (You may remember) in childhood the feet of Ravi had been burned by him.[1]

1. The reference is to the behest of the Sun that Saturn should avert his eyes from seeing good people.

64-65. Then Nārada said to him as he fell with face down: "O Śanaiścara, it is due to the childishness of this boy that you have been made to fall down. Hence do not look at him. He will become very angry. Further, stop falling on the ground by the force of my utterance."

66. After having rendered Śanaiścara stable even as he was in the sky, the leading sage spoke to the boy Pippalāda:

67-71. "O boy, do not be angry. This is the Planet, son of Sun-god. When he is in the eighth house (zodiac) he inflicts pain on even the Devas.

He is all the more malific when he is in the house of nativity. Further he is so in the second house as well.

If he angrily looks at you at all, there is absolutely no doubt that he will reduce you to ash just in front of me.

Even at the time of his own birth, the feet of his father, Sun-god, were looked at by him. The father had joyously come to see his son. Knowing that he was hideous–eyed a cloth had been put over the feet: Still both of the feet were burnt. Even now they are seen covered with skin[1] for a Ghaṭikā (short while, period of time) on the earth."

*Sūta said:*

72. On hearing the words of Nārada, the boy was extremely frightened. He asked the sage:

73. "O excellent sage, tell me how he will be pleased with me. Unknowingly, I have caused him to fall down. I never knew his power too."

*Nārada said:*

74. Planets, cows, kings and Brāhmaṇas in particular, honour (others) when they are honoured. If they are insulted, they burn them.

75. Hence, O lordly boy, eulogize, according to your capacity, the son of Bhāskara, so that he will eschew the anger caused by his fall and become pleased.

* * *

1. Icons of the Sun found in Gujarat have boots on the feet. Is this a reference to icons of the Sun-god wearing boots (but covered with skin), as the Purāṇa states.

76-77a. Then the boy stood with palms joined in reverence. O excellent Brāhmaṇas, this Pippalāda was extremely frightened. He took leave of the sage and bowed down to Śanaiścara repeatedly and eulogized:

77b. "Obeisance to you who are wrathful by nature. Obeisance to the Piṅgala (tawny-coloured one).

78. Obeisance to the deity Babhru (deep brown) in colour. Obeisance to you, the dark-coloured one. Obeisance to you the deity with a terrible body. Obeisance to you, the destroyer.

79. Obeisance to you having the appellation *'Yama'*. Obeisance to you, O Lord, O son of Sūra (the Sun). Obeisance to you known by the appellation *'Manda'* (slow). O Śanaiścara, I make obeisance to you.

80. O Lord of Devas, be pleased with this wretched (boy) who has bowed down to you."

*Śanaiścara said:*

81. O dear boy, I am pleased with this eulogy of yours now. Welfare unto you. Choose your boon so that I can grant it to you.

*Pippalāda said:*

82. O son of the Sun-god, from now onwards you should not inflict harassment on boys and girls,

83-86. O Sūryaja, at my instance you must desist from troubling them till the eighth year.

If anyone gets up early in the morning and eulogizes you by means of this prayer, O Bhāskaranandana, you must not inflict harm to him.

If anyone takes oil bath on the day pertaining to you (i.e. Saturday), you must not afflict him for eight subsequent days.

If anyone makes an iron (metallic) image of yours, puts that image topsy-turvy into oil and then takes his bath with that oil, you must not afflict him. You must accord benefit unto kings.

87-90. During the seven and a half years of your malefic period, if someone tries to consume gingelly seeds with some metal on Saturdays, he should not be troubled by you, O Lord.

If anyone gives a black cow to a Brāhmaṇa with you in view, O Lord, you must desist from afflicting him during those seven and a half years.

If anyone performs Homa unto you with Śamī twigs, covers your image with black cloth, worships you with black gingelly seeds, black flowers and unguents and offers incense burning Guggulu, you must avoid harassing him.

*Sūta said:*

91. On being requested thus by him, Śani said (promised): "Of course, it will be done," took leave of Nārada and went to his resort.

92. Moved by compassion Nārada took that boy and went to Camatkārapura. He entrusted the boy to the care of Yājñavalkya.

93. He told him all the report concerning his birth and the like which had been seen by him with the lamp of knowledge.

94-95. "This is your sister's son born of your seminal fluid. I found him in the forest near an Aśvattha tree at its root.

Now he is eight years old. Perform the holy rites of Vratabandha (investiture with the sacred thread) unto him. In this affair, O great Brāhmaṇa, there is no fault of yours nor of your sister. Accept your own son who is also your nephew."

*Sūta said:*

96. After saying thus, the celestial sage vanished. On hearing all this Yājñavalkya experienced great distress and anguish.

97. Considering that a sinful incident, he had no peace of mind. He despised himself day and night and grieved over it.

98. Through various signs and similarities with him, he recognised him as his son. He brought him up and performed his thread ceremony.

## CHAPTER ONE HUNDRED SEVENTYFIVE

# Gift of a Boon to Yājñavalkya

*Sūta said:*

1-2. O Brāhmaṇas, while he was thus denigrating himself and feeling grief-stricken, Brahmā himself came there and said: "O Brāhmaṇa, you need not feel suspicious about this boy. The boy's birth was non-deliberate and purely accidental."

*Yājñavalkya said:*

3. Still, O Lord, my heart does not feel pacified. Hence, O most excellent one among Suras, prescribe the requisite expiatory rite.

*Brahmā said:*

4. O highly esteemed one, if you feel that your conscience has not become clear (free from feeling of guilt) at all, install the Liṅga of the Trident-bearing Lord.

5-6. When a man knowingly or unknowingly commits any sin, even if it is Brāhmaṇa-slaughter and the like or the murder of a woman, the sin can be wiped off like darkness at sunrise, if he builds a shrine of Hara though it may consist only of five bricks.

7. Especially, O highly esteemed one, in the holy spot of Hāṭakeśvara, it is more effective, as it is sacred and destructive of all sins.

8. Even at the advent of Kali age, there is no sin that vitiates it. I too wish to perform a Yajña here, O excellent Brāhmaṇa.

9. I shall bring here that Puṣkara Tīrtha that is highly endearing to me, lest it should be made inefficacious due to the pernicious effect of Kali age.

10. When Kali age sets in, O Brāhmaṇa, all Tīrthas except this excellent one, become inefficacious.

*Sūta said:*

11-12. Saying thus, the Four-faced One (Brahmā) vanished.

After completely hearing the words of Pitāmaha Yājñavalkya was convinced that the holy spot was very excellent. So he installed the Liṅga. Thereafter, he declared thus in tone as majestic as the rumbling sound of a cloud:

13-14. "If anyone bathes this Liṅga of mine with great devotion on the eighth or fourteenth lunar day, his sin is destroyed.

The Liṅga that has been caused to be washed or adored by others, washes off that sin arising from habitation with other people's wives or even with one' own mother.

15. The adoration performed on this day wipes off the sin committed in the course of a fortnight, if it is perpetrated unknowingly.

16. Ever since then it is well known in that holy spot of Hāṭakeśvara as Yājñavalkyeśvara, O excellent Brāhmaṇas."

CHAPTER ONE HUNDRED SEVENTYSIX

## Origin of Kaṁsāreśvara

*Sūta said:*

1-2. On seeing the Liṅga installed by the intelligent Yājñavalkya he (Pippalāda) installed a Liṅga named after his mother for the sake of her sanctification. O eminent Brāhmaṇas, he was fully endowed with perfect faith.

Thereafter, he bought an eminent Nāgara Brāhmaṇa of the middle region.

3-8. He hailed from Gartātīrtha. He maintained the sacred fires and regularly performed Yajña. He said to him: "Just as this city is holy, so you also are initiated. You are established in the leadership of sixty-eight Gotras. (Brāhmaṇas of) all Gotras will abide by your decision (speech) in all (religious) rites till the sun, the moon and stars last.

O Govardhana, you must think about the ways and means of the worship of this Liṅga. Nāgaras should be encouraged to worship this. By the adoration of the Liṅga, your family will flourish.

By not adoring, there is no doubt about it that the family will meet with destruction. If your descendants adore this

Liṅga with great devotion and then perform their various kinds of activities, O Dīkṣita, those activities will become successful, with the favour of this."

*Govardhana said:*

9. O Brāhmaṇa, I will always adore this Liṅga and for its sake I will extend my devout activities. So also all those born in my family (will do so).

*Pippalāda said:*

10. O Govardhana, bring those Nāgara Brāhmaṇas there quickly. With their permission I shall give merely the name to the deity.

11. He accordingly brought Brāhmaṇas expert in performing Yajña rites, rich in learning and devoted to regular recitation (of the Vedas).

12-14. After bowing down to them, the great sage Pippalāda spoke to them loudly: "My mother named Kaṁsārī is already dead. With her in view, O excellent Brāhmaṇas, this Liṅga has been installed by me. Let it become well-known by your proclamation.

He who bathes this as well as that of Yājñavalkyeśvara on the eighth and fourteenth lunar days shall attain Śreyas (spiritual perfection)."

*Sūta said:*

15. With due reference to that excellent sage, the name of that Liṅga was declared as Kaṁsārīśvara by all those Brāhmaṇas.

16. Thus everything has been spoken to you, O excellent Brāhmaṇas, in answer to what was asked regarding the origin of the deity named Kaṁsārīśvara and how this sin-destroying deity was installed by the noble-souled Pippalāda himself.

17-18. He who reads or listens to this meritorious narrative in the presence of that deity with great devotion, will find his mental sin of thinking erotically of other men's wives destroyed. It is in accordance with the words of Pippalāda.

19-21. If a devotee recites in front of him Nīlarudra Mantras and Prāṇarudras along with Bhavarudra Mantras, even the sin arising from Brāhmaṇa-slaughter perishes. When there is danger from hostile kings as well as from severe drought, Atharva Veda shouild be recited from the beginning to the end. The enemy gets destroyed and it rains immediately in showers.

22. If a king happens to be in a difficult situation (or ill health) he should be righteous and should be devoted to the protection of the subjects. He shall then be rid of all his ailments.

23. If there occurs adverse effect of divine calamity, it shall disappear gradually as Pippalāda himself has said.

24-25. Of what avail is much talk? Whatever great mishap occurs shall get quickly dissolved (removed) by reciting the Atharva Veda before this deity.

## CHAPTER ONE HUNDRED SEVENTYSEVEN

# Creation of Pañcapiṇḍikā

*Sūta said:*

1-2a. Further, there is the deity Gaurī called Pañcapiṇḍikā there itself. The image was installed by Lakṣmī who was in human form. Merely by visiting that deity, a woman attains conjugal felicity.

2b-3. A woman-devotee should place the *Jalayantra* (a pitcher with a hole at the bottom allowing water to trickle drop by drop on the deity below) above the deity in the bright half of the month of Jyeṣṭha when the Sun is in the zodiac Taurus. It shall trickle day and night. The woman shall attain greatest conjugal felicity.

4. By offering *Jalayantra*, a woman obtains the whole of that benefit which she is likely to obtain through the performance of all the Vratas pertaining to Gaurī and making gifts of their choice.

5. Hence in the month of Jyeṣṭha a *Jalayantra* should be offered assiduously to Gaurī by women for the sake of conjugal felicity.

6-7. O excellent Brāhmaṇas, of what avail is the performance of other Vratas, Niyamas, Japas and Homas in the case of women? They are but causes of great pain and strain. At a time when the Fierce-rayed One (Sun) is in Taurus if a *Jalayantra* is placed over Gaurī's (image) with excellent devotion, it is meritorious, O tigers among Brāhmaṇas.

8. If that be done, no woman becomes barren or *Kāka Vandhyā* (having only one child) or one afflicted by misfortune (e.g.death of husband) all through seven births.

*The sages said:*

9. Gaurī, the great goddess, is said to be and is seen as four-armed. How did it happen that she is Pañcapiṇḍā too? Do clarify this doubt of ours.

*Sūta said:*

10. O Brāhmaṇas, when Pralaya occurs she makes herself Pañcapiṇḍīmaya (consisting of five lumps); she assumes this excellent form.

11. She is that great Śakti, the goddess of Suras; she pervades everything. The entire range of the three worlds including mobile and immobile beings is pervaded by her.

12. For the purpose of creation, she preserves the five elements viz. earth, water, fire, wind and ether. Hence, she is Pañcapiṇḍikā.

13. If the Pañcapiṇḍikā is worshipped, the merit is three thousand times more than when she is directly worshipped.

14. The worship is to be carried out in the month of Jyeṣṭha, especially with the use of a *Jalayantra*. In this connection, I shall narrate unto you an ancient legend.

15. O excellent Brāhmaṇas, this befell the wife of the king of Kāśā and this was earlier narrated by Lakṣmī to Viṣṇu on being asked.

*Lakṣmī said:*

16. Formerly, there was a king of Kāśī well-known by the name Jayasena. He had a thousand wives of excellent beauty.

17. Then he acquired another splendid beloved wife. She was a part of my Kalā, in the form of a human being. She was the daughter of Viṣvaksena, the intelligent king of Madra.

18. She used to get up early in the morning and go to the splendid banks of Gaṅgā. She then made the image of Gaurī with five lumps of clay out of the mud from the river.

19-21. She used to adore the idol with five Mantras and the application of excellent scents, garlands, incense, splendid garments, Naivedya offerings with sweet puddings, songs, dances, instrumental music etc. After the ritualistic dismissal of the image of the goddess, she offered various gifts to Brāhmaṇa Gauriṇīs (i.e.married women with husband alive and virgins). Thereafter she used to return to the abode to the accompaniment of various musical instruments being played.

22. As she continued the adoration of Gaurī, her conjugal felicity went on increasing.

23. She surpassed all her co-wives in regard to conjugal felicity.

24. On seeing the day-by-day increase in her fortune and conjugal felicity, all the co-wives became sad and distressed.

25. Some said: There is a special religious rite, she is engaged in forever. She collects mud and clay, makes them into five lumps and worships them.

26. O great sages, others said that she was perfect in the Siddhi of her Mantras. Still others said that she had performed meritorious deeds in her previous births.

27-28. Thus, they spent a long time in their great sorrow. Once, all of them discussed with one another and came to the water reservoir (pond or lake or river) where she performed the worship of Gaurī in the Pañcapiṇḍikā.

29. On seeing them all, she stopped her adoration of Gaurī and hastened to their presence. There she stood with palms joined in reverence.

30. "O highly esteemed ladies, welcome, hearty welcome unto you all. Do mention my duty which I shall quickly carry out."

*The Co-wives said:*

31. It was due to eagerness and curiosity that we have come to you. We are being burned by the fire of absence of felicity fanned by your own conjugal felicity.

32. So, O highly fortunate and esteemed one, tell us why and how you always worship the Pañcapiṇḍikā made of clay.

33. What is the reason thereof? Is it the result of the power of Mantras? O highly esteemed one, if it is not a great secret, do explain to us.

*Padmāvatī said:*

34. O fair-faced ladies, what I am being asked about is really a great secret. It should not be expatiated upon. Yet I shall explain it to you.

35. Since all of you have come at the time when I am adoring Gaurī, you are all my sisters. I am never defiled by the vice of jealousy.

36. Formerly, I was in the city called Kusumapura. I was the daughter of Vīrasena, an intelligent Śūdra. I was given, as per Dharma Śāstra, in marriage to an intelligent son of a merchant by the noble-souled one.

37. At the time of the marriage five excellent letters (Mantras) were given to me for my prosperity by a Yoṣit (a maiden) along with my initiation. Thereafter, I was told to perform the adoration of Gaurī.

38-39. (She said:) "O daughter, till you complete the worship of the Ātman by means of these *Akṣaras* (syllables, Mantras) do not even drink water. Thereby, you will obtain everything desired and desirable."

O splendid-faced lady, I said to her, "So it shall be (done)."

40. Then after the marriage celebration was over, I went with my husband to the place where my father-in-law was present and also the terrible mother-in-law.

41-42. My mother-in-law was dead against my adoration of Gaurī. She always used to prevent me. Naturally, I who was always devoted to Gaurī became frightened. In the water-pond where I used to go to fetch water, I began worshipping Gaurī with devotion and recitation of the five Mantras. (For the sake of image). I took the clay (and made the lumps).

43. Then I used to throw them in the water and go back to the abode. Once my splendid husband set out for some foreign land for mercantile activity.

44. He took me with him affectionately and proceeding along the desert path we came to an arid region, a frightening desert area.

45. So also the time was equally terrible with the Sun in Taurus. The entire caravan took rest in the middle of the spot.

46. They resorted to a deep well comparable to a rain-bearing cloud. At the same time something resembling water was seen in the desert region by me when I thought thus:

47. 'Here plenty of water is seen near at hand. Here I can take bath, become clean, devoutly worship Gaurī and drink the tasty water of the lake.'

48. (Thinking thus) I started and proceeded ahead step by step. I went on and on a long way. It was only a mirage. I became extremely distressed due to thirst in that desert land.

49. In the meantime the Sun came to the zenith of the sky, the Sun in Taurus (zodiac) scorched me from above, O fair-faced ones.

50. Down beneath me there were the hot sand particles all around. I became extremely distressed due to thirst in that desert land.

51. Thereat I fell on the ground and there were boils all over my body. A story mentioned in the Bhārata was then recollected by me.

52. Nṛga[1] performed Yajña by means of sand particles hurled into a well without water, grass or lump of clay.

53. The Devas who can be attracted through devotion became pleased with that noble-souled one. Therefore, I thought I too would be worshipping the beloved of Hara by means of the sand particles.

54. Indeed, the goddess had become pleased. In this birth she has granted me a great realm and plenty of what I have been desiring.

55. At that time, the five Mantras were remembered by me and the goddess was worshipped with five handfuls of sand particles.

56. At that time, O excellent ladies, I fell down dead and was reborn in the place of the king of Daśārṇa well known all over the world.

57. Thanks to the favour of that goddess, I am now equipped with the power to recollect previous births. Though I am junior to all of you, I am well nigh at the top in the matter of conjugal felicity.

58. It is for this reason that I make five lumps of clay everyday and offer them to Gaurī by way of adoration.

59. Undoubtedly this great secret has been divulged to

1. According to Mbh, *Anuśāsana,* ch. 70, King Nṛga who was cursed to be a frog was freed from the curse by Kṛṣṇa and was sent to heaven. Here the legend is adapted to suit Pañcapiṇḍikā Vrata.

you all. Thanks to this truthfulness, may Gaurī grant what is desired in the mind.

*Lakṣmī*[1] *said:*

60. Then all those co-wives stood with palms joined in reverence and told me humbly after repeatedly bowing:

61. "Kindly do this favour to us. Let the five Mantras be given to us—those Mantras whereby Parameśvarī, the goddess, was pleased."

62. All of them were told by me: "Do pray as you please. I shall grant you everything. My words are truthful."

63. Then, O Lord, they were made my disciples and the five Mantras were imparted to them. They were fully rendered true disciples mentally, verbally and physically.

*Viṣṇu said:*

64. O goddess of Devas, tell me too. Of what nature is that group of the five Mantras? Those Mantras were used by you for the performance of the worship and subsequently imparted to them.

*Lakṣmī said:*

65-67. (1) O goddess of forbearance, obeisance to the earth. (2) O splendid one in the form of waters, obeisance to you. (3) O radiant one, obeisance to you. (4) O deity in the form of wind, obeisance to you. (5) O five-formed one, O one richly equipped with the ethereal form, obeisance, obeisance.[2]

With these Mantras the great goddess was formerly adored by me. Thereby the kingdom, extremely rare in regard to all women, was acquired by me.

68-69. Then the goddess was made out of splendid Ratnas (gems) and installed by me there in the holy spot of Hāṭakeśvara, O Lord of Suras. A woman who adores it shall become instantly a favourite darling of the husband. She will be rid of all sins. There is no doubt in this regard.

1. Padmāvatī is the incarnation of Lakṣmī.
2. The five lumps represent the five *Mahābhūtas* constituting the body, (See the next chapter) Dr Kane is HD, V. i p.336 notes that Hemādri adopted this Vrata in *Vrata Khaṇḍa* from this Purāṇa.

## CHAPTER ONE HUNDRED SEVENTYEIGHT

# Origin of Pañcapiṇḍā Gaurī

*Lakṣmī said:*

1-4. O Lord, as a result of the adoration of Gaurī the kingdom was obtained by me. So also excellent conjugal felicity very rare in the case of all women (was obtained).

Still, O great Lord, no child was begotten by me in spite of such a conjugal felicity and the prime of youth.

I was being burnt day and night due to that grief. I did not get any happiness at all.

Once the excellent sage Durvāsas came to the mansion of the king of Ānarta, out of deference to him for accepting Mṛttikā (clay) and for spending the Cāturmāsya (four months of the rainy season when itinerant recluses do not go out of a fixed locality).

5. He was duly honoured by King Ānarta. After offering Arghya and Madhuparka, the king bowed down to the sage and said:

6-8. "Welcome to you, O excellent one among sages, a hearty welcome unto you. No other king is as blessed as I am.

The particles of dust of your feet have been removed by my hair and the feet are rendered clean. O sage, you are a guest in our house. Tell me what can I do for you. I shall offer even my kingdom. What to say about other things?"

*Durvāsas said:*

9. O king, I will conduct my Cāturmāsya rites in your palace. Arrangement regarding *Mṛttikā Grahaṇa* (taking up clay) and attendance upon me may be made.

The excellent king promised, "So it shall be" and spoke to me:

10. "O fair-faced one, he should be attended upon always till the completion of the Cāturmāsya rite, along with the adoration of the deity."

11. After saying, "So it shall be" everything was carried out by me in regard to the activities of service unto him, like a daughter unto her father.

12. After the completion of the Cāturmāsya rite, when the sage started to go, he asked me "Dear daughter, what shall I do for you?"

13-15. Thereupon, after bowing down repeatedly, the holy sage was told by me, "O Brāhmaṇa, I have no child. Therefore; I experience a burning sensation day and night.

This is the condition when the youth of the king is at its zenith and perfect. So, O excellent sage, advise me on that course whereby I shall get a child. Let it be a Vrata, an observance, a gift or a Homa."

Thereupon, he thought for a long time and spoke to me smilingly:

16. "Dear daughter, in your previous life at a time when you were about to die, you adored Gaurī by means of hot particles of sand.

17. Although you attained a kingdom by her worship, yet you still continue to experience the burning sensation in the manner that Gaurī was made to experience by you through the hot particles of sand.

18. The Lord is not present in wood, stone or earth. The deity is present in the feeling of devotion in conjunction with the Mantras uttered.

19. Urged by emotional purity and devout feelings with the Mantras added on, the goddess who came to you through the invocation of Mantras was adored by you with sand particles.

20. Therefore, the burning sensation continues in your body forever. Hence you must make a Pañcapiṇḍikā wholly of Ratnas and install it in the holy spot of Hāṭakeśvara, O lady of splendid face.

21. The installation shall be when the Sun is in Taurus. Thereafter, assiduously fix over it a *Jalayantra* that drips down water day and night.

22. As the idol continues to get the coolness, your burning sensation will get reduced day and night.

23. When the scorching feeling has completely disappeared, you will conceive a son of heroic nature, capable of bearing the burden of the kingdom and of being well-known in the three worlds.

24. Any other lady who adores the idol here in the month of Jyeṣṭha shall also be in the same position as yours."

*Lakṣmī said:*

25-27a. Then the holy, leading sage was told again by me: "I am completely unattached. I have no passionate liking for human birth. I have this feeling because I have noticed that the life of all embodied beings is like the current of a river. Hence, O highly esteemed one, tell me some excellent Vrata by adopting and practising which I can cease to be in human form, O excellent Brāhmaṇa."

27b. Then, O great Lord, he thought for a long time and said to me:

28-30a. "Dear daughter, there is a meritorious Vrata that delights Gaurī much. If that is practised well, a lady shall attain divinity.

The great goddess named Gomayā has been prepared with cow-dung (by many ladies). O lady of excellent complexion, all of them have attained Goloka. O lady of excellent features, perform that rite yourself. You will attain divinity."

30b. Then, O excellent one among Suras, the sage was once again addressed by me:

31. "O excellent sage, on what occasion (month-days) and along what line of procedure should that rite be performed? Mention everything in detail so that I can duly perform it."

*Durvāsas said:*

32. On the third lunar day in the dark half of the month of Nabhasya, the devotee gets up early in the morning and then washes the teeth.

33. Then the devotee observes all regulations pertaining to fast and utters the name of Gaurī with the mind sanctified by perfect faith.

34. At nightfall Gaurī-Catuṣṭaya (four images of Gaurī) is made out of clay. Listen with attention to how it should be done.

35. At the beginning of every *Prahara* (watch of the night) an idol should be made in the form of Pañcapiṇḍa as mentioned before. Then the adoration is to be performed. Listen the Mantras to be recited separately.

36. "(Mantra) O goddess, O favourite of Śaṅkara, you were born in the abode of Himācala, from the womb of Menā. Accept my adoration. Obeisance to you."

37. Then the devotee offers incense and camphor with faith. The Dīpa (lamp) is to be offered with (the wick of) red thread and ghee.

38. After adoring with Jāti flowers, sweetmeat is offered as Naivedya covering it with a red cloth. Thereafter, *Arghya* is to be offered.

39-40. The general rule is that the devotee should use as toothpick a twig of the same tree from which the flower has been taken. For this goddess Mātuliṅga (Pomegranate) is to be used with this Mantra for *Arghya* offering along with scents, flowers and raw rice grain: O goddess, O beloved of Śaṅkara. O splendid daughter of Himālaya mountain, *Arghya* has been offered by me; do accept it. Obeisance to you."

41. For the purity of the body, the same is taken in after the end of every Prahara and the deity Ardhanārīśvara is to be worshipped.

42. Then the devotee worships with (scents?) uttering this Mantra: "O Pārvatī, Obeisance to you who constitute the left half of the body of Hara. May that goddess accept my worship."

43. Then, with devotion Agaru is offered as incense *Gaṇakas* (threads) are placed on the Naivedya offering. The Arghaka is offered with coconut.

44-45. It should be offered with this Mantra: The Prāśana (what is taken in) is the same. "O Ardhanārīśvaras, O two great deities, you are the bestowers of happiness on all. May the *Arghya* be received."

In the third *Prahara,* the devotee worships with *Śatapatrī* (lotus leaves).

46. The devotee shall worship the deities Umā and Maheśvara with this Mantra:

47. "May the deities Umā and Maheśvara who are invariably present at the time of creation and dissolution accept this adoration of mine offered with great devotion."

48. The incense is from Guggula and the Naivedya is in the form of *Ghārikā* (a fried pie). The *Arghya* consists of *Jātī* fruit and the same is remembered as *Prāśana* (things taken in or eaten).

49-51. Thereafter the Arghya is to be given devoutly with this Mantra: "May the deities Umā and Meheśvara who bestow all desires and happiness, take great pity on me and accept this Arghya." The incense is in the form of Granthicūṛna (fragrant powder of Granthiparṇa); the *Arghya* is Madana fruit. For the sake of the purity of the body, the same is taken in.

52. In the fourth Prahara, the devotee worships Gaurī Pañcapiṇḍikā by means of Bhṛṅgarāja, uttering this Mantra with devotion:

53. "O goddess of Devas, your five forms are Pṛthivī etc., that have been mentioned as the five Bhūtas (five elements). Accept this adoration. Obeisance to you."

54. By way of Naivedya, the devotee should give pies cooked in ghee to the goddess with great devotion. The incense is in the form of Granthicūrṇa. The fruit of Madana is used for Arghya. The same is to be taken in as *Prāśana*. The following is remembered as *Arghya Mantra*:

55. "Let that goddess of Suras accept this *Arghya* offered by me to the goddess who appears in five ways consisting of the five Bhūtas."

56. In this manner, the entire night should be passed in front of them (i.e. the five Piṇḍikās) while listening to vocal and instrumental music etc. all the time. The devotee should not go to sleep (during that night).

57. When the day has dawned and the solar disc devoid of impurities has risen, the devotee with great devotion should complete bath and adoration and honour a Brāhmaṇa, along with his wife.

58. O princess of pure smiles, the Brāhmaṇa should be honoured with garments and ornaments according to one's capacity. Food along with sweet pudding should be given to a Gaurī (girl of eight years).

59. Then, O lady of excellent waistline, either a mare or a she-elephant should be brought and the four images of Gaurī should be placed on her.

60. The procession is to be taken out with the accompaniment of singing and playing musical instruments and the chanting of the Vedas. The images are to be immersed in a lake or a tank.

61. The following Mantras should be uttered with excellent devotion. O beautiful lady, I shall mention it to you:

62. "O goddess of great splendour, you have been invoked and adored by me. Now may it please you to grant conjugal felicity to me and to proceed ahead as you please."

*Lakṣmī said:*

63. Thus, O Lord, the adoration was performed by me on that third lunar day in the month of Nabhasya with great devotion.

64. The second and third Praharas passed by and at the time of dawn what do I see? The four images of Gaurī that had been adored by me had become embellished with jewels.

65. Thinking 'I shall perform the *Visarjana* (ritualistic dismissal)' I set off towards the banks of the river. Then the goddess of Suras manifested herself and said:

66-68. "O daughter, do not cast my four images into the water. Listen to my words, Ponder over them and carry out the injunctions.

Do not cast them away. Install them in Hāṭakeśvara Kṣetra. It will remain everlasting and be conducive to the welfare of all women. Do request for the boon. On being adored here I shall grant you everything."

The goddess of Suras, the Daughter of the Mountain was adored by me and told thus:

69-72. "O goddess of Suras, if you are pleased and if you wish to grant me a boon, let me not be born in human womb at all. Let Viṣṇu, the bestower of what is always desired, be my husband. Nothing else such as splendid heavenly kingdom, is desired by me. If any other woman performs this Vrata with great concentration, O goddess, let the satisfaction be the same as with the performance of all the Vratas (collectively). O Pārvatī, you must bring that about solely through this one Vrata."

Gaurī told me "So be it" and then vanished.

73. O my Lord, that goddess, namely the four images of Gaurī, were installed by me in the splendid Hāṭakeśvara Kṣetra.

74. By her power, O great Lord, you are obtained by me as my husband. You are eternal and everlasting. You are always my Mukhaprekṣa (one who eagerly looks at the face of another).

75. O god of Suras, I have entirely told you what I had

been asked. O Lord of Devas, as the proof of the veracity of this I touch your feet.

*Sūta said:*

76. On hearing her words the weilder of conch, discus and club became delighted. He laughed and repeatedly embraced her keeping her close to his chest and said:

77. "O highly esteemed one, excellent! excellent! It is the truth that has been mentioned by you. O lady of excellent complexion, you were asked by me, though I already knew it."

*Sūta said:*

78. Thus, O excellent Brāhmaṇas, everything that I was asked has been narrated to you all as to how the four-armed Gaurī became one of five Piṇḍikās.

79. A man who gets up early in the morning and read this devoutly will never be bereft of Lakṣmī (prosperity and glory) nor will he meet with bad luck.

80. Hence, O Brāhmaṇas, this splendid narrative of Gaurī expatiated upon by me, should be read with all efforts.

## CHAPTER ONE HUNDRED SEVENTYNINE

## Rites Preliminary to Yajñas

*Sūta said:*

1-3. Further, there are other holy sites also in the Hāṭakeśvara Kṣetra that are destructive of all sins. They are the three Puṣkaras.

If they are visited, touched or glorified, O excellent Brāhmaṇas, sin is dispelled like darkness by the Sun.

All the (other) Tīrthas undoubtedly sanctify through holy bath and offering of gifts. But one is relieved of all sins merely by visiting the Puṣkaras.

*The sages said:*

4. The Tīrtha named Puskara, well-known in all the three

worlds in heard about (by us). It was created by Brahmā. It extends to a Yojana.

5. On the north of the river Candrabhāgā it extends upto Sarasvatī. On the south the limit of the three Puṣkaras is Karatoyā.[1]

6. This was formerly spoken to us, O Sūta, as being present in the sky. This is our curiosity. How has it come to Hāṭakeśvara Kṣetra? It behoves you to explain.

*Sūta said:*

7. O highly esteemed ones, what has been said by you all is true. Now, O excellent Brāhmaṇas, listen with concentration in regard to that holy spot.

8. After bowing down to the Self-born Lord, I shall tell everything in detail.

9. While Brahmā, the Avyaktajanman (One whose origin is unmanifest), was staying in Brahmaloka, Sage Nārada, the celestial sage, came there after wandering over all the three worlds.

10. He bowed down the head and touched his (Brahmā's) feet. Then he sat in front of him.

*Brahmā said:*

11. O dear son, how is it that I see you after a long time? Where are you coming from? where have you been wandering? Dear son, tell me the reason thereof.

*Nārada said:*

12. O Lord, I have reached this place hurriedly from the world of the mortals in order to worship your feet. I touch (swear) myself on the truth of this statement.

*Brahmā said:*

13. Tell me the news of the human world. Of what sort are the kings there? Of what sort are the Brāhmaṇas? What sort of dealings abound there now?

---

1. The author seems to have a vague idea of the location of Puṣkara. It is in Rajasthan. Candrabhāgā (Chenab) is in Punjab, Karatoyā formed the ancient boundary between Bengal and Kāmarūpa. (De, p.93).

*Nārada said:*

14. O most excellent one among Suras, there is the onset of Kali in the human world now.

15. The kings abandon the path of the good; they are greedy. For the sake of money they trouble all the people very ruthlessly.

16. They have eschewed the noble quality of heroism. They oppress the wives of others. They do not revere or honour Brāhmaṇas, deities and elders.

17. Brāhmaṇas never hesitate to sell the Vedas. They are devoid of purities. They are greedy to accept gifts even from sinners. They are not regular in the performance of Sandhyā prayers. They are extremely merciless.

18. They are always engaged in agricultural activities. They breed cattle like Vaiśyas. Original Vaiśyas have disappeared from the earth.

19. The Śūdras have become desirous of performing pious rites. These very Śūdras have become ascetics too. All of them are shameless and they laugh derisively at worldly activities engaged in for the sake of earthly existence.

20. On the earth, men cultivate friendly relations with (whatever) person in whose house there is affluence and young women as well.

21. Great lust has entered into the heart of widows, persons observing Vratas and even in religious students.

22. All the Tīrthas undergo great upheaval. They are resorted to by sinful people. All of them are frightened of the Kali age and they run about here and there in all the ten directions.

23. O Pitāmaha, I too was affected while staying there because it was the Kali age.

24. In the Kali age unchaste women are too fond of delicate things. Women argue with their husbands and they are interested in their special work or witchcraft. They ignore the interests of their husbands and perform *Vratas* which are futile.

25. The Kali age has been rendered very powerful by your boons. Whenever there is a battle in the human world I get an itching sensation in the heart.

26-28. When there is a battle in heaven there is an itching sensation in the head and when there is a battle in Pātāla, there is an itching sensation in the feet. Now in the human world mutual quarrels and battles have been seen by me many times between mothers-in-law and daughters-in-law, between fathers and sons, between kinsmen, and between masters and servants. There are fights between thieves and kings and even between married pairs (couples). Clouds contain meagre water and the earth produces very little vegetation (foodgrain).

29. Cows yield very little quantity of milk. Milk does not contain adequate fat content (ghee).

Thus I observed their battles day and night.

30. I wandered over the mortal world for long, having come into contact with it after some time. I will go there once more. There is a great itching sensation.

31. On hearing the words of Nārada, Pitāmaha became worried and all his senses became distressed out of consideration for Puṣkara.

32-35. He thought thus 'My Tīrtha in the mortal world named Puṣkara is well-known. It will certainly be destroyed on being overcome by the Kali age. Hence I shall take it to another place where Kali is not present. I shall leave my Tīrtha named Puṣkara there.

At the advent of the Kali Age that is terrifying unto all living beings, let all the Tīrthas proceed there. When Kali age (being over) departs they will undoubtedly return to their own place.'

36. After thinking thus in mind, after pondering over it mentally, Pitāmaha eagerly spoke to the Lotus in his hand:

37. "O Lotus, do fall down to the ground where there is no (influence or existence of) Kali, so that I can bring my Tīrtha Puṣkara there."

38. Then the lotus sent by him wandered over the whole of the earth and fell on the Hāṭakeśvara Kṣetra.

39. (In the course of its reconnaissance the Lotus saw these things:) The pure Brāhmaṇas, conversant with the Vedas, were enagaged in chanting the texts. Their Yajña rites proceeded without hindrance.

40. All the quarters were full of the Yūpas (sacrificial posts). In the courtyard of the firmament there was the chanting sound of the Mantras of Ṛk, Yajus, Sāman and Atharvan.

41. When this chanting sound rose up and spread over the quarters no other sound could be heard.

In some places there were great discussions and argumentation of Tārkikas.

42. The entire range of the Vedāntas was being commented upon (discussed) in various ways. The sages were seen engaged in their regular observances.

43. Some took only a single meal per day. Some observed complete fast. Some took food on alternate days. Others observed fast for three days together. Still others were engaged in Kṛcchra Cāndrāyaṇa rites (expiation).

44. Others observed the Mahāpārāka rites. Others observed fast for the whole of a month. Still others were *Aśmakuṭṭāśins* (eating only what is ponded between two slabs). A few others were *Dantolūkhalikas* (i.e.they crushed the grains with their teeth used as mortars).

45. A few ate withered leaves. There were great sages having fruits for food. (The Lotus) saw the holy spot rich with different kinds of good qualities and features.

46. It knew that spot as sacred and fell on to the ground. It then rose up from the place where it fell before.

47. O excellent Brāhmaṇas, it then fell down on a second spot. Then for the third time, the Lotus rose up and fell on another spot.

48. Three pits took shape in the three spots. Crystal clear water filled those pits.

49. In the meantime, Pitāmaha himself came to that spot, O excellent Brāhmaṇas, for performing Yajña rites.

50. He surveyed all round the holy place named Hāṭakeśvara full of various Brāhmaṇas who had mastered the Vedas and Vedāṅgas. There were ascetics and many others engaged in pursuing Vrata rites.

51. (Pitāmaha said to himself) Oh, this holy spot is wonderful! It is meritorious, beautiful and liked by the twice-borns. Hence I shall perform a Yajña in this holy spot resorted to by Brāhmaṇas.

52. I shall bring that splendid trio of Puṣkaras to these holy pits–the superior, the middling and the inferior Puṣkara.

53. When the Kali age arrives they will not get destroyed. He thought thus in his mind. Then he sat on the ground.

54. He meditated for a long time and brought the three Puṣkaras–the superior, the middling and the inferior.

55-59. Delighted within himself he spoke: "These three Puṣkaras have been rightly brought here due to the fear of Kali age.

Those who are endowed with perfect faith and take their bath here, will attain great Siddhi that will never get lost with my favour.

Those who perform Śrāddha here on the Kārttikī day with concentration will attain the great merit of performing the Śrāddha in Gayāśīrṣa.

There, from the first Puṣkara, they will get hundred times more merit. Yajña was performed in the Pūrva Puṣkara on the Kārttikī day. Here in the second Puṣkara, I shall perform the Yajña on the Vaiśākhī day."

60-62. After speaking thus, Brahmā commanded the Wind-god: "At my behest, O Vāyu, bring Purandara here. Let him be brought along with the Ādityas, Vasus, Rudras, groups of Maruts, Gandharvas, Lokapālas, Siddhas and Vidyādharas. If they come I can be assisted in all the Yajña rites."

On hearing it completely, Vāyu went to the abode of Śakra and told him everything said by Parameṣṭhin.

63. Then Śakra hurriedly went there along with all the groups of Devas. After bowing to him, he spoke these words to Brahmā:

64. "O Lord, may command be given to me. Wherefore have I been summoned? I shall carry it out. So do tell me quickly."

*Brahmā said:*

65. O Śakra, the highly meritorious trio of Puṣkaras has been brought here due to the fear of Kali age. I want to make them stable.

66. I wish to perform three Agniṣṭomas as I had performed earlier, on the Vaiśākhī day. Bring all the requisites thereof quickly.

67. Bring also the Brāhmaṇas who are worthy (qualified) with the full mastery of the Vedas and Vedāṅgas.

On hearing it Śakra said, "So be it". Hurriedly he brought the requisites and the Brāhmaṇas qualified for the same.

68. Then Prapitāmaha performed the Yajña duly in accordance with the injunctions with the full complement of monetary gifts.

## CHAPTER ONE HUNDRED EIGHTY

# Brahmā Begins the Yajña

*The sages said:*

1. Thus the story narrated by you that in that holy place Yajña was performed by the noble-souled Brahmā is extremely wonderful, O Sūta.

2. There are many Yajñas performed on the earth namely Agniṣṭoma etc. In those Yajñas it is the same Lord of Suras who is worshipped.

3-5. But when he himself performs the Yajña what could have been his desire? Do tell us. Who were the Ṛtviks who performed the rites requisite for the Makha? Mention these. Our curiosity is great. What was the Dakṣiṇā (monetary gift) given by him to those Brāhmaṇas who had been employed as Adhvaryu? By whom was the worship carried out? Who was the Hotṛ? Who was the Agnīdhra priest? Who remained as Brahmā? Who was Udgātṛ? Who was the Ācārya in the Yajña rite?

*Sūta said:*

6. O excellent Brāhmaṇas, I shall explain unto you all the details regarding the Yajña that took place in such a wonderful manner.

7. The noble-souled one gave monetary gifts to the members of the assembly present there, namely the Ṛtviks and the excellent Brāhmaṇas.

8-9. All these things were carried out by Brahmā, the Lord of Devas, who performed the Yajña. He had unmeasurable splendour.

On coming to know that the Four-faced One was desirous of performing the Yajña, Lord Śatakratu came there to extend cooperation and help along with all the groups of Suras. So also came Lord Śambhu with all the deities and Gaṇas (goblins and spirits, his attendants).

10. On seeing that all of them assembled there having resorted to the duties of mortals, Brahmā stood humbly with palms joined in reverence:

11-12. "O excellent Suras, welcome to you all; please do me a favour. Be pleased to be seated in the comfortable and pleasant seats in due order.

I am blessed and contented that you have all taken the trouble to come yourselves in the same manner as you take pains to go to all the Sattras on being invoked by Mantras."

*The Devas said:*

13. O Lotus-born One, tell us quickly as to who has to do what part of the job on hand.

*Brahmā said:*

14. O Viśvakarman, hurry up and complete the construction of the Yajña Maṇḍapa, The Patnīśālās (rooms for womenfolk and domestic activities) and Yajñavedis (sacrificial altars) should be erected.

15. Make all the Kuṇḍas (holy pits) in their respective places. All the utensils, ladles, bowls etc., for the Yajña should be kept ready.

16. The Yūpas (sacrificial posts) should be fixed along with *Caṣālakas* (wooden rings on the top). They should be of the proper size. For the purpose of cooking the oven pits should be dug with the proper sizes and dimensions.

17. Ten thousand eight hundred *Iṣṭakas* (bricks) should be got ready quickly. Twigs should be stacked immediately.

18. The golden image of the Puruṣa should be made there itself.

Saying "So it shall be" Tvaṣṭṛ hastened out.

19. Then the Lotus-born Lord spoke to Bṛhaspati, the preceptor of Devas: "O Bṛhaspati, do fetch all the Ṛtviks qualified for the performance of the Yajña.

20. They should be sixteen in number. It is not proper to entrust this task to anyone else. O Śakra, you must always serve and attend to the Brāhmaṇas.

21. The massaging of their hands and feet should be done. If they are very tired their backs should be massaged duly. O Kubera, O presiding deity of wealth, the monetary gifts should be made at the proper time.

22. They can be given excellent garments, gold and all other things desired.

O Viṣṇu, supervision of what is to be done and what is not to be done is your duty.

23. You must attentively examine always whether the proper things have been duly completed or not.

May all the Guardians of the Quarters keep watch over all directions. The entry of goblins, ghosts and vampires as well as Rākṣasas should be checked.

24. If anyone expresses any desire to have anything, say cloth or cash, the superintendent of all the Yajñas should give them the respective things after due consideration.

25. Ādityas, Vasus, Rudras, Viśvedevas and groups of Maruts shall be the ones serving food to the people who are desirous of taking meal."

26-27. In the meantime, Viśvakarman hurriedly came there and announced to the Lotus-born Lord: "The parlour for the Yajña and everything else commanded by you is fully provided (is ready), O Four-faced Lord."

28-29. Then Bṛhaspati came and told Lord Pitāmaha: "O Lord, Brāhmaṇas to perform the rites of Yajña have been brought by me. The Brāhmaṇas are sixteen in number. Employ them as Ṛtviks, O Lord of Devas. Test them yourself so that the Yajña rite can be faultless."

30. Then Brahmā saw them and tested them himself carefully. Then he employed them as Ṛtviks and duly honoured them.

*The sages said:*

31. O Sūta, do enumerate the names of all the Ṛtviks. Do mention which of them carried out which task.

*Sūta said:*

32. Bhṛgu was chosen by him for the office of Hautra, O excellent Brāhmaṇas. Sage Cyavana was named for the post of Maitrāvaruṇa.

33. Marīci became Acchāvāka priest, Sage Gālava was the Priest Grāvastut (Eulogiser of the rock). Pulastya was Adhvaryu. Atri remained as Prasthātṛ.

34. Sage Raibhya was the priest Neṣṭṛ. Sanātana was Unnetṛ. Nārada was Brahmā priest. Garga was the priest Brāhmaṇācchaṁsī.

35. Bharadvāja was the priest Agnidhra. Parāśara was the Hotṛ. Sage Gobhila was the Udgātṛ in that holy spot.

36. Kauthuma became the priest Prestautṛ in the Yajña rite. Śāṇḍilya was the Pratihartṛ priest and Aṅgiras was the priest Subrahmaṇya.

37. These sixteen Ṛtviks[1] collaborated for the fulfilment of the Yajña. They were respectfully rendered splendid through garments and ornaments.

38. After honouring everyone personally in the manner laid down in the Gṛhya Sūtras, Brahmā respectfully spoke to them:

39. "O excellent Brāhmaṇas, I seek refuge in you all. Do bless me for the initiation in the Yajña rite."

1. The list of sixteen priests required for sacrifices is enumerated in Āśvalāyana Śrauta Sūtra IV.I.6. Out of there Hotṛ, Udgātṛ, Brahmā and Adhvaryu are most important. For details about sacrifice *vide* Kane, HD.II.ii, ch. XXIX.

## CHAPTER ONE HUNDRED EIGHTYONE

# Greatness of Gāyatrī Tīrtha[1]

*Sūta said:*

1-2. In the meantime, a *Madhyaga* (a go-between) hailing from Gartātīrtha was sent by all the excellent Brāhmaṇas, the Nāgaras: "O *Madhyaga* (Nāgara), go to and tell that Kupitāmaha (Evil Pitāmaha) who has destroyed the means of sustenance of the Brāhmaṇas and who has forsaken the path of justice and fairplay.

3. 'This holy spot was granted to the Brāhmaṇas–our ancestors, by serpents.

4. Ending with you, O evil Pitāmaha, one hundred five different Pitāmahas have gone by since the time when that gift was made. There is no doubt about it.

5. With the exception of a being of sinful activities who strays away from the path of justice, contempt was never shown to us as is being done now.

6. He who is outside the clan of Nāgara Brāhmaṇas and performs Śrāddha or Yajña here should be killed by all other Brāhmaṇas.

7. When he (Śiva) granted us this holy place it was assured by him that he (the outsider) would not derive any benefit at all therefrom.

8. Hence, whatever Yajña you perform, get the same done by the Nāgara Brāhmaṇas. Otherwise, you will not get an opportunity to perform it as long as the Nāgara Brāhmaṇas are alive.'"

9-10. On being told thus, the *Madhyaga* went to the place where the Lotus-born One was present, a bit away from the Yajña pavilion, surrounded by Brāhmaṇas. What was said by all those Nāgaras, he told him with special emphasis. On hearing it the Lotus-born One spoke these words in a conciliatory tone:

11-13. Brahmā had adopted human guise and was surrounded by the Ṛtviks. (He said:) "O excellent *Madhyaga*,

1. This chapter describes how, due to the mischief of Nārada, god Brahmā had to marry a Brāhmanised Vaiśya girl without the knowledge of his first wife Sāvitrī.

everything said by you is true. What shall I do? All these have been already chosen by me for the performance of Yajña rites—all these Ṛtviks, Adhvaryus and others. They have been chosen by mistake not wilfully.

Hence bring all those excellent Brāhmaṇas here to this holy spot, so that with their permission I shall go to the pavilion of the Makha."

*Madhyaga said:*

14. You have set aside your divinity and have adopted human guise and features. Therefore, how can those excellent Brāhmaṇas come near you?

15. O Lotus-born One, just as cows are the most excellent ones among all animals, so also the Nāgaras are the most excellent ones among Brāhmaṇas.

16. Hence, if you desire the acquisition of the benefit arising from this Yajña, O Pitāmaha, propitiate all the Nāgaras with devotion due to them.

*Sūta said:*

17. On hearing it, the Lotus-born God became afraid. Surrounded by the Ṛtviks he went to that place where the angry Nāgara Brāhmaṇas were present.

18. With great humility, he bowed down to all of them. Standing with palms joined in deference, he spoke these words:

19-23. "O excellent Brāhmaṇas, I do know that in this holy spot of Hāṭakeśvara, Śrāddha and Yajña rites performed by one excluding you all, are futile.

Due to the fear of Kali, my Tīrtha, Puṣkara has been brought by me to this holy spot. This has been dedicated to you all as a deposit.

These Ṛtviks have been brought by Guru (i.e. Bṛhaspati), O excellent Brāhmaṇas, without knowing the superiority of the Nāgaras.

Hence, the fact of my selecting them, my choice of these Brāhmaṇas, for the performance of Agniṣṭoma may be excused.

This Tīrtha of mine shall undoubtedly be destructive of your sins even during the advent of the Kali age."

*The Brāhmaṇas said:*

24. If you perform the Yajña here excluding the Nāgaras, other Suras also are likely to follow your way. So also the kings of the earth. Hence, the Makha should not be performed by you.

25. In spite of this, O Lord of Devas, if you are bent upon the performance of the Yajña rites disregarding all of us, the Brāhmaṇas, then go away from our vicinity.

*Brahmā said:*

26. From now onwards if anyone performs Yajña or Śrāddha here excluding the Nāgaras, it shall become futile.

27. If a Nāgara too leaves this holy spot and performs Yajña elsewhere, it will become futile.

28. O Brāhmaṇas, this line of demarcation has been made unto the Nāgaras. Hence, be pleased to accord due permission to us, O Brāhmaṇas, so that I can perform the Yajña.

*Sūta said:*

29. Thereupon, Pitāmaha was permitted by those Brāhmaṇas who became pleased. He duly performed the Yajña through the Brāhmaṇas who had been already selected.

30. Viśvakarman who stood by the decision of the Nāgaras came there, O excellent Brāhmaṇas, and embellished the head (of Brahmā).

31. Brahmā became extremely delighted and told Nārada: "Fetch Sāvitrī quickly so that I can go to the pavilion of the sacrifice."

32. As the musical instruments were played by Siddhas, Kinnaras and Guhyakas, when Gandharvas were absorbed in their songs and Brāhmaṇas were engaged in chanting the Vedas, Pulastya took up the Araṇi and spoke loudly these words:

33. "Patnī ? Patnī ?" (Where is the wife of the Yajamāna?) and the leading Brāhmaṇas were seated in their respective places.

34. In the meantime, Brahmā suggested by gesture to the excellent sage Nārada that his wife should be brought there.

35. Nārada (by nature) liked to provoke quarrels. He wished to create a gap in the relations between Sāvitrī and god Brahmā. So he slowly (leisurely) went to Sāvitrī and spoke playfully:

36-38. "O goddess of Suras, I have been sent by my father to you with the message 'Do come; I have taken my bath and am going to the pavilion of the Yajña.'

But, O goddess of Suras, if you go there alone how will you fare there? You will appear like a helpless lady.

Hence let all the celestial women be brought. O goddess, you will go to the great Makha surrounded by those celestial women."

39-40a. After saying this, the excellent sage Nārada went to his father and said: "Father, mother has been called by me. But I have slightly observed her mental predilection to remain unmoved."

40b. On hearing his words, he (Brahmā)became very angry.

41-42. He sent Pulastya to Sāvitrī: "Dear Son, she is slow by nature. Bring her to this place. See how tired I am bearing the weight of the Soma placed over!

Now there will be too much of delay in the performance of the Yajña rite. Very little time now remains for the Muhūrta (auspicious hour) for the Yajñayāna (procedure of the Yajña)."

43. On hearing his words Pulastya hastened to the place where Sāvitrī was present engrossed in songs and dances.

44-45. He said then: "O goddess, why do you stand thus unmoved? Very little time is left for the Muhūrta proper for the procedure of Yajñayāna. Hence come (hurry up). We shall go. Father is excessively agitated and afflicted with the weight of the Soma kept over (his head). He is surrounded by all the Devas."

*Sāvitrī said:*

46. Dear Son, your father being surrounded by all the Devas is settled well. How can I go there all by myself like a helpless person?

47. Go and tell father to be patient for a short while.

48. (He may be pleased to wait) till Śakrāṇī, Gaurī, Lakṣmī and other celestial women gather together in our assembly. I shall come quickly along with them.

49. May your father be informed that Vāyu has been sent by me to invite all of them. They will come presently.

*Sūta said:*

50-51. He hastened to Vidhi who was afflicted with the burden of Soma: "O Lord of the universe, she is engaged in her domestic chores. She is not coming. She tells me, 'I will attend the Makha along with the wives of the Devas. But none of them is seen so far.'

52. Know this, O most excellent one among Suras, and do what pleases you the most. It is rather getting very late for the procedure of the Yajña rite. That woman in her dilatoriness is busy with her domestic chores."

53. On hearing the words of Pulastya, Pitāmaha spoke to Śakra who was nearby, O Brāhmaṇas:

*Brahmā said:*

54. O Śakra, Sāvitrī has not come. She is rather a dilatory woman. But, am I to perform this Yajña with such a wife?

55. O Śakra, go and fetch some other girl quickly so that the auspicious hour for Yajña does not slip away.

56. On hearing the words of Pitāmaha, O Brāhmaṇas, (Śakra went in search) of such a girl. Soon she was met by him, as she wandered nearby.

57. She was a slim cowherd lass, lotus-eyed and moon-faced. A pot of curd was on her head and she was scrupulously taking care of it.

58-59. She was at the threshold to the prime of youth. She was endowed with full complement of all auspicious features. She was asked by Śakra: "O lotus-eyed one, who may you be? Are you a virgin or a married one with a husband? Tell me, whose daughter are you?"

*The girl said:*

60. I am daughter of a cowherd. Welfare unto you. I have come here to sell buttermilk. If you want it, pay me the cost thereof. Do not delay.

61. On hearing it, the Lord of Heaven came to know she was daughter of a cowherd. He seized her quickly and split all the buttermilk on the ground.

62. Even as she went on crying Śakra seized her, forced her through the mouth of a cow and dragged her out of the anus.

63. After sanctifying her thus, O leading Brāhmaṇas, he bathed her in the auspicious waters of the first Kuṇḍa and made her wear excellent garments.

64. Then he joyously spoke to the Four-faced One hastening to him and placing her in front in the assembly of all the Devas:

65-66. "O excellent one among Suras, this girl has been brought by me now for your sake. She is comely in her limbs and is marked by all the auspicious features.

Knowing that she is daughter of a cowherd, O Four-faced One, she was forced through the mouth of a cow and then dragged out through the anus for the purpose of sanctifying her."

*Śrī Vāsudeva said:*

67. Cows and Brāhmaṇas belong to the same family. It is split into two, the Mantras abide in one, while the *Havis* abides in the other.

68. Coming out of the belly of a cow this girl has become a daughter of Brāhmaṇas. Grasp her hand, O Lord, for the fulfilment of the Makha.

69. Let it be before the auspicious hour for the performance of the Yajña slips by.

*Rudra said:*

70. She entered the mouth of a cow and came out of the anus. Hence, she is named Gāyatrī. She shall become your wife.

*Brahmā said:*

71. May all the Brāhmaṇas say collectively that though she is the daughter of a cowherd she has become an excellent Brāhmaṇa girl so that she can be my wife.

*The Brāhmaṇas said:*

72. She shall be an excellent Brāhmaṇa woman free from the nativity of a cowherd. At our instance, O Four-faced One, marry her quickly.

*Sūta said:*

73. Then Lord Pitāmaha married her. Then, O Brāhmaṇas, he held the Soma above the head in the manner it has been enjoined in the Gṛhya Sūtras.

74. The sacred great goddess is standing there even today. She is well-known as the bestower of wealth and conjugal felicity.

75. A man who makes the gift of a virgin there with great concentration, shall derive the entire benefit of a Rājasūya and horse-sacrifice.

76. The girl who gets married there shall be blessed with sons, happiness and conjugal felicity.

77. O excellent Brāhmaṇas, if a man offers balls of rice there the Pitṛs become pleased with him as though libations were offered in a Pitṛtīrtha.

## CHAPTER ONE HUNDRED EIGHTYTWO

## The Yajña of Brahmā: The First Day

*Sūta said:*

1. After having secured Gāyatrī as his wife, the Four-faced Lord became highly delighted in his mind. He started towards the pavilion of sacrifice.

2. Gāyatrī eschewed the despicable state of a cowherdess and proceeded ahead joyously holding the Araṇi on the head.

3-4. Even as the musical instruments were played and the chanting of the Vedas reached the vaults of heaven and the Gandharvas were singing sweetly all round, Brahmā in the assumed form of a human being reached the Yajña Maṇḍapa accompanied by Gāyatrī and all the Devas and the Brāhmaṇas.

5. In the meantime, Viśvakarmā cut the hair of Vidhi and pared the nails of Gāyatrī after him.

6. Then, O excellent Brāhmaṇas, Pulastya handed the Audumbara staff along with the Mantra-charged hide of a deer together with its horns.

7. Gāyatrī was taken to the Patnīśālā even as she

observed silence. A splendid girdle of the Muñja grass was tied round her waist.

8. Accompanied by the Ṛtviks, Vedhas (Brahmā) respectfully followed the instructions in the Vedas. He performed the later rites in the Yajña Maṇḍapa.

9-10. While Pravargya (a prelude to Soma Sacrifice) was begun a miracle took place there. A nude fellow with a hideous face appeared in his hand and requested, "Food may kindly be given." He entered the sacrificial chamber though he was prevented. Though he was threatened by the sages, he wandered there freely and unjustifiably.

The Sadasyas (members of the Assembly) said:

11. "Why have you, O sinner, entered the Yajña pavilion nude in form, holding a skull and bereft of all experience in Yajña rite?

12. O fool, go away quickly before Brahmā becomes angry. Others like the excellent Brāhmaṇas, the Devas including Vāsava also may be furious."

*The Rogue said:*

13. I heard about the Yajña of Brahmā and have come here from very far. O excellent Brāhmaṇas, I am hungry. Why should you censure me?

14. This rite is called Kratu when the wretched ones, the blind and the miserable ones are propitiated. If that is not the case, that should be conducive to destruction as per these words mentioned by Brāhmaṇas:

15. "There is no other enemy on a par with Yajña. If it is without food supply, it will burn the nation. If it is without Mantras, it will burn the Ṛtviks. If it is without monetary gifts, it will destroy the performer of the Yajña."

*The Brāhmaṇas said:*

16. If you have come here with a desire to eat then go quickly to this Sattraśālā (Śacrificial hall) where the ascetics, the blind, the wretched and the miserable ones with parched throats due to hunger, are taking their food.

17. Or, O sage, if you are desirous of money or garments go to the place in the Dānaśālā (chamber of gifts) where the *Vittapati* (Lord of wealth, Kubera) is present.

18. O great fool, this Yajña of Pitāmaha is uncensurable. It is venerated all round. O wicked-minded one, why do you censure this meritorious thing?

*Sūta said:*

19. O excellent Brāhmaṇas, on being told thus, he threw down the skull on the ground and vanished immediately like a lamp.

*The Ṛtviks said:*

20. How can the sacrificial rite proceed as long as the skull lies in the main *Sadas* (chamber)? Hence, throw it away, said the excellent Brāhmaṇas.

21. One of them who was repeatedly told thus by the excellent Brāhmana members of the assembly, lifted up a stick and pushed it out.

22. Then another skull like this one cropped up there. When it was pushed away, another skull took its place.

23. Thus handreds, thousands, ten thousands and millions of skulls rose up there. The Yajñavāṭa (the premises of Yajña) was filled with them all round.

24. A great hue and cry arose in the entire Yajña pavilion on seeing heaps on heaps of skulls that defiled the sacrificial rite.

25-26. Then Pitāmaha meditated and thought. He came to know that everything calamitous was thus caused by Hara. He joined his palms in veneration and spoke to Maheśvara joyously and respectfully. Maheśvara was then in the precincts of the Yajñavāṭa.

27-28. "O Lord, is it proper that there should be deficiency in the rites concerning the Yajña? Hence, O Lord of Suras, withdraw all the skulls. Let there not be omissions in the Yajña rites even when you have arrived."

29-33. Thereupon, the Moon-crested Lord said angrily: "That is my favourite bowl of food. It has always been so. O Pitāmaha, why do these base Brāhmaṇas hate me? They did not offer oblations (saying Svāhā) into the fire with me in view. O Vidhi (Brahmā), the *Havis* offering charged and sanctified with Mantras have not been made to me as (they have done) in the case of other deities. So do you wish that the Yajña rite should be concluded?

Then all the Havyas should be put in those skulls. Further with me in view, a special Homa should be offered in the sacred fire. Then the Kratu will be concluded; not otherwise. O Four-faced One, the truth has been spoken to you."

*Pitāmaha said:*

34. O Lord of Devas, your forms are myriad and different. There is no limit to their number and all of them are to be meditated upon.

35-36. O Three-eyed One, this is called your Mahāvrata. In this manner it shall not be a Makha rite and it is not proper to perform this rite as being outside the scope of the Vedic injunction. But, O three-eyed One, I do not intend to go against your behest.

37. So, O Lord of Suras, the *Havis* may be cooked in a Kapāla of clay (potsherd). That is, the Puroḍāśa should be cooked in them from now onwards by the Brāhmaṇas. When it refers to the Yajña, O most excellent one among Suras, O Lord of Devas, with you in view the *Śatarudriya* should be chanted while performing Homa.

38-39. In the course of all the Yajñas, it should be recited in particular. By means of these Kapālas (skulls), O most excellent one among Suras, your own real form has been revealed by you. Hence, O Rudra, you will be named Kapāleśvara in this holy spot, a twelfth among them.

40. If anyone begins a Yajña here and worships you at the outset, his Makha will be named Kapāleśvara.

41. When this was spoken by him, O excellent Brāhmaṇas, all the skulls, unlimited in number, vanished.

42. Then, the delighted Four-faced God immediately installed the Liṅga of Maheśvara there, called Kapāleśvara.

43-44. And he said: "He who, after taking bath in my Kuṇḍas, worships this Liṅga, will attain the greatest goal. He who performs the *Jāgara* (keeping awake) rite on the fourteenth day in the bright half of the month of Kārttika with great concentration in front of this Liṅga, will get rid of all the sins since his birth."

45. When this was spoken by Vidhi, the Slayer of the Tripuras became very delighted. Reaching the Yajña Maṇḍapa he went near the Vedi (Altar).

46. Then, after duly bowing down to Maheśvara the Yajña rites were started by the Brāhmaṇas with their eyes beaming with pleasant surprise.

*Sūta said:*

47. Even as the Four-faced One was performing the Yajña there in this manner, there came a crore of sages, the inhabitants of the southern region.

48-49. On hearing about the Yajña of Pitāmaha they became inquisitive: "How will this Yajña be, where the Lotus-born Lord himself has become initiated? Of what nature is that meritorious holy place named Hāṭakeśvara? Of what nature are those leading Brāhmaṇas appointed there as the Ṛtviks?"

50-51. The day was Sunday coinciding with the constellation Aśvinī. The Sun was in the middle of the day and the lunar day was Vaivasvatī (second day). The visitors were afflicted with the heat. They came to a certain water-pond and entered the splendid waters.

52-54. All the visitors were hideous and ugly. Some had large ears. Some were spike-eared. Others had crooked noses. There were some with huge bellies; a few with large teeth; many with hanging lips and large heads. Others were flat-eyed. Still others had long necks. Some were dark-complexioned. Some had split feet, long nails and some with nails lifted up. But when they came out and saw one another, they found themselves rid of all ugly features. All of them had become like Kāma.

55-60. They were surprised and they spoke to one another joyously when they realized that the Tīrtha was excellent in view of the change in their forms: "This excellent form has been obtained by us by taking our bath here. Hence this Tīrtha will become well-known in the entire range of the three worlds as Rūpatīrtha. It shall be destructive of all sins.

Those who are endowed with great faith and take their holy bath here will become handsome in features in the course of every birth.

Those who have perfect faith and offer libations with the waters hereof unto the Pitṛs will attain more benefit than that from Gayā Śrāddha.

Those men who make gifts of jewels here will undoubtedly become kings in the course of every re-birth.

We have come to this decision that we will stay here now. We will not go to (another) Tīrtha even if it be very splendid."

61. After saying thus, those sages divided the whole of the Tīrtha (among themselves). Each made his own Tīrtha of the extent of his Yajñopavīta (sacred thread).

*Sūta said:*

62. Even today, O excellent Brāhmaṇas, the Jagadguru (Preceptor of the universe) touches the water in the Tīrtha there at the outset. It shall be loveable and auspicious.

63. A man who is bereft of desire and performs the holy bath with faith shall attain the greatest benefit characterized as Siddhi (perfection).

64. Thus all those sages shared that great lake and carried out elaborately all the rites of the evening.

65. At the beginning of the nightfall they came to the place where Lord Pitāmaha was present in the Yajñamaṇḍapa, observing silence in the course of initiation.

66. After bowing down to him, all of them went to the place where the Ṛtviks were present. They were seated there as they had become tired due to the day-long Yajña rites.

67. With great devotion, Indra and other Suras were massaging their feet. The visiting sages bowed down to all of them and seated themselves in front of them.

68. They held diverse discourses pertaining to the Yajña rites and the relationship with Soma-imbibing and also the change in origin.

69. They spoke among themselves about the origin of Udgātṛ and of Adhvaryu as based on principles. Others refuted this.

70. Other Mīmāṁsakas refuted the arguments of these with their eyes turned red due to anger. They were rather very clever and eloquent in their speech and they maintained their point in the argument.

71. Others who were excellent Brāhmaṇas took up the central (neutral) position as they were aware of the Pariśiṣṭa

(Appendix). They forsook arguments and revealed their opinion as mentioned.

72. Others started discussions about the collection of Mahāvīrapuroḍāśa and other topics defending their own respective positions.

73. Thus the Brāhmaṇas passed that night.

## CHAPTER ONE HUNDRED EIGHTYTHREE

# Creation of Nāga Tīrtha

*Sūta said:*

1. It was on the twelfth lunar day that the second day of the Yajña rites was celebrated. Listen to the news about all the Devas. It can cause great wonder.

2-3. The rites of the Makha were begun by the Ṛtviks who were masters of the Vedas. A mischievously mirthful religious student took a water-snake, entered the assembly and hurled it near the Brāhmaṇas. All along he went on laughing. But it was a terrible act that caused panic unto all.

4-5. The Brāhmaṇas in the assembly were engrossed in their respective duties. The Hotṛ was afflicted due to the long drawn Sattra. Also the water-snake rambled here and there and ultimately coiled round the body of the Hotṛ.

6. He did not move away from his assigned post because he was afraid of the expiation, should it be the case. With his eyes fixed upon the Cayana (collection of sacrificial twigs) he did not speak a word.

7. In the meantime, a great hue and cry ensued there in the assembly of the Brāhmaṇas because they suspected that it was a poisonous snake.

8-9. There was great wailing on seeing the Hotṛ encircled by the snake. His well-disciplined modest son engaged in the duty of Maitrāvaruṇa saw the father encircled by the snake. His activities were like those afraid of a serpent. Therefore, the sage became angry and he cursed the religious student.

10. "O widcked-minded one, a snake has been hurled into the assembly by you, a sinner. Hence be yourself a serpent quickly at my instance undoubtedly."

*The religious student said:*

11. It was for fun that this water-snake was playfully released by me here. I did not aim it at your father. So, O Brāhmaṇa, why do you curse me?

12. In the meantime, the water-snake slipped down from his body and went somewhere else but the religious student remained turned into a serpent.

13. The religious student, the son of Sanātana, who got transformed into a serpent became miserable. He was surrounded by other Brāhmaṇas.

14. With eyes full of tears, he went to Bhṛgu, bowed down before him and spoke these words choked with tears:

15-16. "I am the son of Sanātana and the grandson of Parameṣṭhin. I have been cursed by your noble-souled son Cyavana. O excellent Brāhmaṇa, I am not guilty. So, save me from the curse."

On hearing this, Bhṛgu became merciful. He spoke to Cyavana:

17-18. "O dear one, it is an improper thing that has been committed by you, for this religious student has been cursed. Even a very poisonous serpent cannot harm me. How then can this water-snake, as free from poison as a rope, harm me? Further, this snake has not been hurled by this Brāhmaṇa aiming at me. Hence, quickly redeem this Brāhmaṇa from the curse."

*Cyavana said:*

19. If the ocean transgresses its boundary, if the Sun becomes cool and if the Lord of the night (Moon) becomes hot, then my words shall be false.

20. On hearing his words, Pitāmaha himself came there where his grandson was present in the form of a serpent.

21. "O my boy", He said, "Do not feel aggrieved at all that you have been transformed into a serpent. In this connection, listen to my words:

22. Formerly, I was desirous of creating the ninth family of Nāgas. That shall be introduced on a limited scale on the earth through you.

23. It will not afflict persons who are masters of Mantras and herbal medicines. It will receive excellent worship all over the earth.

24. Here in the holy place named Hāṭakeśvara there is a pond with excellent water. My child, you must take up your residence there always.

25. While you stay there and proceed ahead with your penance, Serpent Karkoṭaka will give his excellent daughter to you. Therefrom, the creation (of your family) will take place.

26-27. The creation of the new ninth family on a limited scale shall begin on the earth. On the fifth lunar day in the dark half(?) of the month of Śrāvaṇa,[1] this ninth family shall receive the highest worship of the earth. From this day onwards the water pond shall be remembered as Nāga Tīrtha.

28-31. It will be reputed all over the earth. It will be destructive of all sins. If devotees take their holy bath on the fifth lunar day here, they will have no fear from serpents till the end of the year. A man who is afflicted with the poison and who takes his holy bath here, shall be rid of the poison instantly and attain great happiness. A woman who is desirous of a son should take the holy bath on the fifth lunar day at sunrise with great devotion holding any fruit in the hands. Even if she is a barren woman, she will become one having excellent sons."

*Sūta said:*

32. Even as Brahmā, born of the Unmanifest One, was speaking thus, other serpents that had been invited for the Yajña came there.

33. They were Vāsuki, Takṣaka, Puṇḍarīka, Kṛśodara, Kaṁbala, Aśvatara, Śeṣa and Kāliya.

34-35. They bowed down to Lord Pitāmaha and spoke thus loudly: "O Prapitāmaha, we have come here at your behest.

O Prapitāmaha, we have come here to be of some assistance. We are well settled in the realm of Nāgas. We may be commanded. We shall carry out your behest quickly."

1. According to Pūrṇimānta calendar.

*Brahmā said:*

36. O great serpents, this shall be your assistance to us. Go along with this king of serpents.

37. Thereafter, all of you should stay there in the Nāgatīrtha well-settled.

38. If anyone with evil intention comes here to create obstacles in the Yajña, he should be quickly set aside.

39. It may be a Rākṣasa, Piśāca, Bhūta or human being. O Nāgas, this form of assistance is the best to be offered (by you all).

40. Then, on the fifth lunar day in the dark half of the month of Bhādrapada, you will all be duly worshipped.

*Sūta said:*

41. They said, "So it shall be" and bowed down to Pitāmaha. Accompanied by the son of Sanātana, they settled in Nāga Tīrtha.

42. Ever since then that Tīrtha is remembered as Nāga Tīrtha. It fulfils all desires of devout men who take their holy bath.

43. If anyone devoutly performs his holy ablution there even once, there shall be no danger from serpents to his family.

44. After worshipping the leading Nāgas beginning with (the son of) Sanātana, a person should offer sweet food to Brāhmaṇas along with good people.

45. For seven subsequent births, he will never meet with misery arising from Bhūtas, Pretas and Piśācas and Śākinīs in particular. He will never have sickness, anguish, defects, blemish or fear from enemies.

46. O excellent Brāhmaṇas, he who listens to this being read will never be afflicted by serpents for the period of one year therefrom.

47. If this greatness of Nāga Tīrtha is duly read before one who is bitten by a serpent, he will survive even if he is bitten by Kāla (god of Death).

48. No serpent stays in the place where the book in which this greatness of Nāga Tīrtha is written down is kept.

## CHAPTER ONE HUNDRED EIGHTYFOUR

# The Yajña of Brahmā: The Third Day

*Sūta said:*

1-2. The advent of the third day was on the thirteenth lunar day, O excellent Brāhmaṇas. All the Ṛtviks became engaged in their respective duties in connection with the Yajña rite beginning with *Prātassavana*. Then the great Yajña of Pitāmaha began, rich in all good qualities and desirable components.

3-5. The one word uttered by the Brāhmaṇas and heard there was "*dīyatām dīyatām*" (Let this be given). The second word uttered and heard was "*bhujyatām bhujyatām*" (Let this be eaten). In that excellent Yajña of Pitāmaha no third word was heard. If anyone wished for anything, say gold or jewel, he undoubtedly got it, nay four times as much as he desired. Splendid mountains of cooked sweet food were seen heaped up there.

6. There were great rivers of ghee and milk (for eating) and heaps of coins for distribution were also seen.

In the meantime, O excellent Brāhmaṇas, a wise philosopher also came there.

7. He was one who could know the past, present, and future always. He bowed down to Brahmā and squatted in front of him.

8. In between the various rites of all those Brāhmaṇas, O excellent Brāhmaṇas, he narrated everything that had happened ever since childhood.

9. The minds of all those Ṛtviks were overcome with fancy and curiosity. With their eyes beaming with wonder, they asked the philosopher:

10. "They (probably) recollected the fact that they had forgotten (or omitted) some of their duties and the innumerable censurable things uttered by them (unwittingly)."

11-14. Then they asked the philosopher once again: "O Brāhmaṇa, how did you attain this extraordinary wisdom?

Oh! Wonderful is your knowledge. Oh! Wonderful is your wisdom. Such a thing as this has neither been seen nor heard by us. Who is your preceptor? Tell us. We are very curious.

O excellent Brāhmaṇa, such a thing as is seen by you has not been heard by us. O Brāhmaṇa, has Brahmā himself enlightened you?

Were you instructed by Hara who was pleased? Or by the Discus-bearing Lord? It is patent that such clear perception can never be had by one enlightened by anyone else."

*The guest said:*

15. These six are my preceptors: Piṅgalā (a queen), a Kurara (sparrow-like) bird, a serpent, a Sāraṅga (black bee) in the forest, an arrow-maker and a virgin.[1]

16. I acquired wisdom by observing the activities of these:

*The Brāhmaṇas said:*

17. O highly esteemed one, tell us, how these became your preceptors. What sort of activities of these was observed by you?

18. In which land and which area were you born? Tell us. What is your name? What is your Gotra? Say everything in detail.

*The guest said:*

19. In this city, there were four Brāhmaṇas who had been banished, vi z. Śunaḥśepa, Śākreya, Bauddha and Dānta the fourth one.

20. Among them Dānta was remembered as enlightened and quiescent. He was well-known as hailing from Chāndoga Gotra. He was a master of the Vedas and Vedāṅgas.

21. He was born in the Nāgara community. He was in the state of advanced age. I am his eldest son, very dear to his heart, clearer than his own life.

22. O excellent Brāhmaṇas, when I entered the prime of youth, my dear father passed away.

23. In the meantime, O Brāhmaṇas, I (met) Sutapas, the King of Ānarta. I was employed as his Kañcukin (chamberlain) by him.

1. Compare BhP XI. 7-14 - The same Gurus are repeated here. In BhP. Dattātreya narrates this.

24. He saw me quiescent and having control over the sense-organs. Hence, the noble-minded one trusted me. There was a queen named Piṅgalā in his palace (Antaḥpura).

25. She was utterly unlucky, being denied conjugal felicity though richly endowed with beauty. Moreover, there were hundreds of other wives in his palace.

26. All of them used to become excessively agitated and excited at nightfall. They used to gather together exquisite scents, incense and flowers.

27. The choicest of fragrant unguents were brought forward; other women gathered diverse kinds of flowers and fine fabrics.

28. This excitement goes on till the time of going to bed. They exhibited great enthusiasm in love-play and experienced horripilation.

29. They used to vie with one another. One thinks "he" will certainly summon her to sleep. Another thinks the same about herself.

30. They used to exhibit rivalry and jealousy, fight with one another and make adverse comments. Ultimately, one among them proceeds to the chamber of the king.

31. Those left behind experience chagrin; they have sighs in their excess of sorrow and finally go to bed. In utter discomfiture, they never got even a wink of sleep.

32. Their eyes became filled with tears and they were excessively afflicted by the god of Love.

33. Āśā (eager expectation) is the greatest of misery. Absence of the same is the height of happiness. Making *Āśā* disappointed, Piṅgalā used to sleep soundly.

34. She never indulged in coquettish make-up. She never exhibited rivalry. Hence, she never became distressed. Piṅgalā did sleep soundly.

35. This excellent behaviour of the lady was closely observed by me and all *Āśās* (longings and expectations) were eschewed by me. So I too have a happy and sound sleep.

36. The gastric fire of those who sleep soundly gets ignited well. Thereby their food-intake becomes very nutritious.

37. This has, therefore, become the cause of the enhancement of my radiance. Therefore, O excellent Brāhmaṇas, Piṅgalā has become my preceptor (preceptress).

38. Those who are entangled within the noose of *Āśā*, men who are thus afflicted, never lie down at night brooding over the non-acquisition of the same.

39. Their abdominal fire never gets ignited thereafter. Nor do they have any appetite at all. Nor is their food-intake conducive to the enhancement of radiance.

40. There is a limit to everything except to yearning or craving.

41. As there is the fulfilment of desires in man so these go on increasing like fire through the addition of *Havis* offerings.

42. Just as the horn of a Ruru deer goes on rising up as its body develops, so also desires of men get enhanced as their effort for the same increases.

43. O highly esteemed ones, after realizing this, a discerning person should be doing that during the day whereby he can sleep soundly during the night.

## CHAPTER ONE HUNDRED EIGHTYFIVE

# Creation of Holy Places

*The guest said:*

1-4. Thus everything has been narrated to you all as to how Piṅgalā became my Guru (teacher). How the *Kurara* bird (osprey) became so, I shall explain to you.

I had much wealth inherited from my father and grandfather. All the kinsmen, relatives, sons and grandsons began to pester me for money and foodgrain.

If I deny anyone anything, he begins to torment me. He exhibits utter exhaustion to the point of extinction of the very life.

5. O Brāhmaṇas, a few of them used to request me for wealth in conciliatory terms. Others thte atened me to give wealth. Others tempted me with bribes for having some share. Some actually meted out physical violence to me (to extort money by force). Thus, I could not find any means whereby I could get peace.

6. So I never had any happiness on account of them. I was worried day and night about the means of bringing about the end to my troubles. I did not find out any means to get peace of mind.

7. On a certain day, a *Kurara* (osprey) was seen by me going hurriedly through the sky holding a piece of meat in its beak.

8. It was being hurt (pecked) and assailed by different kinds of birds all round for the sake of the piece of meat. Then afraid of the other birds, it let the piece of meat fall down.

9-10. The moment it cast off the piece of meat it became happy. All the other birds abandoned it. Similarly, when I was being tormented by my kinsmen, I resolved thus after seeing the *Kurara* with meat being attacked by those without meat and that later after throwing away the meat it regained happiness.

11. After coming to a decision I summoned all the kinsmen, sons, grandsons and all the others and told them:

12. "O my kinsmen, take and share this wealth judiciously. There is nothing else left in my house." Thus I swore three times.

13. Ever since then, O Brāhmaṇas, I was left alone by them and I am happy. For this reason, the Kurara (osprey) became my Guru.

14. Wealth and riches give rise to delusion. Delusion leads to Naraka. Hence hoarded wealth is disastrous. One who seeks salvation should avoid it from afar.

15. Just as a piece of meat is swallowed by fish in water, by beasts of prey on the ground and by birds in the sky, so also a man of wealth (is preyed upon) everywhere.

16. A rich man may be faultless. But he is tormented by kings and others. A poor man might have committed some crime but he is not harassed anywhere.

17. Rich people are like drunkards. They move with the support of others. They falter at every step. They stutter and stammer.

18. As in the case of one afflicted with fever, a rich man hates devoted ones, as a fever-stricken one dislikes cooked food. They show pleasure outwardly liking for heavy and light things but there is bitterness (inwardly) (bitter taste: bitter words) in the mouth.

19. There is trouble in earning money and misery in preserving what is earned. There is misery in loss of wealth or when it is spent. Fie upon wealth, the cause of misery!

20. All the people in the world seek wealth and resort even to the cremation ground (for its sake). Even sons forsake their father and walk away if he is without wealth.

21. A son is a favourite of the father and a father that of the son as long as there is no monetary relationship between the two. Once monetary relationship arises between them, mutual enmity also develops.

22. For this reason, O ascetics, money is abandoned by me. Therefore I stay happy, thanks to the instruction from the *Kurara*.

23. Listen, O highly esteemed ones, as to how a serpent became my Guru.

24. Listen how the house was abandoned by me on seeing the activity of a serpent. Starting the construction of one's own house leads to great misery. It never leads to happiness.

25. A serpent enters the abode made by others and enjoys. After living there comfortably, it passes on to another one like that.

26. It does not have *mamatva* (sense of possession) feeling "This is my house". That does not become its house, because it is not made by itself.

27. After undergoing different kinds of trouble and suffering if a man builds a mansion it does not go with him when the time of his death arrives.

28. After building a house one takes a wife. Then a son and a daughter are born. For the sake of these he begins to do all sorts of things that should be and should not be done later.

29. Like a silk-worm in its cocoon he gets encircled himself and does not realize it.

30. Creatures attached to sons, wives, houses and fields meet with disaster. They get submerged in the mirish sweat of greed like aged wild elephants.

31. One person commits sins but the common people taste fruit thereof; those who enjoy it go scot-free but the doer of it is tarnished with the fault.

32. For this reason, O excellent Brāhmaṇas, the mansion

was left by me. It is an obstruction in the path of salvation. This was the result of my observation of the activities of the serpent.

33. A true ascetic stays in a village for a single night's rest and for three nights in a town. He who (thus continuously) goes (*yāti*) on is called a *Yati*, an ascetic. The other one is an impostor in the practice of Yoga.

34. He who performs the *Madhukarī Vṛtti* (collecting alms like a bee that sucks honey) at the houses of leading Brāhmaṇas where the fire in the kitchen has calmed down and it does not emit smoke, is the (real) Yati, not anyone else.

35. A Daṇḍin (Sannyāsin) may beg for alms but there should be no addiction to it. He who stays behind and does not become detached is not an ascetic at all.

36. The following six cause the downfall of ascetics: Sleeping during the day; eating in excess (i.e. more than what is absolutely essential for sustenance); talking about women; gazing at them intently; and (wearing) white cloth and gold (ornaments).

37. None else but he is proclaimed as a Yati (in Smṛtis) who is impartial towards enemy and friend; who looks at a lump of clay, stone and gold as equals; and who is free from affection for friends and sons.

38. He who meets honour and insult squarely whether in his own land or in an alien country, he who does not revel too much nor hates is a Yati, not anyone else.

39. If in a house special alms are received or food is distributed, a true Yati does not go there again. No one else is remembered to be so (i.e.a Yati).

40. After observing the activities of a serpent and realizing thus eschewal of all associations was pursued by me for the sake of salvation.

41. Thus, O excellent Brāhmaṇas, the serpent became my Guru. By its power, a powerful radiance shone (shines) in my body.

42. I shall tell you how the black-bee became my Guru. A certain black-bee was seen by me. It was closely associated with a tree.

43-45. It resorted to the bit of a branch where it had built a hive before. During spring season the trees began to blossom.

The flowers had fragrant petals. There were fruits as well. The bee collected excellent juice from them and deposited it (in the hive) at the tip of the branch. It was seen to be perfectly happy without any dejection.

46. Vast quantity of honey was thus collected in the course of a long time. With that honey hundreds and thousands became satisfied.

47. I observed this activity of the bee. In the same manner, I extracted the essence from the several scriptural texts, Vedānta works etc., entirely.

48. Like the other bees, other Brāhmaṇas made use of my collection and excerpts.

49. Thus, O excellent Brāhmaṇas, the black-bee became my Guru. Therefore I am refulgent. There is no other cause (for my being so).

50. The expounders of Vedānta who observe Vratas regularly become powerful. They are free from greed and they have cast off desires. They become highly refulgent.

51. If they are devoid of even one of these (scriptures and Vratas) they become sinners and stupidly malevolent.

52. Many Vedānta texts were pored over, studied and pondered over by me. With the intention of the welfare of human world books of the same level were written by me.

53. Thus, O excellent Brāhmaṇas, the black-bee became my Guru. How the arrow-maker became so, I shall tell you.

54. For the purpose of realizing the Ātman, thousands of Yogins were interviewed by me. They were richly endowed with wisdom and they expounded in accordance with their ability.

55-56. They tried to explain how an excellent disciple succeeds in realizing the Ātman. That realization results from the practice of eithty-four different types of Samādhi (mental absorption) and Āsanas (postures) equal in number (eighty-four) including the lotus-posture. There are innumerble other factors too, such as recitation of spiritual texts. In spite of all these, Ātman could not be visualized at all by me.

57. Hence I became disgusted and wandered all over the earth for the sake of a preceptor and guide. I did not meet with a Guru for the purpose of self-realization.

58. On another day, I was going along the royal highway when I saw the king surrounded by a vast army.

59. So I avoided the path taken by the king and came to the entrance of a hut. I stood at the door after going a short distance upwards.

60. There was an arrow-maker there engaged in the simple activity of shaping the arrows of crooked joints.

61. When the king had gone far away,another servant came there.

62. He was in a hurry, O Brāhmaṇas. Even as I was within hearing, he asked the artisan staying upright, engaged in shaping the arrows:

63. "How much time has elapsed after the king passed along this road? Tell me so that I can follow him."

64-66a. The man (artisan) who was sitting with the face bent down, O Brāhmaṇas, spoke then: "O royal attendant, no king going along this royal highway has been seen by me. If you have anything to do with him you may ask someone else. He is likely to tell you. I am sitting here deeply engaged in the work on the arrows."

66b. On hearing his words I thought thus:

67. 'Practice of yoga with concentration of mind will be the means of the knowledge of Brahman. It cannot be gained by other means. Thereafter, I shall begin to curb the mind for the sake of the realization of Brahman. Thereby, it shall be attained by me.'

68. Ever since then I am retaining in my mind always the Lord, the sun of universal form, forever present in the lotus of the heart.

69. Thereafter, O excellent Brāhmaṇas, I see him solely in all the quarters, in the far end of the quarters, in the firmament and on the earth. (I could see) Nothing else.

70. By its power, I am equipped with refulgence.

71. Thus, O excellent Brāhmaṇas, that arrow-maker became my Guru. Listen How a *Kanyakā* (girl) became my Guru earlier.

72. Renouncing all associations, I came out of the house. At that time my wife also closely came behind me and came out.

73. She held the infant son and a splendid daughter. I was then in my Vānaprastha stage. I was thus addressed by my wife:

74. "Follow my advice. You will have salvation here itself. A man may be a celibate religious student, a householder, a Vānaprastha or a recluse. If he has perfect restraint over himself, he shall certainly attain salvation.

75. Otherwise, if you abandon me and go elsewhere. I shall undoubtedly die. This is true.

76. After my death these children of yours, the son and the daughter will die subsequently. Hence, O my lord, have mercy on me.

77. Do not go to any other Tīrtha. You know yourself that this holy place of Hāṭakeśvara is remembered as highly meritorious.

78. It is the greatest of all Tīrthas. O my Lord, this has been heard by me from eminent Brāhmaṇas and other ascetics who extolled it.

79. O my Lord, this verse has been heard by me often repeated orally by Viśvāmitra, the great sage of truthful speech.

80. 'All the (other) Tīrthas undoubtedly sanctify through holy ablution and monetary gifts. But the holy place Hāṭakeśvara shall sanctify even on being remembered.'"

81. Thereupon, with great difficulty, I vowed to resort to the Vānaprastha Āśrama (stage). So I stayed there itself.

82. While I remained there, my daughter in front of me began to play with her wrists full of bangles.

83. As she went subsisting only on roots, fruits and bulbous roots, she became leaner and leaner day by day.

84. Thereupon I became unhappy fearing that the bangles may fall down. Once it happened that only three bangles remained on her wrists. When they clashed with each other, a sound was produced.

85. After a long time only one of them remained. There was no clash and no sound when it was on the wrist.

86. Thinking deeply over this, the hermitage was forsaken by me. After deciding thus I thought as follow:

87. 'If there are many there is perpetual quarrel. With two there is mutual clash and struggle. Therefore, I shall move about alone by myself like the single bangle of the daughter.'

88. Then as my wife and children were asleep I forsook them and went away to a long distance where she could not find me out.

89. I have left off all mundane ties and fetters. I am roaming over the earth taking in whatever is obtained and lying down for sleep whenever the sun sets, wherever it may be.

90. Thereby, O Brāhmaṇas, I slowly acquired wisdom and knowledge of the past, future and the present in particular.

91. Thus my own daughter became my Guru, O excellent Brāhmaṇas.

92. Thus I have narrated everyting that I was asked in regard to my Gurus. I do not narrate anything untrue before you, at any cost.

93. Thus perfect knowledge dawned upon me in six different ways. It is through these that I acquired the perfect superhuman knowledge that caused credence in you all.

*Sūta said:*

94. Then, O excellent Brāhmaṇas, all those Brāhmaṇas asked him: "After forsaking the Vānaprastha stage and leaving off your wife and children, where did you go? How long did you stay thus. Tell us."

*The guest said:*

95. I was in great fright. I roamed over hundreds and thousands of villages where, O excellent Brāhmaṇas, I practised the Vrata of going to bed (stay at the place) when the sun set. That had no reckoning and hundreds of years passed by.

96. All important Tīrthas and shrines were visited. Many excellent mountains and rivers of pure waters were seen.

97-98. While I was in Vārāṇasī, I myself came to know that the Yajña pertaining to Brahmā was about to be begun in the holy spot of mine. So, O excellent Brāhmaṇas, I have come here eagerly to know how that Makha will be performed, where Pitāmaha himself is *Yajvan* (performer of a sacrifice).

*Sūta said:*

99. In the meantime, all the Devas, including Vāsava, came there keeping Vāsudeva and Maheśvara ahead of them.

100. So also Pulastya and other Ṛtviks came there for the sake of other rites. Brahmā too came there wearing the skin of an antelope.

101-102. Then all those Heaven-dwellers became pleased with his wisdom and perfect knowledge. They all said: "All of us shall grant you boon. Hence do choose a boon. Welfare unto you. Request for whatever is desired by you. Surely, we shall grant you the same even if it is very rare."

*Atithi (The guest) said:*

103. If the Suras are pleased with me and they will grant me the boon I request for this that I must attain Devahood with this self-same body.

104. Also like other Heaven-dwellers I must have an equal share in *Yajñas.* O excellent Suras, a position above them too.

*The Devas said:*

105. Certainly you will become a *Vibudha* (Deva) and live in the world of Devas with this self-same body but you will not get a share in Yajña.

106. O Brāhmaṇa, if we were to give a part of the fruit of the Yajña to you, a human being, the Vedas are likely to become invalid. It is against the injunction of the Vedas to give it to you.

*The guest said:*

107. I have nothing to do with that Deva-hood devoid of a share in Yajña. Therefore, I shall practise that which will yield salvation.

108-110. On hearing it the Lotus-born Lord spoke to all the Devas with palms joined in reverence: "May all the deities listen to the beneficial advice that I offer to you.

This Brāhmaṇas has come from a distant place to take part in my Yajña. Moreover as a Nāgara he is a worthy recipient. He is endowed with perfect knowledge.

Since a boon has been promised to him by all the Vibudhas, O excellent Suras, let whatever is desired by him be given to him."

*Maheśvara said:*

111. I shall tell you a means whereby he will have

perpetual satisfaction more than what can be derived from share in Yajña. May all the excellent Vibudhas listen.

112. Hari is proclaimed as the Lord of Yajña that is being performed. For this reason, that Lord is called Yajñapuruṣa (Divine being of Yajña).

113. From now onwards, whenever a Yajña pertaining to Devas or Pitṛs is to be performed in the human world, its conclusion shall be decided thus.

114. O excellent Brāhmaṇas, after uttering this Brāhmaṇa's name, the mane of Yajñapuruṣa should be glorified. Food should be served then.

115-117. Thereby he will have more satisfaction than from a share in Yajña. If any Śrāddha is performed without offering this, it shall become entirely futile like oblations offered in the ash (instead of in the sacrificial fire).

If at the end of the Vaiśvadeva, the devotee honours him along with the name of Viṣṇu that rite shall have everlasting benefit. Even the least thing that is offered with the mind sanctified by perfect faith shall in general become everlasting.

118. If any person does not worship him in the course of Śrādda or Vaiśvadeva, everything shall be futile in respect to the same.

119. If he is pleased all the Suras will become pleased. Even the Pitṛs with averted face before will come face to face with him.

120. On hearing the words of Maheśvara all the *Vibudhas* (Devas) said joyously, "So be it". The *Vibudhas* with Brahmā and Viṣṇu at the head acclaimed Maheśvara's words.

121. Ever since then the reception and worship of Atithis (guests) came into vogue. Hence the adoration of guests and not merely that of the Yajñapuruṣa should always be practised by all efforts in the course of a Yajña.

*The Atithi said:*

122. Here there is my Tīrtha where penance has been performed by me for a long time in the holy spot of Hāṭakeśvara, O excellent Brāhmaṇas.

123. On the fourth lunar day when it coincides with a Tuesday, all the Devas should be present there.

124. If a person takes his holy bath there on that day, let him get the benefit of all the Tīrtha with your favour.

125. "So it shall be", said all the excellent Suras to the Atithi. In the meantime Sage Pulastya said to Pitāmaha:

*Pulastya said:*

126-127. The Ṛtviks and all the Devas are sitting wonderstruck. Let them rise up quickly for the performance of the rites of Yajña.

In the meantime, all the Ṛtviks rose up and resorted to their own respective places. Then, O excellent Brāhmaṇas, the Yajña was resumed with the performance of Homa.

## CHAPTER ONE HUNDRED EIGHTYSIX

## Importance of an Atithi

*The sages said:*

1-3. O highly esteemed Sūtaja, do narrate further unto us the excellent greatness of Atithi in its entire detail.

*Sūta said:*

May all the sages listen to this excellent greatness. Merely by listening to it the sin of day will perish.

This splendid greatness was heard by me from my father.

4. There is no greater duty of householders than worship of a guest. There is no fault attributed to an Atithi, if there be transgression on his part.

5. If an Atithi goes back disappointed from a house actually he hands over his sin to him (the householder) and takes away his merits.

6. If anyone does not honour a guest, everything good in him perishes such as truth, personal purity, power of penance, acquisition of learning, gifts made, and the performance of a Yajña for a hundred years.

7. Only he can be called a (real) Gṛhastha (householder),

to whose house eager and joyous guests flock together. All the rest are *Gṛharakṣiṇaḥ* (watchmen of the house).

8. The following three are never disallowed in the house of men who have performed meritorious deeds earlier: Śrāddha, Dāna and splendidly pleasing words.

9. If the guest is pleased with the householder, all the Devas are also pleased with him. If he is displeased (keeps his face averted), all the Devas are also displeased.

10. Hence, a guest must always be satisfied by a householder even by sacrificing himself if he wishes for his own good.

11. O excellent Brāhmaṇas, guests of householders are of three types. I shall tell you the time when they appear. Listen with attention.

12. (They are:) Śrāddhīya, Vaiśvadevīya and Sūryoḍha the third. The others are ordinary ones. At best they can be mentioned as Bhojanārthīyas (seekers of meal).

13. Śrāddhīya is that guest who comes at the proper time to partake of the food when the Śrāddha of the Pitṛs has been concluded in the manner resolved upon.

14. That guest should be considered Vaiśvadevīya, who has traversed a great distance, has become weary and arrives at the conlusion of Vaiśvadeva rite and not one who has come before time.

15. A guest who arrives at the conclusion of the Vaiśvadeva is one who transports one to heaven. He may be a beloved one or one worthy of being hated, an illiterate one or a great scholar.

16. The host should not ask him about his Gotra or Pravara, place of nativity or the Veda of special study. After seeing the sacred thread, the host shall feed him with devotion.

17. If the (invited) Atithi does not come at the time of Śrāddha or Vaiśvadeva, the host should utter his name and offer ghee Āhuti in the sacred fire.

18. If the host is incapable of offering full food, he should give him some little food with great devotion whereby he shall be satisfied.

19. The third type of Atithi is called *Sūryoḍha* (carried by the Sun i.e. the evening guest) if he arrives after the host has taken food or even at night. To him the householder should offer some vegetable dish within his capacity.

20. After arriving, if the *Sūryoḍha* guest is forced to depart without being honoured, such a poor disappointed man hands over his own sin before leaving.

21. These things are not short in the house of good people: grass, place (to study), water and pleasing words (i.e. a guest should be offered something).

22. By extending welcome the fires of the householder attain satisfaction. By offering a seat the Self-existing Great-grandfather becomes satisfied.

23. Śaṁbhu is pleased if he is given *Arghya* and all the Devas including Vāsava, if *Pādya* is offered to him. Viṣṇu shall become pleased if food is offered to the guests. Hence the Atithi is full of all the Devas.

24. Hence, O Brāhmaṇas, the other Brāhmaṇas (guest) should be hououred always, fed in particular or at least after uttering the name.

## CHAPTER ONE HUNDRED EIGHTYSEVEN

# Greatness of Rākṣasaprāpya Śrāddha

*Sūta said:*

1-3. When the fourth day of the Yajña rite dawned, the scrificial rite was duly started by the Ṛtviks with Somapāna, cutting of the animal etc.

The Prasthātṛ priest (i.e. Atri) took the *Guda* (anus) of the scrificial animal and placed it in an isolated place in the middle of the assembly, O excellent Brāhmaṇas, for the sake of Homa (later). While he was engrossed (in his work), a certain Brāhmaṇa came there.

4. The young man (Brāhmaṇa) who entered thus there was desirous of eating meat. On seeing the anus of the sacrificial animal he eagerly and enthusiastically began to eat it.

5. In the meantime, the Prasthātṛ came near him. On seeing him tasting (the meat) he cursed him:

6-8. "Fie upon you, O sinful one! The anus (meat) that was kept for the purpose of Homa has been defiled by your voracious greed. You have thus caused an obstacle in the Yajña.

It is not proper now for me to perform the Homa with what is left after being eaten. What has been done by you is an act of Rākṣasas. Ere long you shall be a Rākṣasa on my word."

9-10. Instantly, at the very moment he was transformed into one with hairs standing upright, red eyes, spike-like ears, black teeth and terrible appearance. His face was hideous. The lips were found hanging down. He had only the skin, the bone and the sinews left with flesh and fat missing. His form was terrible.

11. He happened to be the sage named Viśvāvasu, the son of Pulastya. He had come there for tasting the meat sanctified through Mantras

12. He was the grandson of Parameṣṭhin Brahmā and a through master of topics in the Vedas and Vedāṅgas.

The Brāhmaṇas all round trembled with fear on seeing him like a Rākṣasa with hideous features.

13. Some repeated the Sūtras expected to destroy Rākṣasas. Some of them sought refuge in Viṣṇu and others in Rudra.

14. With the minds agitated with fright, they prattled, "Save us, save us", and sought refuge in Pitāmaha and others in Gāyatrī.

15. O Brāhmaṇas, on seeing himself turned into a Rākṣasa, he became highly distressed. He rushed to Pitāmaha with the eyes filled with tears.

16. After bowing down he spoke these words with palms joined in reverence:

17-19. "O Lord of Devas, I am a Brāhmaṇa and the son of Pulastya. Hence your grandson. O great Lord, I have been turned into a Rākṣasa today by the Prasthātṛ in his rage.

Due to covetousness of the tongue and being ignorant that it was reserved and kept aside for the sake of Homa, I tasted the meat from the anus of the sacrificial animal.

Hence take pity on my body and bless it with acquisition of human form. Let some means be employed so that (my) Rākṣasa-hood can be dispelled."

20. On hearing his pleading, Pitāmaha took pity on him. he then spoke the following conciliatory words:

21. "My grandson is only a boy. He does not know what should be done and what should not be done. Hence, O excellent Brāhmaṇa take away the Rākṣasa-hood of (this son)."

22-24. On hearing it, the sage said: "O Lord, an occasion for performing expiatory rite in this Makha of yours has been created by him by defiling the anus meat.

Hence this man, the creator of an obstacle to the Yajña, has been cursed by me. I will not at all take away the Rākṣasa-hood from him. A lie has never been uttered by me even as a joke."

*Brahmā said:*

25. I shall perform the expiatory rite for the due completion of this Yajña. I shall offer monetary gifts and cows as laid down and perform the Homa in accordance with the injunctions. Do take away his Rākṣasa-hood at my instance.

26. He said: "O Prapitāmaha, if fire becomes cool and the moon hot-rayed (like the sun), then the statement (curse) uttered by me shall become otherwise."

27. On hearing his words and realizing his determination, Vidhi said to Viśvāvasu in the form of Rākṣasa:

28. "O dear one, stay in this form till I tell you again. Do as I tell you so that I can offer an excellent position to you.

29. There are other Rākṣasas resorting to the western region of this Camatkārapura. They have confined themselves to the limits of decorum.

30. The Rākṣasas in Laṅkā aspire for the excellent state (Mokṣa). They come to that spot and perform penance adopting good Vratas.

31-34. Accept the Lordship there and act in a way beneficial to the Nāgaras. There are many Rākṣasas, Kūṣmāṇḍas, Piśācakas and many other Rākṣasas of evil intention.

All these Bhūtas, Pretas, Piśācas, Kūṣmāṇḍas and others cat- ch hold of all those who go there. But on seeing a Nāgara in front, they go away due to the fear thereof . Hence, Son, go there and be the Lord of all the Rākṣasas. This is the Kingdom given to you by me now."

*Rākṣasa said:*

35. O Pitāmaha, tell me, what should be eaten by me there and what should be given to them after becoming the Lord of those Rākṣasas.

36. O Lord, this is in view of the fact that food should be given to the attendants by a king. Hence, O Lord of Devas, take pity on me and tell this.

37. Indeed this has been heard by me that a king who does not duly maintain with food the group of his attendants goes to the Raurava Naraka.

*Brahmā said:*

38. All that Śrāddha devoid of monetary gifts, gingelly seeds and Darbha grass has been given to you even if it has been performed at excellent Tīrthas.

39. If a pig, a woman in her monthly course, a dog or a donkey looks at a Śrāddha it shall be yours entirely.

40. If the Śrāddha is offered flouting the injunctions laid down, or if Darbha grass used is longer than a *Vitasti* (a span) or devoid of the root, it shall be entirely yours.

41. If gingelly seeds, pies etc., fried in oil or Śūka cereal (barley etc.) are not given in a Śrāddha, that shall be yours.

42. If the Śrāddha is performed by persons who have smeared themselves with oil, who have not bathed and who have not worn washed clothes, that shall be yours entirely.

43. If the Brāhmaṇa fed in a Śrāddha is a Māhiṣika (husband of an unchaste woman), a Śvitrī (one suffering from white leprosy) or a Kuṣṭhin (leper), that Śrāddha shall be entirely yours.

44. If the person fed in a Śrāddha is one deficient in one limb, one having a superficial limb, one who is censured, afflicted with a fell disease, a thief or one who practises usury, that Śrāddha shall be yours.

45. If the person fed is one with black teeth or a husband of a Śūdra woman, a *Vinagna* (excessively hypocritical one), that Śrāddha shall be yours.

46. You will get the benefit of that Yajña which is without monetary gifts, which is performed by those polluted by death of kinsmen and by those without celibacy.

47. If an *Atithi* is not duly honoured in a Śrāddha or Yajña rite on coming at the conclusion of Vaiśvadeva rite it shall be entirely yours.

48. If after inviting a Brāhmaṇa, the person offering Śrāddha

does not observe silence, or if the Brāhmaṇa who takes food does not observe silence, that Śrāddha will be yours.

49. If a man performs Śrāddha in pots of clay or broken utensils, that shall be yours entirely

50. If salt is openly displayed, if the buttermilk gets spoiled or if *Jātī* flower is offered, that shall be yours entirely.

51. If the householder or the Brāhmaṇa does not observe celibacy in a Śrāddha (i.e. on the Śrāddha day) that is offered to you. One without three deserving persons (or three pots) is also offered to you.

52-53. If the food is offered in an iron utensil, that Śrāddha is offered to you by me. If a rite is devoid of Mantras and proper and requisite activities it is despicable. Except in the case of Saṅkrānti and lunar eclipse, whatever is offered at night is despicable. If a Homa is performed at night it is despicable.

54. After saying thus Brahmā, the grandfather of the worlds, stopped abruptly. That Rākṣasa duly obtained the position of Rāksasas at that place.

